SONIC SOVEREIGNTY

# POSTMILLENNIAL POP

General Editors: Karen Tongson and Henry Jenkins

# Sonic Sovereignty

*Hip Hop, Indigeneity, and Shifting*
*Popular Music Mainstreams*

Liz Przybylski

NEW YORK UNIVERSITY PRESS
*New York*

NEW YORK UNIVERSITY PRESS
New York

www.nyupress.org
Library of Congress Cataloging-in-Publication Data
Names: Przybylski, Liz, author.
Title: Sonic sovereignty : hip hop, indigeneity, and shifting popular music
mainstreams / Liz Przybylski.
Description: New York, New York : New York University Press, 2023. |
Series: Postmillennial pop | Includes bibliographical references and index.
Identifiers: LCCN 2022045734 | ISBN 9781479816910 (hardback) | ISBN
9781479816927 (paperback) | ISBN 9781479816934 (ebook other) | ISBN
9781479816965 (ebook)
Subjects: LCSH: Indigenous peoples--Canada--Music--History and criticism. |
Rap (Music)--Canada--History and criticism. | Popular music--Social
aspects--Canada--History. | Hip-hop--Canada. | Radio and music--Canada.
Classification: LCC ML3563 .P78 2023 | DDC
782.4216490971--dc23/eng/20230426
LC record available at https://lccn.loc.gov/2022045734

This book is printed on acid-free paper, and its binding materials are chosen for strength
and durability. We strive to use environmentally responsible suppliers and materials to the
greatest extent possible in publishing our books.

The manufacturer's authorized representative in the EU for product safety is Mare Nostrum
Group B.V., Mauritskade 21D, 1091 GC Amsterdam, The Netherlands.
Email: gpsr@mare-nostrum.co.uk.

Manufactured in the United States of America

10 9 8 7 6 5 4 3 2

Also available as an ebook

*To everyone who finds the courage to share music with others,*

*even and especially when you are not sure who will listen*

# CONTENTS

# Introduction

*Flow, Break, Backspin, Repeat*

If you were standing on the steps of the legislative building in Winnipeg on January 28, 2013, you would have witnessed a pivotal moment in history. In the early evening, looking down from the provincial capital, you would have seen hundreds of people gathered, wearing jackets and toques and scarves to protect against the winter cold, people holding cameras to document what was happening because they, too, knew it was going to be something to remember. Later, they would want to know where they were at that precise moment. And you would have seen the news crews gathered there, too. The publicity had been intentional. This was a watershed moment in Idle No More, a global Indigenous rights movement, and already, Indigenous and non-Indigenous people across Canada and around the world were paying attention.[1] People could tell this was big.

An array of sounds fill that space: cheers, singing voices, and resonant drums. Musician and social justice fighter Buffy Sainte-Marie greets the crowd, recognizes how many people are present, and speaks to how good it is to have so many different people present. She calls it the "educational opportunity of a lifetime"—to learn about what is being proposed by the Canadian government and how it will affect Indigenous communities, to think about how it intersects with what communities have been living with for generations. A member of the Piapot Cree Nation, she says this is the chance "for Aboriginal people to learn more ourselves," to read the treaties and proposed legislation, and "for non-Aboriginal people to finally understand what it is that makes us so proud to be Canadian Aboriginal Indigenous people with inherent rights guaranteed by the treaties, guaranteed by not only the Crown but Canada itself." If you were there, you would have heard her rally the gathered people: "I'm so proud that we all have the opportunity to stick up for what's best in Canada." A cheer erupts from the crowd. As hand drums play together under her voice, she continues, "I'm so proud of you. It's not only about our leaders and our celebrities; it's about every single one of you." Over applause, she calls to the many: "Our neighbors and our friends, our generations past, and all of the generations coming up. We think seven generations into the future when we make our decisions, about interacting with the environment and the world." She offers a song that will resonate across borders, and she starts to sing. The hand drums find their step supporting her voice and the voices of others who join her, and bodies start to move in time with the beat and with the call and response. Over the course of Idle No More, this public space would reverberate with music of many genres, and in Winnipeg, local musicians would help set the tone. Round dance took over this space—as it took over so many others during this time—the music and movement inviting those who participated in the moment and then including new audiences, as participants shared videos online. In turn, these actions made their way into tweets, news reports, and hip hop videos.

If you had been me, you would have heard something a little different. Standing in the snow, I saw and listened to the gathered people, with jackets and toques and scarves. And I heard my boots and my neighbors' boots crunching in snow as we walked across the lawn, then felt my feet and legs move in time with that music and those neighbors as we connected in the widest circle of people I had ever seen. We heard those singers and those drums and moved together in a round dance. Never mind the legislative building, we were making a circle with ourselves and each other, each other and ourselves, taking over the space of that government building with bodies and music and singing and speeches and movement and dance. And I was grateful for holding hands but also frustrated that I couldn't keep my hands in my coat pockets because I had forgotten my mittens. My hands were gaining warmth from the mittened hands of others as the backs of my hands and fingertips were going red with cold. I was drawn in, fully immersed in this moment, holding my friend Robert's hand, his daughters next to us, amid people we knew and did not know, moving together to a very intentional music. And my mittens were sitting in a friend's house in Minnesota where I'd left them earlier that morning, before completing my drive and crossing a border to get here. Blistering cold like this was not new to me after my many winters in Chicago. But I was swept up in the moment, so it was only later that I realized how much of a mistake forgetting mittens was.

Because there, I saw a city light up the winter dark, I heard song reverberate, I moved with a crowd that was figuring out what to do, as we listened and responded and linked hands and moved. If you had been my friend Robert, you would have seen me, your eccentric friend up from the States, back again, having just driven across the border to come participate in an epic winter music festival. You would have remembered me from the past year's music festival, when my partner and I had accepted your invitation to come up to Winnipeg and listen and take part in this festival, in this place your family had lived from before it was a city or Canada was a country. You would have seen firsthand the aspects of me that are a language teacher, singer, and musician you'd known for years and also this new facet of me, this scholar side. You would have seen me arriving—as a non-Indigenous person and a white person and a non-Canadian in the midst of a very public conversation about Indigenous rights and the settler state—coming back to see you and your family in your home. And mostly, you would have been bringing your kids and your friends into this space because, you, too, could tell that this is a moment to be present in and a moment to remember. You, so used to being at the center of things, the life of the party, quick with a joke and a story, could tell that this was a center to be part of. And so you, like hundreds of others, came.

If you had been at the legislative building that day, and maybe you were, you would just have gotten to be in one pair of boots. On the steps, or moving across crunching snow, your hopefully mittened hands holding this hand or that one, playing a drum or holding a camera, but you could not have been everywhere. You could have been a young leader, who walked to Winnipeg from a neighboring First Nation reserve, a Winnipeg resident, drawn in by the call for the flash mob, someone at their first round dance, or a singer who had led many public demonstrations across years.

So I invite you to listen, to reflect, to remember, and to think forward, with me and with others, because in daily life you only get to wear one pair of boots at a time, but in reading and listening we can be much more. This book coalesces reflections from multiple perspectives, across time and vantage point and space, so you can be on those steps and in that snow, who you were, who you might have been, yourself and the person standing next to you, looking back now and looking forward in the future.

## The Backstory behind This Book

What does sovereignty sound like? I listen for the answer by learning with musicians and media professionals who are dedicated to making and circulating contemporary Indigenous popular music. The research that underpins this book is rooted in cities of the Central Plains and Great Lakes regions of the United States and Canada. I started to become involved in the questions that germinated this research in Chicago. In early 2011, a group of musicians and community members at the American Indian Center began organizing a hip hop show that would showcase Native musical culture to the wider community. I became a participant in this process. During this time, I gained interest in ongoing group questions of how it might be possible to fuse powwow and hip hop styles and what effects this performance might have. Further, participants continued to raise questions about how and whether Native culture was audible in Chicago. Listening for places where these discussions were being taken up, I heard loud messages about Indigenous urban culture coming from Canada. Winnipeg was home to two of the three hosts on the CBC (Canadian Broadcasting Company) Indigenous popular music show *Ab-Originals* that aired across the country and played online around the world. Winnipeg was home to an Indigenous hip hop–format radio station, Streetz, that played Indigenous artists alongside non-Indigenous musicians.

Sonic Sovereignty is informed by this exchange of ideas and movement of music, spurred by artists and media personnel whose influence is heard far beyond the limits of a single city. Hip hop and heritage musical forms met in festivals including Aboriginal Music Week, the Aboriginal Peoples' Choice Music Awards, and Festival du Voyageur. These presences gave a loud public platform for artists, one that was still developing in Chicago. They showcased some of the same Anishinaabeg musicians who played in Minneapolis and Chicago. They also offered a venue for musicians from farther away to play city stages: Inuit, Algonquin, Apsáalooke, Stó:lō, the list went on and on. And of course, these presences brought together a much wider set of geographies: popular music citing intertribal powwow styles from the North and the South, hand drum songs played in the East, Indigenous-language rap learned in the West.

But when I began the research that developed into this book, there was little academic scholarship on any aspect of Indigenous hip hop. Adam Krims offered an analytical strategy for analyzing rappers' flow, or delivery style, including Cree rapper Bannock.[2] Conference papers and dissertations were some of few sources early on.[3] As a result, I began by talking with artists, listening to music, and learning from hip hop industry insiders about their understanding of the shape of the scene. *Sonic Sovereignty* analyzes information from my research with musicians and broadcasters in Winnipeg and neighboring cities, as well as subsequent participant observation as a musician and scholar, contributing to a growing interdisciplinary area. This hybrid ethnographic research spans an online-offline divide, following musicians and producers as they, and their music, circulate across digital/physical networks. *Sonic Sovereignty* contributes to the emerging interdisciplinary field of Indigenous popular music studies, which draws from a strong history of public scholarship and practice.

## Sonic Sovereignty

In this book, I propose and apply a framework of *sonic sovereignty* that connects self-definition, collective determination separate from the nation-state formation, and Indigenous land rematriation with the immediate and long-lasting effects of expressive culture. Sonic sovereignty is profoundly related to understandings (and workings) of time. It responds to gaps in some existing sovereignty discourses. Sovereignty is often limited to Eurocentric ideas of legal rights, which fail to adequately address non-European cultural contexts. Many Indigenous groups are thinking toward sovereignty in the future that connects back to precolonial ideas of sovereignty in North America. Sometimes, public discourses around sovereignty suggest that it is something that can be granted—for example, by a federal government. Indigenous sovereignty does not make sense on these terms: peoples are already sovereign. This can be recognized or not by a nation-state, but government actors are not vested with the power to grant it.

Sonic sovereignty is different from some other ideas about sovereignty because it works beyond these limitations. And of course, sound is at the core. Why does it matter that sound is at the center? First, there are some obvious reasons: people express ideas verbally and musically. This takes some direct manifestations: rapper Chase Manhattan spans the US-Canada border with his performances, rapping about holding it down for "sovereign nations," naming Native American and First Nations groups for vibing crowds. Rapper/producer Beka Solo engages ideas of belonging and self-determination as she collaborates with Sto:lo singers for a hip hop track. Sometimes these functions connect directly to the way in which sound works: sampled sounds and evocative timbres play with memory and create experiences that extend beyond what is possible in written language.

Sound contains or implies its own absence. Every time sound is produced, it is remarkable because it is not-silent. And silence is critical to (sonic) sovereignty and self-determination. Choosing who can hear, who should witness, who can have a chance to understand, to participate, and who cannot, choosing what to tell and what to keep, creating moments of no-sound, no-information, and letting the space do work through silent noncommunication—all of this is how individuals and groups can express power, and it is a mechanism through which that choice and that power is felt.

Music making is a sound practice that is often practiced with others. And in hip hop specifically, it is enacted together. That "together" can be collaborative to various degrees; it can involve traces of others through sampling or directly through in-person creative work with others. Sovereignty comes into being through relationships. Sonic sovereignty requires a multiplicity of readings and a holding of multiple and even conflicting viewpoints and approaches. Groups are often heterogeneous: this is crucial. And the "together" may be with people who are no longer physically present in the same world—samples and recording strategies allow those who have passed to still be heard with those who are still physically present in this place and time. Also, these processes allow participation by more-than-human actors. Rather than an exploration of the posthuman, which has been addressed in scholarship on music technologies in the past, I instead refer to the ways in which nonhuman actors are part of composition and performance and to the fact that musicians reject hierarchies of beings; artists are choosing to engage with nonhuman animals, wind, water, the sounds of place and land, through sampling and audio effects to expand those in the music beyond the human.

In some cases, Indigenous hip hop artists utilize public venues, including face-to-face and online spaces of protest, to call for governments and nonstate actors, such as energy corporations, to respect their sovereignty. This has been the case with artists who advocated for ongoing legal recognition of the land rights held by Lakota groups at Standing Rock and for the respect of Treaty rights of peoples of multiple Indigenous nations during the legal challenges that Idle No More took on.

Inasmuch as these artists insist on being listened to and proclaim the manner in which audiences should listen to them, this is an assertion both of sovereignty as defined in a legal manner elsewhere and of sonic sovereignty as it unfolds here: artists are actively taking part in a public effort to have Indigenous sovereignty respected. These actions are one part of sonic sovereignty. So, too, is asserting how one should be listened to, choosing one's audience, identifying when one does not wish to speak to certain audiences, and choosing when to be silent. Silence, the ability to not speak, can supersede the desire of others to hear.

Sonic sovereignty, too, is about storytelling and exploring how musical expression is framed. Mainstream industry spaces often advance colonialist heteropatriarchal ideas, yet there is possibility in broadcasting and streaming audio. Shaping an urban Indigenous community image through popular broadcast, in the face of popular media's history of erasure and active stereotyping, is part of asserting that sovereignty must be recognized. Individuals and groups already hold the ability to say how they should be heard; sonic sovereignty is enacted as artists and media professionals rearticulate this and charge audiences with listening as they are asked.

Decolonization is inseparable from land rights and sovereignty.[4] Multiple and overlapping forms of sovereignty—cultural, bodily, linguistic, and others—are interlinked. Moreover, land rights need not be understood simply as power over a particular piece of land for extractive purposes; multiple forms of sovereignty are imbricated with land rights, and even the power to determine how relationships to land are defined is part of Indigenous land rights projects. The key here is not to think of multiple forms of sovereignty projects as opposed to each other; there is nothing metaphorical about musical sovereignty.[5] Instead, these projects are interrelated.

## Making and Marking a Decade of Change

Even at the time, the moment that opened this chapter felt weighty, and its importance has crystallized since then. The moment, and the movement, emerged from a much longer set of actions. As musician and Indigenous governance scholar Leanne Betasamosake Simpson (Michi Saagiig Nishnaabeg) asserts, there have been "400 years of Indigenous resistance" in North America.[6] The moment, too, led to others that were part of that winter, the following year, and the events that grew from those public interactions.

In this long arc of resistance, 2008 stands out as a crucial year in Indigenous-settler relations in the United States and Canada: the prime minister in Canada, and then in 2009 the president in the United States, formally apologized for their governments' treatment of Indigenous peoples. The possibilities that these apologies recognized, and their limitations, led toward a decade of action and contestation. 2008 was also a watershed year in popular music distribution, a turning point for the possibilities of access to wide listenerships, notably for minoritized artists, and a loosening of mainstream industry forces. Again, the following decade would prove some of the potential in this shift and also show how industry decision-makers would craft and recraft their strategies to retain control of listening publics.

Politically, there was a significant shift from 2008 to 2018. In Canada, a federal apology for Residential Schools was issued in June 2008. Then–Prime Minister Stephen Harper made a long-called-for announcement, which acknowledged the government's culpability in harming Indigenous children and communities and acknowledged that the assimilation policy was wrongheaded. Concrete reconciliation efforts include monies awarded to survivors, increased resources for survivors and families, a public listening process, and changes to educational standards to more accurately reflect history and suggest appropriate actions in the present. This process has had thoughtful critiques and notable limitations. There has been no parallel reconciliation process in the United States, though in December 2009, President Barack Obama made history by quietly signing into law an Apology to Native Peoples of the United States. On both sides of the nation-state boundary, activity around multiple aspects of Indigenous sovereignty was vibrant throughout—and continues beyond—this period. There was a well-attended public ceremony that accompanied the release of the Truth and Reconciliation Commission's findings in the summer of 2015 in Ottawa. Dialogue around the celebration of Canadian confederation in 2017 owes its richness to public conversations: protests by Indigenous peoples and others that this was a festival of colonialism were heard and discussed around the country. As Pamela Palmater (Mi'kmaw) and other Indigenous leaders have pointed out, celebrating confederation is one way of celebrating colonialism.[7] Discussions continue about changing relationships between Indigenous peoples, settlers, and newcomers.

Concurrently with these social shifts, changes in the Indigenous music industry reflected larger transformations in the popular music industry. Technological possibilities for recording and distribution were rapidly developing. The way people listen was changing. 2008 was a big year. MySpace peaked and was surpassed by the first time by Facebook. Spotify launched in Sweden and five other countries. And in Indigenous music media specifically, the first Indigenous hip hop station, CIUR-FM (Streetz), launched in Canada. From 2008 to 2018, listeners and distributors made the move from MP3s to streaming audio. After Spotify's 2008 launch, it grew in market share, and by 2017, it was the most downloaded music app in the United States. And its impact is global: the Swedish company "had over 140 million active users in 61 markets at the end of 2017, with over 30 million songs in its archive."[8]

At the same time, there was a market move from album sales to touring, merchandising, branding, and live-event ticket sales as crucial revenue streams for the music industry.[9] There has been some shifting in industry gatekeepers as a result. Some new platforms for people to be able to share music have emerged, and others have disappeared or faded into relative insignificance.

Between 2008 and 2018, there was a rise in the importance of social media for musicians. It offered avenues for musicians to tailor their images and helped fans "read" their work. Social media interactions create connections beyond the space of the show or one-way transmission-like interviews. Furthermore, social media also entails (unpaid) labor: artists are expected to spend an increasing amount of time and work interacting with fans. Major shifts in social media and music/video sharing around this time are numerous: Google purchased YouTube in 2006. Facebook opened to all users (not just college and high school students), also in 2006. MySpace launched in 2004 and had five million users by November of that year; by July 2006, it had 80 percent of social networking traffic in the United States. MySpace slipped from the largest social media platform from 2008 to 2009. Its popularity declined steadily after 2011, and while still technically active in 2018, MySpace operated with only a small staff. In other words, MySpace died the internet death of LiveJournal and others. Its ghost still haunts us in archived pages.

And yet the relevance of radio has remained strong. As many artists have identified, having their work played on the radio continues to have cachet. It conveys an imprimatur of professionalism onto the artist, marking an achievement within the music industry. Even as new media offer opportunities, radio reaches a large number and wide geography of listeners in Canada and the United States—in 2018, 85 percent of Canadians and 92 percent of USAmericans listened to the radio at least weekly, if not more frequently.[10]

An Indigenous media industry is influential within Canada and beyond its borders; broadcast and streaming music is part of that influence. The creation and decline of Streetz is a significant part of this story. After multiple visits, I moved to Winnipeg in 2013. In the year to come, I would witness the day-to-day workings, contributions, and ultimately the transformation of Streetz FM. Licensed in 2008, Streetz started broadcasting in 2009, rebranded in April 2014, then folded as an Indigenous urban-format station, becoming a country-format station in July 2016.[11] In today's prolific digital world, the end of a radio station might sound insignificant, but this hip hop station—a once bold and hopeful experiment by and for urban Indigenous voices—provided a microphone and a playground for a new Indigenous sound.

In addition to broadcast and streaming audio, podcasts play a role in Indigenous music media. The CBC *Ab-Originals* podcast was heard across the country and beyond; Indigenous media hosts focused on multiple genres of music and showcased artists, connecting them with listeners. Suzette Amaya, David DeLeary, Melissa Spence, Wab Kinew, and Kim Wheeler presented regularly; Rosanna Deerchild hosted special programming on this podcast. It started in February 2010 and was absorbed into the CBC Aboriginal programming stream in 2012. Winner of the 2019 Indigenous Music Award for Best Radio Station Program Promoting Indigenous Music, author and broadcaster Rosanna Deerchild (Cree) has hosted the weekly program *Unreserved*, which airs on CBC Radio One and can be heard internationally as a podcast. *Unreserved* began in 2014 and went national in 2015, and its 2019 award reflects how prominent it had become by 2018.

In the past, music programmers often assumed that music by Indigenous artists was exclusively of interest and relevance to an Indigenous listenership. Hip hop and electronic music by Indigenous artists does not exist in a kind of echo chamber. Its audiences are large and mixed. It is produced by people of many Nations, including artists of mixed heritage, and is relevant to heterogeneous audiences. A popular music "mainstream" or mainstreams are changing, as I examine in subsequent chapters. Popular music by people who foreground their Indigenous identities was first heard primarily in specialized audiences, then was understood to be a market or genre characterized by identity rather than just sound, and now is much more heterogeneous and widely heard. Power imbalances still keep many Indigenous musicians—especially Indigenous female or nonbinary and/or not white-passing musicians—from having egalitarian access to mainstream listenerships and support systems. Yet, over the period of study in *Sonic Sovereignty*, the amount of pop music by Indigenous artists in "mainstream" venues has increased, in Canada and globally: artists and media professionals are reshaping a mainstream sound. The mainstream that is changing is not just what is sometimes called an Indigenous music industry. Rather, the popular music industry is shifting, because of the activities of artists who had been previously, by choice or by circumstance, speaking to a largely Indigenous and mixed-heritage audience. And of course, completely distinct audiences are themselves a fiction.

I come to this writing as listener, participant, and observer, one voice among many. I have a background broadcasting live on radio and have shifted to podcasts and digital media; I have been actively engaged in ethnographic research with Indigenous media throughout these shifts in Indigenous-settler relationships between 2008 and 2018. I participated in and documented Idle No More, a worldwide movement sparked in Canada in 2012 through 2013. As a volunteer with fellow arts practitioners, I participated in the Winnipeg installation of Walking With Our Sisters, a public event that responds to the crisis of missing and murdered Indigenous women and girls. I took part in a public ceremony for the release of the Truth and Reconciliation Commission's findings in 2015 and performed in musical responses to the commission's calls to action in 2016. From the 2008 apology to the 2017 conversation about Canadian confederation, public dialogue increased around relationships between Indigenous peoples, settlers, and newcomers.

## The Political Is the Performative Is the Political

Political shifts and music-industry shifts in the first two decades of the twenty-first century were mutually influential. In *Sonic Sovereignty*, I document, analyze, and reflect on the period between 2008 and 2018 because it is one in which two profound shifts occurred simultaneously and in a mutually influential manner: The ways in which people listen to, consume, and interact with popular music have changed radically. The presence of discourses of urban Indigeneity, the prevalence of scholarship about Indigenous popular culture, and the publication of scholarship by Indigenous academics in large numbers have paralleled a presence of public conversations about Indigenous culture, including contemporary Indigenous music culture, settler identity, colonialism, and what is possible in the future for music, for scholarship, and for settler colonial states. Tanya Tagaq invoked the presence of twelve hundred missing and murdered Indigenous women through her performance at the 2014 Polaris Gala in Toronto. When A Tribe Called Red[12] won a Juno Award in a mainstream category (Breakthrough Group of the Year for 2014), it was changing what mainstream music sounded like, even as its members participated in public calls to, for example, end the practice of using Indigenous peoples as sports mascots. The point is this: this period of time has been tremendous with regard to change. That change is not over.

Violence targeting Indigenous women and girls has been longstanding, but there were significant turning points in Canada in the 2010s. In 2014, the Royal Canadian Mounted Police (RCMP) released a report on missing and murdered Indigenous women, and then it produced a 2015 update. A federal inquiry was established in Canada in 2016. Community-led antiviolence events include the multicity long-standing art and community project Walking With Our Sisters, the multiyear arts and activism gathering No Stone Unturned, Jaime Black's moving-installation art REDress project, and Tanya Tagaq's aforementioned Polaris focus, which was enacted live, was broadcast on television, and incited a heated Twitter conversation. All of these include arts and music elements, attract national and international attention, incorporate an online aspect, and invite Indigenous, settler, and newcomer participation through Indigenous leadership.

Idle No More (#IdleNoMore) ignited in Canada in 2012. It grew and flourished in the winter of 2013 and moved into Solidarity Summer later that year. The moment that opened this chapter was one of many crucial events in this Indigenous sovereignty movement. The ongoing effects continued after 2013: light was shed on existing action, people were inspired to newly participate, groups formed, actions were undertaken across Canada and around the globe, and connections were made between individuals, groups, and causes.

In 2016, international attention again focused on efforts led by Indigenous activists. The Standing Rock Sioux led an effort against the Dakota Access Pipeline (stylized online as #NoDAPL). Thousands of people traveled to South Dakota to participate in physical protests. Online protests emerged simultaneously, and around the globe, sympathetic demonstrations and fund-raisers gained traction. As in Idle No More, Standing Rock activists connected to regional and local issues as well, while keeping Indigenous rights and environmental concerns at the center. And once again, participants committed through music made at the events in both in-person and online activities. These events spanned the US-Canada border and reached the wider world. While engaged resistance is not unique, international participation was significant in both cases. Across online and in-person activity, including musical activity, Indigenous people of many Nations participated, and significantly, settler news sources and settler celebrities became involved as well: narratives changed, and many listeners understood peoples and destinies as linked.[13]

This whole time, hip hop has been continuing. Critics may keep saying that hip hop is dead, and yet it continues to reinvent itself, look back toward foundational techniques, and engage local issues and communities globally. Some journalists lament that it is on its way out, but new artists and audiences keep emerging, existing audiences keep listening, and foundational artists and old records keep being played for new ears. There is something about the method, the teaching that is part of hip hop, intergenerational learning, improvising together, that appealing story of a voice from the streets that keeps resonating as folks all over the world, young and not so young, keep feeling like they have not been truly heard yet.

## Broadcasting the Local Globally

Every time I enter the radio station, I immediately encounter two things. First, the entry follows right alongside the rows and rows of albums that we can play on-air. In the last station where I worked, these were tucked away, a kind of secret cove I had to make a special effort to enter when I was looking for new material or trying to find just the right song to complement an upcoming set. Here, it's right in the middle of every-thing. At UMFM, I sometimes hear other folks planning their shows as I browse, and vice versa. Since the albums are sorted and tagged, it's easy to find albums by genre or that are recommended, and unlike in my radio experience in the States, there is a special sticker if they ful-fill Canadian Content (CanCon) requirements. Right next to this large library is the second immediately notable feature: the desk of Jared, the station manager. He is generally at his desk, at least daytime and week-days. I often find myself tempted into an enthralling chat, regardless of why I entered the station on a particular day. Today, my destination is a little farther. Sandwiched between the small broadcasting studio and the desk of Michael, the program director, is a door that opens into a windowless room, a postage stamp of a production studio. I have an evening slot scheduled, and I get ready to patch an artist through. As in my radio broadcasting experience in the United States, I've already completed much of the work for today's interview even before I step into the studio. And to polish the audio so this show can be both aired and released online as a podcast, I anticipate more time at the editing desk once the conversation is over.

This is an interview for which we planned a distance interview over video chat, so I've been working with the equipment to make sure the recording will function properly. I met Beka Solo in Vancouver, at yet another radio station. We had so much to talk about there, and we've been communicating through a combination of phone, text, and Facebook Messenger since then. Through our conversations and my listening to more of her music, I've made a list of songs I want to listen to with her and dialogue about. When we start talking, it's easy, verbally, for ideas to flow from where we were on text and chat. I ask her about songs she created with a drum group back at her home, and suddenly, she's telling me a story that puts me in yet another studio, the one where they recorded together. When they recorded, this MC and DJ generated ideas to spark the collaboration, in addition to operating the mixing board. So a talented Tsilhqot'in rapper/producer from Williams Lake and ten traditional Sto:lo singers from Chilliwack are in studio, vibing off each other, trying things out and getting into a groove. We travel back to the present, and Beka tells me about that experience of engineering in studio. She so clearly has fun with that kind of work. Beka's stories take on enthusiastic energy when I ask her about delay effects and the use of environmental sounds on two tracks with a totally different vibe. She finds joy in mixing her own music. Some is the joy of controlling the sound and getting it just so and also that wide-eyed excitement of creating, of finding the right effect to craft the exact atmosphere she was going for. I feel this too, and I think about it as I'm monitoring incoming sound levels, thinking toward what parts of which songs I can mix in when I move to producing our interview, thinking through how I can help our listener feel the energy, creativity, and urgency that I hear in the production room.

## Listening and Hearing

I have come to this music and this scholarship as a listener. I attune my ears as someone who has taken time to pay close attention to the music that surrounds me, observe the way audiences are responding to it, ask artists about their process, listen to their answers, listen to what my own ears can tell me, listen in context, listen to how the music is circulating. And I come as someone with knowledge of and interest in music technology and circulation. Throughout the book, I differentiate listening from hearing, continually refocusing on the attentive, relational, and physical process of listening. *Sonic*

*Sovereignty* works through the potential of music, in the words of musician Pauline Oliveros, to "shatter the indifference of hearing."[14]

Multiple modes of listening are active in interpersonal interactions. The physical process of hearing connects bodies—human and other-than-human—as sound waves move through space. While some of this physical process is beyond individual control, we can each impact modes of listening through our choices, postures, attention, and even reciprocal sound-making. Complex structures impact hearing and listening beyond the individual. Factors in recording, broadcasting, streaming, programming, funding, and the multilayered process of accruing cultural capital impact who is heard, by whom, and to whom attention is paid through careful listening. These structural and interpersonal levels are interconnected. There is no single way to listen. I offer readings in order to provide possibilities, sometimes multiple possibilities at once, and sometimes a layering of options with rehearings. There are many more options than those suggested here and a varied range of affective responses to possible listenings; this is the point.

As a whole, *Sonic Sovereignty* invites the reader, too, to attend to multiple and intersecting modes of listening. The book also listens to strategies of silencing as part of willful not-listening. This is taken up through racialized mishearing that limits politically charged songs in chapter 2, structural forces for not-listening that contributed to the folding of Streetz in chapter 3, and not-listening that minimizes the voices of women and nonbinary artists on-air and online in chapter 4. Overall, popular music for broadcast is easiest to share when it fits into existing regimes of racialized listening, yet each chapter provides examples of refusals.

## Backspin, Repeat

The spoken rhythmic voice sounds distant. While completely audible, it contains a crackle like a bad connection. "The virus took on many shapes." The repeated beat that supports the voice propels the music forward, even as other aspects of the vocal bring it back. Two words, "the people," are articulated once, then repeated more quietly each time, an echo that fades and disappears. "The germ traveled faster than the bullet." Where are you and I and we as listeners? When are we? Listening alone in a moment of global pandemic, I wonder, is this now?

A virus seeks hosts, to which some are more susceptible than others; a virus, in some ways indiscriminate, unleashes much more damage on some whose armor is thinner for all the reasons that we know but sometimes ignore. I listen to this song emanating from my computer speakers, between teaching a class on Zoom and having another meeting online. I relisten to this song again as the news cycle around me is full of news about COVID-19, speculations as to whether a cure can emerge, if a vaccine can be found. I listen as a white person in California as the racial and class-based disparities of COVID become distressingly obvious. I have listened before many times, alone and with others, with friends and students and strangers. Some of what I present here is my listening wheres and whens, and some is informed by my listening to others listenings. When my students have listened to this music, they have responded by focusing on a variety of ideas, often protest and survival, or on specific musical elements: vocal timbre, wordplay, intricate electronic drumbeats, deep bass.

A drum beat crystallizes, and then a voice sings over the mix. A melodic arc with a focused timbre, it repeats high in the song's pitch range. This sound is familiar, grounding. Together with the drum, it brings me from this unstable sonic world to the known place of a powwow. The Black Bear Singers' voices and drum anchor my sailing ear. In time with the instrumentals, the voice articulates, "drum beats by region," and I travel with it. I am in a gymnasium or an arena or on a grassy field. And I breathe, because around me, across unique faces and stories, people sing and dance, shake hands, sip coffee. But this wave crashes, splatters on the beach, and I am thrown with the surf. The rapper's voice cuts loud: "The compound was on fire." Electronic instrumentals change timbre, evoking sirens. This could be fun. It could be a height of energy built up by a DJ in a club, but I feel anxious; sirens mean someone is coming, someone I don't want to see.

The groove continues. A listener could still dance here, and maybe you are. The layering sounds are maybe a mounting energy that keeps feet and knees from stillness, maybe a cacophony that throws hands in the air in celebration or resignation. Then rapper Saul Williams's voice continues, making the narrative arc forward into the past: "The missionaries never hid their perspective." He works with his collaborators to tell the terrifying story of the virus, of land prospectors, and the orchestrated efforts to make (Indigenous) people disappear. And the "people" articulate and rearticulate, the singers continue; this is a story of resilience. The refrain comes back, "the compound was on fire," and the sirens return. I hear them differently on this repeat, though they "sound" the same. Maybe you are still dancing; maybe your movement changes as the beat distills at the end of the song, clarifying into a less frenetic form. Maybe you clap slowly with the electronic sounds that pulse as if palms together. Musical practices of sampling, layering, and speech-sung verse, drawn from hip hop and embraced by related genres, bring listeners back and forth in time and let us travel in space. Here, DJ trio A Tribe Called Red and collaborators Black Bear Singers and Saul Williams play with ruptures. This song, "Virus," was released in 2016, yet through listening, it does not exist solely in that moment.[15]

In hip hop practice, it is common to create moments when time extends or even stops. Breaks repeat, and the audience gets into a groove, reliving a moment through sound and dance, again and again. Samples bring music, and its feelings and memories, forward in time or bring listeners backward. This is a sonic practice and an embodied one. The following chapters offer moments that invite the reader-listener to travel with the music and musicians out of time and make space for each reader-listener to have their own experience of the music and its context.

## Flow, Break

Just as music invites multiple readings, *Sonic Sovereignty* invites multiple readerships. Music industry professionals, including media regulators, and music and arts funders are welcomed to listen through the experiences relayed here with broadcast radio, streaming audio, and alternative venues for music recording, performance, and distribution. Artists' and broadcasters' experiences navigating regulatory and funding structures can both showcase how these have worked in the past and open up space to consider how they can function in the future. Scholars in music studies, other media fields, Indigenous studies, and ethnic studies, as well as music practitioners, can all find entry points; intentional variation in prose style is designed to speak to multiple readers and invite unique readings.

Broadcast media provides a space for urban Indigenous communities to be understood—or misunderstood—by internally diverse Indigenous and non-Indigenous audiences. On Streetz, Indigenous media producers retooled existing mainstream channels for their own purposes, a phenomenon that has been previously analyzed in the context of Indigenous-led television.[16] My interactions participating and observing with Streetz DJs, interviewing management and featured musicians, and joining in community events reveal a nuanced view of how the station positions its music and allow me to analyze discourses of Indigenous participation in hip hop. *Sonic Sovereignty* situates musicians' choices within the regulatory environment of broadcast radio. Tracing the circulation of online media, I analyze how musicians use streaming audio networks when regulatory and financial barriers make it challenging to circulate controversial ideas on-air.

Interactions with media professionals determine the theoretical approaches that are most productive for this interdisciplinary research. I scrutinize official policy and scholarship on regulations and funding structures.[17] My ethnographic research connects broadcasting regulations to industry professionals' experiences of regulation within a settler colonial state in other aspects of their lives as Indigenous people. This allows me to extend previous work on the function of music radio.[18] Close readings of music selected for air, alongside my experience with media experts and hip hop artists, shed light on how professionals navigate conflicts and changes in broadcasting rules, funding priorities, and community needs. Connecting to research on the whitening and masculinization of mainstream radio, I assess the implications of this trend on how Indigenous artists are heard—and silenced—through popular music distribution.[19]

Continuing over the following chapters, this book plays with ruptures. Experimenting with possibilities of listening, I deploy moments that mirror musical listening when a tool such as a sample, lyric, or musical reference moves a listener out of time. This stylistic choice is an effort to mirror my conceptualization of sonic sovereignty—drawing on ideas of Indigenous futurity, I argue that part of the sound of sovereignty is the possibility to break with linear time. Begun with colonization, the majoritarian Euro-American time scale imposed a particular notion of time. Linear majoritarian musical ideas reinforce ideas including themes, variation, and development that collectively suggest an ever-forward movement in time. In contrast, though, hip hop welcomes nonlinear listening, and many North American Indigenous listening practices, drawn from storytelling, visit and revisit moments. Thus, in the music in this book, I explore how musicians use tools to help listeners embrace rupture and listen in a nonlinear way and how the out-of-time listening creates a kind of freedom from an imposed time scale.

Sometimes these moments may sneak up on you, like a song someone else was humming sliding its way out of your own lips before you even realize you heard it. At other times, they may be jarring: a neighbor's stereo interrupting your quiet thoughts, a DJ making a transition where the beats do not match up and you are not quite sure how to arrange your dancing body. Some moments I will play and replay, but listen again—every time we hear a song is different, even if it is from the same record.

Chapter 1 is grounded in a critical multisited ethnography and expands from narrative into a focused summary of the media terrain in which twenty-first-century hip hop by Indigenous authors circulates. I synthesize studies on race and gender in popular music industries with particular emphasis on hip hop, which may be of special interest to industry readers. This background provides regulators, such as people working for the Canadian Radio-television and Telecommunications Commission (CRTC), Federal Communications Commission (FCC), or related body charged with creating policy about Indigenous music broadcasting, with a breadth of relevant information about how Indigenous people in general and Indigenous women and nonbinary individuals in particular are currently interacting with mainstream media channels. This information is also designed for granting agencies, including government grantors charged with supporting Indigenous media and private grant makers seeking a better understanding of the unique position of Indigenous musicians as applicants. Some academic readers and musicians will already be familiar with the general sense of these trends yet may find it helpful for data on representation to be detailed here and then connected to theorization of the raced and gendered implications of media circulation. A tailored history of Indigenous hip hop in Canada and the United States connects with relevant literature on colonization and gendered racialization, building toward notions of futurity that are possible in musical practice.

After establishing a ground in chapter 1, chapter 2 centers ethnographic fieldwork with musicians and media professionals to reveal the particular positioning of Canada's most innovative Indigenous music station, Streetz, and the ways in which "mainstream" and "Indigenous" audiences have been articulated and rearticulated over time. The chapter begins at the start of the radio station, traces the factors that motivated its rise, and analyzes work by Indigenous artists who help solidify the station's brand as an Indigenous youth broadcaster, on-air and online. Musical examples and information from interviews demonstrate how Indigeneity in popular sound has been articulated through language, instrumentation, vocalization, or sampling of genres such as competition powwow. In particular, music of Anishinaabe rapper Lorenzo that was chosen for broadcast shows how the station actively shaped an Indigenous community sound during the height of Idle No More. The role of online streaming and the increasing importance of social media parallel a larger trend in music listening, which is revealed as I identify shifts over time from the station's beginning in 2008. Tracing how Indigeneity, Blackness, and masculinity and femininity circulate in popular music discourses, the chapter argues that when contemporary Indigenous hip hop is distributed to an audience that is diverse in race and gender, the frame of sonic sovereignty shows how the music challenges stereotypical constructions of Indigeneity.

Based on the way the online and broadcast media context was described in chapter 2, chapter 3 explores the financial and regulatory environment in which Streetz operated and the barriers it faced. Interviews with industry professionals and musical close readings with Ojibwe rapper Plex, Stó:lō producer/singer Inez, and Ojibwe rapper-turned-politician Wab Kinew show how musicians respond to broadcast regulations and commercial pressures. It begins with the end of Streetz as a radio broadcaster and works backward, tracing what is to be learned from the station going off-air, even as the audience for the music persisted. Thinking through sonic sovereignty, I examine this moment of transition for what it tells us about shifts in the mainstream: aspects of Streetz's successful broadcast and streaming strategies were subsequently taken up by mainstream stations, and some Indigenous artists went on to find success in mainstream venues. This chapter sets the stage for chapter 4, which analyzes the responses of artists who are emphatically not making the jump to mainstream listenerships.

Offering alternatives to the broadcast space, chapter 4 grows from research with Streetz DJs about limitations of official venues and asks what is possible when female, nonbinary, and gender-nonconforming artists create spaces that are explicitly not for all listeners. Building on moments from previous chapters in which certain music was not broadcast, the chapter explores ways in which Indigenous media professionals seek other spaces in which to address timely concerns—notably violence against Indigenous women and girls. Streetz DJ Miss Melissa's experience off-air serves as a pivot point to spaces in which nonmainstream audiences are intentionally created by artists, connecting sonic indigeneity with overtly political activities of the ongoing Missing and Murdered Indigenous Women justice movement. An intersectional analysis connects Eekwol and T-Rhyme's *For Women By Women* project with earlier cyphers for women and nonbinary artists and shows how musicians respond to discrimination within the music industry.[20] It analyzes sonic sovereignty within the context of alternative publics, provides an analysis of hearing versus listening, and establishes the role of silence and refusal in the sound of sovereignty.

In chapter 5, *Sonic Sovereignty* continues to build on the premise that colonization and its attendant logics of conquest can be understood as the transformation of free subjects—including lands, waters, peoples, and nonhuman animals—into owned objects. In this chapter, I demonstrate the ways in which sonic expression and relational listening can create spaces of possibility for decolonial practice. Through relational listening, the chapter invites the reader-audience to listen into a generative space in which the auditor hears subject-voices articulate themselves, displacing object-sounds and dehumanizing logics. Thoroughly analyzing the sound of sovereignty and inviting the reader into generative listening throughout the book prepares the reader to conceptualize, and even participate in, the sound of decolonization.

1

# Hip Hop and Contemporary Urban Indigeneity

It is a cold, snowy evening, though the weather does little to deter the crowds. The thick white plastic of the giant tent blocks the wind from outside, and heat is blowing in through tubes connected to temporary vents. While the temperature is not quite warm, this protection, along with the mass of bodies inside, keeps the indoor/outdoor music festival from being unpleasant in this February winter in a city on the cold prairie. Picnic tables are set with plastic tablecloths. Spectators are seated here, enjoying hot food and drinks from the temporary restaurant at the back. The main focus this evening, however, is the stage. A crowd is gathering. Audience members have walked over the wood chips that cover the snow to place themselves right at the front of the performance area. An emcee grips the mic and greets the crowd in French and English. Behind him, stagehands set up for a band: turntables, keyboards, guitar mic, drum kit, backup singer's mic, and the central mic for the main rapper and singer. In the small partially visible backstage area, band members are preparing to take the stage. This is the thirteenth show for the band in less than that many days, yet the group seems to have a source of energy that keeps them lively this evening. The rapper, Samian, greets the crowd's applause. The musician speaks to the crowd in a mix of English and French, offering shout-outs to the many places from which audience members hail: Québec City, Ottawa, Paris. A cluster of several friends standing near me has come from Ontario, and I have arrived with a group from Minnesota. Of course, Samian elicits the biggest response from the audience when he offers a shout-out to the city in which he is performing: Winnipeg.[1]

A few numbers into the set, Samian starts a song with a rapped list: "Anicinape, Atikamekw, Mi' kmaq, Mohawk, Innu, Cree, Huron-Wendat, Inuit, Abenaki, Maliseet, Naskapi." This list of Indigenous band names includes groups living in and near the present province of Québec, from which he hails. The names of this culturally diverse group form the bulk of the lyrics of the chorus to this song. In his first rapped verse, Samian offers words that recount his understanding of Indigenous history in North America, starting with land loss and extermination and moving through assimilationist policies. The end of his first verse brings history into the present, when he tells his spectators,

| | |
|---|---|
| On ne veut pas juste nos territoires | We don't just want our land |
| C'est une question identitaire | It's a question of identity |
| L'identité c'est primordial | Identity is primordial |
| Et c'est ce que le peuple perd. | It's what people lose.[2] |

At the end of this song, Samian explains that he is Algonquin and makes a connection between his experience in Montréal and the Anishinaabe presence here in Winnipeg. While audience members are mostly in their twenties and thirties, the crowd is diverse in other ways: Francophone, Anglophone, Indigenous, and non-Indigenous, fans who have arrived ready for hip hop social dance, hipsters who shout excitedly at the front of the crowd, and folks who hang back to watch while standing or seated by the far edge of the tent. We are a mix of neck tattoos, skinny jeans, and practical sweaters, dancing together on wood chips covering snow.

The rapper works to animate the crowd, teaching the audience a word that fits into one of his songs and leading everyone in waving a hand in the air. These strategies get a response and encourage the audience to shout and dance with him. Samian invites his guest MC, Anodajay, onstage, and they perform the song "Les Mots" together. François Lalonde animates the drum kit, Sola sings backup vocals, DJ Horg mixes behind them, and Jonathan Tobin alternately plays guitar and keyboard. The DJ plays sounds of pizzicato strings layering with a three-note melody of a legato violin. At the same time, block chords come from the keyboard. The melancholy minor melody cuts out when Samian starts to rap, delivering a text about the power that words can express. After his first verse and a sung chorus, Anodajay raps a second verse with a speech-effusive flow, consistently producing a barrage of syllables, almost without pause. He keeps a strong forward motion with his text, taking a breath only occasionally and always on a weak beat.[3] Samian takes over again for the third verse, his presence polished and confident in front of the dancing crowd. Sola sings backup on the chorus, offering a combination of sung and spoken text. Like Samian's words, hers emphasize how words can be sincere and how they can be harmful. The crowd gets into a groove with the band, moving more or less with the beat emanating from the temporary stage, hands in the air. Just across the river from downtown Winnipeg, in the heart of Francophone St. Boniface, this rapper and this band ignite the crowd. Though some listeners can follow the words in French or Algonquin, many may not. Yet the messaging and the feel of the show are palpable. The mixed crowd takes it in, and this assembled group too becomes part of the event that illuminates the city on this Friday night.

This musical mix that Samian and his band offer is somewhat unusual for a rapper in the first decades of the twenty-first century: Algonquin lyrics appear with French and English, samples are mixed in from intertribal powwow music, and lyrical topicality addresses colonialism, Indigenous pride, and environmentalism. What the musical fusion stands for, however, is quite significant. In the US and Canada, a growing segment of the Indigenous population lives in cities. Many musicians, like Samian, are relying on overlaps between heritage and hip hop musics to tell current stories about contemporary Indigenous culture. Not erased by assimilation, musicians share messages of community pride in the face of challenges; Indigenous, non-Indigenous, and audiences of mixed heritage are listening.[4]

## The Transformative Potential of Hip Hop: Space, Language, and Sovereignty

Musical moments like this one thread together varied ways of listening in hip hop: attuning to flow, beat, samples, lyrics, or references, moving through sound, sensing together, experiencing music as a wholeness with a past-present-future. Listening to musical sound and performance through theories presented by musicians, scholars, and scholar-musicians, this book analyzes how artists and media professionals actively craft their listening publics, at times by bending the mainstream ear toward Indigenous sonic expressions.[5] In addition to lyrical topicality and rhyming techniques, for Indigenous hip hop, choosing or integrating rappers' own First Languages is connected to sovereign articulations.[6] This book suggests that all of these aspects of the music transform space as it is performed. Alongside a focus on space, I synthesize attention to layering and flow with analysis of sampling and technological processes.[7] In Indigenous music contexts, sampling and citation invoke concerns about protocol, ownership, and responsibility.[8] Thus, *Sonic Sovereignty* listens to Indigeneity specifically, which is often omitted in analyses of a black/white sonic divide.

*Sonic Sovereignty* continues the scholarly purpose of writing against misconceptions and does so from a particular position: at the nexus of hip hop music scholarship and Indigenous studies scholarship. Indigenous hip hop faces a double bind in that Indigenous music is sometimes cast as—even defined as—music of the past.[9] Ideas of "pastness" discursively limit expressions of contemporary Indigeneity. Popular music, and hip hop in particular, serves as a counternarrative to rurality and pastness.[10] Further, this music marks the city as undeniably Indigenous, of particular relevance to the artists and genres rooted in urban expressive culture. This contrasts to narrow ideas of what Indigenous music can or should sound like, which can inappropriately circumscribe what Indigenous musicians are expected to play and say. In Canada and other settler states, efforts at the level of the nation-state to deploy Indigenous cultural markers as part of the country's face to the world are part of the ongoing effects of settler colonialism.[11] Reading Indigenous hip hop specifically, *Sonic Sovereignty* builds on Rinaldo Walcott's finding that Black Canadians are consistently rhetorically located in an elsewhere[12] and finds that Indigenous peoples living in North America are regularly discursively located in an elsewhen. People and groups who identify as one or both of Black Canadian and Indigenous thus face one or both of these kinds of removes, as the book describes more fully in chapter 4. As efforts to render Indigenous peoples as premodern underpin the colonialist nation-state, Indigenous music can be miscast as not having a future, so that those who hear it might misinterpret it as static tradition. The vibrant circulation of Indigenous hip hop is a living sonic counterexample to narratives that would locate Indigenous music in the past to make sense *as* Indigenous music or miscast hip hop as divorced from its long and strong roots. *Sonic Sovereignty* is part of a larger, continual reshaping of discourses and narratives as performers musically draw through lines connecting past and future, and careful listening connects audiences through these articulations.

Detailing the ideas proposed in the introduction, this chapter grounds the book's use of terminology that invokes conversations that layer upon each other in each subsequent chapter of the book, weaving together sovereignty, history, futurity, and the time-bending possibilities of hip hop practice. Both grounded in place and relevant beyond borders, musical moments offer readers ways to listen and relisten to voices that resonate differently across audiences. There is meaningful overlap between hip hop contexts in Canada, Australia, Aotearoa–New Zealand, and the United States; some musicians seek and find international audiences in these markets. This chapter offers some context for these connections, while setting up the rest of the book to focus specifically on media markets in Canada and how these resonate in the United States. Recognizing the varied readership of this chapter, the next section provides context on how race is understood in relationship to Indigeneity, details how hip hop's global spread connects to narratives of rebellion as well as the genre's relationship to capitalist consumption, and explores the ongoing effects of the gendering and racialization of hip hop practices. Readers who already have a strong background in all of these concepts may wish to rejoin the flow in the following section, which connects a musical reading of race and belonging to the past, present, and future of Indigenous hip hop. Finally, a history of Indigenous hip hop in Canada leads into questions about mainstreaming and decolonial listening that appear throughout the remaining chapters of the book.

*Sonic Sovereignty* finds that we cannot understand music without a sense of its contextual relationship to space. Throughout this book, I incorporate the quotidian elements of hip hop practice as lived experience that appear in studies of hip hop as a daily reality of urban life. Bridging what has become an international popular music genre with specific references to a particular location, Indigenous hip hop complicates notions of the local and the global in hip hop.[13] As hip hop moves across borders, adopters face the challenge of articulating belonging despite discourses of authenticity derived from specific place, knowledge, and experience. While sometimes racialized similarly to African Americans, urban Indigenous musicians in Canada carry forward culturally and historically different experiences. Throughout the book, examples from twenty-first-century hip hop demonstrate how the music can facilitate localized expressions of Indigeneity while artists continually honor Black musical innovators. Recognizing that hip hop knowledge comes from a hybrid musico-cultural scene rich with Afro-diasporic and Latinx musical performance, these practices demonstrate how artists move their listeners across time and place, even as Indigenous artists honor a hip hop past that is intermingled with, yet not identical to, their own.

In this chapter, I continue in the trajectory of scholarship that interrogates the social context of hip hop, namely, the roles of Indigeneity, racialization, gender, and class on cultural production. Starting from and extending beyond the idea that masculinity in hip hop in the United States is based largely on particular social ideas of African American masculinity, Indigenous artists of many nations and gender identities copy and complicate these tropes.[14] Understood as a practice with pedagogical and performance elements, hip hop is gendered by the way male, female, and nonbinary participants are and are not invited to participate in learning and performance.[15]

As Shawn Wilson, who is Opaskwayak Cree and has lived in New South Wales, Australia, summarizes, "research is all about unanswered questions, but it also reveals our unquestioned answers."[16] *Sonic Sovereignty* questions the (sometimes) unquestioned, reasking and refining questions by inviting conversation across place and discipline. To hear the sound of sonic sovereignty, readers are invited to listen through the many aspects of decolonization. In her influential writing, Linda Tuhiwai Smith, who affiliates with two iwi, Ngāti Awa and Ngāti Porou, theorizes the struggle for decolonization through five dimensions: critical consciousness; reimagining; the intersection of disparate ideas, events, and the historical moment; movement or disturbance; and the structure of power relations.[17] Musicians whose work informs this book proceed through varying aspects of decolonization, often choosing multiple aspects of this struggle in their own creative process. Further, following Tuhiwai Smith's attention to a multiplicity of viewpoints, I proceed from the vantage point that music is inherently multivalent. Through the deep listening moments presented across this chapter, you as reader-listener are invited to open your ears for layering—and potentially divergent—musical meanings. These musical passages are already analytical; some are designed to show, rather than tell, the possibilities for multiple listening perspectives, whether they occur online, in person, over the airwaves, or in spaces that span all of these.

It is not coincidental that possibilities come into being through musical practice. Affective encounters, always more than that which can be understood through text alone, engage expansive experiences of time and of relationship. As Deborah Kapchan observes, listening to music invokes memory and transforms perception: "Even more than language, music also invades the unconscious, re-organizing perception, and creating iconic links between aesthetic experiences of audition and emotional responses such as awe, rapture, or ecstasy."[18] Sometimes this magic feels deceptively simple: a DJ samples a song with its own story and history, a listener feels their own experience of that song history crash into the new signification created in the present articulation, layers of meaning build on and change each other, a present moment is perfumed with moments of past memory and meaning. And yet these moments create the opening for that which does not make sense, for the possibility for that which cannot be made to fit the present systems of value and meaning. These unsubsumable moments hold incredible power. Kara Keeling explains this destructive—and I would add transformational— power: "Whatever escapes recognition, whatever escapes meaning and valuation, exists as an impossible possibility within our shared reality, however that reality is described theoretically, and therefore threatens to unsettle, if not destroy, the common senses on which that reality relies for its coherence as such."[19]

A decolonial future mutually implicates everyone impacted by settler colonialism. As Laura Harjo (Mvskoke) describes it, Indigenous futurity is a "form of collective power" and "is space and place produced via relationality and connections to humans and more-than-human entities."[20] The project of futurity is specific to individual Indigenous nations; it also connects and extends beyond group boundaries. The interconnectedness between the survival of Indigenous peoples and Black peoples can be listened to through storytelling. Tiffany Lethabo King recalls having an unsettling response when she listened to an Anishinaabe woman talk about how Indigenous people are "stalked by the death shadow of genocide daily"; King narrates a tactile response as her own narrative of slavery is changed by the listening: "There was something about the way this Anishinaabe woman spoke of genocide. I knew that it had everything to do with now, with tomorrow, with yesterday. With then. And more so, it had everything to do with slavery." This was not transference but "a different kind of vision of yourself that you experience in a truly ethical encounter, a kind of co-witnessing that enables people not only to mirror back pain but also to also implicate one another in our survival."[21] The possibility for a future is an interconnected one.

The contexts of Indigenous musics expand Keeling's theorization in multiple directions. Indigenous futurity also necessarily brings forward creative expression from the (often precolonial) past, troubling linear time in order to instantiate—however fleetingly—the impossible possible future in the present. Artists, we are reminded by Qwo-Li Driskill, Chris Finley, Brian Joseph Gilley, and Scott Lauria Morgensen, will bring forth this future.[22] The figure of Métis leader Louis Riel looms large in discussions of a cultural future that never loses its link to the past—Riel's statue stands by the Winnipeg provincial capital, and Manitoba celebrates Louis Riel Day each February, even as other provinces do not. The story of Riel, the Red River Resistance, and the North-West Rebellion are told in conflicting ways to audiences in Canada. These histories have been polarizing at times and speak to ideas of nation and legitimacy that change based on an audience's geography, ethnic identity, and when they are told. Even Riel, as a military leader, makes expressive culture central in his figuration of Métis survival. Riel's tenacity and dogged pursuit of rights for those who were not represented by the Eastern Canadian government in the 1800s are celebrated in Western Canada by many Anglophone, Francophone, Indigenous, non-Indigenous, Métis, non-Métis, and mixed-heritage people to the present day. The battles for Métis self-rule are celebrated and mourned in song. A telling example is "La cloche de Batoche," which remembers the 1885 battle in present-day Saskatchewan, using a minor-key refrain to recall the strength of Métis resistors and expressing the ways these experiences resonate—including positively—to this day.[23] I have heard many people in this region—both those who identify as artists and those who do not—refer to Riel's vision for the future that he reportedly spoke before he was executed by the Canadian state: "Mon peuple dormira pendant cent ans. Lorsqu'il s'éveillera, ce seront les artistes qui lui rendront son âme" (My people will sleep for one hundred years. When they awake, it will be the artists who will give them their soul). For many people, the story of Riel's words carries meaning into the present, in which artists perform a special role for physical and cultural survival. Contemporary musicians from the overlapping groups of women, nonbinary people, queer performers, Black artists, and Indigenous artists take up versions of this charge; listening attentively to varied interpretations builds into potentiality. So listen for myriad possible futures.

By being produced by specific groups of people in particular places and times, the musical utterances that I analyze in this book become more than themselves. Rapped lyrics are not simply commentary about the topic at hand; they are part of the work that makes ideas manifest in the world. When musical words or gestures are the acts that do work in the world, they can connect to articulations of sovereignty. Sometimes, sung stories articulate sovereignty and self-determination in band-specific legal ways.[24] *Sonic Sovereignty* listens through music that people make to articulate the city as already Indigenous, that asserts Indigenous or band-specific ways of knowing through their voicing in music, and that temporarily realizes a sought-for future that brings forth the past and transforms the present.[25]

## Popular Music and Indigeneity

Within hip hop scholarship, the word "Indigenous" takes on a variety of meanings. Because the nexus of Indigenous studies and hip hop studies is relatively recent, terminology does not always move fluidly from one field to the other: some scholars use the term "Indigenization" to indicate any use of non-English colonial or local languages or musical forms in hip hop. This does not correspond to the way the word is used to reference First Peoples.[26] There is nothing neutral or given about terminology; the word "Indigenous" is defined and redefined and deployed in contexts with specific resonances.

The reader is likely to notice a shift in terminology over time and based on the positionality of the speaker. Published texts, interviews, music festivals, and events, notably those in Canada, used the term "Aboriginal" with regularity in 2008, but by 2018, the term "Indigenous" was much more common. In US contexts, terms such as "Native American" continued to be common in 2018, yet with a growing focus on international organizing and connectivity, the term "Indigenous," too, was used increasingly frequently by that year.[27] Some people and groups in North America continued to prefer the term "Indian" or "American

Indian" as a self-designation, while others chose band- or tribe-specific terms, such as "Lakota" or "Nehiyaw," first or exclusively. Participants have chosen to identify as Indian, Native American, Aboriginal, Native, and by more specific affiliations; the same individuals may refer to themselves with different terms across contexts. The term "Aboriginal" is used in the Canadian context when referring to specific policies or organizations that employ this term. In Canada, the term "Indigenous" is employed to encompass First Nations, Inuit, and Métis groups, and historically the word "Aboriginal" has been as well. The term "Indigenous" is particularly helpful in border areas because terms such as "Native American" carry with them linkages to nation-states.[28] Rather than referring to Anishinaabeg peoples residing in Canada as "First Nations" and those in the United States as "Native Americans," terms like "Indigenous" that lack markers of nation-state allow for no distinction to be made unless it is relevant. Mishuana Goeman (Tonawanda Band of Seneca) writes that "Indigenous," as a term applicable in multiple global contexts, "refers to peoples in various regions of the world whose history, culture, kinship ties, and land and water practices are prior to and extend beyond European colonization."[29] After Goeman, I use the word "Indigenous" in reference to past, present, and future expressions. In this research, many participants talk about commonalities across Indigenous groups and make music in response to these, though Indigenous nations are heterogeneous.

Literature and guides for writers already exist to inform readers on the history and implications of terminology and to advise on appropriate usage.[30] Here, I offer a brief discussion that responds to topics that have emerged in conversation related to Indigenous media circulation and sonic sovereignty. First, musicians and industry professionals use "Aboriginal" or "Indigenous" as adjectives, not nouns. This common approach in speaking and writing is codified as a recommendation in a 2018 manual and shares significant similarities with a collaboratively written style guide, including capitalizing the term "Indigenous" to align with much contemporary scholarship and recommendations for journalism and other writing.[31] "Indigeneity" is used as the nominative form of "Indigenous." Unlike ideas of Aboriginality or Indigeneity that construct them as opposite to modernity, I argue that many popular musicians operationalize Indigeneity that is utterly contemporary and in large part already urban. Popular musicians including those in this book who circulate their music through social media, online streaming, and other web-based networks manifest Indigeneity that is always already digital.[32]

For political and legal reasons in an international context, many descriptions refer to documents created by the United Nations, such as the 2007 Declaration on the Rights of Indigenous Peoples.[33] Some definitions incorporate multiple layers in an effort to avoid oppositional or overly general wording. Klisiala Harrison, for example, elaborates: "While in many ways heterogeneous in experiences and cultural features, Indigenous peoples share: self-identification as Indigenous, a continuation of historical pre-colonial or pre-settler societies, strong links to territories and natural resources, a distinctness of social, economic or political systems as well as language, culture and beliefs, a non-dominant position in broader society, and a resolve to sustain their ancestral environments and social systems."[34] The deployment of the term "Indigenous" in scholarship acknowledges the existence of a connection between first inhabitants of a variety of places beyond North America, referencing overlapping historical conditions and political struggles between peoples. Engaging the term "Indigenous" both demonstrates an understanding of many distinct cultures as linked in important ways and reflects that this connection has been critical to the actors involved.[35]

Indigenous music and representation can also be interrogated in matters of cultural appropriation. Consider, for example, the following: (1) the controversy around throat singing when Inuit musicians critiqued a Cree singer for using throat singing in an album entered for the 2018 Indigenous Music Awards; (2) the activism of members of The Halluci Nation (and its former incarnation as A Tribe Called Red) against using Indigenous peoples as mascots; or (3) the scholarly critique leveraged by Joanne Barker (Lenape) against persons claiming that they should be able to wear headdresses as a fashion choice.[36] In a written statement about contemporary music in Canada, ten Indigenous composer-performers—Cris Derksen, Melody McKiver, Ian Cusson, Beverley McKiver, Jeremy Dutcher, Sonny-Ray Day Rider, Michelle Lafferty, Corey Payette, Jessica McMann, and Andrew Balfour—explain their term "Indigenous Musical Sovereignty": "Maintaining ownership and

control of our stories and artistic projects is of vital importance for Indigenous creators." They juxtapose this statement in contrast to music
made by non-Indigenous people that claims to be "Indigenous-inspired."
Definitionally, Derksen et al. assert, "Simply, a work is Indigenous when
it is created by an Indigenous artist, regardless of theme or topic. A story
is Indigenous whether it comes from ancestral knowledge, lived experience, or imagination."[37]

## Indigenous Popular Music and Industry Mainstreams

Cultural connection and community acceptance of an artist by their
Indigenous community is consistently used as a metric for appropriateness; for the purposes of discussion within popular music industries,
"Indigenous music" is created by those who are recognized as Indigenous people by their communities and, with respect to artists who
wish to be seen as "musicians" rather than "Indigenous musicians,"
who choose to make some kind of connection to their heritage and/
or Indigenous community through their music, performance, or public
personas.[38] It can be made in any genre. It can be made by people who
are of mixed ancestry. It can be made by people living in urban, rural,
reserve, or reservation locales or who move between these. Community
standards of acceptance and articulation are paramount.

Indigenous hip hop operates at an intersection of ideas about race,
ethnicity, and belonging. Like any genre category, "Indigenous hip hop"
is a term circulated to make sense of a diverse array of musics. While its
application is dynamic, the use of the term in this book reflects its common circulation among musicians and media-industry professionals.
Understandings of Indigeneity necessarily intersect with conceptions
of race, gender, and sexuality, which are all entrenched in the history
of popular music. The USAmerican popular music industry, which has
long held influence across borders, historically distributed music on the
basis of racial classifications; as a result, sexual-racial categories, ideas of
class-based authenticity, and gendered expectations continue to impact
media distribution, genre categorization, and performer expectations.[39]

Hip hop practitioners, journalists, and scholars have argued for wide
recognition of the aesthetic and cultural significance of the practice.
Through sonic and embodied layers, it can be heard and experienced as

an assertion of its own rich history. At the same time, hip hop scholars, practitioners, and scholar-practitioners have countered some popular discourses that touted the romantic, and limiting, story of a culture that emerged from nothing and have striven to inscribe its significance and meaningful aesthetics. This critical work confronts what Tricia Rose identifies as the "hyperbolic and polarized public conversation about hip hop" that "discourages progressive and nuanced consumption, participation, and critique."[40] Hip hop culture is rooted in Afro-diasporic practices and has been shaped by African American, Afro-Caribbean, Latinx, and Indigenous innovators. Blackness and Indigeneity are refracted differently through music, as well as through interpretations of the present and future and past. Hip hop ethnographer Cheryl Keyes explicitly historicizes the artistic influences of West African storytelling practices, music from the period of slavery in the southern United States (e.g., the "ring shout"), music of the urban North after the Great Migration (like the radio DJ's "jive talk"), and influences of the Harlem Renaissance and a long poetry tradition, including luminaries Gil Scott-Heron and Nikki Giovanni.[41] Portia Maultsby, a professor of ethnomusicology at Indiana University, began teaching a course on hip hop in a university setting in 1989, introducing it as an academic subject even before the hip hop culture wars of the early 1990s. Cornel West articulates the ways—and reasons—that American popular music has repeatedly been profoundly changed by African American musics.[42] They and others took on this task because, as they explain, if this music's history is underappreciated, then the skill and artistic creativity of those who make it is also occluded.[43] Heard in context, hip hop rises from West African bardic traditions; survives forced migration and slavery; moves through sharecropping, urbanization, and the Great Migration; and then emerges in an era of white flight, the war on drugs, and the solidification of a school-to-prison pipeline.

Narratives of Black music as being organic tend to erase or minimize creativity, undervalue the technical mastery of Black cultural producers, and also downplay or efface the relevance of Black musical expression to the history of (American) music. This whitewashing writes out individuals and also tries to depoliticize, or make available for co-optation and other use, musical expressions that have come through a long and culturally situated musical history. It is crucial to keep articulating how hip hop—as a practice associated with communities of color—draws from a rich past. Hearing an urban Black music as one with a long history helps current listeners recognize Black cultural production, as well as the skills of those who perform or adapt it. Expanding to a degree into graffiti and breakdance as well, this same legacy is vital to Tricia Rose's 1994 book *Black Noise*, which showed an academic audience and a general public readership that hip hop is a serious, enjoyable, skilled practice stemming from a long aesthetic and cultural history. As hip hop continued to circulate outside the United States, sometimes that limiting and racialized narrative of music without a past came with it. In 2018, Fernando Orejuela explained, "I must ask my students to confront race through hip hop studies because it is easy for them to look at rap as just a style of music-making disconnected from human agency."[44] Orejuela had found that his university students who were studying hip hop often failed to recognize its significance as a cultural form rooted in communities of color.

Sonic sovereignty operates within and through the refusal to continue to prop up colonial structures, the bending of structures to decolonial purposes, and the resurgence of structures of relationship that predate and transcend settler colonialism. As colonization persists, its effects continue.[45] Put simply, "the colonizers never left, were never driven out."[46] Haunani-Kay Trask and Patrick Wolfe have argued for a now well-known conceptual shift in which colonialism is understood as a structure, not an event.[47] This move suggests that anticolonial theorizing and praxis must engage a host of systematically linked power relations, creating or re-creating alternative structures in their wake. It also reflects decolonial scholarship that had previously argued that colonialism is a process and that it is not over. As Trask has articulated, colonization is a "historical process" that proceeds through the policy of genocide—its ongoing effects span cultural erasure, discriminatory policies, state-sanctioned and rogue violence, including gender-based violence, economic structures at the nation-state and multinational level, and so much more.[48] In the phrasing of Tiffany Lethabo King, conquest and resistance to conquest are "not an event, not even a structure, but a milieu or active set of relations that we can push on, move around in, and redo from moment to moment."[49] My argument unfolds with the understanding that the power structures through which colonialism is maintained must be actively supported to continue to stand and so can be resisted and redrawn through individual and collective action.

Through this confluence, listeners perceive theory on sounds of Blackness and sounds of Indigeneity speaking to each other. In both literatures, which are increasingly overlapping, the "invisible," or inaudible, emerge as responses to "mainstream" perception.[50] It is imperative, too, to recall that practitioners, including artists, theorists, and audiences, may identify as Black *and* Indigenous and/or affiliate with other groups. So after Simone Browne, I ask, what is "inaudible," and what is simply unheard by many? Who is ignoring sound or otherwise failing to listen to it, and what responsibility do those ears have to the music and musicians they are failing to perceive? In a Canadian context in particular, historical and ongoing erasures of Black Canadian culture impacts the way hip hop—including Indigenous hip hop—is heard in the twenty-first century. As Katherine McKittrick finds, "Black existence is an actuality, which takes on several different forms that do not (much to the surprise of some) always conform to the idea of Canada."[51] Musical practice is often coconstitutive of ideas of nation, nations, and belonging. Planted in my memory are conversations in which people I talked to about this research were shocked by the existence of Indigenous hip hop or questioned the importance of Black music in Canada. Moments in which some listeners feel surprise or experience cognitive dissonance can be those in which they must rehear, listen, and rethink. These opportunities to reconsider preconceived notions are consistent with what Walcott finds: Black popular culture "forc[es] the recognition of a different kind of Canadianness."[52] This recognition, though unwilling for some, is of a Canadian identity that is not based in whiteness and a sanitized version of confederation.

In hip hop and other popular genres, female, trans*, and nonbinary musicians, producers, and other industry professionals are significantly underrepresented.[53] Over more than a decade, I have heard a variety of producers and sound engineers talk about their experiences in behind-the-scenes music roles. In one such conversation, an engineer explained how much she likes doing her work and also that she is not always seen or heard doing it—people, especially men, in the studio look past her or explain things to her that she has known for quite some time. I hear a knowing nod in her voice; I have heard men explain things to me that I already know many times; she relates these events factually and without surprise. For many women and nonbinary people, experiences like these happen over and over.[54]

The lack of self-representation of womxn[55] (a term that I discuss further in chapter 4) in music is felt in hip hop and urban genres. In chapter 4, I delve into more detail on the popular music industry and the urgency of race, gender, and ideological diversity on multiple levels. Dawn Norfleet explains that Black women in hip hop "contend with three complex, overlapping identities: *females* operating within a male-defined realm; *Black female artists* operating within the context of the White-male dominated music industry, and *artists* operating in a commercial realm that places restrictions on artists in general."[56] Other racialized women, who become what Norfleet calls "representatives of economically disenfranchised classes," experience these three overlapping positionalities in a similar manner.[57] As will be further explored in chapters 2 and 3, music industry gender inequity can be heard on-air in music broadcasting and online through streaming of broadcast sources as well as streaming-first content, such as playlists generated for online music-listening platforms and programming decisions made for podcasts.[58] In response to structural exclusion, chapter 4 traces the ways in which some womxn musicians are creating spaces of strategic exclusivity, curating their own listenerships to do their intended work. This lack of mainstream recognition for music by womxn in general and womxn of color in particular is an audible silence, notably across musical mainstreams in the industry. The nine male songwriters with the most songs in the Hot 100 are credited with nearly 20 percent of all songs between 2012 and 2017. This means that "these individuals are driving the work product and content of popular music and setting an agenda for the entire music industry."[59] Stories, perspectives, and sound worlds are limited when just a few individuals with a limited range of experiences are setting such an influential agenda. In these instances, an unhearing of voices starts from a direct cause: womxn, womxn of color, and Indigenous womxn are not in the room or on the air.

This is one of many ways to listen and one of many ways to speak. An actor, with a studio mic before her, delivers her lines. Her ears are covered by headphones. Behind her, the clear full-pane windows cut the edge of this resonant space. Her hands gesticulate emphatically; her voice, too, is insistent. More hands, and more voices, join her. Three people sit by a fire. Each one holds a drumstick in their right hand and uses their left to steady the sewn edges of a two-headed drum. Two hands manipulate a computer, the left using a keyboard and the right on a mouse; waveforms appear on-screen as the hands manipulate recorded audio files. A dancer gently moves his hands in front of and behind his body. Each one arcs with the flow of the music and then stops with the electronic percussive hit that marks the beat of the song. Hands hold signs aloft, grasp an ear of corn, shake a rattle, touch a blade of grass, and form fists raised into the air.

A voice, echoing as if it were a chorus, says, "Stand up." A solo flute repeats a slow melody; its woody timbre blends with the resonant human voices that sing a complementary melodic line. The first rapper begins, "Stand up with the First Nations and a people that be living here for thousands of years." He shares a list of past heroes, uses language of unity, and ends his verse with, "One people one tribe, now it's us against the pipeline. Get on your feet for Standing Rock, and we'll show you how strong we can be when we unify." Across verses, rappers and singers share the language of solidarity, of sovereignty, of Indigenous land and water rights.

The next chorus is sung by a literal chorus, the recording studio filled with people who sing together. They sing back to the processed vocals of a solo singer whose address is wide: "To all my Native people, to all the original people, to all my Indigenous people." One after another, rappers reference oil in the water, the black snake, sacred grounds. Their vocal inflections, rhythmic patterns, rapped speeds, and wordplay vary widely, but all these styles hang together. Bridging the verses and choruses, individual people say, "Mni Wiconi," "Water is Life," Lakota and English words bringing the core message through each segment of the video. They insist on respect for the earth and a respect for the legal sovereignty of the Lakota people. The images of a studio full of people, interspersed with individuals speaking, give the video an air of earlier activist music videos. Maybe a viewer sees and hears flashes of "Almost like Praying," "Un geste pour Haiti Cherie," or even "We Are the World." With communication techniques distilled through relief concerts designed to inspire, like Live Aid and A Concert for Hurricane Relief, these efforts have an imprint on "Stand Up / Stand N Rock," made in 2016. This time, the music video's audience sees many artists, activists, and artist-activists, mostly from the US and Canada, including actress Shailene Woodley, flutist Tony Duncan, traditional and popular singers Perry Cheevers, Gerald Danforth, Spencer Battiest, Kahara Hodges, PJ Vegas, and rappers Taboo, Emcee One, Drezus, Doc Battiest, and Supaman. The variety across speakers and singers and musical styles, timbres and instruments, musicians and activists, actually helps this well-produced video make sense as a unit; the range makes it hold water.

In this video, Indigenous hip hop artists with a wide stylistic range collaborate. Artists and activists from many nations—Lakota, of course, and also Apsáalooke, Cree, Osage, Potawatomi, Delaware, Seminole, Shoshone, and others—work together on the song and video. It shows how song is already connected to sovereignty, and land rights to daily life. It hits a nerve. It circulates on YouTube and social media and wins a mainstream music video award: the US-based 2017 MTV VMA award for the Best Fight Against the System category. This song courts a mainstream listenership, locking in with known tropes of fund-raising (and emotion-raising) music videos that have sought audiences for decades. It shows its diversity of voices and perspectives by focusing on the wide range of musicians, actors, and activists, Indigenous people of many nations and non-Indigenous allies, singing solo and grouping together. Some of its listeners also hear music videos by Lakota rappers and musicians who speak specifically to the concerns of the Oceti Sakowin; some just hear this more general message. How are these stories told, who does the telling, and what are all the ways listening can happen?

## Sonic Sovereignty in Context

Native nations had multiple and specific notions of sovereignty that they theorized before European contact; the European-derived legal concept is not sufficient to encompass these theorizations. Music, language, and gesture are at the core of decolonial acts.[60] Sovereignty, as Michelle Raheja (Seneca) describes, is "an ontological and philosophical concept with very real practical, political, and cultural ramifications that unites the experiences of Native Americans, but it is a difficult idea to define because it is always in motion and is inherently contradictory."[61]

A Euro-American definition of legal sovereignty is just one notion of sovereignty; far more have been operational in North America since long before colonization began. The English word "sovereignty" is a mere placeholder, so it is worth continuing to define, redefine, and redeploy this and related terms in a variety of contexts and conversations. As the previous example shows, "Stand Up / Stand N Rock" insists on a particular kind of legal sovereignty and also articulates land and water rights through a musical call that invokes the participation of non-Indigenous people and Indigenous people of many nations.[62] Raheja explains that "it is critical to insist on a much bigger notion of sovereignty that takes seriously the importance of sovereignty as it is expressed intellectually, politically, socially, and individually . . . in cultural forms as diverse as dance, film, theater, the plastic arts, literature, and even hip-hop and graffiti."[63] Jolene Rickard (Haudenosaunee [Tuscarora]) contrasts sovereignty as self-determination through law, which she associates with her own upbringing. Sovereignty is active. Specifically through her art practice, in community with others, Rickard determined, "the idea of our art serving Indigenous communities reinforced my understanding that sovereignty is more than a legal concept."[64] Beverly Singer (Tewa, Dine) demonstrates in her writing and filmmaking what she refers to as "cultural sovereignty," "which involves trusting in the older ways and adapting them to our lives in the present."[65] This enactment of sovereignty does involve defending treaty rights, and it also incorporates practicing ceremony, speaking First Languages, and continuing long-standing food-harvesting practices.

What these enactments all share is an emphasis on legal control of land as a right (respect for treaty, ability to live on ancestral land, right to control government structures on said land) *in addition to* one or more other forms of self- and group determination. While land rights are centered in these sovereignty practices, sovereignty practices have become (and perhaps always were) about more than rights under a liberal state. Following Rickard, Singer, and Raheja, as well as Joanne Barker, Taiaiake Alfred, Robert Warrior, and Elizabeth Cook-Lynn, I listen for an expansive conception of Indigenous sovereignty as one that includes, and is emphatically not instead of, a legal framework that determines land ownership, use, and rights through the courts of the settler state.[66] Sonic sovereignty transcends land use and includes unfettered creative expression and linguistic freedom by engaging with creativity through sound, how narrators recount stories, how musicians use heritage musics and popular genres to mutually transform each other, and the ways in which relationships are forged through listening. Like cultural sovereignty, and unlike some sovereignty formations that focus on the individual, sonic sovereignty is experienced and enacted in relationship with others. Like many kinds of musical practice, it comes into being through the body and is relational in nature.[67]

These definitions resonate with that of scholar and musician Leanne Betasamosake Simpson, who extends her own definition from a conversation with an elder: "My understanding of 'Kina Gchi Anishinaabeg-ogaming—the place where we all live and work together,' means something vastly different than a defended tract of land. . . . Sovereignty is not just about the land; it is also a spiritual, emotional, and intellectual space that spans back seven generations and that spans forward seven generations."[68] Bodies—hearts and minds, as well as performing bodies—perform a crucial link to the sonic sovereignty that can be enacted through music. I define sonic sovereignty as an embodied practice of Indigenous self-determination through musical expression. Framing our inquiries through sonic sovereignty invites a way of thinking that takes seriously the lived effects of expressive culture and recognizes that these are inextricably linked to a range of possibilities for self-determination. This form of sovereignty is enacted through musical expression specifically because music can create realities in a manner that transcends the direct signification of symbolic text. Musical practice, so often undertaken collectively, offers a space in which to enact the mutual responsibility that sovereignty entails. Notably, this collective may be internally heterogeneous; practically, this requires opening our ears to ways of listening that allow for multiple interpretations. As a practice, sonic sovereignty can be exercised through established media circulation channels, but it also questions the customary uses of these and pushes into new and ancient forms of creative musical storytelling.[69]

Storytelling is a practice of sovereignty. Simpson is a storyteller; her stories take forms that span intersecting media including verbally recounted narration, songs, short stories, poems, and essays. Simpson uses storytelling as action: "a decolonizing process with the power to recall, envision, and create modes of resurgence and contesting cognitive imperialisms."[70] *Sonic Sovereignty* reads hip hop and electronically based music performance as a stage on which interweaving forms of storytelling are possible: artists tell stories in music, through lyrics and non-verbal elements of the songs they create, through the stories they tell onstage, and through interactions with fellow musicians and audience members as stories unfold. Poetics, multidirectional references, text, and subtext that simultaneously speak to multiple audiences, the ability to take over public space with sound, creative uses of and contributions to changes in emergent technologies—all of these are reasons that hip hop has particular resonance for sonic sovereignty. The specific practice of hip hop is also relevant because of its grounding in Afro-diasporic music making and its ongoing connections to Black music in Canada, in the United States, and globally.

Listening to and telling stories is part of the manner in which a person can constitute one's self and one's community. Historian Angela Cavender Wilson (Dakota) reflects on her experience learning from her grandmother Elsie Cavender: "it is through the stories of my grandmother, my grandmother's grandmother, and my grandmother's grandmother's grandmother and their lives that I learned what it means to be a Dakota woman, and the responsibility, pain, and pride associated with such a role."[71] Highlighting and challenging the cultural power of telling histories happens through interventions both in form and in content, as I explore in further detail in chapter 2. As a practice of sovereignty, storytelling enacts relationships in particular ways. Reflecting on what is heard and listened to can make space for transformation at multiple levels.

## Beyond Traditional versus Modern: Self-Definition and Self-Determination

Living musical expressions extend into twenty-first-century hip hop in the Americas. Due to the specific histories of First Nations and hip hop musics, these practices are well positioned to critique narratives that characterize diverse contemporary urban Indigenous cultures. Aesthetic and social concerns that crystallize in this music open up space in which shifts toward increased audibility of urban Indigenous communities and the retelling of stories are both possible. The research presented here indicates that in large metropolises in the US and Canada, hip hop that employs signifiers of Indigenous culture advances musical messaging that complicates established relationships between Indigeneity and presentness as well as challenging assumptions of cultural loss and assimilation in urban settings.[72] By specifically examining music made during the rise of streaming audio in the first two decades of the twenty-first century in North America, *Sonic Sovereignty* places these musics within a wider context of global Indigenous popular music practices. Hip hop contexts in territory now named Canada, Australia, Aotearoa–New Zealand, and the United States demonstrate significant overlap. There are limits to these parallels, as far as racialization, regulatory and funding structures, and official reconciliation and recognition practices are concerned, yet listening for resonance is productive. As Leonard Sumner, an Anishinaabe musician who has rapped as Lorenzo, explains about traveling from his home in Manitoba to perform for crowds from Australia and Aotearoa–New Zealand, "There's a very similar history, with the relationship between Indigenous people and the colonizers." Playing on the Commonwealth, he elaborates, "Where there's common wealth, there's common poverty. . . . One of the Maori women I met told me that we are united by our struggle." In Canada, as well as in other former British colonies, Sumner finds, "Where we've been able to preserve languages or preserve cultural artifacts or ceremonies, we have to celebrate the things that we are able to maintain. Sharing that with each other is a victory for everybody."[73]

The increased popularity of streaming audio and related changes to star structures at the end of the first decade of the new millennium ushered in, at first, an array of voices. When paired with social attitudes as well as broadcasting and funding structures that encouraged at least a cursory listen to nonmajoritarian artists, these changes invited listening for and with Indigenous urban musicians. Yet the ears attuned to this music had already been shaped by social expectations based on genre, geography, gender, race, and status. Pathologizing discourses about Indigeneity continued to function in wide circulation; a legacy of silencing Indigenous creators, especially in urban areas, perpetuated its ongoing effects. Given tension between the possible and the actual, a framework of relocated Indigeneity, described here and further applied in chapter 2, speaks particularly to how Indigenous culture is produced and mediated in cities. In order to get a sense of how hip hop was falling on postapology ears, listeners are invited to understand the variety of stories that had been told to different people and how the loudest stories were already impacting what each could and could not hear.

Cultural transformation brings to the forefront both theoretical concerns, namely the position of Indigeneity vis-à-vis contemporary culture, and practical ones, notably the strategies surrounding cultural learning and practices that facilitate the creation of hybrid forms. For contemporary musicians, continuing what Joshua Tucker calls "traditional ways" can affirm cultural practices, as well as enforce limitations. As Tucker elaborates, musico-cultural activities that trouble false binaries linking Indigeneity to the rural and the past can actually break the stranglehold of the either/or.[74] Contemporary culture has often been juxtaposed with fixed historical tradition. As Joanne Barker clarifies, "imperialism and colonialism require Indigenous people to fit within the heteronormative archetype of an Indigeneity that was authentic in the past but is culturally and legally vacated in the present."[75] While she writes specifically about offensive misuse of symbols of Indigeneity as costume, her argument could be productively applied to more instances that disaggregate culturally relevant practices associated with Indigenous cultures from the Indigenous peoples who have practiced and continue to practice them. When the power to represent remains with those who wish to do harm or who are unconcerned if they do so, misuse of these practices and objects continues to undermine respect for Indigenous sovereignty.

An interdisciplinary body of literature on contemporary Indigeneity in the Americas has wrestled with a near-endless set of dyads: proximal versus remote, traditional versus modern, central to versus outside of a locus of power. Relocated Indigeneity moves beyond these binaries in two important ways. First, this framework imagines the city as already Indigenous. At its most basic, when urban areas are framed as non-Indigenous spaces, the Indigenous people who live and work in them risk being seen as less legitimate as Indigenous actors.[76] As Bear Witness, a member of A Tribe Called Red, finds, "There's been a long history of Indigenous people in urban settings. We've always been here." He continues, "We've been largely invisible because if you're not wearing the beads, if you're not wearing the feathers, if you're not doing the things that have been made O.K. for Native people to exist as, then you become invisible."[77] Given that urbanization is a reality, how might artists, producers, and listeners grapple with the challenges and possibilities that urban living presents? How does this negotiation influence the renewing of traditional culture for urban communities?

Second, relocated Indigeneity allows for a rethinking of cultural change as generative rather than necessarily diluting heritage culture. This corrects enduring popular misconceptions of urban/nonurban and traditional/modern divides, shattering what Carol Edelman Warrior (Dena'ina, Athabascan, Alutiiq, and Gros Ventre) calls "settler-colonial flexibility and Indigenous fixity."[78] Although scholarly approaches have built outward in multiple directions, false truisms in these power hierarchies—whispered, shouted, and sung—have permeated brains. Even as attitudes shift and scholarship nuances, government policies, status definitions, and resource formulas have largely not wavered. Individuals and communities may see rights denied based on outmoded (and, in some cases, never appropriate) definitions of Indigeneity: contemporary urban Indigenous communities can be framed paradoxically as "too modern" to be authentic to cultural heritage and "too Indigenous" to be full members of contemporary society. While maintaining cultural practices that help establish links to Indigenous identities can be beneficial for community building, it runs into difficulty when tradition is defined in an exclusionary manner, which impacts scholarship and praxis. Both acknowledging the existence of and defying the validity of a prominent dyad, Silvia Rivera Cusicanqui explains that as Indigenous people, "We . . . were and are, above all, contemporary beings and peers, and in this dimension [aka pacha], we perform and display our own commitment to modernity."[79]

Next, I reframe the discussion toward self-determination and away from a possible perceived inevitability of cultural assimilation in cities. Cities can act as vibrant locations of cultural activity. Since 1900, there has been a significant shift in where Indigenous North Americans reside and how people are counted. While at the beginning of the century most communities were located in reserve or reservation areas, a majority of Indigenous individuals lived in cities by century's end.[80] In Canada, over half of individuals of "Aboriginal Origin" in the 1996 Census resided in urban areas, and about 70 percent of nonstatus Indians and Métis people lived in urban areas by the beginning of the twenty-first century.[81] Across the following chapters, specific examples from urban Winnipeg—and extending into neighboring cities—detail how urban areas have already been Indigenous and show the many ways in which urban communities maintain ongoing connections to rural, reserve, and other more geographically removed areas. Listening closely, it is possible to hear not just how these adaptations result in creative reperformances of Indigenous traditions but also how they impact mainstream music and dance. Expanding on previous work on Indigeneity in cities, I ask how contemporary musical expression can provide a way to think outside a false prospect that changes in culture are necessarily instances of loss. While the structures that have pushed urbanization are not neutral, urbanization can result in cultural creativity.

Across cities in Canada in the twenty-first century, urban Indigeneity has been contested even as large and diverse Indigenous communities shape urban centers from Vancouver to Toronto to St. Johns to Iqaluit. While adapting cultural expressions is sometimes called a break with tradition, many musicians instead find it a way to continue Indigenous expressive culture for a changing world.[82] Thinking through relocated Indigeneity frames the work of contemporary musicians in a space that opens between the poles of the binaries discussed previously. Rappers can continue to speak through tradition when it is not associated exclusively with the past. As a point of comparison, Australian Aboriginal rapper Wire MC raps through his understanding of himself in his song "B.L.A.C.K.," which he stylizes as "born long ago, creation's keeper." This links Blackness with Indigeneity, a topic taken up later in this chapter.[83] Further, Wire MC constructs his contemporary identity through both a heritage claim to land and a working of Indigeneity connected to care for the earth. The valences of land stewardship and its connections to legal sovereignty resonate through many Indigenous hip hop performances; they echo across signifiers of traditional, contemporary, urban, reserve, rural, and much more.

Emphasizing the city as Indigenous, *Sonic Sovereignty* details the functioning of musical communities in urban areas. Popular music, and hip hop specifically, moves with people as individuals visit and live in cities, reserves, and rural areas.[84] As Jolene Rickard finds—and in a direct connection to this book's ongoing discussion of sovereignty—these moves are part of sovereignty as action: "Artfully deployed within

Indigenous communities, traditions are a reinvestment in a shared ancient imaginary of self and a distancing strategy from the West. Tradition as resistance has served Indigenous people well as a response to
contact and as a reworking of colonial narratives of the Americas."[85]
Following Rickard, what happens when we listen for the ways in which
music can be of the present, continuing a process of tradition that is re-
sistant, or generative, that collides the past-present-future? When artists
create performances that play with tradition in new ways, they choose
how to alter and maintain heritage practices for their audiences.

## Borderlands and Settler States

Even when we started by talking about music and technique, my conversations with musicians have expanded as I listened to their thoughts
about settler-state policies, blood quantum, continuing effects of colonialism, and possibilities for decolonial activities. Rappers, DJs, and
producers have many ways of engaging these ideas, spanning scholarly
writing, lived experience, hearing from elders, and the hip hop knowledge sharing that comes from listening to a mentor. Musicians, music
industry professionals, and audience members learn, apply, and speak
to and through these ideas in myriad ways. This section is inspired by
these conversations and observations and is designed to offer context
for them. Based on your own experience, perhaps you, reader, feel a
sense of familiarity with this context. Meet us again when Kinnie Starr
plays her music in a few pages. This section asks, and then lays the
groundwork to address, questions about settler colonialism, Blackness's
relationship to Indigeneity, racialized ideas of Indigeneity in hip hop,
and decolonial praxis.

Here, I synthesize ideas across disciplines to reflect that which
emerges through winding in-person conversations: How is race understood in connection with Indigeneity? What does it mean for Black and
non-Black Indigenous artists to use inspiration and themes from Black
USAmerican and Black Canadian music? What does it mean to sell
music that reflects an artist's deep and personal beliefs about identity
and spirituality? How does protocol about music and knowledge affect
what is shared in commercial hip hop? What does it mean to groove to
commercial party-rap rhymes *about* womxn's bodies while being asked

to be part of antiviolence efforts, given ongoing colonialist violence against Indigenous womxn and girls specifically? How might musicians enact bodily sovereignty through rap? How does the settler state in the United States or Canada relate to others globally, and what might this mean for potential Indigenous solidarity across borders? What policies have attempted to curtail Indigenous sovereignty, and what tools are musicians using to reassert it?

The ongoing effects of colonization and assimilation efforts, movements to assert Indigenous rights in the face of violations, and a narrative of hip hop coming from adversity affect hip hop produced in the United States and Commonwealth countries. In settler colonialism specifically, Eve Tuck and K. Wayne Yang explain, "settlers come with the intention of making a new home on the land, a homemaking that insists on settler sovereignty over all things in their new domain."[86] Similar to US history, in Canada, Australia, and Aotearoa–New Zealand, phases of colonial policy vis-à-vis Indigenous peoples typically include first institutional contact, then domination, paternalism, integration, and finally, pluralism.[87]

In response to the destructive effects of assimilation, musicians tell how colonization has affected them and espouse themes of self-determination. For audiences who have not learned about this from school or community, music shares how residential schools, adoption of Indigenous children by non-Indigenous families, and the criminalization of cultural practices all had profound effects, creating shame around music, language, and other aspects of culture. It tells how these policies resulted in the deaths of children and adults, as well as family disruption and ongoing intergenerational trauma.[88] These stem from state policies, which Patrick Wolfe describes in the US as post-1871 legislation and judgments that "notionally dismantled tribal sovereignty and provided for the abrogation of existing treaties, relentlessly sought the breakdown of the tribe and the absorption into White society of individual Indians and their tribal land, only separately."[89] Legal and cultural assimilation aimed to remove Indigenous peoples from their land and integrate them into colonial society, in which groups were forbidden from maintaining unique cultural traits or rights. In response, contemporary Indigenous musicians are reasserting cultural specificity from within mainstream society. Given this colonial history and ongoing colonial present, many

Indigenous artists repeat a hip hop genesis narrative in which this cultural practice comes from adversity, a story that resonates in hip hop's global spread.[90]

Artists who embrace hip hop and its narrative of being a type of music based in creative resistance to caustic power structures face a complicated paradox. Despite liberatory origin stories, rap music has come under fire in public discourse because some stars enact misogyny and homophobia, celebrate criminal behaviors, or advocate extreme consumerism. Other rap musicians critique these very issues as social problems; sometimes these same concerns are given a pass when expressed in other music genres. Even as rap became associated with hyperconsumerism in the 1990s, some artists were critiquing extreme forms of materialism. Other critics such as Jayna Brown have celebrated hip hop *for* its focus on consumption and physical pleasure yet suggested that audiences did not have to derive these from capitalist purchasing.[91]

Even as Indigenous hip hop celebrates hip hop as a way to assert antiauthoritarian messages publicly, it exists undeniably in a commercial sphere. Decisions about what music to broadcast, stream, and promote cannot be disentangled from revenue potential. Indigenous popular music media can be revenue drivers even while they impact cultural narratives.[92] Indigenous music awards provide a prime example. The industry-building activities wrapped in the prestige and publicity of awards shows are designed to drive financial solvency. While maintaining a commercial orientation, Beverley Diamond explains, music awards mechanisms create counternarratives as "part of the larger project of creating a positive image of Indigenous people in a public arena, of recognizing creative achievement, entrepreneurship, and voice."[93]

Hip hop has entered institutional settings through educational programming. Classes and workshops comprise part of the commercial potential of Indigenous hip hop. A combination of artists' desire to positively impact communities, musicians carrying on the hip hop legacy of "each one teach one," and availability of some funding streams for education encourage many performers to take on musical labor that links educational aims with their own teachings. For example, Frank Waln, winner of multiple Native American Music Awards in the US, brings both Lakota-specific and intertribal musical sounds to listeners, participates in community programming as a speaker and educator, and speaks of his desire to create a positive impact on other Native youth.[94]

Hip hop has maintained its role as a flashpoint for media commentary and public discourse around what is or should be socially acceptable, a role it came to play during the culture wars.[95] To emphasize historical context surrounding the heated public debates about hip hop in the early 2000s, Mark Anthony Neal notes that "much of this activity was driven by the need to give voice to issues that privilege the local and the private within the postindustrial city—thus the overdetermined constructions of masculinity, sexuality, criminality, and even an urban patriarchy."[96] According to Davarian L. Baldwin, however, "this form of identification is no different from most young men in patriarchal societies who come to associate masculinity with aggression and violence."[97] This racialized and ritualized masculinity "entails behaviors, scripts, physical posturing, impression management, and carefully crafted performances that deliver a single, critical message: pride, strength, and control."[98] Yet whether expressed by butch female or male actors, such portrayals of overdetermined masculinity often fail to grasp the insidious complexities of power.[99] Artists and music professionals faced challenges because mainstreaming had concretized the specific roles available for artists, based on race and gender, in the first two decades of the twenty-first century. While changes into the 2020s point in more directions, many artists have struggled as they are labeled with a particular category and niche.

Rather than treating race and gender as separate facets, the remaining chapters of this book take an intersectional approach toward the performing, recording, and circulating of Indigenous hip hop and explore the question, What are the consequences of gendering and racialization processes that are constitutive of hip hop practices? Chapter 2 critiques the collapsing of Blackness into a single cliché, which became part of commercial rap genre expectations. It argues that anti-Black racist discourses are linked to settler colonial gender policing, both of which impact contemporary Indigenous hip hop. Chapters 3 and 4 probe the role of stereotypes about race and gender on the circulation of hip hop music. In particular, I critique race- and class-based genre assumptions. Listening for the ways that gendered power is expressed helps to explain which voices are present, which voices may be silenced, and the ways that artists shape their public personas.[100] Unequal access to hip hop spaces and creative opportunities for womxn have created a situation that, Rashad Shabazz finds, "perpetuates the unequal advantage men have outside the home, restricts access to the kinds of mobility hip-hop fosters, constrains the ability to talk about Black urban life from a different perspective, and undervalues the talents of women." This inequity "normalizes misogyny, homophobia, and narrow forms of masculinity within hip-hop, all of which undermines the revolutionary potential of hip-hop space."[101] When considering the influence of borders and belonging for Indigenous artists, moreover, gendering and racialization processes in hip hop magnify these deeply rooted inequities.

In the circulation of hip hop music made by Indigenous artists, ideas of Blackness and Indigeneity breach borders to interact with Native American, First Nations, Inuit, Métis, and band-specific affiliations. In relationship to hip hop, I follow David Jones's definition of Blackness, "not as a fundamental essence but as a constructed, even fractured, cultural identity within a postmodern social landscape."[102] While Indigeneity is not identical to race, Indigenous communities are racialized in practice, and the definition and use of the category of race in Indigenous contexts has changed over time.[103] Hip hop has been imbued with such pronounced racialization since its origin in the United States that whether or not actors consciously do so, Indigenous hip hop artists invoke these indexical meanings, particularly those related to Blackness. A perceived uniformity of monoracial Blackness—advanced in commercial rap—impacts Indigenous hip hop both when these musicians are racialized similarly to Black artists and when their social location as non-Black people forces a consideration of the settler-native-slave dynamic. Because of hip hop's rootedness in a variety of Afro-diasporic practices, it is often characterized as a transnational Black musical form and one that continues to develop in relationship to ideas of USAmerican Blackness.[104] Throughout a discussion of commonalities within cultural expressions created by contemporary Indigenous artists in a hip hop genre that is associated with USAmerican Blackness, it is important to recall that there is no singular "Native" or "Black" cultural identity.[105]

How and when hip hop is associated with Blackness is significant. Connections between race, nationality, and hip hop are unique in the United States, Canada, Australia, and Aotearoa–New Zealand. Despite

HIP HOP AND CONTEMPORARY URBAN INDIGENEITY | 53

differences between individual authors and participants, thematic trends permeate these national contexts. In Australia, Aotearoa–New Zealand, and Canada, narratives sometimes include differences between US-based hip hop and its counterpart practices globally. For example, Indigenous Australian hip hop artist Brothablack explains, "It's important to teach young Indigenous people in regional and remote communities that we have our own rapping and breaking culture. That way, we can explode the myth about it just being an American thing."[106] Hip hop's connections to the United States are often cited, and musicians acknowledge Black Americans in particular, even as Indigenous hip hop musicians reference their own experiences rooted in specific cultures and geographies. Although individual artists can play with ideas of race and belonging, larger systems impose limitations and police possibilities at the structural level.

Contemporary expressions of sovereignty (including sonic sovereignty) reassert something that has long been true: Indigenous groups have a profoundly different relationship to the nation-state than "visible minorities" or nonwhite racial groups because they are engaged in nation-to-nation relationships with settler states and other Indigenous nations. A significant part of sonic sovereignty as practice is to continually reassert, in audible terms, group sovereignty that already exists. These relationships and needs are qualitatively different from those related to racial inequity, though they are linked through settler colonialism and capitalism. Across genocide and assimilation—birth citizenship officially began in 1924—the category "Indian" was maintained in a way consistent with US government policy to contain and then assimilate Indigenous peoples. Blackness and Indigeneity were constructed differently from each other in the nineteenth century because government policy focused on minimizing "Indian" populations and furthering westward expansion, whereas increasing a "Black" labor population was advantageous to slaveholders and later to white business owners. Patrick Wolfe describes this process: "Indians and Black people in the US have been racialized in opposing ways that reflect their antithetical roles in the formation of US society, . . . [which] automatically enslaved the offspring of a slave and any other parent. In the wake of slavery, this taxonomy became fully racialized in the 'one-drop rule,' whereby any amount of African ancestry, no matter how remote, and regardless of phenotypical appearance, makes a person Black. For Indians, in stark contrast, non-Indian ancestry compromised their Indigeneity, producing 'half-breeds,' a regime that persists in the form of blood regulations."[107] In both the US and Canada, when Indian women married nonstatus men, both women and their children typically lost status. State-run assimilation practices aimed to minimize the number of people who qualified as "Indian" and to regulate and discipline those who were so defined. From the mid-nineteenth century, Indians were wards of the state in the United States, defined through legal dependence. These policies were contemporaneous with negative images of ethnic groups in the United States that circulated to police Native Americans, African Americans, and other people of color.[108]

In both USAmerican and Canadian contexts, band or tribal affiliation constituted through precontact or ongoing lived practices confronts settler-state legal policies.[109] In the early 1800s, official affiliation began in response to treaty regulations and government displacement of Native groups. Increases in Indigenous populations are partially due to how race and ethnicity have been categorized, as well as through an increase in reporting of Indigenous identification since 1960 through official measures such as the US Census.[110] In Canada, the number of respondents reporting an Aboriginal self-identity rose 22 percent from 1996 to 2001.[111] This sometimes overlaps with but is not identical to the number of Canadians who are considered "Registered Indians" per the Indian Act.[112] More specific categories, such as tribal or band affiliation, are used by individuals and communities regardless of how categories are used in nation-state data collection. The imposition of these policies did not supersede the maintenance of kinship and relationship structures in Nation-specific ways among Indigenous communities.

For Métis identity in particular, Monique Giroux finds that external expectations of belonging are not sufficient: "Métis identity is not about having a certain list of individual characteristics (blood, cultural competence, etc.) or a membership card, although these are often part of what makes a Métis person Métis. Rather, it is relationships with people and land—with kin and place—that are at the heart of the development and continuation of what it means to be Metis; these relationships define Indigenous nations."[113]

Complicating this process, some settlers, too, have begun claiming Indigenous ancestry. Julie Burelle, who identifies as a white person and a French Québecois de souche, critiques forms of self-Indigenization by which some white Québecois attempt to claim Métis status.[114] This move can be attempted through performance and renarration, through which settlers equate the experience of French white settlers in Nouvelle France with the experience of members of the Abénaki, Anishinaabe, Atikamekw, Cree, Huron-Wendat, Innu, Inuit, Maliseet, Mi'kmaq, Mohawk, and Naskapi nations. By distancing themselves from Anglophone settler populations, Québecois who descended from early French colonists, Burelle argues, often cast themselves as "settlers no more, colonized by the British first and, later, by the Anglo-Canadians."[115] Settler "moves to innocence" can extend to self-Indigenization, a process by which individuals take advantage of gray areas in legal definitions of Métis and nonstatus Indian peoples and attempt to gain status through the Canadian state rather than through long-standing membership practices of specific Inuit, First Nations, or Métis communities. The move to claim status is made, as Adam Gaudry (Métis) and Chris Andersen (Métis) describe, by "constructing their share of Indigeneity via often distant Aboriginal ancestors," making distant genealogical claims where community and cultural connections are absent. Problematically, when settler individuals and groups self-declare a generalized Métis or nonstatus Indian identity, Gaudry and Andersen summarize, they attempt to "gain something at the expense of Indigenous peoples, perpetuating Indigenous political disempowerment in the process."[116]

In a Canadian context, the Indian Act brought matters between Indigenous peoples and the Canadian government into federal control; the Canadian federal government afforded itself the ability to determine "Indian" status and effectively made recognized Indigenous people wards of the state.[117] The 1876 amendment of the 1868 act unilaterally made status blood-linked and patrilineal, regardless of membership systems that individual bands practice. Control shifted from individual bands to the Department of Indian Affairs and Northern Development, which was given the ability to alter band governance and oversee the "Indian Registry."[118] Since the 1970s, federal regulations have included some shifts away from assimilationist and paternalist policies; the 1981 Constitution

Act reaffirmed Indigenous treaty rights.[119] Notable in this context is the gendered manner in which the Indian Act has been deployed and interpreted over time. Native identity has, as Bonita Lawrence finds, been regulated in such a way that Native women have lost their status by marrying nonstatus or non-Native men. As a result, Native women and their descendants have been denied legal status for generations.[120] Recent discussions focusing on sovereignty propose new policies of self-determination and self-government; these would also impact how blood, heritage, or other factors would determine group inclusion and status.[121] As more Indigenous individuals and groups live in cities, these potential policy changes resonate further.

Cultural sovereignty and legal sovereignty are mutually influential. The banning of musico-cultural practices indicates the degree to which they have long been deemed powerful. Practices that threatened the settler colonial process were precisely the ones that were banned. These include those that strengthened Indigenous nations generally, as well as musical and spiritual practices led by Indigenous women specifically.[122] As part of the Indian Act amendments of 1884, which went into effect in 1885, the "Potlatch ban" declared,

> Every Indian or other person who engages in or assists in celebrating the Indian festival known as the "Potlach" or in the Indian dance known as the "Tamanawas" is guilty of a misdemeanor, and shall be liable to imprisonment for a term of not more than six nor less than two months in any gaol or other place of confinement; and any Indian or other person who encourages, either directly or indirectly, an Indian or Indians to get up such a festival or dance, or to celebrate the same, or who shall assist in the celebration of the same is guilty of a like offence, and shall be liable to the same punishment.[123]

As an effort to control Northwest Coast Indigenous peoples, the ban sought to interrupt music-dance practices that enacted sovereignty.[124] The Indian Act also specifically named the sun dance as a banned practice, demonstrating awareness of its power. These bans were used to limit and punish enactments of Indigenous cultural and legal sovereignty by Indigenous peoples of many nations and remained in place until 1951.[125]

## Many Voices Activating the Mic

The diversity of sound, goals, and commercial success within Indigenous hip hop practice has become almost as wide as other segments of the hip hop market. Kinnie Starr, whom broadcasting network Native Communications Incorporated (NCI) names as a leader for Indigenous hip hop and dance music in Canada, has produced innovative music that has captured a wide listener base. A gifted MC, she has incorporated sounds from other genres during her career, including acoustic folk and R&B. As with other artists cited by NCI in its bid for an urban Indigenous broadcasting license in Winnipeg, her music speaks to a wide range of topics in its musical messaging. Her professional persona includes her speaking to her Mohawk heritage and mixed-heritage status. A reflection from Starr about her audiences frames the listening: "With live shows, I always enjoyed how strong people looked after they left my shows, in particular women and Indigenous people."[126]

Across the album *Anything*, Starr tells stories from her life. She explains, "'Black Brown Eyes' is based on a visit my dad and I took to visit my great auntie—she is my namesake, Alida—when she wouldn't talk about her Mohawk blood."[127] This song describes a story that gets lost, one that Starr is seeking again. "Hey now, how'd it come this far," Starr sings, "Why don't we know who we are? / Love changed hands from red to white, stories gone into the night." She goes on to sing, "I asked my old graying Auntie, 'Tell me, tell me history.' / She just laughed and turned her head, 'Hush now, child' is all she said."[128]

Starr, who is of Mohawk, Dutch, German, and Irish ancestry, brings her family's story to this album. It is also a story that could resonate with other stories, notably Starr's question, "Why don't we know who we are?" Across the album, Starr's lyrics are always more than words. A regular percussion line and minor-key melody are part of a story she tells on another song; an electronic instrument line sets a comfortable four-beat pattern: lower bass like a drum, high hit as a snare, punctuated by a percussive shaker. Through a forceful whisper, Starr articulates the song's title: "rock the boat." Evocative of a flute, another line repeats a melody around just three pitches, G, E-flat, and D, creating a descending minor feel. After a short sung chorus, the rapper hits the first verse. She dedicates the song "to every shade of red." In the verse,

her lyrics pile on fractions, listing blood quantum alongside pheno-
type attributes: eye color, skin shade, the details that make people's faces
uniquely theirs, like "cheekbones that cut glass." The rapper's focus is
clear, her range of inclusion wide. To everyone she calls in, she says,
"stay strong, and rock the boat." Each chorus is rock inflected, sung
vocals and guitar speaking to each other. In the second verse, Starr
personalizes the lyrics from her narrator's perspective: what she wants,
what she hears that she is supposed to do, be, and want. She raps, "I like
writing rhymes, but I'm not supposed to / Writing rhyme's not what
fair-skinned girls do. I just bounce off the sounds and the tones / The
beat and the bass make the day less lonely." Midline vowel sounds play
off each other. An extended chorus-turned-bridge strips down to hand
claps and voices alone; then the instrumental lines come back in, and a
high-energy voice invites, "go ahead." "Everybody."[129] Starr may seem
here to be speaking to "everybody"; she has elaborated in interviews
about her varied listenership. Starr sees that she has "sort of a broad
group of listeners." At her shows, she reflects, "It's hip hop heads, white
people, Native people, intellectuals, and hippies, and a lot of metal
heads, oddly enough. . . . I like that idea that people come together, because I'm super mixed both in my bloodlines and in my taste." Starr has
a goal for herself vis-à-vis her listeners: "I like to put people into a state
of contemplation and a state of personal empowerment."[130]

Individual MCs and crews can be located from the mainstream to the
underground, using influences from gangsta to rock to electronica and
referencing Indigeneity through lyrical topicality, musical signifiers, and
visual representations. This set of artists is not exhaustive, but rather it
indicates some of the directions taken by Indigenous hip hop musicians
over time and in "mainstream"-style venues. It includes and extends beyond Starr and others celebrated by broadcasters. Indigenous rappers
and DJs based in what is now the United States and Canada who have
gained prominence since 2008 through awards shows, particularly the
influential Aboriginal Peoples' Choice Music Awards (now the Indigenous Music Awards) and the Native American Music Awards, music
programs such as the Indigenous Music Countdown, and Indigenous
popular music festivals, include The Halluci Nation (formerly A Tribe
Called Red, as well as current and past members Bear Witness, 2oolman,
DJ Shub, DJ NDN, and Dee Jay Frame), JB the First Lady, Wab Kinew,

Rezofficial, Ostwelve, Supaman, Frank Waln, Drezus, Eekwol, T-Rhyme, Chase Manhattan, Samian, Winnipeg's Most,[131] Tall Paul, Beka Solo, Kinnie Starr, Joey Stylez, Sly Skeeta, Dioganhdih, RedCloud, Crystle Lightning, MzShellz, Artson, Hellnback, Jah'kota, Snotty Nose Rez Kids, Prolific the Rapper, Pooky G, Quota EMG, DJ Kookum, DJ Krazykree, DJ O Show, DJ Paisley Eva, Dakota Bear, J25, The Raıın, Rellik, K.A.S.P., Jayohcee, Miss Christie Lee, Shauna Seeteenak, Lil Mike & Funny Bone, Culture Shock Camp, Buggin' Malone, Sten Joddi, Shining Soul, Gabriel Yaiva, Valkyrie, Def-i, Savelle Tha Native, Violent Ground, Indigenous Barbie, Stun, Rey, Thomas X, Boslen, City Natives, and more. Many others have chosen to move through underground scenes, participate in cyphers, and otherwise make music in community. It is a testament to a growing movement that any published list is partial and will quickly go out of date.[132] Joey Stylez is a Cree and Métis rapper who has gained fairly wide mainstream success. He is profiled on multiple Indigenous music sites, incorporates some rock influence in his musical style, and has opened for musicians such as Pitbull.[133] Even as, musically, he presents sounds that fit within rap genre expectations, he and his collaborators use visuals and lyrical references to tell stories that link together past and present trauma.

Joey Stylez's music video opens with red letters on a black-and-white flickering photo. Rows of boys and girls in uniforms stand in rows in front of institutional-looking brick buildings. A siren plays, previewing where the music video is headed, as the text projects, "Thousands of Indigenous children were forced into Residential Schools between 1880 and 1960," and then changes to, "Now their descendants fill Canada's prisons." The video cuts to fit sound to image: ambulance on a city street, a young man is placed on a stretcher. Flashbacks into the recent past and more distant past intercut the scene of bystanders watching his body: a figure stabs a young man, who falls to the ground; the red-tinged figure of a boy in a school uniform, silently looking ahead. A person pushes through the crowd of onlookers. His presence on-screen coincides with a sonic shift from diegetic sound to the decided start of the song in this music video. His baritone voice rumbles, "yeah." He pulls his hands out of his hoodie pockets so he can gesture, throwing down his arms as he raps. The chorus repeats a male voice, pitch shifted down low and boomy: "Boys in the hood / Boys, boys in the hood."

Past, present, future, rural, urban, institutional, the music video is this and that and also this. Visually, it shows the face of rapper Joey Stylez clad in wraparound sunglasses, a baseball cap, a red-and-white-striped hoodie, baggy jeans, and sneakers, his gold grills glinting during close-ups. Images of a residential school building appear with flickering, red, ghostly figures of nuns, priests, and children. Intercut with these, the viewer sees images from the present: young men on camera. They don't sing or speak. But they pose, arms crossed, facing the camera directly, even if their gazes are obscured by sunglasses. In the next verse, the rapper calls himself "living proof" of the history that plays in front of the audience's eyes and ears. Young people have their hair cut; a child is beaten with a ruler. The rapper narrates what he has heard and seen. In a nearer present, video footage shows a person in a hoodie flanked by two police officers, who roughly handcuff him and thrust him against a nearby police car. Sonic and visual images flood in: a rapped reference to poverty, an image of stacks of cash, a group of men standing in a city street, posing for the camera, people running across a busy street, a man pausing to embrace a grandmother. A compact, repeated melody creates a taut loop: an electronic string sound that plays a seven-note melody around a descending minor-scale segment on D, C, B-flat, A, G continues without stopping for a full three and a half minutes. The tension never releases.[134]

## Popular Media Terrain for Indigenous Hip Hop

When I listen to the album *Tribal Tribulations* years after it was released, I think about how the rapper delivered his music at the live shows of his that I have seen over the years. I remember hearing Chase Manhattan perform after a powwow in Chicago, energizing an already lively crowd. I feel the humid August evenings, moving from venue to venue in downtown Winnipeg, when he came to perform before a music award ceremony in that city. I hear Chase laughing as we talk over lunch and then the serious focus coming into his voice as he tells me about what drives him to make music. At the same time, particular aspects of Chase's music make an impression on me: the wide variety of samples, his strong nasal vocal timbre, the minor-key electronic melodies that vibrate across the album.

Are these musical layers disambiguated in your ear? Do they arrive as a wholeness that does not need or want to be disentangled? The timbre of drum beats that open the song "One on One" evokes the resonant character of a big drum. This regular drum pattern is the heartbeat around which all the rest of the sounds are structured. Rapper Chase Manhattan worked with producer Jeezy to create this beat from a sound library. This sonorous percussion is pitched at a D. The buzzing and overtones create a full, realistic sound. This drum sound, typical in Anishinaabe music, is also now heard throughout much intertribal Native North American music. If transcribed to a four-bar pattern, the easy duple beat would hit as repeated dotted eighth sixteenth notes. While this beat is less rhythmically complex than the beat on some of Chase's other songs, the vocals play with this regular pattern. The rapped verses contribute syncopation and a relatively faster flow that complicate the overall rhythmic language. An arcing flute line changes less rapidly, and repeats an F, E, A three-note melody.

In his description of the compositional process, Chase recalls, "'One on One' was a real hard beat for me in the beginning." He had to innovate to make it work. As he says, "I knew I had to twist it somehow in order to make it sound good."[135] Like the layered rhythms, the song's form offers some sonic intrigue. The hook is an unusual length—just three bars. This breaks the continuity, placing emphasis on the sampled song that comes in during what would be the fourth bar of the hook but, surprisingly, is the start of a new segment. This lengthy sample, female voices singing a hand drum song, functions as a five-bar lead. The hook features a rapped vocal line, a flute line that repeats at the bar level, and a drum. The hand drum sampled in this segment flows almost seamlessly into the beat after it cuts out: the timbre shifts from sampled hand drum to composed drum beat; but the meter remains consistent, and the timbre is similar. In this way, the sample is integrated into the larger work, and the hand drum feel continues.

The form is a minor variation of rap standard for broadcast distribution. After an eight-bar intro, there are three sixteen-bar verses, intercut with eight-bar choruses and then an eight-bar outro. The first chorus repeats twice in a row, but otherwise the song proceeds as expected. The song gives much that could be heard across broadcast or streaming rap radio, but with timbres, instruments, and samples that are legible with markers from intertribal North American Indigenous musical expressions. Perhaps you hear this song as it fits with club rap of the early 2010s. Perhaps your ear focuses in on lyrics or samples or melodic line. Perhaps the song washes over you as you dance, moving you whether or not you listen in to specifics of the artists' creative choices.

Chase Manhattan released "One on One" in 2010. He has frequently spoken of his Native heritage in his publicity materials and onstage; his mother is Oglala Sioux and Muskogee Creek, and his father is Leech Lake Anishinaabe. Later, he would be nominated for multiple Indigenous Music Awards (first when they were called the Aboriginal Peoples' Choice Music Awards and then again after the name change), as well as for the Native American Music Awards. He would attract press in the US and Canada for the music he made as well as for his mentorship of young musicians. His efforts include teaching with the Project Your Voice program at Little Earth, a Section 8 housing development for Native Americans in South Minneapolis.[136] He would collaborate with rappers of many nations, bringing intertribal references to an increasingly wide hip hop audience. He would play live shows around the United States and across the US-Canada border and find an audience at stages from clubs to hip hop battle showcases to casinos. He would start a clothing brand, Hustle Tribe. But then, he was performing live at shows in the region: at 49s after powwows in the Great Lakes area, in urban and reservation shows that marketed to largely Native audiences.[137] Listening closely to this song is one way to think through changes in Indigenous hip hop music from the 1990s into the opening decades of the 2000s.

Since hip hop began in the Bronx, Indigenous artists have been active in the hip hop scene in the United States. Within contemporary Indigenous hip hop in the United States and Canada, a variety of styles is represented. Artists who specifically foreground their Native identity grew into a larger scene in the 1990s. An important nexus around such artists formed around musicians WithOut Rezervation (W.O.R.), Litefoot, and Julian B, all of whom had significant album releases in 1994. From Oakland, California, W.O.R. members Mike Marin (aka Saint Mike), Kevin Nez, and Chris LaMarr called attention to social issues relevant to Native American audiences on their first album. "Mascot," for example, narrates the racism behind using Native American figures as sports mascots, repeating the central idea, "We're nobody's mascot."[138] Throughout the album, rappers use lyrical topicality of colonialist expansion, land rights, and racism; Saint Mike (Navajo / Laguna Pueblo / Washoe) alternately raps Native pride in general and Navajo pride in particular.[139] This theme of pride is featured in music by other artists who began performing around the same time. Gary Paul Davis, aka Litefoot (Cherokee/Aztec), addresses colonialism and land use in his lyrics. From California and raised in Oklahoma, this funk-inspired rapper also references Native and Cherokee pride in his music and offstage appearances. Julian B (Muskogee)'s *Once Upon a Genocide* includes tracks "Genocide in Progress" and "The Spirit of Crazy Horse" that convey strong emotion through dense rapped lyrics.[140] These artists' twin themes of struggle and pride continued into the work of musicians who emerged in the following two decades.

Indigenous rap in Canada came to audiences slightly later than in the United States. Some groups in Canada were active in the 1980s in underground scenes. By the 1990s some had wider listenerships—notably War Party (Cree) out of Alberta and Eekwol & Mils (Cree) in Saskatchewan— but it was not until 2000 that a parallel movement strongly coalesced. A growth of hip hop performance that actively foregrounded participants' Indigenous identities paired with sustained audience interest in such performance led to the first time that the Canadian Aboriginal Music Awards included a category for Best Rap or Hip Hop Album in 2001. After 2000, Indigenous rap scenes in both the United States and Canada started to expand in multiple directions, making this time period a rich environment for listening and reflection.

As with other genres with commercial appeal, hip hop circulates through broadcast networks, which simultaneously reflect and shape listener preferences. Many Indigenous hip hop artists, like other musicians, have sought the recognition and exposure that broadcast airplay offers. Groundbreaking Indigenous urban radio broadcaster Streetz operated in tandem with the mainstreaming of Indigenous hip hop and electronic music from the end of the first decade of the twenty-first century into the mid-2010s. As described by broadcaster NCI, "The growth of [the] urban music scene within the Aboriginal community can be measured by what is heard on Streetz-FM. Hip Hop and dance music has been a prominent influence on contemporary Aboriginal youth culture, which was spearheaded by artists such as Winnipeg's Most, Kinnie Starr, War Party, Eekwol, Inez Jasper, Joey Stylez, Lil Pappie, Plex, Tru Rez Crew, Samian, The Halluci Nation and Team Rezofficial." With a focus on audibility for artists who were not previously played on commercial stations, NCI emphasizes, "The advent of Streetz-FM created an outlet for the best urban Canadian artists to be finally be heard."[141] Understandably celebratory of its own role in the process, the broadcaster points to artists who shaped Indigenous hip hop sounds for urban publics. This effect began in Winnipeg, where, as the only urban-format station, Streetz broadcast to a wide demographic of hip hop fans—not just Indigenous listeners. As NCI describes Streetz's role, the station is the city's "only 100% urban music format (Hip-Hop, Dance and R&B-inclusive of Aboriginal music). The goal of Streetz-FM is to remain a unique station in Winnipeg and to offer a professional sound for urban music fans."[142]

Home to many influential media entities, Winnipeg plays a crucial role in the Indigenous music industry, as will be detailed in chapter 2.[143] It has been maligned as a city with challenging racial tensions and celebrated as a location of possibility. Winnipeg's role as a city in which larger dynamics can be seen and heard is indeed related to its position as a majority Anglophone city with a minority Francophone population, as well as a heartland of the Métis Nation. Anglophone Indigenous music industry players in Canada have deep connections to Indigenous music industries internationally through cross-promotion and talent development among Indigenous artists in Canada, Australia, Aotearoa–New Zealand, and the United States.[144] To be sure, Francophone and cross-market artists and industry professionals continue to shape and develop the Indigenous music industry in Canada and beyond its borders. Per the 2016 Canadian Census, 88.2 percent of Winnipeg's population spoke English only, 10.1 percent spoke English and French, 0.1 percent spoke French only, and 1.6 percent spoke neither English nor French. In St. Boniface, the English-only population was smaller (73.7 percent), and the French-English bilingual population was significantly larger (24.7 percent), as was the French-only population (0.5 percent). Winnipeg continues to be home to newcomers from a variety of global regions where French is spoken—due to centuries of French colonial expeditions abroad—including France, Algeria, Cameroon, the Democratic Republic of the Congo, Haiti, and Morocco.[145]

Access to French-language schooling, arts programming, city services, and more is directly related to the ongoing and historical Métis presence, which predated the founding of the province. It is also interwoven with the presence of Francophones from Québec and elsewhere who are not of Métis ancestry. The unique position of some Québecois in Canada is invoked in contemporary Indigenous political theory. To explain the outrage many Indigenous people felt when the 1969 White Paper suggested ending the status of Indigenous Canadians as codified in the Indian Act, Arthur Manuel uses the metaphor of the rage that Québecois would feel if their unique legal status were removed and they, too, were assimilated into Anglophone Canada.[146]

In this light, Samian's performance with Anodajay that opened this chapter takes on additional layers of resonance. They performed in St. Boniface, speaking in French, during the Festival du Voyageur, a music festival that celebrates Francophone music and highlights Métis and First Nations cultures while playing for an Anglophone and Francophone audience that hails from beyond the city itself.[147] It is possible to listen for echoes of what Julie Burelle calls Québec's "complex and contradictory status as a colonized/colonizer minority."[148] Samian, who has found success within Québec's Francophone music industry, and Anodajay, who is part of Québec's majority Francophone population, performed a set celebrating First Nations cultures and making connections between Indigenous groups in Québec and Manitoba.

## Listening to Urban Indigeneity

Onstage in a performance tent over snow, rapper Samian spits who he is and how he sees himself connected to other Indigenous peoples beyond his nation. The logo of Winnipeg's only urban-format radio station, stitched into snapback hats adorning heads that move through the city, feature three skyscrapers and a tipi over the stylized graffiti of the station name, Streetz. A rapper tells his story and that of others, taking center screen in the present while ghostly figures of disappeared children from the past flicker throughout the music video. A rapper flows through everything she wants to talk about right now: strength, loneliness, blood, identity. She sings an extended metaphor, inviting listeners to rock the boat, to change things. A women's hand drum song sample grounds and unsettles, setting the tone of a repeated chorus but for an irregular number of bars. A DJ brings a sample forward in time, repeats and extends it; each listener experiences it differently as they access their own memories and associations of it. What does decolonial futurity sound like? How will we listen?

In the following chapters, this discussion probes how perceptions of Blackness, Indigeneity, anti-Black racism, and anti-Indigenous bias influence the mainstreaming—or lack thereof—of hip hop that begins in Native-focused media spaces. Decisions and adaptations by artists and media professionals, including problematic pressures for self-censorship, emerge as community-focused artists confront wider markets. How might tropes that have been concretized in USAmerican hip hop and then sold to a multiracial mainstream audience—such as the celebration of violence, misogyny, and a focus on consumption—also become associated with some Indigenous hip hop? Urban Indigenous communities are pathologized in news sources, with rhetoric similar to that levied toward urban Black communities.[149] As will be further explored in subsequent chapters, anti-Indigenous and anti-Black biases overlap and speak to each other particularly in hip hop; racialized ideas about practitioners and listeners that have accrued to this musical form have informed its circulation.

Long before settler colonialism, Indigenous nations across North America have engaged music and dance for myriad reasons. Since colonization began, First Nations, Native American, Métis, and Inuit music practices have enacted Indigenous "survivance," which is an active process of cultural survival. Gerald Vizenor (Anishinaabe) contrasts "dominance and absence" with "survivance," a term he coined for "heard and read stories that mediate the literature of dominance."[150] Following Vizenor, survivance is not only about physical continuation; performance embodies the active and creative process of cultural survival that presents a narrative more powerful than that of Indigenous erasure.

How does Indigenous futurity sound? What are the resonances of radical kinship? How does a listener start to open their ears to decolonial possibility? To hear openings into these questions, this chapter ends not with my own words but with provocations from, respectively, Laura Harjo, The Halluci Nation (A Tribe Called Red), Joanne Barker, Frank Waln, and Eekwol:

When we enact futurity, we involve community practices, knowledge, and relationships of many kin-space-time-envelopes, and all of these elements guide us. Our invocation of kin-space-time-envelopes places us in relationship to kin, including kin who are not blood kin but chosen. As a consequence of dialoguing and relating with all forms of kin, such as those residing in the metaphysical realm, futurity shifts the ontology of human life, pivoting away from simply an existence on earth bookended by birth and death toward lives conceived of as a life force. Our relatives' life force has the power to move and invoke us to action and responsibility to community.[151]

If you're an Indigenous person living in a country that was forcefully colonized, it's all too common to find yourself underrepresented and misrepresented if not blatantly and systematically devalued and attacked.[152]

Narrating Indigenous peoples back into their governance, territories, and cultures challenges the narrations and policies of US and Canadian imperialism and colonialism.[153]

When I first moved into downtown Chicago, there were 2,000 people in the dorm building. This girl got on the elevator, and she said, "You have really nice hair, where are you from?" I told her I was a Lakota Indian from South Dakota and she said, "You guys are still alive?"[154]

When I talk to young people I always talk about colonization. Just like that, I talk about residential schools. Because my dad went to day school, my grandparents went to residential school, and I didn't know that until I was nineteen years old. I didn't even know. But I knew all of the effects. I had sort of embodied that thinking—we're just genetically inferior. And I know a lot of kids grow up thinking like that. . . . It's hard not to want to speak up or change the conversation around the dinner table. . . . It can happen with Indigenous communities, but it has to happen within settler communities. It has to happen at that dinner table where there's not a single brown face but still the same conversation you would have as if there were a brown face in the room. . . . It's education and awareness. That's a huge thing that has to happen. And it happens through music. It happens through performance.[155]

2

# The Remaking of a Hip Hop Mainstream through Online and Broadcast Media

On a morning in December, I arrive just before seven a.m. for the start of *The Rise Up Show* on Streetz. Radio DJ Miss Melissa is preparing to work in one of the two live on-air rooms. As she does not have guests this morning, she will work from the corner control room. This space has a comfortable setup for one or two DJs. The program runs a wide spectrum of music over the course of the morning. A longtime professional in Manitoba's Indigenous music industry, Miss Melissa has experience as the host of *National Aboriginal Music Countdown Top 40* and has acted as a member of the board of directors of Aboriginal Music Week, in addition to her work with Native Communications Incorporated (NCI).[1] Early on, the show plays American southern rapper 2 Chainz, whose songs have seen success on *Billboard* charts. California rapper Tyga's "Rack City" comes on later, this hit airing alongside older tracks. In response to a request, Miss Melissa plays some Beyoncé, and then the list of US-based male rappers continues with the radio edit of DJ Khaled's "No New Friends." *The Rise Up Show* incorporates throwbacks, including some 2Pac and Coolio this morning. Between songs, song intros, and blocks of songs, show hosts typically offer weather and traffic information as well as commentary on celebrity news, movies, and local issues. Outside of this catered content, the station also plays advertisements. These are largely for local organizations and businesses, and this morning they include the Manitoba government, the General Employees' Union, and a Winnipeg car dealer. While the station sometimes broadcasts ads seeking an Indigenous listenership, such as educational opportunities catering to Indigenous potential students, others address a wider audience. The ads this morning are consistent with those I often hear on the station, a mix of announcements with a public service message and advertisements for sports events, jeans, lunch spots, and car finance. Through a combination of older and new songs, commentary, and ads, the station delivers an eclectic, high-energy program.

This music and commentary hits the airwaves, and streams to listeners online, from a studio in Winnipeg. In this studio, in this city, something crucial and utterly unremarkable is happening. Every weekday, radio DJs get up early, commute to work, and then find the energy to share witty remarks and upbeat music. Across the city, people listen, hit snooze alarms, and listen again, warm up their cars, and press play as they, too, commute to work in the dark, put in headphones as they wait for the bus, or get ready for school. Every day, the banter and the songs continue, some of the songs repeating into a groove of familiarity; people click on the links on the station's webpage or social media, with interest or just as an additional routine, next to morning emails. Yes, there is something special about this station and these DJs, something many listeners actively choose and feel part of. There are musicians on this station who are on no other channel in the city and some who are on no other channel anywhere. And there is also something meaningful in the mundanity of this format. *The Rise Up Show*, on Streetz, is playing hip hop and electronic music by Indigenous artists, and the station is supporting events designed to serve an urban Indigenous community, particularly young people. And at the same time, the station is delivering a commercial-sounding experience to a diverse listenership: in a racially stratified city, it is in the unusual position of speaking into a wide variety of listening ears.

This chapter listens for possibilities for self-determination, collective action, and sonic sovereignty through a medium that may at first seem strange: popular music on broadcast and streaming radio. Indeed, as Elizabeth Cook Lynn has identified, pop culture has facilitated both positive social change for and regressive action against Native Americans.[2] Even without branding itself as radical, commercially inflected music that circulates on-air and online creates possibility through the sometimes subtle and sometimes not-so-subtle work that popular culture performs. First, the very existence of an urban-format Indigenous station, sparked in 2008, challenges still-pervasive misconceptions about Indigeneity. And second, even as artists operate within many genre expectations and connect to the musical histories that have preceded contemporary hip hop, they find space to play with these conventions, both on-air and online.

Listening for sonic sovereignty on radio, and specifically first listening for it on broadcast radio in Canada, presents an intriguing set of
situations. Sonic sovereignty, an embodied practice of Indigenous self-
determination through musical expression, overlaps with, but differs
in scope from, legal sovereignty. Not just focused on rights as articulated through a settler court system, sonic sovereignty entails aspects
of representational sovereignty, cultural sovereignty, intellectual sovereignty, and bodily sovereignty, among others, as well as self-definition
and self-determination. Following Vine Deloria Jr., this is not an individual approach to the sovereign but one of collective action.[3] As
both aural and embodied practice, sonic sovereignty engages speakers,
singers, and listeners in dialogue and relationship. Canadian broadcast
radio, like other regulated distribution media in Canada, is governed
in part by policies that promote the interests of Canada as a nation-
state. Aware of the cultural power of its more populous neighbor to the
south, Canada—like Australia, Aotearoa–New Zealand, and other Anglophone countries awash with USAmerican popular media—enforces
minimum content amounts from its own musicians.[4] Regulatory bodies
carefully define what it means to count as Canadian, and broadcasters
make promises about Canadian content when applying for limited licenses, as this chapter shows in depth.

The Canadian Radio-television and Telecommunications Commission (CRTC) publicly defines its role this way: "To implement the laws
and regulations set by Parliamentarians who create legislation and de-
partments that set policies. We regulate and supervise broadcasting and
telecommunications in the public interest."[5] While it operates at arm's
length from the federal government, it is charged with implementation
of federal laws and regulations. Canadian content, or CanCon, is a chief
example of how Canada uses broadcasting to resist USAmerican cultural
imperialism. The actions of Native-licensed media entities operating
within this system offer a crucial vantage point for understanding how
Indigenous sovereignty interacts with the stated purpose and actions
of national media policies and regulators.[6] Streetz came into being in a
postapology moment, continued to air during Idle No More, and operated at its most influential level as public dialogue about Indigenous-
settler relations was also particularly robust. Listening to Native-licensed
broadcaster Streetz turns the perspective on sovereignty over airwaves

on its head: within a regulatory environment of cultural nationalism, Indigenous voices are enacting sovereignty and self-determination through broadcast media.

Pressing on tensions between ideas of "mainstream" and "Indigenous" audiences, this chapter's analysis visits the way these are constituted and reconstituted and explores the space between them. Whether or not it is recognized explicitly, artists and promoters in Indigenous hip hop must contend with ideas of Blackness that are inseparable from, and constituted by, commercial hip hop. Even as discursive constructions of Indigeneity/modernity binaries are repeatedly shown to be false and damaging, their prevalence has persisted. As many popular music listeners transitioned to streaming audio, Indigenous musicians and broadcasters actively participated in the shift toward new listening practices at the end of the first decade of the twenty-first century and the beginning of the second, and they continue to influence mainstream sounds and listening practices after this period. And yet, for contemporary Indigenous musicians working in popular music—particularly in genres that rely heavily on electronic music technology—the dualistic construction poses a challenge to audibility. There is a parallel with another erasure: that which is created by electronic music's masculinist discourse.

Commercialized stereotypes of monoracial Black masculinity and the image of the rural Indian are ideas that circulate in mainstream popular culture with alarming regularity. The uneasy balancing act required of a broadcaster of urban-format Indigenous popular music demonstrates the overlapping and mutually influential currency of these ideas. Musicians' and professionals' efforts to respond in this fraught space challenge, reify, consume, extend, rework, and recombine them. This chapter explores the possibilities at these junctures. It begins with movement on mainstream airplay and then analyzes online options for artists as well, notably musicians who take on political concerns that exceed the list of topics circulated on mainstream commercial hip hop as influenced by Black social movements and concerns brought by artists who do not fit into mainstream ideas of a masculine MC or DJ persona. Broadcast popular music often plays a role in supporting the colonialist heteropatriarchy, reinforcing racialized norms, and resisting change. It is crucial, then, to reanalyze why and to listen for the possibilities in alternative performances.

The circulation of music by the artists on Streetz challenges misconceptions of Indigeneity and stretches notions of contemporary popular music; when Indigenous cultural production asserts itself *as* contemporary popular music, definitions must expand to accommodate these realities. In a related move, I argue that online communities for sharing and discussing contemporary hip hop offer strategies for community building, communication, and group affinity bonds even—and especially—when participants belong to minority groups within electronically based music scenes. Using participant observation, interviews, social media analysis, and close readings of circulated media, I find that musicians actively reshape presumptions about gender and Indigeneity. They navigate tension with a musical "mainstream," typically read as white and male, though these categorizations go largely unmarked. To trace the way exclusionary conceptions of Indigeneity and femininity circulate in popular music discourses, work with artists and producers who are part of one of the most innovative and far-reaching Indigenous music stations in Canada, based in Winnipeg, offers relevant case studies in broadcast and online media distribution.

Broadcasting is not a soloistic endeavor. Critics mock its large scale; neoliberal streamliners ask fewer people to do more work. There is something audacious about looking to this complex multipart system, asking it to work for minoritarian voices, trusting that it can, and then doing the mundane and repeated labor so that it will. Engineers maintain the upkeep of facilities and manage broadcasting mechanics (and, more recently, also work with web management and livestreaming). Technicians work on facilities and keep giant radio towers in good repair. Public-relations staff handle a range of tasks: receiving visitors in a physical building, being the first face that people see or the first voice folks hear when they call on the phone, and triaging questions; curating, posting, replying, and managing negative commentary on social media accounts; planning and promoting events; handling internal and external communications. In marketing, sales managers, or fund-raisers for nonprofit stations, secure funds to keep the station going. A marketing team connects with programming and works with branding. Staff members manage accounts, write copy, handle billing and financial record keeping, and work with social media. Web managers and technical support staff manage the website and online streaming. Other tasks, like human resources and payroll, might be handled in-house or contracted. Either way, someone is doing the work of keeping a team operating.[7]

Managers are tasked with leading in a way that will secure financial viability, ensuring appropriate record keeping and clearance from licensing (such as the CRTC in Canada or the FCC in the United States), and coordinating staff. Music directors solicit and choose new music additions and manage the music library. Program directors manage the overall sound, working with music and on-air talent. Radio DJs and interviewers create the sound and atmosphere that listeners hear; it is their energy and creativity that make the auditory fingerprint of the station. And the musicians whose work airs have yet another complicated industry behind them.

From a point of view of material and of labor, broadcasting sound cannot be any single person's project. When I invite a reading of sonic sovereignty, then, I am asking you, reader, to consider that which becomes possible between and among this vast network of people, the work that they do with an even larger listener base in mind. When groups choose to use their collective skills and resources so that musical groups reflect their experiences and tell their perspectives—and, in a neoliberal capitalist structure, pay the musicians and industry professionals for their time—what comes into being? Sonic sovereignty emerges from a collective misuse, in Sara Ahmed's phrasing, a dialectic through which music industry workers push and pull between using media industry resources for their own collective ends and pushing parts of that behemoth ("the media industry"), loosening its strictures on the voices that are heard and silenced in the unmarked "mainstream."[8]

## Performing Indigenous Modernity

By enacting a sonic Indigeneity that refuses to be placed outside contemporary culture, artists articulate an urban modernity that is consistent with, and extends from, living tradition. Working with urban Native young people, Renya Ramirez writes, "We can see what previous generations called tradition morphing into the next generation's identity, becoming the new tradition."[9] Focusing on cultural processes that young people participate in allows for expressions beyond a traditional/contemporary binary. The separation of traditional and contemporary stems from the myths on which settler colonialism was built; Malea Powell identifies the pervasiveness of these ideas "that 'the Indian' was (is) a figure against which 'the American' can be rendered from the raw materials of 'the Euro-colonist,' and rendered most effectively by making 'the Indian' a thing of the past."[10] Some previous research took for granted a perceived incompatibility between modern urban living and maintaining Indigenous cultural expressions; often public discourses continued misconceptions around Indigenous modernity even as research attitudes changed.[11] Powell, who identifies as mixed blood of Indiana Miami, Eastern Shawnee, and Euro-American ancestry, challenges audiences to remember where these myths come from and to "believe differently."[12]

Indigenous popular musicians invite audition that moves the listener past tropes of modern versus traditional. This intentional rehearing sometimes presents enduring, if tired, narratives, in order to play with them. In one scene, the video projections of A Tribe Called Red show Hollywood Indians or caricatured cartoons, as the DJs loop contemporary competition powwow, electronic instruments, and the sounds of urban life.[13] People dance with different stories in their own heads, about whom their city is for, where "real Indians" live, what it means to be from the Cayuga First Nation or the Nipissing First Nation, to be growing up in Ottawa, to be of settler descent or of mixed ancestry. These stories from daily life interact with, impact, and are impacted by scholarship. Studies have focused on the potential alienation of city life, or how it may deemphasize band- or tribe-specific traditions.[14] While urbanization was posed as a strategy to assimilate Indigenous people, this policy did not succeed in the cultural erasure for which it was designed.[15] Further, the reality that people frequently move between urban and nonurban locations complicates a view in which these areas are wholly distinct.[16] People live outside a modern-versus-traditional and urban-versus-rural experience; musical performance enacts this reality.

Real life exists within regulatory structures. Contemporary Indigenous musicians still sometimes face expectations of performing otherness and what Joshua Tucker calls "a temporally extended separation from a national 'mainstream.'"[17] That is, maintenance of tradition can sometimes still be seen as necessary for claims to Indigeneity, and it may create at least an imagined distance from "mainstream" national culture. This is congruent with a phenomenon in which, in order to hold together as a category, Native music has risked being defined as outside the mainstream and thus as marginal.[18] As a result, when Indigenous groups continue to enact cultural practices that engage with contemporary culture, this embodiment of modernity is sometimes used to deny group rights. If cities are framed as non-Indigenous, then Indigenous people who make homes in them may be either ignored or misunderstood.[19] Further, a refusal to hear myriad sounds of Indigeneity in urban areas reinforces a false binary between Indigenous and non-Indigenous spaces.

As an example of an urban location that defies false binaries, Winnipeg provides a central example of an ongoing, established Indigenous community in an urban setting. Ethnologist Morgan Baillargeon finds that historically, many Indigenous groups in Canada and in the United States "have been living in urban settings long before Europeans arrived in North America." Winnipeg was a center of trade long before European colonization. The city's vibrant and changing mix of Métis and First Nations residents further evolved during the fur-trade era, particularly starting in the eighteenth century. Since then, Baillargeon explains, "some of the Métis and First Nations communities who settled at Red River, Manitoba in the early 1800s were instrumental in the building and development of cities and towns that grew up around modern day Winnipeg."[20] Understanding the city's urban culture through relocated Indigeneity, as elaborated in chapter 1, involves remembering this precolonial past and the history of cultural exchanges in the area.

In the twenty-first century, Winnipeg provides a compelling counterexample to the distancing discourses that locate Indigeneity far from urban life, if time is taken to listen carefully.[21] In this Canadian city, a hybrid broadcast/online Indigenous hip hop station premiered as a viable part of the urban mediascape. The first of its kind in the nation, and even globally, this station has played Indigenous popular music from across Canada and the United States and is heard far beyond the city limits. Winnipeg is located at the fork of the Assiniboine and Red Rivers, on the original lands of the Anishinaabeg, Nehiyawak, Oji-Cree, Dakota, and Dene peoples and on the homeland of the Métis Nation—the city has long been a crossroads for trade and exchange.[22] Creating and sharing musical expressions also allow participants to express positively felt cultural attributes. With music distribution, these can be shared within and beyond the Native community.

Within the city of Winnipeg, NCI has operated the radio station Streetz, an urban-format radio station that has broadcast hip hop, dance, and other genres of music by Indigenous, non-Indigenous, and mixed-heritage artists to a diverse listenership. Gaining the radio station license in 2008 was significant. It marks an acknowledgment by NCI that there is a sizeable population of listeners in Winnipeg who want to listen to hip hop and urban-format music and that they would do so on a Native station. It shows a recognition by regulators that a Native-licensed station would be an appropriate broadcaster for hip hop music and thus should be awarded a competitive license. Given the struggles hip hop stations have faced in Canada, even in large cities, to gain broadcasting licenses, this meaningful. That the station would go on to play hip hop by Indigenous and Black Canadian artists is also an important step for transforming the airwaves traversing a city to better reflect the people living in it. Leadership and on-air talent negotiate the important role the station can have in Winnipeg, on the Prairies, across Canada, and across borders. The four professionals whose input most closely inform this chapter are Dave McLeod, board member with the Manitoba Audio Recording Industry Association and CEO of NCI, and three on-air DJs: Miss Melissa, an Indigenous music industry leader who also served as the Streetz music director; Alex Sannie, a Black Canadian musician who is a hip hop artist with The Lytics; and Paul Rabliauskas, an Anishinaabe comedian who has performed in a variety of clubs and festivals.

The broadcaster NCI operates as part of a larger matrix of arts and cultural organizations in Winnipeg. This city had an important role in the Woodland School Arts Movement and is home to Indigenous-focused visual arts organizations such as the Urban Shaman Gallery. Graffiti Art Programming and Studio 393, hip hop–specific community-based projects, offer graffiti, breakdance, and DJ and MC programs for Indigenous, settler, and newcomer youth.[23] Beyond NCI, Winnipeg hosts the media outlet Aboriginal Peoples Television Network (APTN), which operates both a web presence with streaming video and traditional television broadcasts.[24] The city is home to numerous musical and cultural festivals and events, many of which include First Nations, Inuit, and Métis artists, such as Manito Ahbee, Indigenous Music Week,

Festival du Voyageur, and the Indigenous Music Awards. The legacy of Indigenous artists in Winnipeg has carried through to contemporary figures, continuing a cultural legacy.

When Indigenous media producers take control of established distribution systems, opportunities arise for the circulation of alternative narratives using mainstream channels. But this phenomenon, experienced on Native-licensed radio, did not begin with Streetz. Previous radio- and television-broadcasting channels have demonstrated the efficacy of such a shift. The Inuit Broadcasting Corporation, for example, established a satellite television station for and by Inuit communities in the arctic, acquiring government licensure in 1981.[25] TV Northern Canada created a dedicated station beginning in 1991 and connected with southern Indigenous content producers to create APTN, which began broadcasting in 1999. Headquartered in the urban South yet broadcasting across Canada, APTN and NCI, the parent organization that began Streetz, take advantage of the opportunity to produce and distribute content relevant to numerous Indigenous groups throughout the province of Manitoba and across Canada. As Faye Ginsburg has argued, securing access to media-distribution channels did not impede Indigenous cultural production, as some people had feared. Rather, she finds that these channels "have played a dynamic and even revitalizing role for Inuit and other First-Nations people, as a self-conscious means of cultural preservation and production and a form of political mobilization."[26] Musicians, too, use broadcast radio as a strategy for cultural learning, as the contemporary popular music of Leonard Sumner will show. At the same time, these opportunities for preservation, production, and mobilization face limitations. Scarcity of financial resources and ideological concerns that inhibit Indigenous cultural expressions both constrain the extent to which potential opportunities can be actualized.

## Turn on the Radio

Bright major-key guitar chords and electronic hand claps set an upbeat feel. It could not be easier to clap along. Where do you feel bright party music? Does it echo in your ear? Do you tap your fingers or move your feet? Does the music move your body as a whole? The rapper's lyrics playfully bounce between a single beat per syllable and six faster ones in a four-plus-two pattern. While the slow lyrics deliver the core message, even the faster ones flow unhurriedly; instrumentals do not overshadow any words. With only a couple of listens, you could probably rap along, too, if you wanted. People all around the world are "equal." They want to have a "good time." The rapper is rhyming so we can "all shine." And, as the song continues, the "good time" and the commonalities between people are given lyrical detail. How are people equal? "We all about the girls / We all wanna find one to put our arm around." This song will share the "new Neechi sound"; it invites all listeners who share this vision. Through double entendre, the lyrics become less innocent as the song embraces a party vibe. Artists play with the party rap export—as opposed to just a carbon copy, they offer a regionalization of something that does not require the listener to stretch their expectations very much, aesthetically or politically. A new voice enters for the sung chorus; a male singer tells a (probably different) listener, "I got some sunshine in my pocket that I put away for you, just for you." The male rapper repeats the singer's lines, "away for you" and "it's just for you."

A listener could strain to hear this duet as men singing and rapping romantically to each other, but the performers on the track make choices that would complicate this reading. The low-register, almost gravelly, singing, might not be just men's voices, but the rapper, Wab Kinew, identifies himself and names producer Boogey the Beat as well as Lorenzo, who sings the hook, all three male-identified artists. As the verses and hook continue, the rapper spits his lyrics about the kind of man he is and speaks his words to "girl" and "shorty." The sunshine in the singer's pocket is more than light, as the lyrics make repeated references to oral sex to be performed by the girl he is addressing. This might be just sex, it might be romance, or it might be something else or multiple things at once. The rapper expresses his desire; a girl catches him looking at her "in the worst way"; even this may be said with a smile. He wants her "fine ass rolling" with him; he wants to "make memories." After the third repeat of the chorus, a voice shouts, "everybody," encouraging listeners to sing along as the song plays out. The chorus lyrics repeat, multiple times, with encouraging shouts from the rapper's voice in the background.

With the song's lyrical focus, catchy duple beat, bright instrumentals, use of double entendre, and grouping of who is talked to and about, this is one of many songs on Streetz that fits with one or more existing commercial hip hop tropes that circulate on both sides of, and across, the US-Canada border. Sumner explained that the song came out of a fun collaboration with Kinew. "You're just in the studio. You're kinda just going with the flow, you know what I mean. . . . It's just like regular life. There's times to be serious, there's times to laugh, there's times to be angry, there's times to be sad."[27] Like the songs Sumner and Kinew would both distribute later, including those deemed more directly political, this song adapts US-based commercial hip hop tropes, solidified through commodification of rap in the 1990s and then exported. These are young men, singing with an almost-pop party rap vibe, rapping about sunshine, (heterosexual) sex, and parties. Brief mentions of Neechi identity and a club party scene suggest that the musicians are urban Anishinaabeg men. And still, these could almost be any boys rapping about girls using known tropes. Sexual references are clear, albeit with some discretion. The romance is heterosexual. The words are not exactly clean, but the musicians never actually swear. They fit their song into a verse-chorus format, alternating rapped verses and sung choruses, use the chorus to emphasize the key elements of the verses, and wrap up the whole thing in about three and a half minutes. This song is an easy fit for broadcast and streaming radio. Listeners often seek an outlet through music to decompress; Sumner reflects, "I have some fun songs that seem to get a lot of traction, stuff that's not too heavy. And I'm OK with that."[28] And as a song that checks the Canadian-content box and also matches the station's goal to play music by Indigenous musicians, it was in regular rotation on Streetz.

Musically, Streetz plays a mix of current hip hop, R&B, dance, and some pop tracks, alongside older hip hop and R&B songs. Local Indigenous artists and Canadian artists air with US-based rappers and groups and some international musicians. While the station maintains a distinct image from popular-hits-format stations in the city, on-air DJs avoid negative comments about successful songs on these more commercial pop stations, regardless of their personal views on them. Many of these songs also make it into the station's rotation. Miss Melissa plays songs like the electronic duo Daft Punk's "Get Lucky" featuring Pharrell Williams, which reached number 1 on the Billboard

Dance/Electronica list. The station also airs the older Rihanna and Jay-Z song "Umbrella," which reached number 1 on the Billboard Pop 100. When Miss Melissa delivers celebrity news, she covers Justin Bieber's retirement and subsequent retraction. While off-air Miss Melissa's aesthetic preferences include an eclectic mix of underground artists, she keeps a professionally neutral tone on-air and thus avoids potentially alienating a more mainstream listenership. She does show her taste through praising artists whose music she appreciates: one morning, this translates to a short rhapsody about the Bingo Players. In the mix of music from various geographies, *The Rise Up Show* also features non–USAmerican artists, including Dutch group Bingo Players, British rapper Tinie Tempah, and internationally popular Canadian rapper Kardinal Offishall. Over the course of the morning show segment that opened this chapter, two tracks by Winnipeg-based Anishinaabeg artists aired on the station: one by Wab Kinew and one by Leonard Sumner. The urban-format station presents local Indigenous hip hop music, sandwiched between widely known non-Indigenous artists, to a wide audience.

On-air sound parallels online messaging: the station consistently expresses its position as Indigenous and urban, using sound, image, and text to demonstrate these aspects of the station's identity simultaneously. The meta title for its "About Us" section on its website proclaims, "STREETZ 104.7 is Winnipeg's Aboriginal Youth Radio."[29] This tagline is designed to appear in several different places for internet users. By embedding the text in the website's code, the staff orient this meta title for potential listeners. It becomes the browser title when readers navigate to the page and also appears as the title in a web search result. This meta title and the associated meta description appear on sharing previews on social media sites like Facebook. Across platforms, Streetz proclaims its focus on urban music for Indigenous listeners. The meta title for streetzfm.ca has been "Winnipeg's #1 Hip Hop and R&B Station."[30] The "About Us" section further identifies the station's Indigenous urban audience (figure 2.1). Set in white on a black background, the station information falls under a bright header, in which yellow, blue, and pink fluorescent lights shine around the station's logo.

Figure 2.1. Streetz, "About Us" (accessed 3 April 2014, www.streetzfm.ca).

On the side of the page, a photograph of the iconic downtown Provencher Bridge at night marks both the city and the time of day, identifying the station with Winnipeg's urban nightlife. The logo further speaks to urban Indigeneity with yellow and white bubble letters that mimic a graffiti-writing style. A tipi is among the four buildings on top of the writing, foregrounding an identity that is simultaneously urban and Indigenous. The juxtaposition of these symbols shows the station wrestling with the representational challenge of making an urban Indigenous community audible.

Bright piano chords vamp, and a treble voice sings, "I've been watching everything." A rapped voice layers over, explaining that the narrator is trying to hold out hope. The rapper, Shad, intones, "And somehow, you expected to have mastered this smooth swagger and move, with the right walk, the right talk, fashion and crews, souls subtly attacked and abused, and what's funny's being Black wasn't cool where I'm from 'til suddenly you started hearing rap in the school hallways. Amidst this madness I grew."[31] The expectations for Black youth—Shad uses the word "limited"—create problems, as does the small range of possibilities shown for and to young people like the narrator. Shad continues, "But after a while, it sort of starts naggin' at you, the crazed infatuation with Blackness, that trash that gets viewed. And the fact that the tube only showed Blacks actin' the fool and I was watching." The rapped voice pauses, almost midsentence, and the treble voice continues to sing about watching everything. The rhythmic sound of a record scratching layers in; the piano continues. After a pause, the rapper comes back in with a fast-paced yet relatively quiet lead-in to the next verse: "saturated with negative images and a limited range of possibilities is strange."[32] Canadian rapper Shad has been heard in rotation heavily on Streetz. His parents are from Rwanda. They gave birth to Shad in Kenya, and they raised him in London, Ontario. His song "Brother (Watching)" traces his experience of the way Blackness is negotiated in Canada. For an MC, this gendered and raced experience is inflected by what Rashad Shabazz describes as the cyclical nature of tropes like the hypertough heterosexual rapper: "this figure has gained so much traction in hip-hop because against the backdrop of profound assault Black boys and men have and remain under, toughness, being hard became an outward expression of subjugation and powerlessness."[33] The narrator describes being interpreted, in Canadian parlance, as a "visible minority," a double bind of a certain kind of cool paired with limited and limiting options for success.

Even as global hip hop reaches across borders, it speaks back to ideas of USAmerican Blackness. Hip hop made and circulated in Canada engages with Canadian Blackness, echoing around an ongoing legacy of erasure of Blackness in Canada; Katherine McKittrick calls Canada "a nation that has and is still defining its history as Euro-white, or nonblack."[34] To what extent does attempting to access mainstream airplay necessitate accepting, and even reifying, commercialized stereotypes of Blackness and masculinity? What does this imply for musicians who are both non-Black and nonwhite? Black Canadians speak from a specific position, rapping in the shadow of USAmerican commercial music, as do musicians who are both Black and Indigenous. An unproblematized acceptance of associations between Blackness, masculinity, and commercial hip hop risks becoming essentialist; even as raced and gendered constructions are recognized as just that—constructions—they carry meaning and have lived effects for listeners.[35] These constructions carry particular resonances when conveyed by people for whom Indigenous masculinities are personally relevant. "Indigenous men and those who identify with Indigenous masculinities," as Robert Alexander Innes and Kim Anderson find, "are faced with distinct gender and racial biases that cause many to struggle."[36]

As will be further explored in chapter 4, a move away from settler heteropatriarchy responds to these struggles while proposing alternatives that offer possibilities for men, women, and gender-nonbinary people. When linked to specific teachings, Indigenous and Nation-specific understandings of masculinity can be understood as connected to duty toward others. In Indigenous contexts in the US and Canada, notions of Blackness intersect with conceptions of Indigeneity, economic marginality, gender, sex, and urban living. Halifiu Osumare describes, "U.S. black American culture continues to be mired in social narratives of 'blackness' that proliferate multidimensionally in the international arena, commingling with other countries' issues of social marginality."[37] Through the 1980s and into the 1990s, hip hop by Black Canadians troubled the notion of the Canadian state as white and challenged a benevolent version of confederation. Hip hop that has emerged from the sometimes overlapping groups of Native and Black artists into the twenty-first century builds on this legacy, bringing together culturally specific forms of Indigenous storytelling and song to disrupt the processes evinced by earlier Canadian rap.

Markers of place, gender, class, and race all are implicated in the construction of hip hop aesthetics. Performers and industry professionals circulate and alter these even as they stretch in multiple temporal and stylistic directions. Across b-boying/breaking, DJing, graffiti, and rapping, hip hop can display an aggressive, and even violent, aesthetic that Imani Kai Johnson calls "clichéd masculinity."[38] For commercial rap, Daniel Traber finds that performers are expected to integrate markers of class, "reputations as genuine street thugs," criminality, and "prison records."[39] The subgenre of gangsta rap influenced mainstream rap aesthetics due to its commercial viability and popularity in the US and abroad in the mid-1990s. While hip hop was stylistically diverse before and after this commercial mainstreaming, some tropes solidified in listening ears. Frequently cited at this moment of transition is N.W.A., a group that Canada-based artists like Lorenzo describe as an important stylistic influence. As Murray Forman characterizes these tropes, they include "uncompromising lyrical depictions of gang culture, gun violence, anti-authoritarian attitudes, drug distribution and use, prostitution, etc.," as well as "homophobia, sexism, misogyny, and anti-social aggression."[40] Tricia Rose calls attention to "the fundamental logic of mainstream masculinity" that hip hop may "convey . . . with excess, bravado, and extra insult."[41] Similarly, Nelson George connects the tropes of gun violence, revenge, and what he calls "cartoonish misogyny" to the rap that became widely popular in the 1990s and continued to impact commercial music into this century.[42]

From the confluence of African American, Puerto Rican, and Caribbean influences in early hip hop, mainstream rap music shifted to focus on limited monoracial Black urban tropes for profit-making purposes. Through an analysis of how a rap group would need to be packaged to meet sales goals, Daniel Traber contends that Blackness became portrayed as monoracial as rap commercialized. He points to "the mainstream, commercial musical industry that sold rap in record numbers as solely a hardcore and gangsta genre." As a result, "the commercial music industry not only sold rap in this form, it also portrayed blackness" as a "monoracial, exclusionary urban identity."[43] This version involves an exaggeration of violence, a masculinity based on heterosexual conquest, and the conspicuous consumption of luxury products; it operates in a way that excludes, that normalizes, and that grants official status to only a particular kind of performance of Blackness.

Destructive stereotypes of hypersexuality, violence, and profligacy are related to earlier "racial colonial caricatures" of African Americans.[44] These stereotypes, sold as part of gangsta-inflected rap's appeal, contribute to a hyperscrutinized, singular vision of Blackness. Why would rappers' celebration of consumerism and excess be read as anything other than a mainstream capitalist dream? Roopali Mukherjee references instances like hip hop headliners wearing Tommy Hilfiger and then being criticized in the mainstream USAmerican press for participating in USAmerican capitalism: "renewing age-old scripts that black Americans are, at base, ill-equipped to manage wealth and are deserving of racist ridicule for their attempts to buy their way into the privileges of participation in public life, such critiques echo those from other historical moments."[45] The performative display involved in this type of commercial rap, what Annette Saddik identifies as the "aggressive display (of blackness, masculinity, wealth, subjectivity),"[46] is sometimes presented as an artist's truth and sometimes shown with a wink: audiences may or may not perceive it as congruent with an artist's experience as performed, but the artists are generally aware that their performances cite known tropes in order to keep commercial backing.[47] The move into successful sales with Black, white, and other audiences was crucial for this shift. Mireille Miller-Young recognizes the related marketing strategy of equating the ghetto with adventure and using its imagery for financial gain when marketed toward a white or mixed-race audience.[48] This goes beyond the phenomenon that bell hooks describes as one in which "ethnicity becomes spice";[49] commercial rap at times participates in the solidification of a stereotyped monoracial Blackness that the artists themselves may well recognize as just a performance.[50]

In the context of hip hop, performance of race overlaps with that of gender and other identity formations. Hip hop feminist scholars like dream hampton reconsider "raunchy rap lyrics and hip-hop's complicated sexual history as alternately liberating and constraining."[51] The movement between the possible and the damaging is difficult to reconcile, as she explains: "I want to tell [my daughter] all the ways hip hop has made me feel powerful. How it gave my generation a voice, a context, how we shifted the pop culture paradigm. . . . I want to suggest that maybe these rhymes about licking each other's asses are liberating. But I can't."[52] As described in chapter 1, the gendering and racialization of hip hop practice over time has been reinforced by limiting commercial rap tropes. Arguing for a queer reading of hip hop's ratchet aesthetic, L. H. Stallings finds that raunchy lyrics and hypersexualized settings allow musicians and listeners to fail to be respectable. Embracing excess and the unproductive does not diminish what she calls "hip hop's objectification of women," but it allows for a focus on "black communities' intent to use sexual leisure to critique Western sexual morality."[53] Even as twenty-first-century artists have reperformed alternatives to these tropes and proposed resilient redeployments of them, these tropes remain powerful references in many musical imaginations.

Similarly, racialized identity construction reflects back on genre in a cyclical manner. While rap music in its international scope consciously or unconsciously evokes characterizations of USAmerican Blackness, the globalization of this music and culture allows for shifting performances of hip hop racialization. The popularity of this marketing genre in the mainstream—Blackness had become "cool" in a limited way, thanks to rap—further contributed to limited racialization.[54] When rappers who foreground their Indigenous identities produce mainstream commercial music, their performances can evoke, reify, or play with tropes of criminality, hypermasculinity, and consumption. At the same time, the rappers' locations—in urban, rural, or reserve locations, their social location vis-à-vis class, or specific relationships to living histories—become additional reference points that can invoke and potentially transform popular culture images of the "Indian" in the contemporary moment.

A hit by a Toronto rapper plays out ideas of Blackness in Canada, layering in conceptions of masculinity, heterosexuality, and national origin. What does it take to sound Canadian? Whose sounds fit in the nation-state? With a distinctly recognizable force, electronic percussion immediately snaps in a catchy four-beat bar. The fully electronic instrumentals offer descending melodic lines, their buzzy timbre repeating through the eight-bar intro. In a call-and-response, two vocal lines converse: "That girl is so." "Dangerous." "That girl is so." "Dangerous." "That girl is so." "That girl." That girl is lyrically typecast, and then, once more, two pieces of an intersecting hocket, "that girl" and "dangerous" zipper together to complete the sung chorus. Akon, the song's featured vocalist, may be singing with himself, but the pauses and sonic panning create dialogue.

Across the three verses on this collaborative song, rapper Kardinal Offishall plays with his voice. He dips into a low-pitch register when he delivers metaphoric innuendo: "the big dog tryin' to get her little kitty to purr." He often stays at a repeated pitch, so each move up or down brings special attention. Talking about her curves, he raps, "Body's like weapons of mass eruptions"; the first syllable of "weapons" strains into the pitch stratosphere, an exuberant yelp. His speech combines multiple vernaculars. By the third verse, the Jamaican patois that has peppered the rapped flow takes it over. Kardinal Offishall's vowels change shape. They stretch and elongate. His references shape-shift, too: "When she do her ting, man can't walk straight / That biscuit fi soak up erry-ting on her plate." Known for his Toronto slang, Kardinal Offishall brings a range of speech patterns that can be heard on that city's streets. The influences of Jamaican dancehall speak through the album as a whole. This single, "Dangerous," from the album *Not 4 Sale* was released on a USAmerican record label (Geffen Records). Released in 2008, the album charted on the US Billboard 200 and peaked at number 3 on the Mainstream Top 40 in September 2008.[55]

Kardinal Offishall's intelligibility as both Black and Canadian can be read through what Rinaldo Walcott calls the "problem" of Blackness in Canada.[56] He was born and raised in Toronto, but his presence in Canada is heard by some through his parents' immigration from Jamaica; his location as a diasporic subject invokes his second-generation status. This understanding could allow listeners to avoid the potentially disjunctive ongoing presence of Black Canadians that stretches back pre-Confederation. The slow and rocky acceptance of Black Canadian music into the Canadian music industry suggests a larger resistance to the idea of Black music being fundamentally Canadian.

Active forgetting is integral to the creation of cultural narratives that whitewash Canada. This lobotomizing is part of the ongoing myth of Canadian Blackness being only post-1950 and urban; it connects to the erasure of the ongoing presence of Indigenous peoples. Despite the centuries-old presence of Black communities and a two-hundred-year history of slavery in what is now Canada,[57] McKittrick finds that Black communities continue to be constructed as "non-Canadian, always other, always elsewhere, recent, unfamiliar, and impossible."[58] Like Walcott, she argues that Canada has erased geographic presences and ignored nonwhite histories. Walcott traces a move to associate Blackness with the Caribbean and recent migration. To these two spaces that Walcott identifies, McKittrick adds USAmerican migration as well, but the result is the same: Black people and Black communities are conceptually relocated outside Canada. Place names from early Black Canada, and places themselves, are bulldozed; with physical erasures comes much intentional forgetting. At the same time, Black communities in Canada are pathologized in similar ways as in the United States. The hypervisibility of Black individuals and communities related to criminalizing and pathologizing state policies operates alongside historical and cultural erasure. National narratives minimize or erase Canada's histories of slavery. Indigenous peoples who were captured and sold as slaves, sometimes called "Panis," labored under both French and British colonial rule.[59]

Re-membering Black and Native histories, and their intersections, is crucial to understand contemporary expressive culture. This begins with recalling histories that have been whitewashed. As Peggy Bristow explains, "A history of Black women's lives in Canada must start with our arrival here as slaves. Black women, like Black men and like First Nations peoples, were enslaved here, beginning with the seventeenth century, first by the French and later by the British. We were brought here to labor."[60] But the story does not end there. Absent, too, from a whitewashed history is the pivotal role that Black Canadians have played in shaping the country. One representative story is found in Mary Ann Shadd Cary, who impacted media creation and distribution in Canada starting in the 1850s and became the first female publisher and editor of a newspaper.[61] One of the pathbreaking decisions Shadd Cary made was that when a Black school teacher, Sarah Armstrong, suffered an attempted sexual assault by a white man, the public should be made aware in a manner that presented Armstrong with respect. As a news writer and editor, Shadd Cary was using the press to work against insidious stereotypes of Black womxn's sexuality.[62] Named figures, like Shadd Cary, and thousands unnamed, can be consciously recalled to piece together a more accurate story.

These stories course through sung histories, as well, notably Webster's collaboration "QC History X." When I first listened to this song, it stood out in part because of its unusual intro. It is not the only song on the album, *Le vieux d'la montagne*, to start with a downtempo minor melody, nor is it the only one to use a violin to deliver part of the tune. However, in this song, there is an interruption that marks the opening: the sound of a record scratch enters, and an English-language voice asserts, "Wake you up, out of your brainwashed state."[63] When I listen again, thinking through the history of the past several centuries in what is now Canada, I hear the interruption that marks the intro as a parallel for interruptions that mark the entire song. The record scratch interrupts the violin, the vocal line in English interrupts the previous songs' French-language flow, and Webster and Karim Ouellet proceed to interrupt recent narratives of Canadian history.

In the first verse, the rapper promises to bring the listener back in history. Webster says he will "Vous dévoiler des faits / Qu'on n'apprend pas forcément" (reveal to us the facts that one doesn't necessarily learn). He promises to teach us what isn't taught in school about Indigenous and Black peoples, reminding his listeners that history is "romancée, manipulée" (romanticized, manipulated). And so the subsequent verses offer what I hear as one interruption after the other: Samuel de Champlain's well-known narrative is nuanced, as the rapper places language inter-preter and free Black man Mathieu Da Costa back on Champlain's ship in 1604. A whitewashed history is again interrupted as the rapper names Olivier Lejeune, a Black man enslaved in Québec City, who is brought there in 1629. He lists the names of specific heroes and gestures toward thousands unnamed over the past four hundred years. Québec history has a problem. The rapper explains that national histories want us to be-lieve that Black people arrived in the 1970s, while in fact, their presence can be traced through business, the army, trade, and more for hundreds of years prior to this time.

Over the verses, Webster and Ouellet continue. They draw parallels between those who have been located outside of Québec's history—even when they are inextricably of it—and, as I listen, I consider, of the Canadian present. The rappers name "Genocide à grande echelle," wide-scale genocide against Indigenous peoples, and describe the kinds of distancing that settlers attempted against Indigenous peoples, the "viol culturel / Être vu en étranger / Sur sa propre parcelle / De terre an-cestrale" (cultural rape, to be seen as a stranger on one's own piece of ancestral land).

In conversation with other tellings of Canadian and Québecois his-tory, this song can be heard to consciously re-member free Black people and Black slaves back into the history of what is now Canada. It also makes explicit connections between Black Québecois and other groups, including Chinese immigrants. It specifically outlines ongoing connec-tions with Indigenous peoples whose presence on their own ancestral lands far predates settlers and settler histories and continues to this day. As historian, scholar, rapper, and storyteller, Webster interrupts and reconnects.

As with selective myopia in the mainstream public imaginary re-garding Indigenous people in Canada, ignoring an enduring history of nonwhite people in Canada both sanitizes despicable instances of state violence and invisibilizes the creative accomplishments of nonwhite Ca-nadians going back hundreds of years, in the case of Black Canadians, and since the very beginning, in the case of Indigenous people in what is now Canada. When popular music today destabilizes dominant racial-ized mythologies, it creates space for conceptualizing belonging differ-ently, in the past and into the future.

## Hearing Winnipeg through Global Headphones

An image flashes and holds just long enough to register. One second, two seconds, three seconds. The camera moves constantly, panning left to right, zooming in, shifting focus during microscenes. Visuals freeze, then transform, though the sound flows without such abrupt changes. Even with two radically divergent speeds, sound and image work together, generic and specific speak to each other in a flowing dialogue. A lone figure walks toward an urban skyline: skyscrapers, parking lots, trees, the many turrets of a church, white steam rising in front of the hazy black-and-white city. Light pings of minor-key electronics, reminiscent of a video game or the cell phone a man holds to his ear, are the most prominent sounds. Then the beat drops with an easy four-beat pattern. Visually, viewers never stay still: stacks of money appear on a table next to an ashtray. The tattoo on a man's forearm comes into focus. Three men in baggy jeans, caps, hoodies, and prominent necklaces stand in the middle of a street in front of industrial four-story buildings. More images arrive in succession: a neon hotel sign, a close-up of a $100 bill, a chain-link fence topped with barbed wire, a wall covered in graffiti tags, a steaming vent covered in icicles, three men backlit, appearing as baseball-capped silhouettes in the street. Women wearing short dresses dance in slow motion holding red plastic cups. A handle of Grey Goose appears, a pool table, a series of quick close-ups in the club and on the rooftop, as the rapper says, "monster," "goonies," "soldiers."

The audience was prepared for this, but barely. A siren wails, sounding the approach of a fire engine, even as visually, the vehicle is already parked outside a smoking building. Ominous drum crashes and minor-key electronics mean viewers could be anywhere, danger both approaching and already arrived. Movie soundtracks have taught us as audience members to be nervous for anyone who enters the scene now. But we're not just anywhere: we're on a street corner; the pole with crossing street names is in focus in the frame. Even as the camera continues to circle around the vehicle and the firefighters, "Powers Ave" remains clearly in view. I can almost hear the crunch of hardened snow, full of foot tracks already. The camera pans to bare tree branches, past the bands on the trunks designed to protect this deciduous urban canopy. Rows of two-story houses and apartment buildings typical of this neighborhood extend into the street beyond. The video cuts to downtown buildings. One bus ride away, skyscrapers reach upward; even from the camera's vantage point several stories up, their apexes are out of reach. Buses pause in the roads below, and some rooftops of multistory buildings are visible, covered in snow with vents expelling hot steam. A government building is branded above its highest windows: "Canada." The hip hop group's name appears on-screen, also naming the city: "Winnipeg's Most."

As in Snoop Dogg's "What's My Name" and Eminem's "My Name Is," the audience has no excuse for forgetting this name. We see it on bandanas, T-shirts, and hats; close-ups zoom in on the group's name on necklaces. Prominent markers of the city's downtown and North End neighborhoods show us where we are, piles of snow, street signs, and specific businesses behind the rappers as they flow, "I'm a Winnipeg boy. That's who I am. And my name more feared than the ghosts of the damned." A "peg city vet" is surrounded by others known in the scene, the "team" a constant presence as the men walk through the streets. The railroad tracks that separate the North End from farther south feature in the visuals and the lyrics, the wrong-side-of-the tracks metaphor hard to miss.

This is not just an ode to a city or an invitation framing how the group wants to be read or a calling card. It's a narrative, a sort of love story, maybe ill fated, maybe fraternal. A woman stares angrily at a man, yells at him soundlessly, and he yells back. Their fight is cut with images of the man in the streets, with his crew. The male rapped vocals on the track tell his story: "My baby want me at the game, but I tell her this is all that I know." Low-pitched vocals repeat, "All that I know." He goes on, "I could've took a nine-to-five, but the hustle life is what I chose," and the vocals echo, "what I chose." We hear him say his family wants him "on the right road," but the woman grabs her coat and walks out—he has made his choice otherwise. The first verse puts us in the street and the club; we're led on a rapid tour by Jon-C. When the chorus returns, we see the woman again; she reaches her hand to touch an empty place in their bed: the singer is overlaid visually and audibly; he is not with her. In the second verse, the singer, Charlie Fettah, raps about her as he walks in the streets without her: she says she's worried ("Every time I leave my house, my girl say that she worried. She say she plagued by dreams of my casket being buried"). But he chooses to move "fast," to make "money in a hurry," to drink and smoke. He can't help himself; he can't sleep. His parole officer is the only one who is really "holdin' [his] leash." By the third chorus, his "girl" has disappeared. The third rapper is outside on Selkirk Avenue: "In the ghetto and I love it. Money making is nothing." Money changes hands; men walk in groups. Brooklyn raps that he has to watch his back because he's so successful, that he's clubbin', that the jacuzzi is bumpin', that his family came around to love that he was "thuggin." The group's name flashes on-screen after the final chorus. The lasting visual is this name and the three men together.

Hip hop trio Winnipeg's Most was frequently played on Streetz. They performed "All That I Know," one of the group's most popular songs, live in studio at the station and shared the video online through the station's official channels. Even as Jon-C, Charlie Fettah, and Brooklyn respond to their lived realities, they make choices to tell a story with sonic and visual markers that come from USAmerican hip hop and that trope Blackness in a particular way. This aural and visual narrative resonated with many audiences. Their music, to some extent, became iconic of Winnipeg hip hop as it solidified. Canadian commercial hip hop was coming into its own in the first decade of the twenty-first century, and then, "All That I Know" became a popular urban anthem for the city—including Indigenous and non-Indigenous hip hop fans—in 2010. Winnipeg's Most went on to win multiple Aboriginal Peoples' Choice Music Awards in 2010 and 2011. The three MCs, Jon-C, Charlie Fettah, and Brooklyn, pursued group and solo projects over the next several years and continued to feature on Streetz.

## Shaping a Community of Listeners

By using on-air music and wrap-around branding to form the station's listenership, Streetz achieves two related outcomes. The station performatively creates its audience. Simultaneously, the station uses focus groups, listener feedback, and staff members' own experience to alter the station's sound and image in response to that audience. As CEO of NCI, Dave McLeod takes a strong leadership role at Streetz over these related audience-forming and audience-reflecting functions. McLeod speaks highly of the mixture of Indigenous and non-Indigenous urban music broadcast by the station, as well as music showing the Indigenous and the urban simultaneously, both clear strategic moves. This hybridity is partially a strategy for audibility, as many Indigenous groups making hip hop and electronic music are not played on other stations. A member of the Pine Creek First Nation, McLeod notes that even rising-star group A Tribe Called Red had a difficult time airing on stations besides Streetz in the group's early days. McLeod sees Streetz's approach as an opportunity for artists to gain a wider audience: "Native artists love the fact their music is mixed with a mainstream-like sound, because it opens the market to them. This gives an opportunity for them to be heard. . . . You look at A Tribe Called Red, who recently won a Juno in a non-Native mainstream category, which Streetz supports. They come to Winnipeg, and they sell out. Is it just Native people at their show? No. They're invited to the Winnipeg Folk Festival. . . . They'll have hundreds upon hundreds of people in front of the stage dancing to their music."[64] Even as the station courts multiple overlapping publics, professionals find a utility in thinking through responses from Indigenous and non-Indigenous listenerships. While these listenerships are never wholly distinct, music professionals respond to real instances of anti-Indigenous bias.

McLeod contrasts what he terms a non-Indigenous "mainstream" with an Indigenous "community," explaining, "There is so much goodness in the community that is often overlooked. And I think a lot of mainstream, they don't know."[65] This speaks to a way in which artists could be heard—likening their music to that which is already accepted by a mainstream ear.[66] Listeners consider music by Indigenous artists that they might otherwise have ignored, but through a "mainstream" normalization. This technique, albeit a controversial one, is not uncommon for commercial media: that which the broadcaster wishes to introduce is featured alongside that which is already popular. Much like a featured artist in a song by a better-known rapper, the lesser-known musician could gain acceptance through proximity. Connecting Indigenous popular music to an audience that may not otherwise be aware of it is part of the station's strength for the CEO. He explains, "Particularly when people listen to our station, they're hearing Aboriginal music mixed with mainstream music. That's a good thing. We're saying this music is good enough to be played with mainstream music. [First

Nations radio host] Paul [Rabliauskas] is good enough to be a great morning-show announcer. . . . So it opens the door."[67] In this instance, McLeod uses the word "mainstream" to clearly delineate Indigenous recordings from those by non-Indigenous artists: these categories can be strategically playlisted together on-air. This strategy serves a pragmatic function and maintains a system of legitimation: early on, A Tribe Called Red struggled to get airtime, likely because of their conscious foregrounding of Indigenous popular forms in their musical mix. Contemporary powwow features heavily in their remixes. This genre brings a high nasal vocal timbre and consistent contrasts in register, uncommon qualities in music that typically charts. Yet, as the group has gained popularity over time, the DJ trio's characteristic sounds attract more audience members, as indicated by both numbers of fans and diversity within the group's fan base.

This increase in audibility can be heard in the music of one artist who has appeared live and on-air on Streetz: Leonard Sumner. The musician was initially showcased on the station when he created his first digital EP and continued as he produced subsequent albums. When I asked him, "How did you get involved with Streetz initially?" he replied,

> They were just coming up. I was living on the rez, and I had my EP done, and I released it digitally. I sent them my tracks, and then they started playing it. They were looking for First Nations artists and Canadian content, so I was able to provide them with that. And the people really liked my music as well, so it was like a win win win. . . . The people got to listen to someone who grew up around with them, and they got to play local Canadian content, and then I got to be on the radio. Everybody benefited.[68]

Native-licensed radio can provide an outlet for music that might otherwise be hard to sell.[69] Often top-down controlled and requiring licensure and regulation by the national government, broadcast radio comes with sets of rules and patterns of behavior that act as barriers for some artists. The distinction between "Indigenous" and "mainstream" music may make sense for some of the programming purposes about which McLeod speaks, yet this cleavage is not neat. A Tribe Called Red won a Juno Award for Breakthrough Group of the Year in 2014. This category is not specifically for Indigenous artists but for new groups in Canada generally. While the group had been attracting a more racially mixed audience before the 2014 win, this award solidified wide recognition and began a stretch of other mainstream accolades. Effectively, this group helped shift a Canadian mainstream toward the music they were making. How then would a group like A Tribe Called Red fit into the station's pragmatic dichotomy? Even groups without such a meteoric rise trouble easy categorization. Joey Stylez, a rapper from Saskatchewan, is of Cree and Métis heritage. His music has a decidedly commercial sound. He raps and sings in English, rather than using Cree, Michif, or other Indigenous languages favored by some other Métis artists. He offers a pop party rap sound and has gained fame opening for mainstream acts like 50 Cent and doing collaborations with the likes of Pitbull. Yet, his music, as described in chapter 1, does sometimes take on social commentary on issues like the effects of residential schools. The "mainstream," then, is already Indigenous: if Indigenous music is characterized as that by Indigenous artists, then the presence of musicians like Stylez within a musical mainstream troubles the notion that mainstream music is made only by settler Canadians. And if Indigenous music is characterized as that which incorporates language, instrumentation, vocalization, or genres from Indigenous sources, then A Tribe Called Red's widespread popularity reinforces the notion that Indigenous music *is* mainstream music.

In practice, musical norms are already informed by Indigenous musical practices because Indigenous artists and musical conventions cannot be separated from the development of popular musics on the North American continent; this aligns with the concept that the city is already Indigenous, which is applied in this chapter through the concept of relocated Indigeneity.[70] At the same time, settler colonial policies informed by what Tuck and Yang call "settler moves to innocence" have furthered public misconceptions that center norms around settler culture.[71] The reinforcing of a whitened mainstream is inextricably linked to the performance of settler nationalism—the regular reinforcement that establishes a "mainstream" or norm as white in a place where white people arrived as outsiders is part of the colonial project.[72] Its incompleteness can be characterized as settler colonialism's "ongoing existence and simultaneous failure," according to Audra Simpson.[73] The stakes of

maintaining these hierarchical divisions relate to larger power structures. Given the degree to which these moves are embedded in music
industry structures, it is unsurprising that Indigenous music industry
insiders would use the term "mainstream" to refer to white listenerships
and artists, even if they do not believe that the music industry must
or should be organized around a white/Indigenous (or even center/pe-
riphery) model. This very tension is the point: uncritical use of the term
"mainstream" in daily language both reinforces and conceals the constructed nature of this concept.

## Limitations of Courting a Musical "Mainstream"

Through accessible distribution, broadcast and online media shape
public discourse about urban Indigenous artists and audiences. Streetz
station staff articulate that in cities like Winnipeg, they often encounter stereotypes about Indigenous people as being linked to crime and
violence. This is a stereotype that some Winnipeg rappers—notably
members of Winnipeg's Most, which later reformed as the duo Winnipeg Boyz—have been criticized for playing into. Some listeners have
noted that these musicians celebrate drug use, misogyny, and violence
and worry that they are not the strongest role models for young people.
Violence, including gun violence, appears in the group's older music videos, as do limiting portrayals of womxn. Rappers admit that their stance
on displaying violence in their music has changed over time; later songs
offer more nuanced messages about drug use. In spite of criticism, rappers like Winnipeg Boyz members Jon-C and Charlie Fettah take on
roles as leaders, speaking from the marginalized urban location of Winnipeg's North End. Yet not all kinds of dissent are equal with regard to
genre and broadcast expectations.

Brooklyn is remembered by many people with affection and with respect for the music he made. All three are recognized for their work
in Winnipeg's Indigenous community. They served as role models for
up-and-coming rappers. They collaborated on many artistic projects.
They called attention to the issue of missing and murdered Indigenous
womxn, which is particularly drastic in the North End neighborhood they consciously represented. In 2012, the three men purchased
headstones for slain Indigenous women Carolyn Sinclair and Divas

Boulanger. Brooklyn explained, "This is what we can do. This is our part. If everyone did something, it would slowly take the target off our people."[74] All three MCs have taken heat from a number of sources, and none claimed to be perfect. Upon Brooklyn's untimely death in 2015, many people took time to reflect on how he, and Winnipeg's Most, had helped change opportunities for Indigenous artists to get onstage, to win awards, to get on the air.

## Artist Promotion

Playing Indigenous popular music on the airwaves and online is a critical piece of the Streetz music strategy. The station has the potential to offer a platform for sonic sovereignty: artists choose to sing or rap in their First Languages, articulate stories using their own terminology and narrative strategies, and select instruments, timbres, melodies, and other sounds without regard for expectations of the mainstream ear. This goal to play Indigenous popular musicians is clearly heard by Streetz's listeners of both broadcast and online streaming audio formats. Fans have also discussed their appreciation for the on-air DJs' attitudes, and for the local music they play, on the station's Facebook page.[75]

NCI touts its ability to provide Indigenous music content to Manitoba and to develop talent notably among youth. In a letter of support for NCI's application for CIUR (Streetz), Jean LaRose, CEO of APTN, praised NCI for broadcasting the Aboriginal Peoples' Choice Music Awards, "an event that draws 6000 people," as well as "live concerts featuring Aboriginal musicians (NCI aired over twenty recorded acts in 2007)." LaRose's letter further attests that NCI is "a force" in "supporting and developing Aboriginal musicians (especially youth)."[76] Regional Native artists in the rotation include Wab Kinew, Winnipeg's Most, Brooklyn, Young Kidd, and Hellnback. Musicians working in Canada include Indigenous artists who are not local to the Winnipeg region, such as Drezus, Inez, Plex, Joey Stylez, Deejay Elmo, and A Tribe Called Red. Musical selections and on-air interviews with nationally known musicians provide Winnipeg listeners with slickly produced music by Indigenous artists working in Canada. These musicians' songs help change discourses of Indigenous modernity through their presence in a mix, demonstrating a professional sound emanating from Indigenous artists and providing a source of inspiration for local musicians, as Streetz on-air show hosts Miss Melissa and Alex Sannie have both expressed.[77]

Streetz has always taken pride in promoting Indigenous artists. Professionals reflect that the Streetz model is not one that exists in other cities, in Canada or internationally. Some have gone so far as to say that it would be difficult to replicate, as the revenue generation is not at a commercial level. However, the professional station presents possibilities to shape the sound of urban Indigeneity for Indigenous, non-Indigenous, and mixed-heritage audiences. Possibilities for Indigenous self-definition—and even simply getting airtime—were limited in the early 2000s. Sonic sovereignty entails taking control of narratives of what constitutes Indigenous cultural production and, to a greater extent, what constitutes contemporary Indigenous cultural identities, letting this be a dynamic process and allowing these narratives to change over time. McLeod touts the radio station's ability to support and promote urban Indigenous music. He references nationally, and then internationally, known artists who had a mouthpiece at Streetz from the beginning: "Now the fact that we exist . . . is actually helping the genre [urban Indigenous music]. . . . So I think artists have a place to go." McLeod explains that he views the station as "there for the community." It is important for NCI, he says, to "play a legacy role" by helping to launch and support artists.[78] In Miss Melissa's description of her vision for the station and newer artists, she focuses on artists who are known across Canada and connects them to local upstart musicians:

> LP: Are there artists that come to mind when you think of artists who've been able to find an audience with Streetz?
>
> MM: Definitely. A Tribe Called Red is huge. They're one of our—they'll probably go on and on to do amazing things. We have Inez Jasper as well, who's really on that top-notch level as far as making music goes, and she's been at it for so long and doing her thing. . . . I'm trying to think local. I know I've seen people get interested in us and then over the four-year period actually become an artist.[79]

As Miss Melissa describes, over time, some music listeners become active cultural agents, creating their own songs and even distributing recordings. The station provides inspiration by showcasing music by

Indigenous artists. In addition, it provides a viable venue for music distribution: local artists can send their recordings into the station, and they are reviewed by the music director. Tracks that fit into the umbrella of the station's sound that also meet minimum audio-quality standards for air are transmitted to audiences through the station's online and broadcast media.

## Developing New Artists

On-air host Alex Sannie describes that Streetz has "produced a lot of really talented artists." In this way, broadcasting Indigenous popular music encourages the development of new artists. Sharing music by Indigenous artists has been important for listeners, new musicians, and the station. Sannie explains, "There have been hip hop stations before here in the city, and there was not even close to as much Aboriginal hip hop on there. And that didn't work out. That wasn't gonna fly with anybody. Everybody's rapping, everybody's making music, and you want to be heard." Airing songs on a mainstream medium, here broadcast and streaming radio, creates audibility to a wider public and ascribes legitimacy to artists' work. Indigenous rappers, DJs, and producers whose work has been showcased in this manner include Drezus, The Winnipeg Boyz / Winnipeg's Most, Leonard Sumner, Hellnback, Young Kidd, Lotto, Inez, Wab Kinew, and Boogey the Beat. Sannie explains that whether listeners tune in to broadcast or streaming, the station helps to develop new artists as it shares their music: "it's a lot easier to find cred when people can turn on the radio and hear your music."[80]

Leonard Sumner, who has performed under the stage name Lorenzo, began having his music played on Streetz when he was starting out as a rapper. Lorenzo had several songs in rotation on Streetz, both on his own and with musical collaborators, as demonstrated in table 2.1.[81] These songs persisted in rotation when the station modified its format in the spring of 2014.[82]

One of the songs that audience members have enthusiastically welcomed at shows, "They Say," is Sumner's musical response to residential school survivors. He played the song to cheers and applause as part of the Idle No More movement. The song aired on some Indigenous media but not others, and it was largely not taken up on commercial

TABLE 2.1. Lorenzo Songs in Rotation

| Song title | Musicians |
|---|---|
| What Becomes of the Broken Hearted | Lorenzo |
| Divine Beauty | Lorenzo |
| Lonely Road | Lorenzo |
| Your Light | Lorenzo |
| Fly | Lorenzo feat. David Hodges |
| Searching | Lorenzo feat. Wab Kinew |
| Heart of Gold | Lorenzo feat. Charlie Fettah |
| One Life | Crown P. feat. Lorenzo |
| Good Boy | Wab Kinew feat. Lorenzo and Troy Westwood |
| Sunshine In My Pocket | Wab Kinew feat. Lorenzo |
| Home Free | Dead Indians feat. Lorenzo |

airwaves. This song's circulation provides an opportunity to ask, What kinds of sociopolitical messaging are and are not chosen for air, and with which audiences in mind? Programming decisions related to commercial viability show how audiences are imagined; examining them helps to reveal the tension between overlapping mainstream, underground, Indigenous, and settler audiences with which Streetz has wrestled.

Native radio can serve multiple purposes: to distribute music and also to shape community narratives, often in the face of known biases. As Clint Bracknell and Casey Kickett identify, "radio broadcasting can be a powerful cultural resource for Indigenous communities."[83] A Tsilhqot'in hip hop musician from Williams Lake, British Columbia, Beka Solo studied music production in Vancouver and has worked as a mixing engineer, producer, songwriter, rapper, and DJ. She has found an audience through CFRO, Vancouver Co-op Radio. On this station, Suzette Amaya's show *Think NDN* broadcasts on-air and streams online, connecting local First Nations musicians to listeners, as well as sharing community news and events. Beka Solo's creativity as a beat producer and skilled collaborator arc across her songs. For example, she worked with Sto:lo United, notably for the songs "Same Blood" and "Salvation," for which she collaborated with the traditional drummers from Chilliwack in studio. She explains her motivation to use drums also in the beats she produces, saying, "Hand drums have a lot of symbolism to me. It's like

Figure 2.2. Beka Solo performing with the duo Rich n Beka. (Photo by Billie Jean Gabriel Photography)

a heartbeat, those hand drums for me. When people are dancing, you're the hand drum. It synchronizes with it. I'm always drawn to drums because that's just what my spirit is. It keeps pulling me that way."[84]

Like other radio stations that focus on Indigenous listeners while keeping a broad audience in mind, Streetz broadcasts for intersecting audiences, with a commitment to sharing positive stories about and for Native communities. Creating and maintaining divisions is part of the project of the settler state. As Helene Vosters describes, "Nations, after all, thrive on divides. On constructed borders fortified by nationalist discourses designed to define outsiders, insiders, and outsiders within."[85] Mutual listening that fails to reinforce these rigid boundaries opens into other possibilities.

## Cultural Continuity

Within a hip hop and electronic music context, cultural continuity is expressed in a variety of ways. Some artists whose songs made it into the Streetz rotation have used musical citation of Indigenous intertribal or band-specific forms, such as A Tribe Called Red's use of contemporary powwow recordings. Few of Sumner's songs use musical citation of this kind, but his popular "They Say" is a notable exception: a traditional hand drum and sung outro appends the piece.

Several songs by or featuring Sumner that were taken up by Streetz work through violence, anger, and social inequality in a way that is consistent with some tropes of USAmerican hip hop. Operating on mainstream and alternative circuits simultaneously is not completely unusual.[86] For the listeners of Streetz's broadcasts on-air and online, the music acts as a form of cultural continuity and recalls a precolonial past. While many of the musicians discussed in this book employ the citation of traditional music styles, there are many ways to effect this continuity. With Sumner's music, some of this connection to an ongoing cultural legacy happens through the form that music takes. Linking storytelling to rap in Anishinaabe communities, Sumner builds on an existing legacy of hip hop storytelling as pedagogy, through which earlier musicians have encouraged listeners to avoid violence, embrace Black and Latinx identities in a racist society, and find motivation to work toward social change.[87] Musically, a constant presence of Indigenous popular music on the radio waves emphasizes that as a city, Winnipeg is already Indigenous; its Indigenous identity is clearly in step with contemporary urban culture.

I propose a parallel between the reading of Black American hip hop as part of a long historical musical legacy with the rereading of Indigenous hip hop as both forward-focused and linked to cultural continuity. Indigenous rappers who grapple with the difficulties of becoming known and financially successful face decisions about how to manage subgenre conventions of commercial rap music. These both limit the artists' expressive possibilities and support limiting conceptions of womxn and nonwhite actors within this music. This process is similar to the one by which commercial rap has come to use the construction of monoracial Blackness as part of its subgenre convention. In response, artists may adhere to simplistic images that commercial rap suggests and may also explore alternatives. In both cases, debates among scholars and participants have shifted over time.

In one collaboration, Sumner worked with Wab Kinew on "Good Boy" when they were traveling from Winnipeg to a show in northern

Manitoba in the Opaskwayak Cree Nation. Kinew, Sumner, and singer Troy Westwood later collaborated with youth through the North End Arts Centre to produce a video for the song.[88] It tells the story of an eighteen-year-old Anishinaabe boy, Matthew Dumas, who was shot by Winnipeg police under controversial circumstances. The song documents a feeling that the shooting was racially motivated and also proposes a way to respond to violence. Sumner explains, "I thought it was an important song because of the content and what Wab was saying. . . . When Matthew Dumas was shot, I was very angry."[89]

"Good Boy" begins with a guitar intro. Wab Kinew's spoken comments reveal that the song is about Dumas. Then, Troy Westwood sings, "A good boy was my son / Oh, I'm no angel, not the chosen one / On that day he did nothing wrong / Oh, those bullets did not belong." Kinew's lyrics address police violence and also suggest that this single incident is part of a larger problem: "It's bigger than the boy shot / Or cop who pulled the trigger / It's a product of our history how Canada's configured." The rapper references residential schools, mentioning the often-cited imperative to "kill the Indian" in the child that is part of the settler colonial process: "Old habits die hard; you want to kill the Indian / But you can't kill us, the Elders taught us to survive." Survival, specifically that which is taught by Elders, stands in opposition to this ultimately unsuccessful goal of completely disconnecting Indigenous youth from cultural knowledge: cultural sovereignty continues through musico-cultural teaching and learning. After Kinew's last rapped verse, Lorenzo sings and then repeats, "I'm wondering if them cops would have took a shot at me." Even as he raps about death and speculates if he too would have been killed, his voice carries forward in time: hip hop enacts the future that Anishinaabeg musicians, because of the colonial process, were not supposed to have.

The identification of Indigenous rappers with Black rappers across—and within—national borders extends what Walcott identifies as the manner in which rap music is able to "disrupt the notion of the modernist nation-state."[90] In Walcott's reading, rap narrates moments in which anti-Blackness and police violence are leveraged against Black Canadians, Black USAmericans, and others. These kinds of violence are practices that "spill their borders."[91] When First Nations rappers identify with the racialized violence leveraged against Black people (across and beyond North America), yet another stick is lodged into the wheel of the settler colonial state: rap artists extend their citational practice to link anti-Black policing with anti-Native policing. Black and Native people move past the boundaries of the nation-state, a boundary whose recent invention is frequently critiqued in Indigenous creative expression.

Relating the true stories of Black and Brown people injured or killed by police officers is a known trope in hip hop; it is also a strategy for survival. Sumner both personalizes and generalizes from Matthew's story. The focus of this song on the life of an individual boy expands into the question of whether the police would have "took a shot at me," creating a humanizing effect. Matthew is a person in this story, a "good boy," rather than a statistic. Sumner's personalization indicates that the rapper sees the connections between Matthew and other people who live in Winnipeg. Sumner has reflected that one of his aims as a musician is to help humanize the history of First Nations people in Canada, as mentioned earlier. The personal connection bridges back to Matthew, as Westwood's repeated chorus places the emphasis again on the "good boy." Over this sung chorus, Kinew delivers a monologue. He speaks about his belief that police and Native Winnipeggers can come together to forge some kind of understanding after this tragedy. This optimistic ending is put on a song that documents a tragic incident. In Sumner's words, "It was a really dark moment in the history of Winnipeg, I think. I wanted to paint that and bring that to the listeners."[92] Telling Matthew's story was one way for Sumner to articulate his response to police violence against Indigenous people. His articulation was part of a demand to be heard, as well as a manner in which to connect to listeners through the grief and anger they were experiencing. It also fit well with stories told in USAmerican hip hop by Black artists, including groups with a large artistic influence on Sumner, like N.W.A. Reflecting about anti-Blackness specifically, Sumner summarizes that it is "a learned behavior from colonialism" that relates directly to anti-Indigenous bias.[93] The experience the artists relate in "Good Boy" is real, personal, and local to Winnipeg. And it is consonant with existing stories about police violence that circulate in commercial hip hop. While this song has a decidedly more serious tone, like "Sunshine in My Pocket" discussed earlier, it works with known tropes: form, length, and instrumentation that are within a realm of expectations for hip hop music on-air.

Based in Indigenous worldviews, rappers like Sumner describe, storytelling operates as part of art's functionality. Telling one's own story in one's own voice, and relying on band- and nation-specific ideas of history and storytelling, sonic sovereignty is enacted through these musical narrations. Consistent with Sumner's framing of the storytelling he engages with through rap, Jill Doerfler, Niigaanwewidam James Sinclair, and Heidi Kiiwetinepinesiik Stark summarize, "Anishinaabeg stories are a form of resistance."[94] In a theory that resonates musically through contemporary hip hop practice, Sumner's stories can be heard as "expressions in the interest of the continuation and innovation of cultural and political traditions. They are acts of survival, innovation, and growth."[95] Stories are active processes, best understood through the engagement of telling and listening. These are relationships through which meaning is made and moved among storytellers, listeners, texts, and sources. As David Stirrup explains, "It is that circulation—in which stories, works of art, and so on exist not as products or artifacts, but as participants and spaces for participation—that constitutes the ground of knowledge of Anishinaabeg Studies and enables discourse around questions of responsibility, personhood, community, and sovereignty." These processes constitute what Stirrup calls "aesthetic/intellectual sovereignty."[96]

Musical storytelling extends oral tradition through the technological mediation of twenty-first-century music practice and engages speaker and listener in a relationship of teaching and learning. Sumner told me, "Music is a teacher, definitely. A lot of people base their lives on the kind of music they listen to. They base their style off of it. They base their actions off of the music."[97] Lessons and stories can emerge from song and are part of the work that songs perform. When I asked Sumner about his views on music's role in storytelling, he connected music and video to oral tradition, which constitutes part of sovereignty:

LP: We've talked in the past about how you have learned more about Anishinaabe culture. Do you see music as overlapping with other cultural expressions, for example storytelling in the Anishinaabe tradition?

LS: I think our people are—a lot of our people are natural storytellers. And we don't really realize that, and we have new mediums now for telling those stories. A lot of it was oral tradition before, but now people are, you know, making videos and making songs, making radio documentaries, and telling a lot of stories that haven't been told and a lot of stories that haven't been heard.[98]

Oral learning is a feature of song. While stories have been conveyed through speech and song over many generations without needing to be written down, contemporary songs like Sumner's can be both relayed directly through performance and recorded for listeners to experience as recorded sound. These stories serve a variety of purposes. "Good Boy," as described previously, is one such story that speaks to the difficult reality of police violence against Indigenous Winnipeggers. The retelling in song serves to commemorate and also potentially learn from the violent episode that inspired this song. Also in rotation on Streetz, "Lonely Road" offers a related function. It is a meditation on how strength and pride can be present even in moments of difficulty. Sumner describes that Indigenous popular music has been "part of the awakening for a lot of people" and that "storytelling and the music helped people open up their understanding of what has happened" over time in and to Indigenous communities.[99]

Musical storytelling's role in teaching and learning resonates through "They Say." The first rapped verse of the song begins, "Sometimes it hurts to be Indigenous, born in this nation. It's not enough to talk about decolonization." When describing the song, Sumner highlighted this line: "that to me is the basis of the whole song." He explained to me that he navigates multiple cultural forces: "I speak English. And it's helping me because I sing songs. And I'm trying to learn my language, and I understand some. And I'm using both of those to help me."[100] Sumner alludes to the national apology and to portions of Canadian treaties that make Indigenous people subjects of the queen. He further explained the reference to land and his Anishinaabe identity as being "about rediscovering myself, making connections to my culture that I didn't have growing up."[101] The process of rediscovering heritage practices is one shared by other artists. Anishinaabe writer Sean Fahrlander called this the "long walk back to our traditions."[102]

Sumner's song "They Say," and embodied audience responses to it, calls for the recognition of Indigenous land and water rights as well as self-determination. Sonic sovereignty, or the enactment of sovereign rights through sound, can and does come into being through these named moments that are widely acknowledged to be both political and related to territorial rights. This form of sovereignty also extends into a call to recognize other forms of preexisting entitlement to self-determination, including through naming, storytelling, language, audience determination, and bodily integrity, as will be further explored in the following chapters. Listening through "They Say," how can musical practice help manifest and put into practice a specifically land-rights-based use of sovereignty?

Sumner's deep engagement with land rights through treaty—which connects to his understandings of Anishinaabe identity—extends into his choice of performance venue. Performing with Idle No More has been part of Sumner's role in using music to claim voice in public space and to keep water and land rights center stage. Idle No More has used song in large public gatherings to inspire participants and manifest collective public identity, both in Canada and beyond national borders. As #IdleNoMore embraced contemporary networking strategies, it used digital music distribution, information-sharing platforms, and the building of virtual group identities as it engaged participants across Canada and around the globe. The participatory and intentionally nonhierarchical movement was first titled as such in October 2012 in a tweet. From this beginning, the first in-person event was held on November 10, 2012, in Saskatoon, Saskatchewan, in which Jessica Gordon, Sheelah McLean, Sylvia McAdams, and Nina Wilson organized a teach-in. Participants gathered to discuss Bill C-45, which proposed removing many water protections and changing the way some reserve land is handled. Concurrently, they launched a Facebook page for Idle No More, and a Twitter hashtag came into use. This first event included spoken-word poetry and a round dance. Many nations have a version of the round dance, a healing song from the Plains that became a hallmark of the movement. The movement spread across Canada, into the US, and globally. Existing simultaneously online and offline, the movement encompassed large events in public spaces, such as round dances in malls and events in front of government buildings such as the one that opened this book, and the online sharing of petitions, videos, songs, and stories.

Sumner's music connects land and water sovereignty, a central organizing charge of Idle No More, with the movement's musical reclaiming of voice in physical public spaces and in online spaces of dialogue. Sumner played at a rally in Winnipeg at the Manitoba Legislative Building on December 21, 2012, at the beginning of Idle No More's first winter, explaining, "I was there because I wanted to be with my people when they were there."[103] His song "They Say" was received with enthusiastic cheers. Sumner reflects, "It felt good. It felt good to be there." When I asked him why he thought music had a role in public events like this one, he explained that music "can help change people's opinions." Singing at rallies, he says, "feels like the right thing to do."[104] In this performance, Sumner spoke to previous silencing, taking over the ability to define. Instead of accepting what "they say" about him, Sumner offers his own voice, and reiterates, "they can't silence my song." This song asserts the existing sovereignty of Anishinaabeg peoples in a way that directly confronts the nation-state. Sumner performed this song at a variety of community events, including at his free daytime concert during Aboriginal Music Week the following summer. At this concert, the song once again was greeted by loud cheers from the crowd.

The relationship between Idle No More and a song like "They Say" provides an opportunity to ask how critiques of setter colonialism, not usually included in pop radio, interact with a commercial focus of music broadcasters. Streetz did not take an official stand on environmental policy or land-rights issues. While the same characteristics that make DJs skilled as on-air talent translate to public event hosting—notably confident public speaking and charismatic verbal improvisation—efforts like Miss Melissa's on behalf of missing and murdered Indigenous women are undertaken in an individual, not a station, capacity, as will be further explored in chapter 4. This distancing of the Streetz brand from active political messaging related to controversial topics—notably sovereignty, civil disobedience, rallies, and Indigenous rights—during periods of contested movement building is consistent with the station's goals of not alienating potential listeners, particularly a "mainstream" audience. In spite of the on-air omission of solo work like "They Say," Sumner has maintained a positive attitude toward Streetz. When I asked him about his experience with the station, Sumner explained, "I used to go there [to Streetz] all the time, do interviews. I played on-air a couple times. I love Streetz."[105]

Some station staff members laud a project of pragmatic legitimiza-tion; the work of circulating artistic presentations of Indigenous moder-nity is performing more revolutionary work. Rather than simply seeking mainstream acceptance for electronically based music by Indigenous artists, its constant articulation takes on a meaningful presence in the soundscape of the city and, through online streaming, throughout the province, the country, and beyond: these songs are part of the fabric of the city not as new additions but as auditory reminders that the city has always been—and still is—Indigenous. Audible in the musical sound-scape, Winnipeg's Indigenous identity is fully in step with contemporary urban culture. To illustrate this, Sumner's popular songs—both those that are and are not circulated on radio—offer insights into musical mes-sages that resonate with broadcasters and audiences. Sumner describes, "People adapt over time. I've adopted this term called 'retribalization,' where you kind of take what is helping you and what's good for you and you use that in your daily life."[106] Taking stock of Canada's colonial past and present and moving into a moment of opportunity, Sumner uses lyrical topicality, storytelling, and teaching to musically exhibit continu-ity in change.

When Sumner and I discussed how he selects his topics when rap-ping, he noted, "As far as tackling the issues, that's what hip hop was. . . . It was antigang. . . . Public Enemy was badass then. . . . Then these big corporations got a hold of it." This legacy of rap music that "tackle[s] the issues," as he states, is one that Sumner takes seriously. In his music, he frequently deals with political concerns as well as portraying positive associations with First Nations culture. When I asked him about which specific areas are foremost for community attention, he articulated a clear project:

LP: What issues do you think are important to address in your music?
LS: I think the history of Canada and the treatment of First Nations people is one—like I said, humanizing that story instead of just read-ing what the newspaper says. . . . There is what they call "intergen-erational trauma," stuff that has happened through being removed from your family, being placed into these situations. . . . [Residential school] was done to kill the Indian in the child. A lot of people are in denial of that. I think it's important they understand, have some

empathy or sympathy, if they can understand what happened to that person's parents, because they like to think of it as hundreds of years ago, but it was within two generations.

Sumner and I spoke at length about Canada's contentious treaty process. Throughout the 2010s, Indigenous, settler, and newcomer residents in Canada and beyond its borders debated how to honor treaties, many people deepened their understandings of residential schools, and the effects of intergenerational trauma were significant topics in mainstream media sources as well as in community programming. As Sumner reflected back on why he has chosen to tell the stories that he has, he recalled, "I have had an urge to speak about the things that I've had an experience with. And the format that was popular at the time was hip hop music. That's just a continued form of my way of expressing my experience as an Indigenous person trying to regain more of a cultural identity and retain some more language." As we talked about different levels of awareness and background of his listeners, Sumner explained, "I don't have all the knowledge. I felt like I was leaving the door open for exploration on their own behalf. They can hear the stories, and they can take that information. The door is unlocked. Now, there's more information for you to go and research on your own behalf if you choose to do so."[107]

The circulation of Sumner's music through online and broadcast radio demonstrates the possibilities in a shift around digital Indigenous modernity and articulations of sovereignty in the city. This music comes to increasingly large audiences even as Sumner articulates his personhood through self-definition and builds through collaboration toward self-determination. Music that has elicited enthusiastic responses includes, though is not limited to, that which asks for recognition of sovereignty that Sumner and Anishinaabeg people already have. Asserting presence on-air and online, music like Sumner's articulates a city wherein Indigenous popular musicians are already audible. Airing songs through broadcast and streaming radio gives musicians access to a kind of credibility that can help a wide variety of listeners hear their work as legitimate. Relying on this system of legitimation has strategic limitations that prevent a shift of the larger status quo.

Further, as Sumner's catalog demonstrates, within the confines of nationally licensed radio, staff perceptions of what might be political issues that are not mainstream enough—and thus would potentially alienate listeners—create a kind of self-censorship that limits which songs contemporary Indigenous artists are able to air.[108] In this case, musicians are able to express contemporary Indigeneity in music for a wide audience, a crucial feat that works against stereotypes that locate First Nations artists in the perpetual rural past. Yet this process has its limits: music that risks falling outside the mainstream in its sound and message risks not being heard because it challenges listeners too much and is too far from a sound that can be accommodated easily by existing ears. This limitation can be heard acutely for artists whose music eschews mainstream conceptions on multiple fronts. For artists whose popular music challenges masculinist discourses of electronically based music as it also pushes the limits of discourses of Indigeneity, mainstream perceptions of racialized and gendered cultural producers work together to create a challenging environment for broadcast success.

## Masculinist Technology Discourses through Popular Music

Audibility in contemporary popular music scenes—specifically in electronically based music that typically airs on urban-format radio stations—is constructed in a gendered manner.[109] When new machinery takes center stage, a cultural masculinization of popular music technology often occurs. At the beginning of the twentieth century, this masculinization was strategically associated with music in order to counter previous feminization. For music relying on analog and then digital machinery, this shift was so effective that DJ performance is often read first through technology, rather than primarily through expression of feelings.[110] The masculinist discourse of electronic music technology exists within a sphere of some nuance. While frameworks cast electronic noise in several different lights, a valuative aspect is consistent. That is, even as electronically based music is described with some gradation, the power dynamic that privileges the technologized qualities is consistent.

As Robin James characterizes this dynamic, femininity is culturally associated with whichever genres are seen to be less "serious" or less "avant-garde" in a specific context.[111] Music may be characterized as raw and thus realistic or amusical and thus unskilled, depending on who is producing it and in what context. Crucially, for value to be ascribed to sound, it is not the music itself that shifts but how that music is perceived. In general, James identifies a cultural tendency to "construct the aesthetic and moral virtue of the artist in terms of qualities that, found in individuals from privileged groups, are valued, yet, when found in individuals from underprivileged groups, are considered signs of weakness, fault, or flaw."[112] With similar findings on the gendering of electronically based music, Tara Rodgers identifies how male musicians are given cultural license to use unusual sounds as a form of creative play, while when female musicians use the same techniques, they are often critiqued for making "mistakes."[113]

As chapter 1 detailed, the manner in which the trope of the "Indian" has been characterized as premodern continues to haunt articulations of contemporary Indigeneity. The lingering power of these outmoded discourses locates contemporary Indigenous urban musicians as outside scenes that rely on modern technology. This continues from a historical process of exclusion that has been an active part of the settler state in Canada and the United States, where, as Julia Emberley summarizes, "discourses of racial and sexual difference rendered the bodies of indigenous people invisible, as in worthless and expendable."[114] In addition to more general racist stereotypes leveraged against Indigenous people, young womxn have noted the particular destructiveness of stereotypes through which they are mischaracterized as sexually available and unintelligent and, through negative characterization of difference, are continually otherized from a mainstream.[115] Indigenous womxn are thus cast as outsiders along multiple axes in electronically based popular music scenes, as racism, misogyny, and specific biases against Indigenous womxn all work together as forces of exclusion. The move to turn womxn from subjects to objects, like the colonialist and neocolonialist sleight of hand designed to transform Indigenous peoples of all sexes from subject to object, is part of the structural project of settler colonialism.

The electronic music discourse of power and control takes on an added meaning when applied to the DJ. Due to what Jesse Stewart has identified as much of hip hop's rootedness in "masculine ideologies," hip hop is gendered by the way male, female, and nonbinary participants are and are not invited to participate in learning and performance.[116] Tracing this phenomenon historically, Mark Katz finds that DJ battles act as are-nas for young men to try out masculinities, which creates institutional-ized sex discrimination that contributes to the dearth of female DJs.[117] This combines with discourses of technology, in which focusing on the record player and subsequent technological innovations allows for a mas-culinized shop-talk feel that avoids the potential risks of feminization that some people equate with music.[118] As many DJs learn in informal settings, when these spaces are male-only enclaves, learning spaces physi-cally limit access for womxn. Focus on the physical objects that produce technologized sound as well as the male bodies that manipulate it are part of the ideological masculinization of DJing, but there is more: already a musician who harnesses new and changing technology to create sound, this figure also controls listeners' movements with the resulting music. The DJ controls the space as master of ambiance and, through sound waves, controls the movement of other people's physical bodies.[119]

To be made audible for the listening ear trapped by a notion of urban modernity, Indigenous gender norms as expressed in music shift to adopt mainstream characteristics. Indigenous masculinity is con-structed around notions of nonwhite masculinity, particularly Black masculinity, and is frequently counterposed to white masculinity. This construction also draws on historical conceptions of masculinity that are band- and region-specific while also operating in conversation with stereotypes promulgated in settler society.[120] For Indigenous artists who express musical facility in mainstream rap, these multiple strands are set up as a contrast to a racialized nonwhite femininity that largely borrows from genre-based tropes that offer a limited set of possibilities for womxn; racialized and gendered stereotypes are at the core of set-tler colonialism.[121] Further compounded with masculinist discourses in electronically based musics, programming and broadcast decisions are constrained by these interconnected and mutually influential ideas about gender normativity.

## Streaming Audio, Online Music Sharing, and the Mainstream

Broadcast and online radio create spaces in which Indigenous musi-cians challenge exclusionary notions of modernity and masculinity, as demonstrated by the way Leonard Sumner and other artists interact with Streetz. Official online media presences, such as the Streetz website, offer a platform for this kind of challenge online. When Streetz began in 2008, music-listening norms for online audio centered on the purchase or sharing of online audio files. By the time it rebranded in 2014, norms had shifted toward increasing use of streaming audio. Streetz livestreamed its audio content, hosted on its own website. While broadcast radio continued to capture significant audience attention throughout the 2010s, the streaming service served two functions: to expand Streetz's audience to listeners beyond the reach of the Winnipeg-based radio towers and to adapt to changing listener preferences for online media streaming.

Streetz served an Indigenous constituency as part of its mandate, which allowed the station to take risks with unconventional messaging, challenging existing stereotypes that are often conveyed on other media outlets. Yet, as a popular music station, Streetz was designed not to push the envelope too far. As radio station staff wrestle with representational concerns, they too must address bottom-line business marketability. Radio programs crafted for specific listening publics provide some possibilities for listenership curation that are absent in traditional broadcast radio. Artists access and deploy sonic sovereignty through choosing how they frame their expressions, as well as for whom they share their music.

The concept of creating community online has gone from being met with unease to being consciously argued for to being largely accepted.[122] While some limitations do exist, in physical scenes for which a specialized subcommunity is hard to access regularly in person, online spaces offer opportunities for connection, exchange, and mutual support. Possibilities and limitations for media sharing and community building affect Indigenous, female-identified, nonbinary, and Indigenous female DJs and other hip hop musicians in urban centers in the United States and Canada. Musicians in these overlapping numerical-minority communities face particular challenges in accessing mainstream venues for hip hop and electronic music, due to biases outlined in the previous section. Participating in online communities offers a needed corrective both to shift discourses around who is included in electronic music and to create a sense of community for participants who are, at present, discursively marked as outside certain popular music scenes. Due to the exclusions of Indigenous musicians and female musicians, exclusions that compound for Indigenous womxn in hip hop and other electronically based music cultures, the need for an online community that capitalizes on digital media comes into focus. As musicians curate audiences through online music streaming and social media, they speak to and with a receptive audience, while simultaneously nudging "mainstream" audiences in new directions.

Online music distribution, especially streaming audio and social media, is reshaping the popular music "mainstream."[123] Members of numerical minorities in physical communities can find solidarity and support through online communities, which offer the possibility to connect beyond the limits of geography. And yet online streaming, like broadcast radio, is impacted by market forces. Social media companies, too, are in the market for consumers' attention. While the move to online distribution offers artists opportunities to curate listenerships, it complicates, rather than resolves, the hierarchies between media companies and musicians. Even so, artists who are underrepresented in mainstream music scenes use the move online to create communities that bolster their success. As online music listening became more commonplace in the 2010s, enthusiasm for the possibilities of decentralization of artist promotion emerged. Social networks function as a source of new music discovery; this can then stimulate listener demand for these musicians across other platforms.[124] That is, though broadcasters have a history of influencing, or even creating, the audiences they attempt to attract, in order to stay relevant to consumers, the "mainstream" must shift to accommodate consumers' desires.

Given the particularities of broadcast radio, many artists are using the bottom-up possibilities of online platforms to distribute media and engage in networked communication distribution. The music adds to a series of flows that shape related processes: artists are using online music distribution to reach specialized audiences. At the same time, broadcasters take note of the listener attention and consumption of music through digital channels that increased across the 2010s. To try to keep listeners in their brand enclosure, broadcast media companies are including streaming audio and social media in their distribution plans. This has multiple effects. One is that media entities are paying attention to what listeners gravitate toward online, to keep their audience, so they may

expand their offerings to accommodate new tastes. Then, as streaming and social media become more incorporated into existing media
companies, some of the reasons people looked toward them in the first
place diminish: they are incorporated (brought into the body of) existing music industry structures, which means that the biases, inequities,
and star focus of those structures are imposed on the newer distribution
networking modalities. Even as Indigenous hip hop is shifting the popular mainstream, there are limits to what individual artists can do within
the media system as set up, even using digital media.

The popular musicians who inform this book continue to circulate
their music and appear on broadcast radio, yet this medium has become
just one of many options for disseminating music and interacting with
fellow artists and fans. Frank Waln and Tall Paul are both rappers who
appear on stages across the Midwest in cities including Chicago, Minneapolis, and Winnipeg. Artists like these actually shift the mainstream
with their music through a combination of live touring performances,
online music circulation, and broadcast media distribution.

The prominence of online distribution for these artists is indicative
of a creative attempt to problem solve; it poses a moment of possibility
for each artist's self-presentation. Frank Waln is a Lakota rapper and
producer who grew up on the Rosebud Sioux reservation in the United
States. He moved to Chicago as a young adult to pursue music professionally. Waln and I met in Chicago, where he has performed frequently
between shows in other urban and reservation areas across the United
States, as well as internationally. When I talked with him about living
in Chicago, he explained that he sometimes feels invisible as a Native
person in the city.[125] To combat this invisibility, his work samples and
incorporates a variety of signifiers of Indigenous culture, from Lakota
Rabbit Dance song samples to collaborations with hoop dancers. As a
result, his work serves in part to rearticulate Indigeneity in large urban
centers. Tall Paul, an Anishinaabe MC, lives and works in Minneapolis. He travels to perform across the United States, as well as in nearby
Canadian locations, both urban and reserve. Paul reflects on his Native
identity in the lyrics of his rap songs and has gathered a geographically
wide following for music in which he raps in his heritage language, Anishinaabemowin. Minneapolis is home to a Native American–preference
housing project, a rarity for the United States, where reservation land is

typically geographically distant from large cities. Many cities host large and vibrant Indigenous communities; it is the official structure that sets Minneapolis apart. Despite Minneapolis's unusually visible Indigenous community, its music communities do not as a whole mirror this trend: Indigenous artists are still numerical minorities in hip hop and electronic music scenes.

In the cities where Waln and Tall Paul live, the number of musicians who self-identify as Indigenous and celebrate their heritage in their music is significant yet relatively small in relation to non-Indigenous musicians. Online community helps to connect the musicians to communities that are not always as accessible in the physical sphere. This kind of online communication allows for participants to connect across space, a process that actively creates new geographies. Rather than being centralized in the single radio station and limited by its broadcast area, virtual configurations take on a webbed form of networked communications. Lateral connections are possible, and even encouraged, between users; the importance of a distributor is diminished. Exploding the notion of Native actors in reservation-only spaces, networked communication between cities and across urban, rural, and reservation areas is crucial for revealing a much more complex contemporary reality.

While social media are designed to feel user-centered (for the consumer), Shelly Knotts accurately depicts the hierarchy of power, with service providers at the top, then software designers, leaving users at the bottom. Even with this structure, users have some control over how they operate inside the platform; Knotts characterizes the "level of citizen autonomy" within social media as "high."[126] Like many artists who self-promote through social media, Frank Waln and Tall Paul take advantage of platforms' possibilities. These artists produce solo work, and each also collaborates for specific projects. To hype their collective work, Waln and Tall Paul have used Instagram and Facebook to share photos and captions. Waln's Instagram post shared an image of both artists in front of a mic, while Paul added text applauding their shared management, alerting their fans to prepare for their collaborative effort.[127] Artists' social media sites are part of the space for audience development and musician identity curation, which later impact the mainstream. As users adapt social media spaces to their own ends, they can also leverage music promotion alongside other messaging, such as engaging users in social and political causes.[128]

For online music engagement, sharing enthusiasm for the work to a sympathetic community offers the artists a space in which positive messages of support are forthcoming. Finding support is particularly relevant for communities that are numerically small in person, that face active discrimination, or both. As studies by Mark Cronlund Anderson and Carmen L. Robertson and experiences recounted by participants during my fieldwork demonstrate, active discrimination against Indigenous groups in the United States and Canada has been documented in detail in scholarship and by artists themselves.[129] Harassment online is a real threat and one of acute concern for women, nonbinary people, and people of color, as will be explored in chapter 4. Yet artists seek and actively cultivate support through social media spaces that are geared toward friends and fans.

Support here is manifest in a variety of ways. First, the number of positive reactions to Waln and Paul's celebratory posts trend relatively high. For Paul, the number of likes and engagements was about five times what his Facebook page sees on other kinds of posts, such as political news about the Dakota Access Pipeline. Additionally, the comments that friends and followers offer share messages of support. Commenters write generally positive posts as they share emojis like hearts. They also direct encouragement to this duo and enthusiasm for the success of Indigenous musicians, for example writing, "Keep up the amazing work Frank Waln & Tall Paul!!" and "Natives With Ambition."[130]

This single interaction reflects a larger trend in online music community building: participants are able to build affective ties across space. In this post, other Indigenous hip hop and electronic musicians who choose to make their identities part of their artistic work are among the respondents, including MCs from across the US and Canada. For all the possibilities for music community forming online, this interaction comes offline and enters a hybrid online/offline space; the photo that Waln and Paul shared with their circles is a snapshot of the two of them together in the same room. The artists traveled to be together so that they could collaborate in person. Internet-based interaction around music does not stop in the online sphere; musicians and listeners build an ongoing network of connections to offline music-making. Completing the circuit, fans share photos from live shows, commenting and sharing positive thoughts after performances. The physical and virtual community come together as photos from live music are posted online, creating a hybrid music scene.

These posts are emblematic of several larger points on the possibilities in online music community. Inasmuch as communities are based on social relationships, it is entirely possible to instantiate a community without being physically co-present. Artists connect to each other through a broader transnational community, creating relevant communal geographies that are felt affectively even if they never instantiate physically in the same form. In an online community, camaraderie over a shared interest or identity becomes the primary organizer. Media that offer success are typically Indigenous-producer led and open for community participation.[131] Musicians give and receive encouragement; share ideas in a community of insiders, making connections not always available offline; and use the online space as a springboard for offline interaction—the inspiration from online communication helps create local instantiations of musical community.

Social media have been lauded for their disruptive powers. This is because, at a structural level, they allow for peer-to-peer communication. The possibilities of networking between participants without a central organizer, and other forms of bottom-up social organization, have played a role in movements such as the Arab Spring, #Occupy, and #IdleNoMore. Because they provide opportunities for artists to self-promote and share music without the intermediary of a record label, social media and user music-sharing platforms have been a source of optimism for the democratization of the music industry, particularly in regard to increasing opportunities for independent artists.[132]

Even as artists explore these possibilities, they face limitations. The actual experience of peer-to-peer information sharing on social media is limited by design. Platforms are made to generate capital; social media companies such as Facebook experienced vast revenue gains throughout the 2010s.[133] While musicians attempt to control their own self-presentation online, sometimes countering existing stereotypes, they speak into a sphere in which disinformation circulates and siloing can occur.[134] Changing, and sometimes opaque, algorithms can make it challenging for individual artists to control how their messages reach potential audiences, unless they pay for advertisements on these platforms. Yet independent musicians continue to attempt to bend these tools to their own needs and may well influence the music industry as they attempt to break into it.

One way to hear the rise of streaming for hip hop in the 2010s is through Chance the Rapper's success with his 2016 album *Coloring Book*. Among many other accolades, it was the first streaming-only album to win a Grammy Award. As Tom Johnson details, this victory at the 2017 awards show has been interpreted as a marker of the democratization of success in the music industry in the 2010s and has been hailed as a breakthrough moment for independent artists.[135] While one single artist's success in one awards show does not prove that avenues for mainstream music industry recognition are open to all, this victory was indeed an important first for more than just this skilled Chicago rapper. Chance the Rapper's win in the Best Rap Album category coincided with a rule change at the Grammys, in which albums only available for streaming could be eligible for the awards. This move both opened the door for future streaming albums and indicated the seriousness with which conservative mainstays like the Grammy organization came to accept the importance of streaming audio in the 2010s. Like the creation of Indigenous hip hop awards in the early 2000s, changing industry categories reflect adapting listener tastes.

One way to hear mainstream music industry players' efforts to maintain centrality in the 2010s is through Chance the Rapper's success with his 2016 album *Coloring Book*. Chance the Rapper's third mixtape was not released with a record label. Yet the independent project was praised by critics as "one of the strongest rap albums released this year" and as having "the sound and feel of a masterpiece, a watershed in the career of a suddenly major artist."[136] Available online for free, it was highly popular with fans and a critical success; it included critiques of the music industry, directly in the song "Mixtape." With this impressive independent success, Chance the Rapper clearly showed that he was not the only one who still cares about mixtapes: originally posted for free download or streaming, *Coloring Book* became an Apple Music exclusive and then was made available for streaming on other platforms as well. When organizations like the Grammys then updated their rules in a way that made this hit song eligible to be included in their awards and recognitions, was the Grammy organization doing a favor for Chance the Rapper, or was Chance the Rapper doing a favor for the Grammys?

The vantage points from which this story can be told meet each other here: independent artists can, in some ways, take advantage of online music distribution to curate and grow their audiences. And mainstream media players are adapting their offerings on the basis of the popularity of independent artists. Chance the Rapper's deal with Apple Music and his win at the Grammys came into being at the meeting place between an unsigned artist using online media distribution to self-promote and the mainstream industry shifting because it was profitable to let his music in. Call it a mixtape or an album, *Coloring Book* was not a sleeper hit. It was Chance the Rapper's third mixtape; his previous music had already created significant fame for him. *Coloring Book* features well-known rappers including 2 Chainz and Lil Wayne. Not just any album could go from a free independent release to landing on the top ten of the Billboard 200, but many independent artists look to him as a model for their own possible success. Chance the Rapper was already skilled, experienced, and supported, all of which made this album's rise possible. But the lesson remains: for music that can become popular, there is a dynamism between independent online music sharing and the shift of mainstream players to capture enthusiasm and listeners (and their dollars).

While some kinds of teamwork are possible remotely, improvisatory group interaction and real-time collaboration remain easier in person. The use of digital networks alone is not enough. Rather, these distribution networks best express the possibilities outlined here when they are engaged strategically. Because revenues from digital music are so low, these other aspects of online promotion have the greatest potential for artists with regard to longer-term financial solvency: name recognition, followers, attracting listeners to live shows, and the intangible benefits of having listeners appreciate and respond to the messages in their music. The move online has made sales worth relatively little, so the other unpaid parts of online music activity, like popularity that could lead to concert ticket sales and licensing contracts, are the primary avenues that could compensate artists for their labor. The use of digital technologies, while prevalent in popular music industries, is not a neutral practice. These systems have limitations, which vary across social context and are seldom as accessible for Indigenous communities.[137] Sometimes celebrated for lowering barriers to entry, these tools do not remove the effects of gatekeepers. Shifts occur as these tools become more prevalent: data sharing can be facilitated, including the sharing of data that participants would prefer not to disclose or would prefer not to share with everyone who gains access. Many kinds of labor, like promotion, brand management, and in some cases early-career recording and distribution, have shifted from labels and professional companies to the musicians themselves. Ways of sensing and knowing—facilitated through digital technologies—can feel different from more immediate tactile experiences.

## Conclusion

Broadcast and online music distribution can be leveraged to form a dynamic scene in which social relationships between participants become part of the musical encounter. At its best, the active process of self-definition and audience curation that musicians enact online plays a role in diversifying mainstream music on streaming audio platforms. Sonic sovereignty is operationalized as artists employ specific forms of storytelling, self-determination, and the development of relationships. There are limits to these possibilities. Official media sources like radio must attend to marketability, which limits how much they may challenge misconceptions and still attract a wide audience. Artists play with existing tropes in hip hop; ideas of Blackness, masculinity, sexuality, and urbanness that have calcified through commercial rap cannot be fully disentangled from twenty-first-century performances. Online music-media-sharing communities create opportunities for bonding across space, but they neither preclude the desire to meet in shared physical space nor fully sidestep bias that occurs offline. Practical restrictions affect media distribution whether music is shared on radio waves or online: messages go out from a central location, they are enjoyed separately, and only some listeners will choose to further engage with the musicians, broadcasters, or each other. Even in the face of these limitations, as musicians harness social media and insist on being heard, possibilities for change emerge.

As intersecting groups of Indigenous, female, and gender-nonconforming musicians are distanced from popular music by overlapping discourses, musicians activate broadcast and online media spaces to share music and create community. When musicians' lived realities are expressed in a way that is audible for a wide audience, these strategic misconceptions are challenged. A lack of audibility in physical music scenes is more than a matter of numerical scarcity: prevailing discourse codes electronically based music as masculine and distances Indigenous music from (assumed non-Indigenous) popular music. My work with musicians in hybrid on- and offline music scenes has demonstrated that seeking community is crucial for individuals fighting to be listened to and that online music scenes offer viable possibilities for connection, support, and community building. This process offers essential support for musicians, but it does not stop there. When listeners start to deeply listen to musicians who had been operating outside the mainstream, there is a possibility for a shift in the prevailing discourses that had de-centralized them. That is, when musical communities that emerge in the wake of exclusions engage with listeners, audiences and musicians have the potential to challenge those exclusionary discourses together, as art-ists demand recognition of sovereignty through sound. When listeners pay attention to artists like Leonard Sumner, Tall Paul, Beka Solo, and Frank Waln in broadcast and online spaces, these artists' work reaches new audiences. The distribution of Indigenous popular music through broadcast and online media demonstrates great potential to recast exclu-sionary conceptions of Indigeneity and racialized gender norms. Yet pop-ular music distribution continues to fall back on a project of legitimation, particularly in the broadcast realm. Online distribution is demonstrating additional viability for rearticulating the soundscape of the city from the perspective of female, male, and gender-nonconforming Indigenous art-ists, articulating a physical and virtual space that is combating limiting conceptions of race and gender from a musical mainstream.

Even as musicians and audience members explore these options, questions remain. How can artists respond to legitimation projects, and what alternatives exist from the perspectives of broadcasters and online distributors? How do regulatory and funding structures—and broadcast-ers' understandings of them—contribute to the mainstreaming of cer-tain sounds, voices, and perspectives? As the interactions with music of Lorenzo, Inez, Shad, Wab Kinew, Tall Paul, Frank Waln, and Winnipeg's Most have shown, myriad social factors contribute to the shaping and reshaping of musical narratives, by musicians in their expressions and by music broadcasters in subsequent distribution. Chapter 3 explores how mainstreaming is structured, placing the regulatory and financial structures in context with the activities of musicians and broadcasters.

3

# Radio Silence

*Changing Mediascapes*

In April 2014, listeners who tuned their radio dial to 104.7 FM in the Winnipeg area heard a steady stream of oldies. Hearing oldies on the radio is not surprising, but hearing them on this station truly shocked people. Since 2008, 104.7, or Streetz, had been known as the city's hip hop station. During the oldies run, I was living in Winnipeg and doing ethnographic research in the city's hip hop scene, including at Streetz. I was in the station's broadcasting office during this time, and I heard surprise, confusion, and even anger. Listeners called into the station, and the receptionist fielded many responses from perplexed and irritated people. What were oldies doing on the air here?

The week marked a change at 104.7 FM that impacted branding, music, and ads. There were nuances to personnel and programming, as well as music continuities and discontinuities. But listeners heard the core message: Streetz was going off the air, to be replaced by a station called Rhythm. The loss of the city's only hip hop station hit people hard. It was even more difficult for listeners because Streetz was a Native-licensed station, so listeners knew to expect urban music by Indigenous artists on-air and streaming online. In Winnipeg, with its large and diverse urban Indigenous population, this loss was felt acutely. Beyond Winnipeg, Streetz had been a leader in playing Indigenous hip hop through streaming radio. With its passionate and invested fans, why did Streetz go off the air? And further, what does its dissolution mean for the circulation of hip hop and related genres by Indigenous musicians?

In many ways, Winnipeg radio station Streetz offers a classic success story. An innovative group secured funding, staff, and a coveted broadcasting license to start something fresh: a hip hop station playing music by and for the Indigenous community. Listeners became inspired, recorded new tracks, and had them played on-air. But as with many innovative media entities, Streetz did not encounter an uncomplicated rise to prominence. Financial pressures and audience expectations tempered that success: grant funding was cut, commercial money was hard to attract, and the great experiment changed its model, sound, and even branding multiple times in response. This chapter delves further into what Streetz's singularity as an urban-format broadcaster meant for both licensing and hip hop music circulation, notably for hip hop marketed toward Indigenous, Black, and Filipinx listeners.

Reflecting with media experts and hip hop artists at Streetz, this chapter interrogates how professionals navigate conflicts and changes in broadcasting rules, funding priorities, and community needs. As contemporary Indigenous expressive culture is increasingly heard in mainstream venues, media that once served a diverse but relatively small community now faces new pressures. Building on chapter 2's theorization of a dialogue between sonic Blackness and Indigeneity in hip hop for a mainstream listenership, this chapter identifies how commercial pressures are intensified as racialized stereotypes circulate about hip hop music and its assumed listenership and connects the circulation of racialized tropes to the underpinning of the settler colonial project. I find that broadcast and streaming radio simultaneously contribute and respond to shifting ideas of urban Indigeneity for a Native and non-Native listenership. At the same time, artists connect by playing through pleasure, offering audiences an experience that is all the more transformative when juxtaposed with challenges in daily life. Changes in practices and policies for mainstream broadcast and streaming radio have had profound impacts on racial representation in urban pop soundscapes. I extend research that explores the whitening of mainstream radio and detail the implications of this trend on how Indigenous artists are heard—and silenced—through pop music distribution. Finally, this chapter further develops the concept of sonic sovereignty, focusing specifically on the ways in which commercially oriented popular music formats can yet leverage their wide reach to confront and alter expectations of Indigenous music. I argue that Streetz's broadcast and streaming music-distribution strategy is part of the phenomenon of sonic sovereignty in which Indigenous musicians and broadcasters take control of how Indigeneity sounds, confront and challenge expectations of mainstream airplay, and expand aesthetic and political boundaries.

## The Streetz Media Context

As the parent organization for Streetz, Native Communications Incorporated (NCI) programming encompasses English-language broadcasts that include music, local news, and commentary as well as weekend Ojibwe-language and Cree-language broadcasts. NCI decided to start a second radio station to cater to a younger audience; this license was approved by the Canadian Radio-television and Telecommunications Commission (CRTC) in 2008.[1] Launched as CIUR-FM, this station was branded as "Streetz," broadcasting at 104.7 MHz. The Canadian Broadcasting Corporation (CBC) described the station this way: "The radio dial at 104.7 FM is a unique format that focuses on the best dance, R&B and hip-hop music. Both mainstream and local music is mixed with a specific focus on urban aboriginal music as well."[2] The station has featured young, energetic radio DJs and has played local, Canadian, USAmerican, and international music in hip hop, dance, and R&B genres. It has functioned as a microphone for local hip hop artists. NCI FM and Streetz have established official presences at numerous music programs and Indigenous community events in Winnipeg. While both stations have featured First Nations and Métis radio hosts and include Indigenous music, they play songs by a variety of non-Indigenous artists and do not exclusively target an Indigenous audience.

In Canada, the process to create and sustain urban-format stations has been more challenging, and slower, than in some other markets. This reality, coupled with the CRTC's mandate to support Indigenous broadcasting, became increasingly audible in the post-apology moment and again in response to the recommendations of the Truth and Reconciliation Commission. For this reason, the plight of Streetz as an urban Indigenous broadcaster is particularly instructive for regulators and funders. While not always deemed cutting edge, broadcast radio is ubiquitous, and through its streaming presence, it continued to transform soundscapes into the decade after the 2008 apology (and the founding of Streetz). Broadcast radio leverages its hyperlocality: weather, traffic, resident personalities, regional events, and even homegrown music are part of its appeal. Yet Streetz seeks and promotes Indigenous artists from around Canada and across borders—who create a kind of connective tissue between localities. At the time of its peak success in the early to mid-2010s, Streetz served a function that did not exist in other places on a national level: to celebrate and share the music of talented Indigenous artists alongside non-Indigenous artists. Even as other cities started to explore the possibilities of their own urban Indigenous music presences years after Streetz folded, its early impact—and lessons from the challenges it faced—resonated.

NCI is headquartered in a two-story studio and office in Winnipeg. Off a boulevard in an industrial area, the station's home is urban, though beyond the city's downtown core (see figure 3.1). A single reception area serves NCI FM and Streetz. The first floor is dedicated to NCI FM, which broadcasts across Manitoba. Upstairs holds Streetz, which broadcasts to the greater Winnipeg area. Each floor holds offices and its own broadcasting studios; the shared boardroom for NCI and the office of the CEO are adjacent to the shared entry. This space highlights events, artists, and accomplishments of NCI FM and Streetz. A changing LCD screen shows concert action shots and smiling promotion photos for popular music artists of many genres. These Indigenous musicians mark this celebrity-reel part of NCI's image as a locally knowledgeable broadcaster with a focus on Indigenous music and programming. CIUR is situated in such a way that it speaks to the realities of media circulation designed for Indigenous artists and listeners and also distributes music to a mixed Indigenous and non-Indigenous public, and so it responds to many of the realities faced by other broadcasters.

Winnipeg is home to Aboriginal Peoples Television Network, the nationally broadcast Indigenous Music Awards, and many other arts programs, festivals, and concerts, as described in chapter 2. At the same time, the media audience in Winnipeg is diverse: Indigenous, settler, and newcomer listeners are all potentially significant to broadcasters and advertisers.[3] Broadcasters, artists, and listeners can learn much from listening closely to Winnipeg, as here, media outlets negotiate overlapping realities. How does an Indigenous-focused station navigate a city that holds a national mouthpiece for Indigenous media and also has a diverse potential audience? The way in which this is maneuvered relies on popular media formats. Enthusiasm for new media creates a space for possible misconceptions about the relevance of broadcast media. Radio broadcasters continue to have wide and sustained reach in both Canada and the United States.

Figure 3.1. NCI/Streetz office signage. (Photo by author)

In Canada, radio "reaches listeners in every corner of Canada regard-less of the size of the market." In 2017, 86 percent of Canadians aged twelve and over listened to the radio weekly.[4] In the United States at this same time, 93 percent of adults listened to the radio weekly, which exceeded TV and smartphone use.[5] Even as streaming audio program-ming grew during the 2010s, research in pop music markets finds that "mainstream consumers want to go directly to the 'greatest hits'"; this audience behavior continues to underscore the "important role" for radio.[6] Media professionals working for Streetz expressed awareness that the kind of music on—and not on—the radio impacted listeners within and beyond Winnipeg.

## The Loss of a Hip Hop Broadcaster

When Streetz went on-air, it was the only hip hop station in Winnipeg. And it was beloved by many people. Streetz had a profound importance to its audience, as evidenced by responses from April 2014 when it ended. My research with Streetz and then Rhythm included looking at their relevant web presences. The primary locations for listener interaction were the official Facebook pages and hosts' public Facebook pages. Some interactions occurred through official Twitter handles, though these more often encompassed announcements from station staff and the musicians whose music they played. The station's website offered listeners online audio streaming of the broadcast shows, provided song and artist information for the streamed audio, and created one-way communication about shows, events, and community announcements for the listening audience. Streetz's use of online platforms is consistent with that of medium- and large-size broadcasters, following Heikki Hellman and Arto Vilkko's assertion that "all prominent radio stations take advantage of new digital platforms and social media."[7] The primary location for listener feedback as well as station communication, Facebook showed a significant uptick in activity in the spring of 2014. Listeners' comments largely fell into three major categories: displeasure at the end of Streetz, confusion about the station change, and appreciation for the station.[8]

On April 2, 2014, Streetz's on-air DJ Paul Rabliauskas posted on his Facebook page that he was saying good-bye to Streetz.[9] Responses to his public post generally followed the themes of confusion or displeasure. One poster wrote simply, "sadness." Other listeners wrote about their concerns for a format change or a general worry that changes at Streetz would be a personally felt loss, writing, "It's a sad day" and "tell me it's still gonna be hiphop bro."[10] The Streetz official Facebook page released a coordinated message about the change, featuring a photo of then-current and former hosts MJ, Paul, Big Will, and Miss Melissa. Responses to the announcement included appreciation for Streetz.

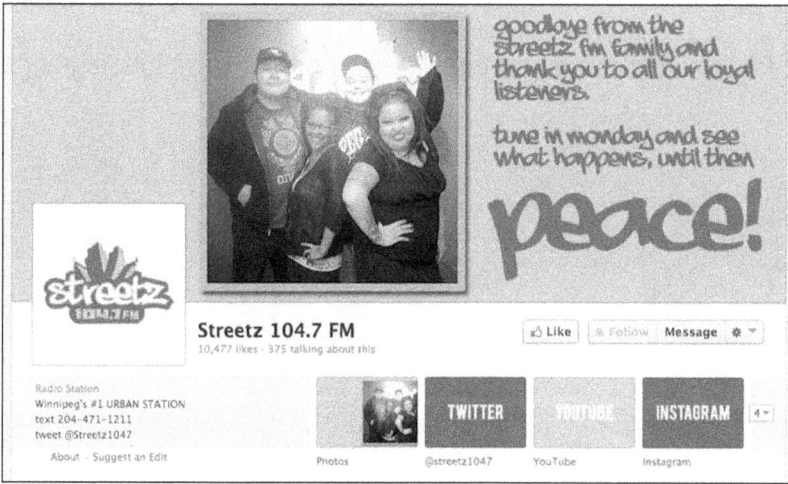

Figure 3.2. Streetz Facebook page, 2 April 2014.

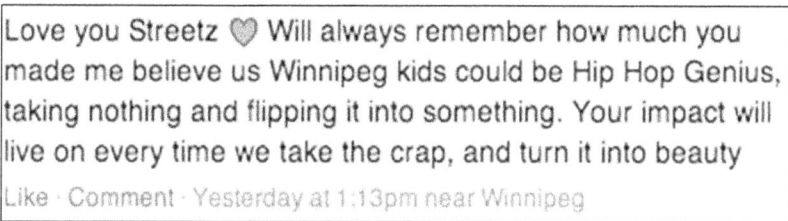

Love you Streetz 💜 Will always remember how much you made me believe us Winnipeg kids could be Hip Hop Genius, taking nothing and flipping it into something. Your impact will live on every time we take the crap, and turn it into beauty

Like · Comment · Yesterday at 1:13pm near Winnipeg

Figure 3.3. Poster comment to Streetz, 2 April 2014.

The Streetz Facebook page reposted youth organizer Michael Champagne's blog entry summarizing the major positive impacts Streetz has had since it started. He wrote, "Because the folks on this station are so real, familiar, relatable to not only me, but most Aboriginal youth I talk to, it is no wonder that they have been voted #1 Radio station by Uptown Magazine with Big Will taking the crown as most beloved radio dude in the Peg. Also, they support community initiatives, and allow opportunities for young people to have their voices heard. It is amazing." About Miss Melissa in particular, Champagne wrote that she exhibits "passion and dedication": "[She] is as passionate about making change for our people of any radio announcer I have ever seen."[11] The station's Facebook page also posted a question asking listeners to share their favorite

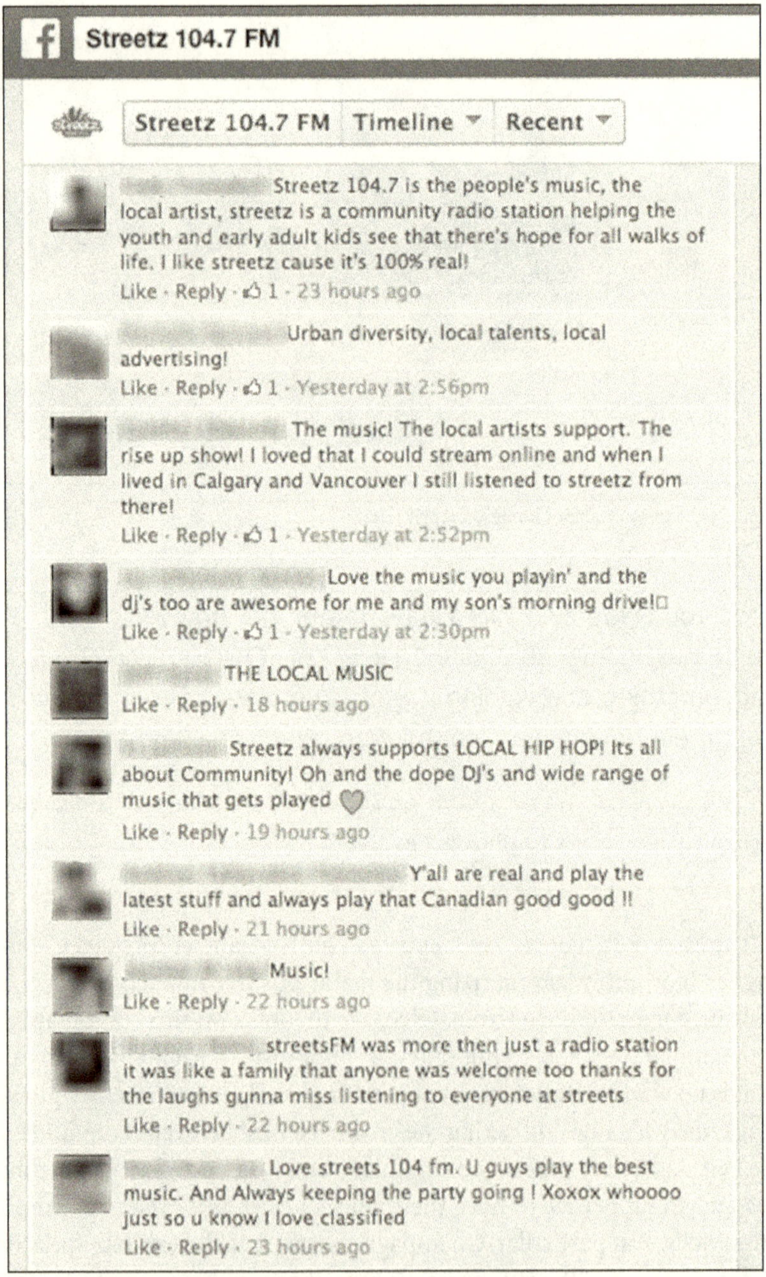

**Streetz 104.7 FM**

Streetz 104.7 FM  Timeline ▼  Recent ▼

Streetz 104.7 is the people's music, the local artist, streetz is a community radio station helping the youth and early adult kids see that there's hope for all walks of life. I like streetz cause it's 100% real!
Like · Reply · 👍 1 · 23 hours ago

Urban diversity, local talents, local advertising!
Like · Reply · 👍 1 · Yesterday at 2:56pm

The music! The local artists support. The rise up show! I loved that I could stream online and when I lived in Calgary and Vancouver I still listened to streetz from there!
Like · Reply · 👍 1 · Yesterday at 2:52pm

Love the music you playin' and the dj's too are awesome for me and my son's morning drive!□
Like · Reply · 👍 1 · Yesterday at 2:30pm

THE LOCAL MUSIC
Like · Reply · 18 hours ago

Streetz always supports LOCAL HIP HOP! Its all about Community! Oh and the dope DJ's and wide range of music that gets played 💚
Like · Reply · 19 hours ago

Y'all are real and play the latest stuff and always play that Canadian good good !!
Like · Reply · 21 hours ago

Music!
Like · Reply · 22 hours ago

streetsFM was more then just a radio station it was like a family that anyone was welcome too thanks for the laughs gunna miss listening to everyone at streets
Like · Reply · 22 hours ago

Love streets 104 fm. U guys play the best music. And Always keeping the party going ! Xoxox whoooo just so u know I love classified
Like · Reply · 23 hours ago

Figure 3.4. Social media praise for Streetz. (Posts to Streetz's public Facebook page, www.facebook.com/streetz1047fm)

things about the station, which elicited a long list that frequently high-lighted listeners' appreciation for local and Canadian hip hop.

Reflecting on the station, fans highlighted how Streetz supported local hip hop. They wrote about the station as "like a family," recalled that it is about "community," that it is "real," that it shares "hope," and mentioned ways in which diverse audiences and musicians are welcomed and supported. Emphasizing the broadcast and streaming dimensions, one commenter wrote that they streamed the radio station when not in Winnipeg. Some listeners focused on specific aspects of the music, like "big bass," "up to date rap and hip hop," and "local artists."[12]

During the week of oldies, the on-air shift and the online announcement combined to create a sense of confusion among some listeners. Displeasure at the loss of Streetz was a theme from other posters. Specifically, listeners noted that the station had been different, provided a service unlike other stations, and played Indigenous artists. The concern

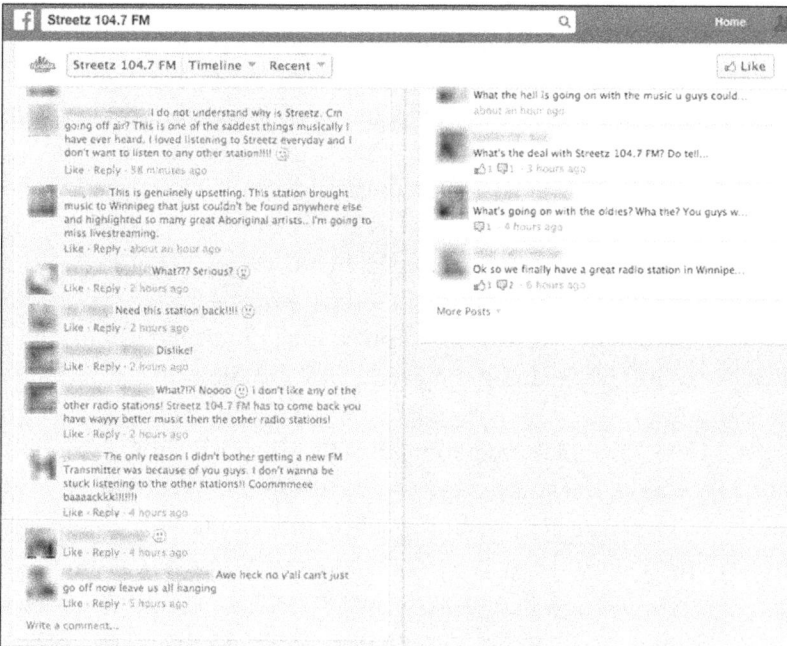

Figure 3.5. Social media confusion and displeasure. (Posts to Streetz's public Facebook page, www.facebook.com/streetz1047fm)

about having an ongoing venue to play Indigenous artists and a station whose format focuses on hip hop was a concern of listeners such as these. It was also a topic that staff at CIUR discussed seriously before and after the format shift.

Streetz's folding was a loss to dedicated listeners. And it was more than that. Streetz played a unique and valuable role broadcasting Indigenous hip hop to a diverse audience within and beyond the city of Winnipeg, including overlapping Indigenous, Black, and Filipinx listenerships. Its five-year airing suggested the viability of playing urban-format music by Indigenous artists; its subsequent branding shift and folding raises questions about how commercial pressures and mainstreaming are affecting Indigenous pop musicians.

## Community Radio, Commercial Radio: Positioning an Urban Broadcaster

After gaining a license in 2008, Streetz charted a new path for a Native-licensed station. Into the early to mid-2010s, it was the only dedicated urban-format station that specifically played urban Indigenous musicians. In order for musicians to take control of their own narratives, they first needed to access a platform to which a wide audience could listen. As an on-air DJ and station music director, Miss Melissa brought her years of expertise in the Indigenous music industry in Canada to Streetz. She has described her background as an urban Indigenous person as impacting her experience in Winnipeg. In recounting her vision for the station, Miss Melissa focused on how it supports local upstart musicians. But how, exactly, did Streetz help support urban Indigenous music and musicians, and while doing this work, why did the broadcaster meet resistance?

NCI CEO Dave McLeod and on-air DJs Miss Melissa, Alex Sannie, and Paul Rabliauskas navigated Streetz through a niche position in media broadcasting. Neither fully publicly funded nor fully ad funded, Streetz operated in between, initially somewhat like a "community" radio station that had significant in-house control over the material it aired. Community radio has the potential to reach listening audiences that public or commercial broadcasts do not capture. In Gillian Turnbull's study of community radio, she found that "while public radio aims to educate and serve a large population, and generally does so with considerable financial support, and commercial radio looks to serve a target audience defined by interested advertisers and the generic categories offered by major record labels, both types neglect to pursue the interests of minority groups, alternative artists, and small communities defined by their locality."[13] The interests of these numerical minorities, as well as a listenership tempted by alternative musical sounds, would ideally be served by community broadcasters. Canadian broadcasters under the government of the Conservative prime minister Stephen Harper saw decreased resources. These cuts sparked conversations comparing CBC funding to the less robust public-broadcasting funding available in the United States, though levels of public funding in Canada remained significantly higher. Even after a change in federal administrations, a secure future of funding for public broadcasting in Canada remains an open question.[14]

The CBC operates provincial stations that record and broadcast from across Canada. Affiliates deliver local news, stories of regional interest, and music by homegrown and national artists. CBC Manitoba, in both its French- and English-language radio iterations, brings a microfocus on local issues and musical culture.[15] Yet purely commercial radio and publicly funded radio fail to attract some potential audience members. In Manitoba, commercial radio broadcasts content that is similar to other stations across Canada; this programming is designed with advertisers in mind. Public broadcasters serve a wide range of audiences; hip hop and other urban genres are not a major focus for music played on CBC radio. During Streetz's peak broadcast years, the CBC offered only three programs that included hip hop music content, and these all included other music genres as well: *CBC Radio 3 Podcast*, *The R3-30*, and *The Strombo Show*. There were no Indigenous-specific music shows that were broadcast at the time Streetz rebranded (2014). This was in contrast to eleven classical shows and ten other pop music shows at that time. Individual Indigenous hip hop artists such as Hellnback did have pages on music.cbc.ca, though they lacked regular inclusion on a show platform.

NCI fails to fit squarely into categories of a public, commercial, or community broadcaster, instead exemplifying some characteristics of each. Unlike commercial stations, it is organized as a nonprofit company. Distinct from a public broadcaster tasked with reaching all Manitobans, it has a board of directors that aims to represent First Nations and Métis communities in Manitoba, as well as the province's large geographic diversity. The station's funding structure indicates that it is neither fully public nor fully commercial. NCI has received some support from the Northern Native Broadcast Access Program (NNBAP), funded by the federal government. This program's purpose is "supporting the production and distribution of relevant Aboriginal programming to Northern Native people."[16] This program's budget has decreased, both in terms of real dollars and purchasing power, from the 1980s to the early twenty-first century. NCI's proportion of funding from government sources has also decreased over time. In 2003, this was at about 46 percent.[17] By 2008, "close to 80% of NCI's more than $2 million annual budget [was] generated by NCI itself."[18]

When NCI operated Streetz, it received support from Canadian Heritage. Public funding had decreased to only 8 percent of NCI's operating costs by February 2014, and NCI was not permitted to use any of this funding for Streetz.[19] During the same period, Streetz received no grant funding. With a staff of thirty-three for both stations during this time, NCI needed to fund operations, including its production, accounting, sales, promotions, leadership, and support staff, along with producers and on-air talent. To attempt to cover costs, both NCI FM and Streetz solicited sponsors and played advertisements on-air and online.

The CRTC divides radio stations based on their licensing.[20] The CRTC names the "public" broadcaster in Winnipeg as the CBC/SRC, while the "private" (commercial) list encompasses Rogers, Jim Pattison Broadcast Group, Golden West, Evanov Communications, Corus, Zoomer Media, and BCE. The CRTC sets up different categories for "Campus," "Community-Based," "Religious," and "Native," the latter category being the one in which CICY-FM (NCI FM) and CIUR-FM (Streetz) were operating.[21] Compared to other markets, notably in the United States across the southern border, this is a relatively small number of stations. Due to population differences, the potential listenership is also smaller than in the United States, even in urban centers like Winnipeg. Because of the limited number of stations, pressure to specialize with regard to format is not particularly intense. Home to only the third urban-format station in the nation, Winnipeg, cosmopolitan though it may be, follows the larger and even more diverse city of Toronto in this regard. For listeners and advertisers, even in the 2010s, hip hop continued to be a tough sell; it was crucial for stations including Streetz to court mainstream listenership to stay afloat. To a certain extent, most stations have to be aware of, and palatable to, a general mainstream listenership to draw a sizable audience.

Crucially, not all of these ideas about listenerships and their appetites are born out of experience; some continue as part of received ideas within industry settings. For example, hip hop in Toronto was very popular for years before the license was issued for the city's first urban-format station. Beyond the station's placement in a policy subcategory, Streetz itself had a role in Winnipeg. McLeod characterized the Streetz mission and mandate as community oriented. He elaborated, "The mission and mandate of our radio station is to be representative of the people we serve and also to provide a professional service that is inclusive of different age groups and target audiences and to utilize and work with the community including the talent as much as we can within our given annual budget."[22]

As a broadcaster, NCI FM reaches throughout the province of Manitoba, over seventy-five communities, with fifty-nine transmitters.[23] CIUR has a more localized reach, transmitting via radio to the city of Winnipeg and the metro area. Through online streaming, however, the potential audience for the urban-format station became global. Streaming plays an important role in contemporary radio delivery, though listeners continue to access programming, including new music, on the radio dial.[24] With regard to the traditional radio reach, McLeod explains that Streetz "is local, it's Winnipeg, and it's youth orientated." He identifies why the format was chosen: "because we did focus groups, and when we picked the genre of music and that was the winning genre as opposed to going rock or other genres."[25] McLeod's comments reveal both his understanding of the station's community focus and his aim to use directed market-research techniques to achieve results.

Station staff aimed for Streetz to target audiences that were not primarily tuning in to public or commercial radio. At the same time, precisely because these audiences were not pursued by other stations, providing an urban music format offered a unique marketing opportunity. The publicity materials for Streetz highlight that the station markets itself to "Aboriginal youth" as "the fastest growing demographic" in Winnipeg. As described in chapter 2, meta titles on the station's website as well as sharing previews on social media sites like Facebook clearly emphasize the tagline, "STREETZ 104.7 is Winnipeg's Aboriginal Youth Radio" and "Winnipeg's #1 Hip Hop and R&B Station."[26] While listeners may understand themselves as the users of a radio station, defining the consumer is more complicated for ad-supported broadcasting. On-air and online, clients who pay a station are the advertisers; commercial stations match them with potentially receptive customers. Radio developed the process of delivering consumers to advertisers, and continues it. Media companies in the streaming music business are able to further target advertisements to listeners for their clients, using data from listening behavior, subscriber-provided information, and in some cases data passively provided by users, such as location information for smartphone listeners. Streetz's tailoring of its programming occurred at an illustrative intersection: it needed to secure advertising revenue and so sometimes operated like a commercial station, yet it was also licensed as a Native station with a directive to serve an Indigenous listenership. For Streetz and then Rhythm, the bottom line is not just financial: station programming reflects a community image.[27]

When station music directors make choices about what is on-air, they necessarily also decide what does not enter station rotation. This audibility or inaudibility presents a high-stakes choice. As described in chapter 1, the silencing of voices racialized as Native in music genres racialized as Black plays into a larger narrative of intentional not-hearing.[28] This situation invites careful attention to who is and is not listening and opens possibilities for audibility when the scope of the listenership is widened. Within the station, discussion of how CIUR operated as Streetz and then as Rhythm has reflected change over time. Alex Sannie recalls, "At the beginning, playing so much local content, it got this community vibe quick.... When [station music director] Melissa took over, ... the quality control stepped back up. Now you have this hybrid where ... we have a lot of commercials, we're selling ad time, [and] going out to community events."[29] In my conversations with station management, staff, and on-air talent, it became clear that these professionals think very carefully about how the station is positioned and how its messaging can impact images of Indigenous communities and individuals.

## Distributing Indigenous Music, Shaping an Urban Indigenous Community Image

Shout-outs in the intro name exactly whom listeners will be hearing: Jon C "The General," Inez, and Heatbag Records. The drums have established a duple rhythmic pattern, but little else has coalesced by the time the MC starts locating himself after the eight-bar intro: "I'm that Winnipeg Boy, these rappers they know my name. I'm that Native from the hood, the boss who's walked the game. I'm drawn to the flames, I'm cursed by the fame. The city needs a bad guy, so I'm the one they blame." The musicians emphasize how they can be heard and read by listeners. Local. Urban. Native. Known. Halfway into Jon C's first sixteen bars, he leaves no mysteries. His very first lyric references the song for which his (former) group is best known. He drops two verses in a row, telling the listener about his tangles with the police and maintaining that he will rise above. He is in the streets; he is making money on his music; he is, with some comedic wordplay, a "dope track dealer." A high-pitch synth melody enters, then a female vocalist starts to sing. A low-register processed male voice echoes her, extending the pitch range but maintaining the melodic content: the narrator is strong; he is a boss. Inez offers syllables on a three-note descending melody, easy to repeat and sing after: "nah nah nah, nah nah nah, hey hey hey hey." This, too, repeats. The sound is clean and skillful. It's relatively easy to sing with her. The song breaks from the male rapper / female R&B-style vocalist trope with the next verse: Inez offers a speech-sung flow, and she too raps, "I'm a boss, every day." Her sung vocals and speech-sung lyrics take over the rest of the song, "The Takeover," which ends with the low-pitched processed voice. Officially named as Inez's song featuring Jon C, their collaboration can be read and reread, heard and reheard, variously interpreted by different listeners. "Boss need a boss, yeah," "We're taking over." For hip hop listeners of the first two decades of the twenty-first century, much would be familiar in timbre, text, style, form, collaboration, and effects. And yet something in the second half of the song is not quite so easily captured and defined. The way this song plays with mainstream hip hop sounds of those decades, while inflecting the artists' interpretations of a specific urban environment and musician positionality, exemplifies how urban Indigenous broadcasters navigate sonic vocabularies and audience positionings.

As a popular music broadcaster within Canada, Streetz felt the familiar shadow of the USAmerican pop music industry. While this musical
hegemony is familiar to many people in Canada, CIUR also faces unique
challenges as a Native-licensed station. The charge to promote Indigenous music to a wider public stems in part from the station's mandate
to serve Indigenous musicians and listeners. This mandate, which comes
from the mission of NCI, is reinforced by the broadcaster's commitment
to the CRTC. In the application for the license for CIUR, NCI stated,
"approximately 50% of Canadian content category 2 [popular] music will
be performed by Aboriginal talent and approximately 5% will be in an
Aboriginal language."[30] This desire to play Indigenous popular music
is further underscored by a lack of opportunities for Indigenous artists
on other stations. McLeod spoke to the need for NCI to play these artists because "commercial stations generally will not play . . . Aboriginal
[musicians] as independent artists."[31]

Indigenous artists' songs are interspersed with those of non-
Indigenous artists, yet Indigenous-identifying and mixed-heritage musicians' works are important to the station's overall image. When Streetz
first went on the air, the first song the station played was by Ojibwe rapper and producer Plex. When the station later rebranded as Rhythm, its
first song was by Stó:lō artist and producer Inez Jasper.[32] By playing these
artists in moments of symbolic importance, the station affirms their overall centrality. Additionally, Indigenous artists appear as guests on-air at
the radio station. These features include artists from outside Winnipeg,
like Inez and A Tribe Called Red, who have made appearances on-air
and online. Local artists like Leonard Sumner, an Anishinaabe musician
from the Interlake, have also appeared on-air, as discussed in chapter 2.[33]
For McLeod, a major goal is the station's legacy: "If we can reach out to at
least two generations of young people, that would be very fulfilling in the
work we do. . . . And when I'm an old, old man, I can look back and say I
was a part of that point in Aboriginal radio history."[34]

## Sonic Sovereignty: Articulating Urban Indigeneity

Music and associated language and gesture are at the core of decolonial acts. As Silvia Rivera Cusicanqui articulates, "the possibility of a
profound cultural reform in our society depends on the decolonization

of our gestures and acts and the language with which we name the world."[35] Enactments of sovereignty, suited to the medium of musical culture, are inextricable from this larger project. While the situation in which Cusicanqui writes is culturally distinct, she writes from her position in Bolivia, recognizing that her conclusions are relevant to the larger region and globally. Even within the North American continent, there was a wide variety of governance structures that predated European contact; these continue to impact differing conceptions of sovereignty that exist among Native nations to this day. Indigenous presence in Canada stretches back into the distant past, much longer than the several hundred years of Black presence. Histories of slavery and forced labor differ across and among Black and Indigenous groups, as do patterns of movement and migration, both forced and chosen. Yet the contested movement and ongoing exclusions of Native and Black musics (and musicians) from a Canadian industry mainstream speak to multiple kinds of unwillingness to hear Afro-diasporic and Indigenous peoples as integral to the Canadian nation-state.

Indigenous media broadcasters, DJs, and other musicians can argue for the recognition of existing sovereignty through pop culture practices. Sovereignty, as described by Jolene Rickard, "is the border that shifts indigenous experience from a victimized stance to a strategic one"; these strategies extend beyond legal ones, which constitutes a larger move.[36] A conception of sovereignty that extends past legal definitions of a Euro-American nation-state is both practical and necessary; this includes cultural sovereignty, bodily sovereignty, food sovereignty, linguistic sovereignty, representational sovereignty, visual sovereignty, radical sovereignty, and intellectual sovereignty, as well as self-definition and self-determination.[37] As Maile Arvin (Native Hawaiian), Eve Tuck (Unangax̂), and Angie Morrill (Klamath) have productively theorized, decolonial action in the present requires supporting Indigenous sovereignty struggles that recognize varied lived realities across Native communities.[38] Sonic sovereignty, expressed through musical practice, is part of a decolonizing process that extends into all areas of life. Musical expression is relevant to self-determination, community building, and the inseparable project of connecting to land. As described in chapter 1, Leanne Betasamosake Simpson operationalizes sovereignty that is not simply about maintaining control over a particular spot on a map.[39] Working through the body, music creates vibrations that physically connect musician to listener; forms of community are actively enacted through participatory performance. Language, musical references, instrumentation, lyrics, timbres, and musical forms are all involved in the expression of the self, as well as the manner in which individuals and groups demand to be recognized. And, following personal preference and community protocols, determining one's audience, electing what to share with whom, and invoking the power of silence by not speaking or sharing are all part of sonic sovereignty. Like other aspects of Indigenous sovereignty, sonic sovereignty takes place whether or not it is recognized by a nation-state.

As an embodied practice of Indigenous self-determination through musical expression, sonic sovereignty offers a frame for listening for the effects of expressive culture in the world and seeking the ways in which self-determination in performance is part of decolonization's projects that span other times, places, and venues. While commercial-sounding radio might seem like a surprising space for self-determination, it offers many opportunities for collective enactments: relationships are created between musicians and carefully crafted audiences. The heterogeneous groups, created through broadcasting, online streaming, and in-person events, include a variety of listeners, possible vantage points, and interpretations. There is a specific power in taking a medium that often contributes to the colonialist heteropatriarchy—mainstream popular music and its distribution systems—and finding space for counternarratives. Engaged Indigenous musicians are not waiting to be recognized by the Canadian or USAmerican nation-state. Sonic sovereignty is about being heard, and building on audibility, it interrogates the power structures that seek to silence Native voices.

Much urban Indigenous hip hop music draws on references that speak to articulations of Indigeneity that transcend individual nations or bands, yet rootedness in specific place continues to be crucial.[40] Band- and nation-specific concepts of sovereignty contribute to more widely translatable sovereignty concepts; these are based in regionally specific understandings of land. Anishinaabe writer Waaseyaa'sin Christine Sy identifies that political struggles with settler colonialism are associated with land, and that land is inextricably linked to Indigenous relationships and knowledge. Her understanding of land as more than stagnant geography is articulated through the shift toward the use of the Anishinaabemowin word aki, meaning "the physical universe that makes up Anishinaabe life as well as the unseen movement that manifests this physically."[41] Personal story, or dibaadjimowin, enacts a form of relationship with land.[42] This form of storytelling can convey both long-ago stories and more recent ones; these narratives and their form require listeners to pause and pay attention.

Pause. Pay attention. What do you hear? "What the mic means? a chance to reach the people," he raps. And here, it is exactly that. Over his verses, rapper Wab Kinew mixes together lessons and odes to hip hop and to spiritual practice. The laidback tempo over an unchanging beat allows for his relaxed flow, a perfect fit for the lyrical reference to "old-time rhyme and flow." "Praise to the gods of the hip hop religion," he starts, and later he turns to the powerful and storied figure of the white buffalo.[43] The musicians look to the past for the future: this is a song about ascending. Kinew raps, "Natives on the rise," while making space for pain and wondering how he "rose above this shit." At the chorus, musician Iskwe sings about traveling far and being grounded close to home: "I've been all 'round the world. I've seen all kinds of people, but still there's only one for me." Always a dialogue, rapped and sung lines weave across and speak to each other. Iskwe's and Kinew's voices interlock to finish the chorus, as she sings "give it up" and he raps what to give it up for: old-time ways. For hip hop, for longtime spiritual practices, respect for homeland (and getting it back), this song is an ode to enduring history. Each listener to the 2010 song "Give It Up" might hear one kind of history more than others or read something more specific into some of the more open signifiers.

Pause. Pay attention. What do you hear? A rhythmic voice repeats "electric, electric 49," the emphasis falling on different syllables as the rhythmic patterns change. This lower-register female voice contrasts with the singing voice in the higher pitch range, the two playing off each other in the established groove. You might hear this as a dialogue or even as the same voice, speaking across its range of sonic possibilities. Both voices work together to deliver the theme. Across short melodic phrases, snippets of metaphor heighten this energy: "power up," "throw the breaker," "hit the switch." Electronic instrumentals play up this feel. A timbre reminiscent of lasers sets the scene, and then the song's instrumental melody loops using high pitches and a diffuse synth timbre.

Vocal echoes and shouts evoke the sound of a crowd and hype up the singer's vocals. Instrumentals, timbres, lyrical content, sound processing and effects: all of these locate the sound in an electrified communal dance space. And Inez's vocals tell us this "party" is specifically a "49."[44] So it's late in the evening, the powwow is over for the day, and the sounds, the dance steps, and the energy are all shifting in character. After a competition powwow, the audience might already be listening for displays of dance and musical skill, but now, the music has clearly established the shift toward a participatory environment for social dance, levity, a party. The sound is polished and balanced. The song has a clear narrative arc, a musical build and a fall. It sounds professionally produced.

Why listen closely to this heavily electronic track from 2013 when thinking about sonic sovereignty and mainstream radio airplay? Inez released this song, "Electric 49," on her album *Burn Me Down* on her own label. She promoted it at Indigenous music industry events. It earned her a Juno nomination and an Indigenous Music Awards (IMA) nomination. This album is self-produced, and the sound is professional. "Electric 49" has the build and arc that make it an easy radio version of an EDM-influenced pop hit. With this music, Inez won an IMA for best producer/engineer in 2014.[45] With this music, she was a guest on Streetz, and her music played on-air. Radio professionals spoke about the possibility for Streetz to launch new artists. This included artists like Inez from across Canada and beyond its borders. The station also prided itself on attracting listeners to local Indigenous artists in particular.

Through sonic sovereignty, Streetz's role in playing music by artists who foreground their own Indigeneity demonstrates the Native-licensed station's active role in shaping narratives of what urban Indigeneity sounds like. This forms a refusal to accept stereotypes of rurality and pastness. Sannie describes Streetz as providing an important opportunity for Winnipeg musicians, noting Ojibwe rapper Wab Kinew as an example. Originally from the Onigaming First Nation in Ontario, he was a member of hip hop group Dead Indians and then released two solo albums, *Live by the Drum* (2009) and *Mide><Sun* (2010).[46]

After initial airplay on Streetz, Kinew went on to success in multiple spheres. He transitioned from working as a rapper to being a public radio host. He ran for office—and won—in 2016 as a New Democratic

L to R : Kenny G, Wab, P-nut

*"Three young Ojibway warriors who fell on the battlefields of North America hundreds of years ago awaken today to find their once proud nation reduced to rubble. The mighty Ojibway, who were once warriors and shamans, are now gangsters, addicts and prostitutes. Amidst the barren post-apocalyptic landscape of modern Winnipeg, these* Dead Indians *set about to turn the tide in their people's struggle, using the power of the microphone."*

Figure 3.6. Dead Indians public webpage, April 2005, Wab Kinew at center

Party (NDP) candidate in Winnipeg and was elected Manitoba's NDP leader in 2017. Sannie, a hip hop artist himself, reflected on the importance of showing that rappers can be serious and intelligent people. His band, The Lytics, also aired on Streetz. Sannie has talked about his experiences being underestimated and being subjected to stereotypes as a Black Canadian and as a rapper. He spoke with empathy about the ways in which hip hop artists are heard by mainstream ears and noted how Kinew has used his exposure on Streetz to launch other projects: "It's amazing how he's transitioned from being an artist to being a media person to now just being a little bit of a person, like a celebrity. . . . That's probably the biggest hip hop success story of anything. . . . He's been like, 'I said I was smart when I was rapping, and you may not have bought it, but now I'm in a suit and my table is higher than yours, and

I'm still telling you the same thing.' So he does bring a lot of credit to everybody in that regard."[47] Kinew's success beyond hip hop has the potential to bolster the idea that Indigenous hip hop artists can be smart, engaged community members. His career demonstrates an exceptional trajectory of what is possible through musical expression. In this case, he honed skills presenting as a public figure and crafting language first in hip hop, which he used for music with a wide range of lyrical topicality. His collaborations include party anthems and responses to police violence, as analyzed in chapter 2. His solo work released before the beginning of his political career also shows a wide range, but his 2009 and 2010 albums signal his shift toward more community-focused rap that previews his political career.

Wab Kinew's solo voice speaks unaccompanied: "I hear a lot of people say that the Native community needs heroes. But we already have our heroes. So let's just take a minute to remember them." This song is an homage to these heroes. It's also an homage to K'naan. A repeated sample from this artist musically frames "Heroes." Inspired by this prominent Black Canadian rapper's "Take a Minute," Kinew's lyrics tell a story of collective strength. He draws a musical line through refugees' experiences in Canada to the experiences of Indigenous peoples in Canada. In Somali-Canadian K'naan's song, the musician tells the stories of his heroes: Nelson Mandela, Gandhi, K'naan's mother. Across his verses, he references his own experience as a refugee, names his pride in continuing to represent Somalia, and talks about successes he has found through music. In "Heroes," Kinew brings names and stories of Indigenous heroes from across time and space on Turtle Island. This honoring sounds meaningful to Kinew, even while he acknowledges that many others fail to listen to these heroes. Right before the hook in the first verse, he raps a response to anti-Indigenous bias: "Yeah, I'm a live real lavish, for all the times that you called my people savage."

While K'naan's song tells about the rapper's personal life and journey, Kinew focuses more on each individual hero's story. He stretches back in time and across profession and calling: spiritual leaders, politicians, sports stars, freedom fighters. Kinew honors Louis Riel, Phil Fontaine, Waneek Horn-Miller, and Tommy Prince. Musicians like Buffy Sainte-Marie get special mention. As he does across the album, *Mide><Sun*, Kinew also brings his own experience with healing medicine to the

song, notably the experience of the sundance. Through the song, Kinew encourages listeners to reach out. Since the stories of these heroes aren't in the history books, he raps, "Go ask an elder. Go ask Grandma. Go ask Kookum. Better yet ask Wab Kinew. I've got opinions for days." Kinew encourages respect for elders' knowledge. He urges his listeners to reach out to their grandmothers, using endearments in English and Cree. And he also establishes himself as expert and dominant figure in this narration.

After this album, Kinew transitioned through public media channels to institutional leadership and then into the government itself that he had formerly critiqued. Kinew claimed a position in which he could exercise decisions that impact the relationship between Indigenous and non-Indigenous communities, and he did so at a time of social and political transformation. However, this is not the only trajectory that has a potential impact on Indigenous sovereignty, nor is it one everyone would choose, or to which all musicians have access. Kinew's move from speaking through hip hop to speaking through electoral politics occurred at a moment of transition. Even as media professionals attempt to court specific listener segments, these listenerships are changing.

## Sonic Indigeneity and the Mainstream

The Idle No More movement in Canada and internationally was a watershed moment in which Indigenous sovereignty gained mainstream attention among audiences spanning settler, newcomer, and Indigenous identities, which influenced social change throughout the 2010s. Musicians note the increasing knowledge of inclusive history among Indigenous, non-Indigenous, and mixed-heritage audiences as well as active involvement with political issues involving Indigenous-settler policies. Sumner reflects, "audiences have a better understanding now of intergenerational trauma, of the history between Canada and Indigenous peoples. . . . Slowly but surely people are being educated to the atrocities committed against Indigenous peoples by the Canadian government."[48] CIUR staff talk about the musical "mainstream," which includes Top 40 songs and those that chart on *Billboard*, principally in Pop, R&B/Hip Hop, and Dance/Electronic categories; this word is applied to both listeners and music. The range of the station's musical repertoire demonstrates how it attempts to court multiple audiences simultaneously. Staff talk about the "mainstream" audience as those whom they infer are listening to this music: urban or suburban, primarily white, young to middle-aged listeners.[49] Another audience is that composed of Indigenous listeners, typically an urban and young to middle-aged group for the purposes of the station. A third subgroup that is important to programming decisions is composed of fans of more underground music, particularly those whom Miss Melissa and others call "hip hop heads." These listeners enjoy older music as well as newer releases and tolerate—and even prefer—sounds that do not appear on current-hit radio stations. This group is typically urban and in a similar age range to the other two groups but is potentially racially mixed. In order to attract mainstream and underground music fans and to court Indigenous and non-Indigenous listenership, the station must consider the needs of these overlapping constituencies and attempt to alienate none of them.

The association of "commercial" music with non-Indigenous artists has been furthered by industry categorization. In the CRTC's decision approving CIUR, it identified, "Musical component will focus on 40% Aboriginal selections and 60% commercial content; mix of Rock, Pop and Hip Hop." The very licensing distinguishes between "Aboriginal" and "commercial" music; they are quantified as wholly distinct categories.[50] The change to Rhythm maintained the distinction between "mainstream" and Aboriginal/Indigenous music; it also elaborates on the genres and genre associations made under the new branding. Rhythm's content is a 60 percent "mainstream playlist," which NCI categorized as "a playlist that includes up and coming rhythmic hits, R&B classics, and throwback beats," notably not using the hip hop genre marker, though these were the "throwback beats" on-air. The station identifies the rest of its playlist as "airing local and national aboriginal [sic] artists" and says it maintains its "current ratio of 40% Canadian content."[51] CanCon regulations are a Canadian effort to resist USAmerican hegemony; they paradoxically present opportunities for people of many nations who live within present-day Canada to broadcast their music.

Furthermore, when envisioning their audience, NCI staff also contrast their work with that of university stations. University station formatting commonly offers block programming, unlike commercial stations and those like CIUR, which maintain a level of consistency in music genre throughout the day and the week. Professionals including Miss Melissa spoke positively about the role of university and community stations but made careful distinctions between these broadcasters and CIUR. Message rap, for CEO McLeod, is best suited for broadcasters whose have the freedom to embrace an alternative music mission. Because he sees this music as not financially sustainable, he explained, "I think that's where university stations have a role to play. . . . University college stations, I respect the work that they do very much. I think if you want the underground hip hop, and the message based hip hop that's very vocal, there are outlets for that."[52] The combination of university stations' freedom to offer block programming and their access to funding sources beyond commercial revenue does open up options for these broadcasters to provide specialty programming and even potentially controversial music, including politically hard-hitting hip hop. Staff at CIUR did not express this kind of freedom when describing their own programming. Over time, our conversations revealed an increasing focus on the commercial aspects of broadcasting.

The way CIUR positioned itself over the years it was broadcasting as Streetz and then as Rhythm demonstrates changes both in mainstream radio and in the manner in which popular Indigenous music has been heard as part of the soundscape of contemporary Winnipeg. During the moment of branding transition between Streetz and Rhythm, McLeod told me, "We're not here to compete with commercial stations at all. . . . Our audience, I think, will tend to be a little older." This distinction of a slightly different market was sometimes subtle. He mentioned, "When people came into the focus groups, they talked about what they heard in commercial radio. And some of them like what they hear." In the focus groups, McLeod noted, "some [listeners] said they were looking for something different. So I think that's what we listened to. What do people want that's different? . . . People want to hear more local music." Providing local music programming hosted by local personalities could help CIUR speak to a regional market in this way. The amount of money the station aims to make, staff report, is modest. McLeod asserted, "Our goal is not to be the number 1 station in the city. Our goal is to have it pay for itself and turn a small profit so it can remain stable."

As Indigenous urban music was heard more regularly as part of a mainstream sound beyond the station, playing commercial-sounding music on CIUR also increased as a station goal. The station aspired to play music that professionals described with words like "good," "good quality," "best," and "professional"; these overlap with their descriptions of commercial-sounding radio. These valuative terms are subjective. In some situations, "good" and "quality" convey race or class subtexts. Professionals might talk about playing higher-"quality" music while referring to a goal of attracting consumers with more income, for example.[53]

After the station rebranding from Streetz to Rhythm in 2014, staff described that the station would aim to play "the best possible music that will sound professional."[54] Miss Melissa explained that Rhythm was designed to court a more mainstream listenership: "We don't want to play a lot of heavy hip hop on our day parts, like Monday to Friday, six a.m. to six p.m. That's usually where we save the more commercial mainstream-sounding artists for. Then in the evening and into overnight, it turns more into a hip hop, urban-heavy station." This argument is familiar to broadcasting professionals, as well as people who worked to get hip hop on the radio in earlier decades. The idea that hip hop would not appeal to advertisers or that the music would hurt audience numbers during prime daytime hours was used to minimize hip hop airplay when Black artists were trying to break into mainstream airplay. This argument resurfaces here, with the addition of minimizing Indigenous hip hop content during the highest listenership (and most lucrative) airplay hours. Miss Melissa detailed that, while the station will maintain Canadian and Indigenous music in the playlist, "we just try to make it sound as mainstream as possible during the day to compete with the other stations."

Though Miss Melissa acknowledges the role of market research, she also makes her aesthetic determinations based on what she termed the quality of music.[55] "I think it just sounds, quality-wise, . . . better during the day. And that way, a lot more people would be inclined to play it, for example, in their businesses, in stores, or around their children. That's what we want."[56] In these statements, there is a conflation of "good" music, music with high production values, and music that is likely to attract an audience that is doing business. This slippage fails to acknowledge "good" local music that maintains a grittier sound or speaks to a listenership that is not likely to purchase goods and services that station advertisers wish to sell.

These discussions of musical quality and listenership inherently engage changing representations of race and ethnicity. As some listeners and professionals later reflected on the station's legacy, they connected the station's nonwhite listenership with some of the challenges that it faced. Politically, Indigenous studies scholars and community leaders frequently emphasize that Indigeneity is not a racial category; Indigenous identity is linked to the sovereign rights of Indigenous Nations that existed prior to colonization, whether or not these rights are always acknowledged.[57] At the same time, stereotypes that are leveraged against "visible minorities" in Canada are often deployed against Indigenous individuals and groups, particularly people who do not "pass" as white. As Bonita Lawrence explains, "For Indigenous people, to be defined as a race is synonymous with having our Nations dismembered. And yet, the reality is that Native people in Canada and the United States for over a century now have been classified by race and subjected to colonization processes that reduced diverse nations to common experiences of subjugation."[58] The station did not attract the same level of advertising support as other broadcasters; as grant revenue fell, the necessity of advertising became clear. In order to attract sustained investments from advertisers, the hip hop station had to confront stereotypes about its listeners. Anti-Black racism and anti-Native bias both functioned as barriers, as advertisers had to be reminded that listeners could indeed have income to spend on their products.

Alex Sannie, who worked in Winnipeg public schools with Indigenous and non-Indigenous students, is aware that Streetz listeners include children and teens. He noted that the station is reaching young listeners, as well as courting financially independent listeners. Sannie echoes Miss Melissa's perspective linking "quality" to sales: "if I can play you at work, people buy more ads." He views an older audience as still engaged in hip hop and other kinds of urban music, while also having the capacity to purchase advertisers' products. He explained that young professionals "are still buying albums on iTunes": "We have been trying to really cater to them." In informal conversations with station staff, the distinction between numbers of listeners and listeners likely to patronize advertisers was also emphasized. The shift toward considering ad revenue encouraged leadership and hosts to be conscious of which kinds of listeners they anticipated would be a good fit for station sponsors in addition to how many listeners would tune in. This is consistent with economic pressures that media critic Eric Weisbard identifies in radio formats, as "formats needed to convince advertisers that the public being addressed separately was commercially worthy."[59] Merely having raw numbers of listeners, without those listeners being considered a viable ad audience, was not a sufficient argument to convince businesses to generate ad-based revenue in the long term.

In the September 2014 application for the broadcast license renewal of CIUR, NCI broadcast technical manager Hoa Bui's document clarifies the rebranding from Streetz to Rhythm this way: "In the Spring of 2014, Streetz was rebranded as Rhythm as a means to continue our relationship with our Aboriginal core audience as well as to align with the teachings of the Medicine Wheel and be inclusive of all cultures."[60] This application, for a Native-licensed station, continues to focus on a Native audience, which is unsurprising given its licensing category. The general reference to the Medicine Wheel is not further explained, making it read as an intertribal reference, and the idea to be "inclusive of all cultures" is consistent with station discussions and branding changes that also include non-Indigenous and mixed-heritage musicians and listeners. NCI specifies that Rhythm's "primary intended audience is a balance of male/female between the ages of 25 and 40 newly entering the workforce or in the process of establishing themselves in their chosen career path."[61] Even while articulating that Winnipeg has a large Aboriginal listenership, NCI emphasizes that Rhythm is not just for this market: "we have created Rhythm 104.7, a new radio station with a format designed specifically for young professionals, young families, and young adults from all ethnic backgrounds."[62] This is a marked difference from Streetz, which emphasized a younger audience demographic, focused on Aboriginal listeners, and did not make reference to employment status or gender balance. Rhythm's intended audience is akin to other radio markets, which connect advertisers to working adults.[63]

Station staff members talked directly and indirectly about the role of "Top 40" radio. The Top 40, Contemporary Hit Radio (CHR), or hits format is familiar to a wide range of listeners. Its ubiquity makes it a force that shapes the known range of sonic possibilities for music radio. Whether or not individual listeners profess to like contemporary hit radio, they have likely experienced its effects. Top 40 is a form of hit radio that operates on the principle of playing and replaying a subset of songs, presumably those that broadcasters anticipate their listeners will like and want to hear reaired. Born in 1952, the hits radio format replays songs to create familiarity, which, up to a point, can also encourage listeners to enjoy a song because it is known. A popular origin story of hits-format radio typically places KOWH owner Todd Storz at an Omaha diner in the post–World War II era. He watched a server pay the jukebox to play the same set of songs over and over. She explained that she liked to hear these while she worked, so Storz started experimenting with not delivering novel content all the time but offering listeners the opportunity to rehear their favorites on-air.[64] So, regardless of the specific music, CHR delivers a repeated set of songs. Listeners who flip through their car radio channels, go to spaces like malls or other businesses that play pop radio, or attend bars and clubs that offer this mainstream music experience the hit-parade format, hear and rehear the same songs, and thus get to know them.

But there are structures in place that influence hit radio: it does not simply reflect listener taste. Currently, Top 40 stations do not play the hits of the Billboard Hot 100 Chart. In October 2000, *American Top 40* started getting its charts from the iHeartRadio subsidiary Mediabase, which no longer uses direct data on the forty most popular songs based on sales, streaming, and airplay. However, it has the ability to create hits because of its omnipresence: the show *American Top 40* airs on 150 iHeartRadio-owned stations across the United States, streaming online at www.at40.com, and through the iHeartRadio app, with additional content on its YouTube channel. Owned by iHeartMedia, *American Top 40* is headquartered in New York but owns stations in the United States, Canada, Aotearoa–New Zealand, and Australia.

This USAmerican program, heard in Canada, influences the mainstream sound in Canada as well. *American Top 40* plays in a broad range of stations across Canada, with the exception of Nunavut and the Northwest Territories and near but not on Prince Edward Island. Online streaming and accessibility through increasingly available fiber connections add to the program's ubiquity. The sample listing of stations in table 3.1, gleaned from *American Top 40*'s distribution map, shows some of this breadth, noting city, province or territory, and time that the program is played.

TABLE 3.1. *American Top 40* Saturation

| Station | City | Time |
| --- | --- | --- |
| CKBZ | Kamloops, BC | Every day 6 a.m.–12 a.m. |
| CKRW | Whitehorse, YT | Sat 6 a.m.–12 a.m. |
| CFMG | Edmonton, AB | Sun 6 p.m.–10 p.m., Sat 8 a.m.–12 p.m. |
| CFGW | Saskatoon, SK | Sat 6 a.m.–12 a.m. |
| CKLF | Brandon, MB | Sat 9 p.m.–1 a.m. |
| CKMM | Winnipeg, MB | Sun 8 a.m.–12 p.m. |
| CHUM | Toronto, ON | Every day 6 a.m.–12 a.m. |
| CJFM | Montréal, QC | Sat 9 a.m.–1 p.m. |
| CJCJ | Woodstock, NB | Every day 6 a.m.–12 a.m. |
| CJCH | Halifax, NS | Sat 6 a.m.–12 a.m. |
| CKCW | Moncton, NB | Sat 5 p.m.–9 p.m. |
| CKIX | St. John's, NL | Sun 10 a.m.–2 p.m., Sat 2 p.m.–6 p.m. |

Source: Compiled from *American Top 40*, "How to Listen," 28 October 2018, www.at40.com.

Strategies to capture audiences in broadcast radio are updated, but not abandoned, for streaming audio. Playing music that will keep listeners tuned in is the point of commercial music radio; broadcasters are able to sell ads based on the listener demographic they attract. When a program like *American Top 40* is available through a website and mobile app, in addition to broadcast radio, iHeartMedia reaches listeners in more places, following them online. As online streaming became more popular during the 2010s, media companies used their apps to collect user data, such as location information, personal contacts, and detailed demographic information.[65] Media companies can make the leap from selling listeners' attention to radio advertisers to also selling their attention and their data; it becomes possible to further stratify listeners in this process. In response to changing listener preference as some audiences move online, broadcasters like NCI look to larger trends to figure out what might work for them. To keep tech-savvy and younger listeners engaged, Streetz offered its music through digital streaming, hosted independently on its own website. While community-based and not-for-profit broadcasters typically lack the resources (and/or the appetite) of media giants like iHeartMedia, Spotify, and Apple (via Apple Music) to collect and monetize user data, many have adopted the streaming-audio format to try to keep listeners as they move from a car radio to a smartphone. As they do so, media organizations, musicians, and listeners participate in a shift: some musics and musicians that were previously outside the "mainstream" begin to be captured in general audience programming.

Streetz staff members have had shifting ideas about how useful it is to intentionally model the Top 40 in their broadcasting. Indeed, it seems to be an open question about how best to balance the unique perspective that a Native-licensed station can bring with the expectations of a broader audience for what popular music radio should sound like. The specific categories underrepresented on CHR—nonwhite artists, female and nonbinary artists, and independent labels—are exactly what an independent broadcaster like NCI has the potential to add to the soundscape. Yet, as NCI received less grant and government funding to meet expenses, it had to look more for other sources and thus shifted some of its strategies to adapt to new financial realities and court a more broad-based listenership.

## Regulating the Sonic Environment

Image management for a hip hop broadcaster involves calculations related to potential listener response as well as to the regulatory environment in which the radio station is situated. Radio stations are subject to standards and obligations from multiple sources. These include the more specific category of regulations, particularly the Radio Regulations, and acts, notably the Broadcasting Act.[66] All radio stations are expected to adhere to policies laid out in these documents. As the entity that created the policies, the CRTC aims to ensure that these are enforced. Commercial stations are required to become members of the Canadian Broadcast Standards Council (CBSC). The CBSC is tasked with handling complaints lodged against commercial radio stations, and all commercial stations are required to become members.[67] Stations are also obliged to follow standards not specifically outlined in CRTC or CBSC policy, such as those discussed in decisions or determined by past practice.[68] When Native media professionals attempt to showcase Native artists on a channel regulated by Canadian parliamentary legislation and mainstream financial pressures, it is not surprising that some tensions emerge.

Hosts and programmers mentioned two major factors related to regulation: Canadian content and decency. Management, too, expressed a combination of ideas about audience that shape music programming within its regulatory environment. While CIUR staff acknowledged that songs about issues relevant to Indigenous communities may have a "positive aspect," some that appeared too gritty or realist, including "conscious" or "message" rap, were cut from circulation. Authorship is the other major factor in the broadcaster's regulatory environment. A dive into regulatory policy *as written* helps to reveal regulatory policy *as enacted*. This dynamic then impacts the implementation of decency standards, shaping the messaging to which audiences can listen.

Stations are expected to make some of their music choices based on the musicians involved. The CRTC enforces a policy that a certain percentage of music that broadcasters put on the air must be of Canadian origin. This protectionist action exists in an environment in which many Canadian consumers purchase music from USAmerican and other foreign artists, while directly across the southern border, US-based listeners tend to purchase domestic music. In Canada, only 12 percent of record sales in 2000 were domestic; domestic sales were at 92 percent in the United States that same year.[69] The specifics for what counts as Canadian are detailed, yet even some professionals express confusion about how exactly the "CanCon" rules apply in various situations. To be considered "Canadian content," a piece of music must meet at least two of the following criteria:

- *M* (music): the music is composed entirely by a Canadian
- *A* (artist): the music is, or the lyrics are, performed principally by a Canadian
- *P* (performance): the musical selection consists of a live performance that is recorded wholly in Canada, or performed wholly in Canada and broadcast live in Canada
- *L* (lyrics): the lyrics are written entirely by a Canadian[70]

The rationale for this policy is that it would have the effect of increasing the amount of music by Canadians on Canadian radio. As the CRTC website contends, "Canadian content is about Canadian artists having access to Canadian airwaves. CRTC broadcasting policies and regulations support all Canadian talent that contributes to the Canadian broadcasting system. Policies and regulations support the artists themselves as well as the industries behind them."[71] The veracity of this statement is not at issue here; rather, the policy's impact on the music that broadcasters choose is central.[72]

Sannie has expressed optimism about how this regulation can encourage Canada-based artists and bolster both listening and pride: "Here, you have a station. And every time you have a new song, it can get played. And you can get Streetz online too," he explained. When he broadcasts music that is Canadian or local on-air, Sannie frequently announces these facts. In part, this has to do with CRTC regulation: "I figure if anybody is listening and checking, it's just a nice quick little, 'Hey, this is happening again.'" In addition, Sannie expresses passion for introducing listeners to Canadian hip hop. As an MC, producer, and performer with the hip hop group The Lytics, Sannie has a wealth of experience making music. This background makes him sympathetic to other artists, particularly other Canadian hip hop artists. He told me, "I'm an artist myself, and I think it's really important for Canadian artists to get recognition, especially in their own country." This recognition can both help grow an artist's fan base and remind listeners that Winnipeg and Canada are producing quality rap music. Sannie narrates, "When somebody hears a good song, I try to tell you if it's local and also if it's Canadian. If it's local and you love it, people text in like 'Who was that?' and all of a sudden locally this person has five new fans. And if it's Canadian, they go, 'Oh, wow, who is that? I didn't know I liked Canadian hip hop.' You do!"[73] For some listeners, the idea of Canadian pop music did not already include homegrown hip hop and hip hop by Black and Native artists. There is power in the moment of realization for these audiences to shift their expectations.

Sannie's experience as a listener further influences his decision to flag local music on-air: "When I was growing up, I was shocked to find out how many [Canadian artists] I really loved. I used to listen to Saukrates all the time." When Sannie heard that Saukrates was from Toronto, he remembers feeling, 'This is amazing.' Now I really really love him. . . . Knowing that you share a bond, at least country-wise, with an artist is really important." Listeners might not initially be aware that the Black Canadian rapper and singer Saukrates is from Ontario. He signed to the USAmerican Warner Bros. Records in 1996 and then released music through the United States–based label Def Jam in the early 2000s. Like many Canadian rappers, he pursued opportunities in both the US and Canada, a strategy often necessary for Canada-based rappers to succeed at home. Sannie wants listeners to experience Canadian music as well as the material they associate with the States: Since it can feel as if "everything" comes from the US, he says, "it's really nice to know that what you like is coming out of your own backyard."[74] When Maestro Fresh Wes, who is often credited as the godfather of Canadian hip hop, was rapping in the 1980s, he was not signed to a Canadian label. Because there was no hip hop or rap category in 1990, his Billboard-charting hit "Let Your Back-bone Slide" was nominated for a Juno Award in the Best Dance Recording category. About that performance, the rapper says he could tell that the music was new to Canada: "We knew we were doing something special."[75] In the music video for this popular track, a tuxedo-clad Maestro raps in a fast flow, "I'm not American," and then references the money he makes everywhere he goes—in France, England, and the United States. This Ca-nadian had to head abroad to make money at home. His hit single show-cases this story through lyrical references to international money pouring into a Swiss bank account. Drake is one of many Canadian rappers who cites Maestro's music as an inspiration. It has not been easy for hip hop from Canada's own backyard to find commercial success at home first, so naming rappers who come from Canada aids this process.

CanCon regulations affect Indigenous music play in nuanced ways. In a curious turn, the promotion of Canadian national interests buoys the airplay of some Indigenous musicians who live in present-day Canada, even those who do not identify with a Canadian nationalist project.[76] At the same time, it fails to incentivize airplay by international Indigenous artists, including those who share stages with Canada-based musicians at the Indigenous Music Awards and other high-profile industry events. The border between the United States and Canada becomes concretized in a regulatory setting; it bisects Indigenous lands and interrupts move-ment.[77] Author Thomas King (Cherokee/Greek/German descent) sum-marizes that though "the line that divides the two countries [Canada and the United States] is a political reality" and "the border affects bands and tribes in a variety of ways," the Canada-US border is "a figment of someone else's imagination."[78]

Canadian content regulations impact airplay significantly. Miss Melissa confirmed that when she selects music, CRTC requirements shape when Canadian content airs: "It's their rules and regulations that we have to play Canadian artists between six a.m. to midnight at a 40 percent quota."[79] The CRTC oversees Canadian content requirements at different percentages across stations. Unlike policies regarding decency, both how many songs must be Canadian and how this quality is established are quantified by the policies that the CRTC enforces. As in the case of Leonard Sumner, sometimes Indigenous music has the benefit for broadcasters of ticking both Native and Canadian content boxes simultaneously. Many other stations operate at a 35 percent Canadian content requirement.[80] NCI filed a request with the CRTC to reduce Canadian selections on-air. However, as both Streetz and Rhythm, CIUR was required to play 40 percent Canadian content.

Responses to the percentage-based CanCon policy raise questions about how professionals evaluate hip hop and electronic musics. When NCI made the request to decrease CanCon, it argued, "there are not enough Canadian urban musical selections to support a 40% level of Canadian music so the station has been rotating Canadian selections to a level where listeners tire of them." It also argued that "the Canadian urban music scene is small compared to that of other countries including the United States" and that hip hop lyrics often contain "inappropriate" language that makes the music unsuited for air.[81] This argument was rejected by the CRTC. It raises compelling points about how broadcasters respond to the hegemony of USAmerican hip hop and the USAmerican popular music industry as a whole. Given the large reach of this industry, what music made in Canada is being heard and by whom? What are the standards by which music is deemed "suitable," particularly for the "urban" music category, which is racialized as Black within the industry? Hip hop does have a history and presence in Canada, so what does it mean when this history is not heard by certain decision-makers?

With regard to differentiating Canadian content from notions of decency, Hoa Bui, broadcast technical manager at NCI, submitted the Canadian content reduction request on September 7, 2012. The letter states that reducing the Canadian content would "greatly assist NCI in reflecting the current radio play music available in the 'urban genre' which is inclusive of Hip-Hop, Dance, and R&B. The station has had a successful history in profiling local artists and those from other regions of Canada, particularly from Vancouver and Toronto."[82] Even as this letter touts Streetz's record in getting Canadian artists to listeners, the station requests decreasing its responsibility to do so. Interestingly, the request highlights Streetz's ability to attract attention not just to Winnipeg artists but also to those from urban centers in Canada's most populous city and reaching all the way to the West Coast. The letter suggests that a decrease is warranted precisely because the urban-format music content that listeners desire is generally less than 40 percent Canadian. The incongruity of these statements is striking. The application was denied, but because the CRTC determined that the 40 percent content agreement had been an attractive reason for CIUR to gain the competitive license and that the station did not articulate a sufficiently compelling reason to reduce it. It made no comment about whether there is enough Canadian urban content to air or if stations like CIUR have a special obligation to increase the amount of available content if not.[83]

The application itself refers to what it deems a lower audio quality in Canadian urban content, which makes the music unsuitable for air: "tracks are commonly released in a lower quality MP3 format, the music director often spends much time in attempting to contact urban artists to seek a high-quality version which some artists do not have."[84] The majority of the supplementary brief notes the progress toward airing urban Canadian content, of which Streetz has been part, while suggesting that there is not enough content available. Part of the application suggests that some Canadian hip hop is unfit for airplay because it contains profanity, sexism, or violence. Including the statement, "The decision is not however based on the financial viability of Streetz-FM," NCI explicitly states that the question is one of content availability and not profitability.[85] Taken at face value, this invites larger questions about access, training, and the structure of the mainstream music industry. Regardless of audio-quality indicators, the inclusion of content concerns indicates a focus on perceptions of potential listeners.

## Mainstreaming and Its Costs

When music professionals play saleable music on state-licensed airwaves, they face questions about efficacy and acceptability: What sells? What passes muster of the regulatory bodies? The larger nexus of commerce, government regulation, and artistic practice presents a complicated and often-changing dynamic. How do the ideas of acceptability relate to ideas of national belonging on licensed airwaves? How and by whom is potential marketability determined, and what role does actual sales data have in presenting the idea of the popular? Amid commercial and regulatory pressures, how do musicians navigate creative agency? In Canada specifically, the state policy of multiculturalism is often reflected through the metaphor of the mosaic: communities are created as disparate pieces that are all placed alongside each other to create the whole of the nation. National narratives often describe Canada as being founded by British and French colonists, with more recent versions including First Nations and other Indigenous groups as well. Those who are counted as "visible minorities" within Canada, through official multiculturalism, are often constructed at a remove, discursively decentered regardless of how long they have lived within, or been citizens of, the current nation-state. As referenced in chapter 1, these representational concerns are particularly acute for expressive culture. In musical and other staged celebrations of neoliberal multiculturalism that feature Indigenous culture performance, essentialized stereotypes of musico-ethnic difference risk being performed, naturalized, and sold, as Silvia Rivera Cusicanqui notes.[86] Multiculturalist policy, Rinaldo Walcott observes, "characterizes these others as people with static cultural practices located both in a past and elsewhere."[87] Reflecting deeply on the ongoing presence of Black Atlantic cultural practices in Canada, Walcott discerns, "official multicultural policies at both the federal and provincial level support this idea through a discourse of heritage—in Canada heritage always means *having hailed from somewhere else.*"[88] This is related to a well-documented process in which Indigenous groups are discursively located in the past in order to serve state goals. Bruno Cornellier particularizes this to a (white) Québecois desire for a departicularized "indianité." This extends to the rest of Canada through Canadian state attempts to co-opt and generalize markers of Indigenous identity for its own use.[89] Building on Walcott, I find that the Canadian modernist multicultural nation-state locates Black Canadians in an elsewhere and Indigenous people in Canada in an elsewhen. Heritage, as frequently performed in music, can be problematically dislocated in space and time.

Musical representation is inseparable from representation in other media. Indigenous people and those who are deemed "visible minorities" face the oscillating problems of hypervisibility and invisibility. Consequently, these issues of visibility lead to both overscrutiny and underresourcing—overscrutiny by state and rogue actors at the same time that official channels underinvite group members into meaningful participation—which affect groups beyond the sometimes-intersecting groups of Black Canadians and Native peoples in Canada. Reflecting on the representation and consumption of Filipina/o queer culture as part of what she calls the Canadian "multicultural art scene," Casey Mecija found that she and her band "felt burdened with the task of responding to what others demanded" of them.[90] As Marissa Largo explains, "When minoritized subjects are made visible within official multicultural discourse in Canada, such visibility often continues to legitimize the interests of the nation-state, and reproduce colonial and neoliberal narratives. . . . Simply being visible in various sectors of society such as arts and culture does not guarantee social justice and inclusion."[91] To what degree does getting on-air, gaining the potential to be heard, relate to the possibility of actually being listened to?

In its commercial form as recorded sound that can be played on-air and online, rap music is imbricated in layers of perceptions and perceptions about perceptions that people hold about this music and its authors. Artists, media personnel, and audiences bring a variety of ideas about class, consumption, violence, gender, and sexuality that shape how this music is heard. Public rhetoric about hip hop has been charged for decades.[92] Discourse about rap music as a genre is mutually influential, with perceptions (including self-perceptions) that people nourish about Black and Indigenous men, women, and nonbinary people. The objectification of musicians—of the people whose voices are heard on-air and whose bodies appear in music videos on-screen—occurs in consort with racialized and gendered ideas that listener-viewers nurture about labor, worth, value, and agency. The settler colonial project props up and depends on the circulation of tropes of sexual and racial difference. At the same time, when hip hop focuses on physical pleasure, including that which can come from consumption, luxury, experiences of power, and sexual gratification, it can offer musicians and listeners a space for embodied possibility. Even if this pleasure is only temporary, it can be experienced and reexperienced through live shows and relistenings, providing space for both sensorial enjoyment and the political implications of being in control of one's body.

Questions about decency meet questions about marketability in uncomfortable ways. How does an awareness of anti-Black racism and its connections to structural and personal biases against Indigenous people impact the choices broadcasters make about representing these groups? How do raced and gendered ideas that various audiences hold about certain people's pleasure conflict with settler colonial state policies of control and regulation? What does it mean for music to be "suitable"? What kinds of messaging are "objectionable," and who is doing the objecting? Which stereotypes are suitable for airplay, and which are not?

Streetz provides a salient example of how media personnel attempt image management in the face of a pointed ongoing public debate about hip hop music. Industry professionals express apprehension about how their station is perceived based on associations of criminality, violence, and sexism in commercial rap. McLeod worries that "hip hop is sometimes stereotyped to be gangster, to be crime ridden, to be people in jail, to be something that's threatening: And those are some of the stereotypes our salespeople have dealt with, our announcers have dealt with. Some of the community has reflected on us that way."[93] Racially inflected genre associations are carried in this concern; the very reliance on a neoliberal structure—the station has little public funding so must sell ads to survive—is part of the economic system that forces the mainstreaming of sound in order to turn a profit. Misperceptions trouble the CEO, as he sees these stereotypes as potentially damaging to both the station's image and its bottom line. The stereotypes about which he worries connect back into anti-Blackness, other forms of racism, and anti-Indigenous biases that pervade the structure of the settler colonial state.

One strategy for clarifying subjective standards is to set up measurable limits. For example, music distributors may home in on a presence or absence of certain swear words and use this as a measure of whether to air songs. This is a strategy followed by the Federal Communications Commission (FCC) in the United States. The creation of a list of words deemed offensive is still a highly subjective process; listening for specific words risks ignoring the larger context in which the words are used. Still, this strategy has the appeal of being quantifiable. It is one that NCI has attempted, as demonstrated by its communications with the CRTC. As part of its application to the CRTC to change its broadcasting requirements, NCI "submitted that in many instances Canadian urban music is not intended for radio but rather for personal and club use, and that the lyrics in hip-hop music often include inappropriate language. As a result, many urban selections are not suitable for airplay."[94] In this passage, NCI connects "inappropriate" language as suitable for individual listening or airing in a club venue but not for radio broadcast. This fixes a location but does not answer for whom or to whom music might be appropriate or inappropriate.

McLeod shared a combination of personal preferences and ideas about audience that shapes his vision for music on the station within its regulatory environment. In the beginning, the station played a lot of what he calls "edgy" music, as part of a more open-door policy for new singles. The station became more discerning over time with new music because, he said, "What we found was that the consistency and the quality of the music plus some of the messaging we found to be negative at times, even songs that had to do with issues. You know, there's some music that has to do with Native issues in a positive aspect, while others may lean towards being negative in terms of drug use, disrespect towards women." McLeod sees these themes as better suited to "the hip hop fans' own listening habits" rather than for broadcast. He elaborated, "There's some that has to do with living life on the streets. It might have been sexist, it might have been demeaning to women, and we found that we agreed with that when we surveyed our audience and we began taking a lot of that out of the format. . . . Now . . . we want to play a larger role in the community. We want to be family orientated so a family could listen to us. So we began making some major changes."[95] McLeod acknowledges that songs about issues relevant to Indigenous communities may have a "positive aspect," yet all of these songs that dealt with community concerns in a realist light were slated for removal early on in the station's lifetime. In the station's early days, staff weeded out some songs that related to gang activity or violence. These songs, which McLeod describes as having negative content, were the first cuts from a more open policy that included much local music. Then, staff listened for other kinds of content that might be controversial. There was concern about topicality referring to history and current political realities in the Native community. As a result, some Indigenous conscious or message hip hop was excluded from CIUR. Professionals make decisions on content on the basis of a variety of factors including their understanding of the CRTC's enforcement of the Broadcasting Act and Radio Regulations and the sometimes nebulous standards of decency to which they are held.

CIUR, like other broadcasters, faces the difficulty of making decisions about what exactly might be objectionable, whom it should use as the standard for the imagined audience with standards of taste, and whether it should or can differentiate between songs that respond to difficult lived realities and those that hyperbolize them. Hip hop's ability to deal head-on with conflict is part of what can make it appealing. During Leonard Sumner's rap career, he has discussed the appeal of rap, especially gangsta rap, for Anishinaabeg artists. He reflected, "People feel like there's something against them all the time, that there's racism, that the police treat us differently. . . . It's almost like N.W.A. in the early '90s. That's Winnipeg now, and instead of Black people it's Native people."[96] Borrowing from a gangsta musical type allows for artists and listeners to respond to racism and police violence. Importantly, as traced by critics such as Rinaldo Walcott, responses to anti-Black police violence are also found in Canadian rap and related genres. Hear, for example, the connections that the rapper Devon draws in lyrics between the Royal Canadian Mounted Police (RCMP) and Los Angeles Police Department (LAPD) or his rapped directives to police to stop shooting young people, in his most famous single, "Mr. Metro."[97] Amid anti-Black racism and stereotypes against Indigenous men and womxn, musical vocabulary—and the corresponding musical and situational connections—can elicit concern from broadcasters about how they think the music will be perceived. In this case, broadcasters worry about how the music will publicly present Winnipeg's urban Indigenous community—and the sometimes-overlapping categories of Indigenous musicians and Black musicians—to a wider public.

Presenting this subtlety through music distribution is not a straightforward process. Failure to present rap with a wide range of lyrical topicality and depth of content, however, can play into images of hip hop musicians and fans as simplistic. As a hip hop performer and radio personality, Sannie is invested in demonstrating "that hip hop people aren't dumb." He has spoken about racism, including white audience members wearing appropriative and caricatured dress at shows. Sannie expresses that special weight is placed on Black Canadians and that he feels pressure as a rapper and as a Black professional. He explains that it is important for young listeners especially to know that rap musicians can be smart: "I want everyone who's listening to know that you are a smart person, you are an interesting person. . . . You're allowed to talk about genome breakthroughs or whatever as long as it's interesting." This derives in part, he says, from working in schools. He explains, "I was working with a lot of kids that didn't really have the highest self-esteem, and . . . I want everybody to know, I take hip hop very seriously and I'm very passionate about it." This is part of a larger effort against negative images of rappers and rap fans as brash but substantively empty: "I think it's sad that people think we're kind of like a one-shot, or a one-trick pony, loud and in your face or whatever. There are a lot of really smart great qualities about people involved in the music, people that listen to the music."[98]

While CRTC policies outline expectations for programming that will not violate community standards of decency, the specifics are hard to pin down. Policies have changed over time. CRTC policy for broadcasters regarding profanity, sexually explicit material, and objectionable material can lack clarity.[99] Despite this, the CRTC expects that stations will provide listener warnings if they do intend to broadcast potentially offensive content. Complaints to the commission have focused on broadcasts that filers worried were offensive, sexual, or inappropriate for children yet played during hours when children may be listening.[100] Commercial broadcasters also adhere to the CBSC codes. Rhythm publicly proclaims to follow the standards of the CBSC. Displayed on its official website after the station change, the broadcaster highlighted a "Code of Ethics" section, which states, "Rhythm 104.7 FM reserves full rights to ensure that all commercial and programming content is in accordance with the Canadian Broadcast Standards Council code of ethics."[101]

Broadcasters need to keep track of standards, obligations, and requirements set out by parliamentary legislation, enforced by the CRTC, and expanded on by other policies that the CRTC has the ability to put into practice.[102] Because of this complexity, the perception that radio broadcasters have about their regulatory environment and how this influences their programming overshadows the decisions that a lawyer might make about requirements in a given case. An individual broadcaster might hold its station to a stricter or looser standard of decency on the basis of its perception of radio policy or might use its own ideas about decency, as regulatory bodies can be vague in this regard.

When I asked Sannie if he received complaints about violent content or sexual content in the music on-air, he replied, "I used to get it quite a bit." He explained that some of his friends and personal acquaintances were surprised about music on-air whose lyrics were misogynist or sexual in an over-the-top manner. Sannie describes the CIUR atmosphere as one that is open with regard to musical style but that aims to limit "distasteful" lyrical topicality. Because a diversity of musical styles are heard in twenty-first-century hip hop, Sannie finds that "the gloves are off. Anything goes nowadays. It's more the content that will get you." Rather than adherence to a specific subgenre of music, he articulates, this means simply "whether you're swearing or not: There is one song we played before. . . . We stopped playing it. I remember the first time I heard it, I was just like, no. Swears or not, that's just not something that I felt comfortable playing. So first step was we moved it out of my time slot, and it came up a couple times in the evening, and now it's out of the system. . . . It was just a super graphic song. It's distasteful."[103]

Sannie's own judgments of appropriate lyrical topicality are impacted by his knowledge of the station's audience. Listeners seeking a hip hop radio station in the Winnipeg market have scant options. While some other stations, such as UMFM, include hip hop in block programming, CIUR is the default choice for a radio format that plays urban music all day. The station's music may be playing in public places, including schools; Sannie is aware of and feels responsible to a young audience: "Even before I started working here, one of the schools I was working at, . . . towards lunch, we'd have to give them [Sannie's students] a solid half an hour of floor hockey or something to burn off some energy, and they loved listening to Streetz during that time. And I didn't really think much of it, but how many kids and young people are listening all the time? Because if you like hip hop, this is the station you listen to." He says he doesn't want to "police" music, but "if we're not playing your favorite song, upload it to your YouTube account and make a whole playlist and do that or get satellite. But there's certain things you don't wanna hear."[104] Here, Sannie's preferences about lyrical topicality that is tasteful enough for air, CRTC guidelines regarding what stations can play during daytime hours without content warnings, and his concern for how the station could influence young listeners all contribute to the musical content he wants during his afternoon show. CRTC enforcement and CBSC codes affect radio programming, but perceptions about what these regulations are have an even greater impact on the music that is circulated.

Broadcasters often voluntarily impose standards of perceived appropriateness that are not directly required by the CRTC. This influences the type of content played during and beyond daytime hours. On-air DJs are conscious of profanity when selecting local content, as would be expected given the regulatory environment. Yet neither the station nor the CRTC has a clear line for regulating material, particularly song lyrics, that may be perceived as overly sexually explicit, misogynist, politically volatile, or otherwise negatively charged. As a result, much of what stays on the station parallels commercial music on CHR stations. Conspicuous consumption and misogyny are more likely to get a pass, while actively politicized messaging, such as that related to specific causes in the public eye, may get flagged as objectionable.

## Creating and Reflecting Changing Listenerships

A station that needs to build commercial ad sales into its business model would reasonably look to stations that are bringing in ad dollars for models of what can attract listeners. Focus groups show that some existing listeners enjoy what they call Top 40 radio, which suggests that it could be useful to incorporate more CHR programming into an overall station sound. Comments like McLeod's about music that sounds the "best" or most commercial, Miss Melissa's remarks about mainstream music, and Sannie's discussion of commercially successful programming reveal two important concepts in the crafting of a music strategy that depicts the urban Indigenous music community in specific ways: the idea of "mainstream" and the idea of "community." Artists are characterized and audiences constructed in specific categories through the use of these terms.[105] In the music industry, the label "mainstream" is generally "associated with hits, stars, and corporate production."[106] Taking a cue from CHR stations and programs such as *American Top 40*, recordings are more likely to play on radio when they fit the existing standards, lyrically and sonically, of music already in the mainstream.[107] The examples from Leonard Sumner's output discussed in chapter 2 demonstrated how, even within the music of a single artist, songs that better fit existing standards enjoy more broadcast plays. For radio that relies on sponsors and advertisers, the form and style of this music must fit into the existing schema for stations to turn a profit. Commercial rap material is generally most desirable for airplay when it fits with standard structure and is deemed both nonalienating in lyrics and accessible in musical sound. This fits the rough three-minute length with verse-chorus form, with extended songs and remixes being reserved for alternate formats or late-night broadcast. For professionals at CIUR, the word "mainstream" overlaps in usage with the word "commercial"; it also tends to signify "non-Indigenous." Miss Melissa's use of "mainstream" sometimes even slides into "commercial mainstream" music.

Radio broadcasters attempt to fix a "community" in order to be able to target or serve a particular audience. This is a difficult process, as defining a community is contentious. The groups of people and even individual identities involved are fluid; even self-described communities change over time, and individuals may belong to multiple communities at once. Yet, in order to make choices about which music to air, which events to participate in, and how to shape a station's image, radio professionals must thoughtfully construct an imagined audience. This notion of community is often geographical, particularly in the case of radio, which has a distribution area that is fixed by the station's wattage. Radio stations like CIUR expand their distribution through online streaming. At the same time, the city that airs the program and provides the on-air talent and station staff forms the station's geographic center. Beyond geography, additional criteria for "community" membership for broadcasters may include "commonalities in age, education level, ethnic background, gender, and special interests."[108] The "community" may also reflect a perception of shared goals or values.[109] As with the focus groups, station staff focused on two kinds of "community": the "general" community and an Indigenous community. Internally to the station, the unmarked term "community" refers to a local Indigenous community, while marked versions of the term refer to other group constructions. For example, McLeod explains, "There's the community connection there. Paul is a First Nations comedian, and he's on the morning show. And he makes people laugh. And MJ who is part of the Black community, so the diversity is there, and the humor is there. And it's a point of community pride."[110] While simultaneously referencing multiple constructions of "community," McLeod again refers to the potential for the station to court a Black audience as well as an Indigenous audience and uses the unmarked word "community" to mean Indigenous listeners. These are overlapping groups, and they also intersect with a Filipinx listenership courted by the station.

Broadcasters, including CIUR, both create and reflect their listenerships, as chapter 2 outlined. The urban-format radio station uses signifiers of the city in its branding; visual and sonic markers of hip hop culture simultaneously reference urban location and USAmerican cultural expressions. Positioned from within a Native-licensed station, some conversations about Black listeners and Back music professionals suggest that these audience members and cultural producers add something to the city's hip hop station. In the exchange just quoted, McLeod suggests that MJ, a Black radio DJ, adds "diversity" to CIUR. A propensity to hold racialized listenerships as discrete categories is common in the radio industry, yet it collapses lived realities.[111] This move occludes individuals and groups of mixed Black and Indigenous and/or Latinx or Asian Canadian heritage; it downplays the cross-referencing of Afro-diasporic and Latinx and Indigenous musical expressions that have been occurring since before hip hop began. These categorizations also minimize intersections of gender and race among listening publics, a topic that will be taken up in further detail in chapter 4. The branding shift over time reflects the implicit awareness that Streetz is crafting the aural perception that listeners have of their neighbors, which has larger implications for relationships between listeners across racial and ethnic lines; the stakes are incredibly high.

The songs easiest to fit onto commercial-sounding broadcast, as well as other industry formats such as award shows and headlining stage shows, are those that conform to existing sound expectations. Musical examples in this chapter, "The Takeover" and "Electric 49," take cues from these sonic expectations. In mainstream hip hop, this extends beyond high production values and sound quality, the three-minute format, and lyrical topicality on a set range of topics. These expectations are raced; Indigenous artists often borrow tropes of USAmerican sonic Blackness, particularly in Canadian settings where Indigenous urban people are racialized in similar ways to Black, and sometimes Latinx, Americans. Artists may well be speaking from realities of their lives— sharing, for example, lived experiences with racism, resource disparity, illicit commerce, and gang culture. Yet it would be naïve to imagine that music professionals are unaware of how these images and stories circulate in hip hop, particularly that which can access a mainstream audience.

These tropes and stereotypes, circulated through musical performance, are at the core of settler colonialism. When a rapper projects the image of the hypermasculine, sometimes armed, sexually potent, and/or impoverished (though possibly accessing capital through drug or other illicit trade), these stereotypes risk flattening the range of possibility for how artists of color can be heard.[112] At times, artists play into what is expected—trying to access an Indigenous audience or playing music that listeners who are not steeped in a particular tradition may hear *as* Native. As musician Chase Manhattan described in chapter 1, a creative team may look for intertribally recognized sonic signifiers in order to speak across the wide variety of music practiced by internally diverse Native North American communities. The effects of playing into certain signifiers (e.g., powwow music cues, drum beats, and flute samples) or gesture and topicality (e.g., racially coded language and themes common in commercial rap music) can both recirculate old tropes and function as a strategy for audibility in a crowded soundscape in which the hegemonic ear is trained to hear only certain sounds.

With regard to audience feedback, listener communications conducted for CIUR polled the station's aspirational audience about their musical preferences and interests. For station professionals, this offered an opportunity to create the listenership the staff hoped to attract based on the music and commentary that the station produces. Approximately seventy people participated in the group discussions that were subdivided into three separate events, with plans in place for additional groups over time. The "general" audience group included Indigenous listeners as well as "the Black community and the Filipino community"; a more specific constituency included what McLeod calls "the up and comers," which includes current college, university, and graduate students.[113]

For the name change from Streetz to Rhythm, the station gradually released information to listeners. In spite of these efforts, listeners I spoke with who were not affiliated with the station expressed some confusion about the unusual music on the station during the shift from Streetz to Rhythm, as well as the reason for the switch afterward. Some were even unaware that Rhythm was connected to Streetz, a confusion that was also reflected on social media.

NCI tried to incorporate elements of CHR that leadership thought would bolster listenership at CIUR. With the rebrand from Streetz to Rhythm, the station attempted to court more "mainstream" listeners. To do this, it walked a fine line between keeping hip hop and Indigenous-specific content, while broadening the station's scope. This attempt at balance was expressed on social media at the time of the branding change: "The station is owned by Native Communications Incorporated (NCI), as a manager it was the goal of our team, to successfully swap the former hip-hop format with what we call 'rhythmic hits.' To date, Music Director, Melissa Spence has added over 3000 songs that includes everything from dance, R&B, throwback hits and electronic dance music. Rhythm 104.7 is a big supporter of Canadian music, Indigenous artists and the incredible talent that exists within the diverse cultures of our city."[114]

This branding change includes support for "Indigenous artists" on the new station, even though these musicians are not prominently featured on the webpage. It contrasts the term "rhythmic hits" with "hip hop." However, three of the four kinds of music included in "rhythmic hits" are typically played on urban-format radio stations, which is consistent with Streetz. In this sense, the branding change was more severe than changes in music programming. While social media messages like these would not reach all radio listeners, those who stream online saw the new station page, and radio hosts on-air pushed listeners to connect to the station's new social media presences at the start of the transition. Yet feelings of loss and questions raised by listeners lead to a wider inquiry. Within regulatory structures and market pressures, can broadcast radio act as an adequate medium for artists to convey an ample range of aesthetic and political expressions?

## Sonic Indigeneity and the Mainstream

Listening through sonic sovereignty, we can ask, How is it possible to use broadcast and streaming radio to present music made on Anishinaabeg terms, on Métis terms, on Indigenous terms? What are the material and imaginative conditions that would facilitate expansion beyond European-derived standards for music performance in highly standardized and commercially driven media circulation formats? On the one hand, there is a space created through interaction with mainstream media players in which Indigenous actors are making and distributing contemporary music. This music acts as an extension of culturally grounded production from a historical lineage. New expressions are created in dialogue between Indigenous actors and industry professionals, some of whom are non-Indigenous. Something forward-looking, something contemporary, and something old that reaches back before broadcast radio is created and re-created. On the other hand, in mainstream venues, it can be a struggle to present musical performance that maintains, for example, an Anishinaabeg sensibility for a mixed Anishinaabeg, Indigenous non-Anishinaabeg, and non-Indigenous audience. Through sonic sovereignty, artists assert a frame of reference and insist that it should be respected. Like legal sovereignty, it may be respected or not, but the people expressing it are already sovereign. Decolonial projects come from what Bonita Lawrence and Enakshi Dua call "talking on Indigenous terms" and consistently recognize the reality of ongoing Indigenous sovereignty.[115]

With this frame, one way to interpret changes at Streetz is that as the station moved toward a more "mainstream" sound, some of what made it special was lost. Its appeal came in part from its local sound, from its willingness to air new artists, and from its ability to reflect a mixed Indigenous audience, all qualities that hit-format radio and broad-based public programming alike fail to present. Many of the decisions the broadcaster made, however, are understandable in the circumstances. Station staff hosted focus groups, listened to what other streaming and broadcast channels were offering, and made plans based on revenue needs. Media landscapes are changing, and online distribution channels impact what audiences hear. In Canada, the United States, and globally, however, the established players continue to impact who is heard. Real people's listening habits show that broadcast radio still matters.

## Emerging Musicians for Emerging Audiences

Streetz listeners and staff alike have pointed to radio's key role in another area that is not going away: developing new artists. As a Native-licensed station, Streetz played a crucial role in inspiring, supporting, distributing, and celebrating up-and-coming Indigenous musicians. Groups that support emerging artists will be crucial to the future of Indigenous sonic sovereignty. Streetz's support of A Tribe Called Red is illustrative of how it can take early exposure from sympathetic ears to launch Indigenous musicians into mainstream circulation. There are many more stories of musicians who have found increasing professional success in part through the promotion and support provided by a constellation of Indigenous arts and media organizations.

This confluence of organizations extends past markers of genre. Whereas broadcasters hew to a set format and deliver content within an expected range of genres, Indigenous music labels, collaborative arts spaces, awards programs, and even funders need not maintain such rigid categories. Many organizations even offer funding in multidisciplinary projects that connect music with dance, theater, visual arts, and other media. This potential for genre flexibility is already sounding in mainstream venues. And these mainstream venues are being changed by the sonic force of Indigenous popular music. Between 2008 and 2018, four winners of the flagship Polaris Prize have been Indigenous musicians, and all four of those were in or after 2014.[116] All of them play with sound in a manner that exceeds traditional pop genre categorizations. For example, Jeremy Dutcher won the Polaris Music Prize on September 17, 2018. The operatically trained singer and piano player learned his own Wolastoqey language and worked carefully with archival recordings of songs from his home community. Elements of opera, singer-songwriter pop, and the crackle of historical antiquarian recording technologies all intermix in his aesthetic. He won the prestigious award for his debut album, *Wolastoqiyik Lintuwakonawa*, an impressive feat that is no doubt due to his skill as a vocalist, pianist, and composer and his creative approach to integrating archival songs. His developing career has also been supported by groups dedicated to getting Indigenous voices heard. In 2017, he developed a new composition with the Winnipeg-based vocal group Camerata Nova, an ensemble that intentionally collaborates with Indigenous composers.[117] His music circulated on RPM.fm, a web-based music-promotion site dedicated to sharing and celebrating Indigenous musicians. His songs were distributed because of the establishment of RPM's record label, which describes itself as "a new label dedicated to promoting innovative, genre-crossing, and contemporary Indigenous music."[118] He was part of the New Constellations tour, which brought Indigenous and non-Indigenous artists together in concerts and workshops in front of intentionally integrated audiences. And of course, he learned from his own elders, carefully studying language with elder and song-carrier Maggie Paul.

Other histories of support show similar patterns. Tanya Tagaq has worked for years to reach listeners and has been bolstered by the artist-centered Six Shooter Records, Indigenous- and Indigenous-feminist-focused performance tours, and collaborations with arts organizations and universities that actively cultivate positive working relationships with Indigenous artists. A frequent cross-genre collaborator, she has worked with groups such as The Halluci Nation. Her version of throat singing is in line with the heritage practice of her Inuit community, though she herself learned from cassette tapes. Her music incorporates punk rock aesthetics and performance art stylization and creatively folds in live electronics and sometimes also video projections. Support networks that augment talented voices have real effects on how—and whether—musicians reach listeners. This support has significant implications for the future of Indigenous sonic sovereignty.

Continuously articulating sovereignty is part of a demand for recognition, even as self-definition, self-determination, and land rights have never gone away. Music that circulates sonic sovereignty demands changing ways of being, moving, and sounding in the world: a shift from paternalist regulations and destructive assimilationist policies toward a strategy of copresence. Experiences with regulatory systems, including the ways in which people experience the force of these systems, shape what is heard and by whom. CIUR was not the force that created a long-term commercially viable mix of hit radio and Indigenous hip hop. But it was a force that supported and amplified voices of Indigenous artists in hip hop and related genres, and with other Native-focused groups and media actors, Streetz has been a part of a shift in the mainstream Canadian sound. It is a shift that is still ongoing, and it is not yet clear how this new mainstream will flow or precisely where it is headed. The top-down (and internally self-referential) Top 40 format may not be the most likely one for expanding Indigenous audibility, but other people and groups are creating a variety of avenues for making and distributing boundary-pushing music. Artists working in and through these deepening channels express sonic sovereignty as they innovate, re-member, and insist on being heard.

The movement to possession, from subject to object, that underpins settler colonial logics is expressed on Black and Brown bodies. The ways in which heteropatriarchy is integrated in a mainstream commercial hip hop industry are necessarily linked to the ways that heteropatriarchy is inextricable from racialized and gendered violence. There are groups—including broadcasters, programs, labels, award shows, and arts organizations—that support Indigenous artists specifically, and their significance should not be understated.[119] In response to artists being shut out of mainstream venues, these groups help develop talent, get artists recognized, and widen their scope of influence. And sometimes, they help catapult artists into mainstream recognition. Many people who are now attracting this kind of success have had significant support along the way, often from their own Indigenous communities as well as from groups focused on Indigenous music promotion.

Listening through sonic sovereignty, it is possible to identify people creating alternative pathways, new organizations being developed, existing ones adapting to better support Indigenous composers and performers, and artists doing the hard work of using these supports to share their sounds. Yet some musicians—Indigenous musicians in general and Indigenous female and nonbinary musicians in particular—face steeper barriers to audibility and must create workarounds because the system as set up does not adequately serve them. The realities of the biases in both the current structures and the systems created to supplement the biased system leave room for improvement.

From the folding of Streetz, it becomes clear that good-faith efforts to pair marketability with Indigenous audibility meet barriers, face those barriers, adapt, and sometimes, go silent. Artists and media distributors face a mainstream that still does not always hear Indigenous music as already central to it. It is also clear that radio play still matters; consumers across international borders and age categories listen to music on the radio. As gatekeepers, broadcasters convey a sense of legitimacy in music and musicians that they choose and thus attribute a lesser value to music they do not choose. This has financial implications: the loss of broadcast venues for artists and host opportunities for media professionals has a real impact in the lives of creative workers who lose a platform, royalties, and job opportunities.

The depth of experiences of loss at the end of a single broadcaster demonstrate that, on Streetz and in other venues, being on-air matters. Accessing listening publics matters to artists and media professionals. Yet this potential for being heard is not enough. As this chapter has explored, the ways in which music is presented for potential listening and the ability for musicians to make choices about their own presentation and about what to play and not play are all crucial, and sometimes underappreciated, next steps beyond simply vibrating the airwaves. Without radio that actively listens for and airs urban music genres by Indigenous artists, the playing field continues to not be level. And yet, as in the definitions of sovereignty articulated and expanded by Rickard and Simpson, paying attention solely to the mainstream continues a limiting myopia. The Halluci Nation, Wab Kinew, Jon-C, Jeremy Dutcher, Tanya Tagaq, Inez Jasper—all of these artists have navigated multiple ways of making and sharing music. Dutcher, for example, started learning in his community from his elders and from archival recordings. He did research, sang, studied music at university, and collaborated with Indigenous and non-Indigenous musicians to start creating new works. His music found an audience as he did interviews and distributed his music online and on the air, and he used what are now considered alternative venues to get heard.

Sonic sovereignty starts in community, works through collaboration, and navigates media circulation to access a platform for national and international listenership. Just as Indigenous sovereignty is more than a takeover of European-derived juridical forms, it does not simply replicate a mainstream music industry for Indigenous artists. As a strategy, sonic sovereignty adapts to unique needs and visions. Musicians do not have to reproduce all of the same problems of the inherited mainstream music industry, though this takes careful critical attention. The future can be more than the old mainstream with a new face. It can be a way to listen and be heard that expands audibility for everyone.

Chapter 4 addresses limitations of this model, particularly those faced by artists whose music does not translate into mainstream formats for political and aesthetic reasons. It further explores silencing and willful mishearing, focusing primarily on ways in which artists are taking control of their listenerships under challenging circumstances. The end of Streetz as a broadcast space was coterminous with multiple new avenues for listening. The local rebranded station Rhythm offered some options to the Winnipeg broadcast listenership, as well as a much broader streaming audience. As streaming platforms continued to expand in listenership after 2014, these avenues, too, provide spaces in which mainstream and alternative sounds dialogue with, and change, each other. While Streetz primarily focused on broadcasting, its role as a studio for small live performances and a sponsor for in-person concerts demonstrates how inextricably linked performance and distribution are. As artists and other music professionals take charge of their self-definitions and craft their audiences, these concert spaces again enter into the conversation about media distribution.

4

# This Music Is Not for You

*Humor, Rage, and Hip Hop*

Outside the stadium, a red carpet lines the sidewalk. Velour ropes separate the walkway from the rest of the sidewalk on which fans have gathered. The pathway winds from a spot just west of the corner where cars drop off guests to the entry of the stadium. A camera crew runs up and down, documenting the arrival of nominees and leaders to be broadcast on Aboriginal Peoples Television Network (APTN). Photographers snap pictures as well, contributing to the atmosphere of celebrity. Each group of VIP guests stops and answers questions from two smiling hosts. Some appear very polished; others respond quietly or seemingly surprised by questions about fashion or the event. The pre-show coverage is live on television and the web on APTN, and a crowd of onlookers watches from the street. On the sidewalk, audience members snap their own photos and consult the program while waiting. This event is about more than just the musicians winning awards: community leaders arrive on the red carpet, as do leaders from the powwow and festival Manito Ahbee.

Inside the stadium, the seats on the floor start to fill in. The arena is set up for a show, with a giant stage taking over one end of the space. The stage is dark before filming begins. With an eye toward television optics, production staff start to ask ushers to move the audience into seats as close as possible to the stage for the filming. This gesture crystallizes how much this performance is created for television. The audience in the room is part of the optics for the APTN cameras, curated for maximum effect. Before the show begins, a warm-up announcer prepares the audience for our role as part of the show. For the filming, the on-screen announcer appears, participating in a variety of bits, telling jokes in short sketches between performances and awards. As the audience, we appear on camera as well, both on the large screens on the sides of the

Figure 4.1. Drezus being interviewed on the red carpet outside the award show. (Photo by author)

stage and on the television channel and website that broadcasts into people's homes. The video crew moves smoothly, for example, focusing on a child seated in my row when an invited speaker talks at length about kids. From the moment when the first band emerges with flashing lights and fog, this is a stadium show, playing to the back rows of the space. The venue transforms temporarily only for the grand entry, as dancers enter the space to a very different sonic background and atmosphere.

Absent the grand entry grounding moment, the Indigenous Music Awards (IMAs), filmed and broadcast from Bell MTS Place in downtown Winnipeg, could almost be any music award show. Presenters follow their scripts, read their lines, and make a little space for awardees' acceptance speeches. Hosts heighten moments of drama: opening an envelope in preparation for a big reveal, holding the audience for a beat before the news hits. As in many awards shows, the high-profile awards that air live add drama and excitement to the evening: nominees are announced, and then the cameras find the winners, who deliver remarks that range from very prepared to delighted but off-the-cuff. The live musical performances and prerecorded video segments run according to a plan. The well-executed show is actively family-friendly, fun, and above all, polished for viewers at home watching on TV and online.

The mainstreaming of Indigenous popular music operates through connecting vectors. On the one hand, groups that foreground Indigenous aspects of their music have gained recognition in venues that were previously off-limits to them. Awards for Indigenous musicians moved from a rarity to a regularity at Polaris, a Canadian juried music prize awarded to one album each year in any genre. Increasing numbers of Indigenous musicians are winning Juno Awards in mainstream categories, which are awarded based both on sales data and on the votes of Canadian music industry judges. At the same time, structures that Indigenous music industry insiders initially set up in response to exclusions from mainstream-industry power structures have themselves become more mainstream. Indigenous media gain national and international attention. Indigenous, settler, newcomer, and mixed-heritage audiences pay attention to red-carpet events, such as the IMAs. The interaction between these forces creates a space of negotiation. Increased audience has brought risks of increased appropriative listening. Mainstreaming brings the prospect of additional financial rewards for musicians and management. It also brings potential softening of the political potential of music that is chosen, the nonchoosing of some repertoires, and pressure to conform to popular music conventions, as discussed in the previous chapters. This rapprochement both signals and creates a change in the mainstream itself, as music by Indigenous and mixed-heritage artists retunes popular sound. But not everyone is invited to, or chooses to, participate in the mainstreaming. As with the music industry more generally, female and gender-nonconforming artists, producers, and other professionals experience fewer supports and more barriers to participation. And some have responded to bias with strategic refusal.

The career trajectory of MC Eekwol intersects with, and influences, Indigenous hip hop as it has developed in present-day Canada. An active rapper in Saskatchewan in the 1990s, she was part of hip hop's development as people north of the Canada-US border created styles that were distinct from regional US-based scenes that emerged during that decade. Eekwol performed and recorded with Mils and performed alongside a sometimes-changing group of other rappers. She released a self-titled album in 1998 and a sophomore album in 1999. Throughout the 1990s, thematic and musical tropes from the mainstreamed versions of commercial US-based rap influenced international artists as regional and national styles formed. In the 2000s, Indigenous music industry structures and groups included hip hop by Indigenous artists in Canada. The Canadian Aboriginal Music Awards started a rap/hip hop category in 2001 (won not by Eekwol & Mils but by another group started in the 1990s, War Party). The awards ceremony had previously recognized some contemporary Indigenous music, such as rock and folk, alongside traditional recordings but did not have a rap category prior to this date.

The Aboriginal Peoples' Choice Music Awards, later rebranded as the Indigenous Music Awards, which I describe in this chapter's opening, began honoring rap/hip hop artists in the early 2000s as well, both through a dedicated category and by recognizing rappers, DJs, and producers as entertainers and music creatives. Podcasts and radio shows that included significant hip hop content came before audiences, such as *Think NDN* and *Ab-Originals*. And in 2008, Streetz got its license in Winnipeg; in 2009, it began broadcasting Indigenous hip hop music. During the next several years, Eekwol found a following outside of Saskatchewan. Her music aired on Streetz. She released five additional albums. These expanded her aesthetic footprint and included Cree language as the decade wore on. Eekwol, working with her brother, producer Mils, won the 2005 Canadian Aboriginal Music Award (Best Rap or Hip Hop Album) for *Apprentice to the Mystery*. In the 2010s, the Indigenous music industry saw some shifts: artists sought accolades from non-Indigenous-industry kingmakers, some of whom had previously felt out of reach. At the same time, some intentional tours and billings attempted to more openly attract settler, Indigenous, and mixed-heritage listeners. While fully separate audiences had always been a fiction, the marketing of these events reflected a post-apology moment. Eekwol released another album, *Good Kill*, in 2015. She has mentored and collaborated extensively with up-and-coming artists. Her 2018 release, a collaboration with T-Rhyme, was not written with awards shows, airplay, or playlisting in mind.

MCs Eekwol and T-Rhyme released *For Women By Women*, stylized as *FWBW*, as an album with eight tracks available as a digital download.

For *FWBW*, the rappers booked performances across Canada and the US, such as the sākihiwē festival in Winnipeg, the Regina Folk Festival, Megaphono in Ottawa, and Show and Prove in California. Both musicians have previously released and performed music that tells personal stories and responds to contemporary social realities, as is typical for many rappers. At times, this music responds to their lived experiences as women and particularly as women with Nehiyaw roots.[1] T-Rhyme also takes pride in her Denesuline roots. She grew up in northern Saskatchewan and later relocated to Saskatoon. Her music in the 2000s brings forward an old-school vibe; she frequently references 1990s rappers and cultural touchstones in her lyrics. Eekwol also lives and works in Saskatoon on Treaty 6 territory, and her family is from the Muskoday First Nation. Both musicians have performed throughout Canada and internationally. *FWBW*'s marked focus on being both by and for women is different from their previous work—at least in messaging. The rappers are clear that this is a joint project, not the start of a duo. It is one in which the musicians collaborate and specifically address their experiences as women across the tracks and during performances. It is also one in which they unabashedly state that the music is *for* women: they will not apologize that the music is not for everyone.

For musicians and audiences, it is important for some spaces to be dedicated to womxn.[2] The cypher Tribe Called Queenz, an earlier collaborative project in which T-Rhyme participated, is a case in point: it was created to support Indigenous womxn in particular. Other womxn have been buoyed by the space; non-Indigenous womxn have played roles in creating these productive artistic spaces. The reactions of audience members and media have revealed some of the expectations they hold about music that supports Indigenous womxn. When the four rappers of Tribe Called Queenz started performing together, T-Rhyme explained, some people assumed that all members were Indigenous, though one of the cofounders is white. T-Rhyme remembers that the cypher was focused on Native values and that everyone, including the non-Native rapper, was dedicated to creating a good community space. This attitude echoes the "for us." It is the work of being allies that created a cohesive project, not just heritage or upbringing. *FWBW*, too, is able to be heard because a variety of people work to support Indigenous womxn. As Eekwol puts it, "We're hoping that this project grows, because of allies."

Figure 4.2. Eekwol performing at Show & Prove 2018 Hip Hop Studies Conference, December 9, Riverside, CA. (Photo by Jonathan Godoy)

Figure 4.3. T-Rhyme performing at Show & Prove 2018 Hip Hop Studies Conference, December 9, Riverside, CA. (Photo by Jonathan Godoy)

T-Rhyme expands, "It'll be like a ripple effect."[3] Through their reflections and insights, readers hear how the work done by the "us" of this
project is at once personal and connected to community.[4] In this chapter, *FWBW* provides the case study that crystallizes an intersectional
analysis of power in popular music industries.

The popular music industry is structured in such a way as to amplify
insider voices and to deprivilege listening to creators and creations that
are too far from established norms. Of acute concern for articulating Indigeneity in popular music, this mainstream sound comes from a commercial orientation of recorded popular music, as described in chapter 1;
the financial and cultural pressures of hits-focused radio reinforce it,
as developed in chapters 2 and 3. The musical projects explored in this
chapter enter a popular music reality constrained by current power
structures, but their authors explore alternatives. Commercially oriented music is not always distinct from that which is understood to be
politically or community focused.[5] Building on the examples of Drezus,
Frank Waln, Inez, and Lorenzo explored in the first half of this book,
this chapter listens through music that urges recognition of an expansive
notion of sovereignty. Musical activity can call for more than just an acknowledgment of legal sovereignty through respect for Indigenous land
rights. Through sonic sovereignty, artists articulate their preexisting
rights to define their audiences, tell stories on their own terms, create
sovereign space through interactions with others, and maintain bodily
sovereignty. Musicians work to shape how they are heard, though they
are sometimes not listened to at all. Thus, a tension emerges between
structural exclusion, or the way in which Indigenous womxn artists face
barriers to being heard within a mainstream media industry, and strategic exclusivity, in which the artists make the choice not to cater to the
whole industry but to create their own listening publics. This tension
resurfaces in chapter 5, which explores the further implications of decolonial listening practices.

Using *FWBW* and live performances of the music as a point of
departure, this chapter asks what it means to make and circulate
music that is for womxn and by womxn. In a larger context in which
Indigenous artists and broadcasters navigate and renavigate musical mainstreams and their alternatives, music by and for women—
coming from Indigenous women, non-Indigenous female allies, and

nonbinary and gender-nonconforming allies—is faced with an industry tightrope. Musicians balance multiple goals and pressures to
walk this line, and sometimes, they choose to jump off. The *FWBW*
project connects with previous collaborations First Ladies Crew, an
all-women Indigenous cypher out of Vancouver, and Tribe Called
Queenz, an all-women Indigenous and non-Indigenous cypher
started in Saskatoon.[6] All of these projects emerge in a pop music reality in which female and trans* musicians continue to be largely underrepresented across the music industry. In this context, what might
it mean for music to be created for womxn and by womxn, and why is
such a project relevant in the twenty-first century? Popular musicians
often feel pressure to create something agreeable for the mainstream
ear; this chapter offers framing that builds on what Jennifer Stoever
calls the "sonic color line" to question what is possible when artists
acknowledge bias in a mainstream listenership and respond with various kinds of refusal, most notably in ways that challenge hierarchies
and pursue alternative structures. Rather than jockey for position in
a crowded pop field, these musicians forbid listening by those who
would have them silenced.[7] The MCs convey their message using hip
hop's twin powers of humor and rage. This chapter proceeds in two
parts. By undertaking an intersectional analysis of the power dynamics that surround this project, the chapter extends into other performance contexts, ultimately circling back to what makes the project
new—or not so new—to begin with. From frustration with racial bias
and heteropatriarchal conditions that had minimized the reach of Indigenous womxn's voices, the artists create music that is specifically
not to be heard by all.

As Audra Simpson explains, refusal is a political strategy. It stymies.
To refuse is more than to shut down; it can even reveal the (to some, formerly hidden) nature of that which was refused. Indigenous refusal can
take many forms: refusal to disappear, refusal to recognize the nation-
state, refusal to use a settler passport, refusal to pay taxes, ethnographic
refusal, and armed refusal.[8] For Simpson, refusal subverts settler colonial state policy directly when subjects insist on being seen and read
as citizens of Kahnawà:ke and refuse to accept the need to be seen as
citizens of the United States or Canada. Even as Mohawk people express

their sovereignty and insist on controlling group membership, she explains, "At times, though, their notion of nationhood is driven by their refusal of recognition, their refusal to be enfolded into state logics, and their refusal, simply, to disappear."[9] The possibilities of and tensions between recognition and refusal are applicable to situations beyond the use of passports and control of membership rolls. In the case of *FWBW* and other womxn's cyphers, musicians and audiences have created and re-created spaces that are tailored to their own needs. In the face of being shut out of some structures of support, including award shows, sometimes artists make the decision not to try to pry their way in but instead to create other spaces and structures in which they can share, build, and validate their own musical expression. Together with audiences, musicians intent on circulating these messages access power by making their own spaces and, in them, refusing to disappear.

In this chapter, I follow Simpson's use of refusal, finding that musicians say no in their cyphers and projects as a form of generative refusal. Synthesized with what José Esteban Muñoz calls a "critical hope," this is a strategic and forward-thinking no, an "active refusal and a salient demand for something else."[10] To refuse that which is, in the neoliberal music industry, so heavily sought after—an audience that will pay—provides a moment of interruption. Instead of accepting a paying audience at any cost, musicians insist on asking questions first. Who is paying? What do they think they are paying for? What kinds of control—creative, political, bodily—is being asked of performers, even by entertaining the notion of this audience? In hip hop cyphers and projects by female artists, musicians name and cultivate participation by women, girls, nonbinary, trans*, and two-spirit people. *For Women By Women* allows for an exploration of what becomes possible when musicians specifically do not include men in their cultivated listenership—they refuse. Some listeners have pointed out that those who are not invited to listen could continue to do so anyway. This is true and is part of the point: *FWBW* and womxn's cyphers are not attempts to re-create structural, cultural, interpersonal, and disciplinary barriers in such a way that they would limit men's access to hip hop. Creating music for, and also with, a particular audience instead makes space for generative activity that is aligned with musicians' goals.

## Who Are "Women"?

The use of the category "women" opens up questions about terminology. For some listeners, this term may seem like it reifies a gender binary. Musicians in *FWBW*, Tribe Called Queenz, and First Ladies Crew frequently use gender-expansive language, bringing in trans*, two-spirit, and nonbinary individuals.[11] The English language is limited in this regard: there is no concise word for women (specifically referencing all who identify as women and not just those who are sex-assigned female at birth), two-spirit, nonbinary, agender, and gender-nonconforming people. This limitation is part of the ongoing effect of colonization. Eekwol identifies that a rigid gender binary came with colonization and English: "There was no him or her in our Cree language." The Cree words iskwew (ᐃᔥᑫᐤ) and napew (ᓇᐯᐤ) are descriptive words translated as "woman" and "man," but as Eekwol explains, "in Cree, a lot of the words are so descriptive that it's hard to translate into English. . . . In the language, those terms were only used specifically when needed."

The entire project, which creates space for womxn, could seem retrogressive. I have seen some raised eyebrows about a project that centers on the idea of "women" in the twenty-first century. Isn't a gender binary and a separate space, I have heard, something that was left behind in the second half of the twentieth century? This viewpoint is itself a situated one. There have been several moves toward women's spaces in popular music specifically. In response to women's underrepresentation on mainstream labels, women-owned record labels and management have created their own structures within the industry. In the United States and Canada, there was a flourishing of these in the 1970s and into the 1980s, including in lesbian separatist circles.[12] Some of these spaces were primarily white, others were headed by Latina or Black artists, and some were more racially mixed. However, the majority of the performers in these spaces were non-Indigenous. In Indigenous communities, women-only spaces did not rise so dramatically, or disappear, in the 1980s and 1990s. Intertribal events have held a place for girls' and women's music and dance; singing and drumming continues to be taught within groups of women in some Nehiyaw and other Plains and Woodlands Indigenous cultural spaces. Speaking to womxn in this context becomes part of a strategic effort to choose audience and to increase the likelihood of being truly listened to.

The album *FWBW*, and the approach it represents, does not stop at being *for* women; it is also unapologetically *by* women. In one sense, the idea of being "by" women can be read narrowly: this is a project that has been completed by two female-identified performers. Their gender identification is far from tangential to the project, as the intersectional analysis illuminates—their experiences as women in the music industry cannot be separated from experiences of erasure and bias, as well as joy, that motivated the project. While accurate, this straightforward conceptualization of "by women" does not encompass all of the meanings of the phrase. Being "by women" is a way both to make space for other womxn's experiences and to provide the MCs opportunities to investigate what it means to them for a project to be *by* women. Eekwol and T-Rhyme are both clear that this project stems from not just their experience but that of other womxn.

> EEKWOL: We're saying 'For Women By Women' because we're speaking English and for lack of better terms. . . . But it's definitely not specific to a small category of who constitutes women. So it's kind of like for us, by us.
>
> T-RHYME: Yeah it's FUBU!

On the title song "For Women By Women," like Solange's 2016 song "F.U.B.U.," the musicians own their authorship and speak directly because they are aware of the unequal power dynamics around them. Solange speaks to anti-Black violence, explaining that she "felt like society acted in fear of Black people and how that automatically escalates into violent, awful experiences along with the demonization of Black men and women." In the song, she reads through the symbolism of the brand FUBU, a commercial venture that "exhibited Blackness . . . on a huge global level," using its connection back to the "Us" of Black creatives, she explains, "because I wanted to empower."[13] Naming their audiences and claiming their own authorship, Eekwol and T-Rhyme, like Solange, speak to racialized gender hierarchies.

The motivation for *FWBW* imbues every aspect of the project. When the album was digitally released, T-Rhyme announced in a public post

Figure 4.4. *FWBW* album cover; album art by Joi T. Arcand. (Spotify, https://open
.spotify.com/album/opuxhTjyXHzZydMAV5tBqF)

on Facebook, "This project was birthed by wonder, excitement, frustration, fear, laughter, tears, happiness and most importantly LOVE. We
did this not only for our own healing, but for every single woman, girl,
mother, daughter, grandmother, aunty, cousin and friend out there to
unapologetically accept. This project is for us all 👊 🔥 💜."[14] The post
linked to the album on Spotify and iTunes.

Without apologies, T-Rhyme writes a generationally expansive post,
amplified by a raised brown fist, fire, and love emojis. Fire has become
an ongoing image of power for the MC, as she has come to understand her power as an Indigenous woman. By strategically excluding

unsympathetic listeners, the artists are creating a supportive listening public. When the three of us discuss *FWBW* together after one of the performances, Eekwol grounds the conversation, and the album, in whom the work is for. She explains, "The first song is 'For Women By Women.' You know it's really for us by us." T-Rhyme affirms, and Eekwol continues, "We literally continuously asked ourselves throughout the whole project who are we doing this for. And it is for predominantly those that are oppressed, which happens to be mostly women: violence, missing and murdered, all of those experiences that are *us*, that are—that we're living in at the time right now." This expansive "us" brings in individual women who are left out of other social polities; the formation and leveraging of an "us" critically brings to light the continuing effects of settler colonialism. Indigenous women and girls are murdered and disappear at rates significantly higher than non-Indigenous women in the United States and Canada.[15] As singers and listeners pay attention to missing and murdered women and girls, it further becomes clear what gender-based violence indicates on a structural level: as Audra Simpson argues, Indigenous women "have *historically* been rendered less valuable because of what they are taken to represent: land, reproduction, Indigenous kinship and governance, an alternative to heteronormative and Victorian rules of descent."[16] Through Eekwol and T-Rhyme's "us," attending to women who experience gender-based violence offers care that is necessary because the lives of individual women are valuable.

This "us" can make space for a variety of people who understand what it is like to experience unequal treatment and who are open to hearing musicians' message. Their address, however, is unapologetic: they are not catering to anyone. As Eekwol elaborates, "We're not trying to please." Because women and girls are often raised to please others, this gendered refusal carries particular power. Listening to this music requires more than just opening one's ears; witnessing the message requires action. T-Rhyme explains, "If you stand with us, then you *stand with us*. And if you don't like it, it's not for you." She repeats, and Eekwol echoes, "It's not for you." The MCs point to commitment as that which will solidify the listenership: those who truly want to listen will be those who will ally themselves with the musicians.

## Gender, Race, and Listening

In *The Sonic Color Line*, Jennifer Stoever builds on W. E. B. Du Bois's notion of the visible color line and identifies how a mainstream listening ear marks voices, sounds, and soundscapes based on raced and gendered assumptions. As Stoever explains, "white-constructed ideas about 'sounding Other'—accents, dialects, 'slang,' and extraverbal utterances, as well as ambient sounds—have flattened the complex range of sounds actually produced by people of color."[17] Limitations too are placed on musical expressions of voices interpreted as female, and "sexism disciplines the cultural meanings attached to perceived gendered differences in the voice, impacting expressions of race and sexuality."[18] Asymmetrical relationships and regimes of value are enacted through listening practices. Indigenous female artists, like the musicians of color in Stoever's analysis, are not heard in their fullness. The continued forcing into the straitjacket of modernity versus tradition underscores this problem. Musicians heard as pop artists may not also be heard as Indigenous individuals who are well versed in their musico-cultural traditions; those who continue to practice heritage music and dance or speak their First Languages are not always taken seriously as contemporary pop artists.[19] When language, speech patterns, tones of voice, sounds, and particularly for Native musicians, instrumental timbres and patterns must fit a coerced range of options in order to sound "Native," Indigenous artists are faced with limitations to their creativity.

Listening with a hyperawareness of gendered and raced sonic expectations performs two related functions. First, it is not uncommon to encounter a narrative of female, Indigenous, and other minoritized musicians as being "unheard"; it is crucial to press on this narrative and ask, Unheard by whom, and why? This is the racialized move toward the imperceptible that Katherine McKittrick identifies, in which a subject is "rendered invisible due to [their] highly visible bodily context."[20] The not-heard cannot exist without someone not-hearing. An artist like JB the First Lady, founder of the cypher First Ladies Crew, started rapping as a teenager and has been making evocative hip hop music since the early 2000s. She has not been quiet. So who is failing to listen? And second, this notion of the gendered color line points out the creative limitations that a mainstream listening ear places on Indigenous womxn artists and artists of color. When groups such as Tribe Called Queenz use genre-typical sound vocabularies, if not everyone hears them *as rappers*, because they are waiting to hear them *as women*, the problem again rests with the ear of the audience. If, in the face of gender- and race-specific expectations of musical sound, projects like *FWBW* choose to define their own listenership, it is worth considering what an assumed default listenership would have been before the musicians so confidently articulated their own.

Musician-audience interaction engages the related but nonidentical practices of hearing and listening. It is not coincidental that a rhetoric of being or not being heard is often phrased in the passive voice. Hearing itself can be a passive activity. On a physical level, soundwaves enter the ear and vibrate the eardrum; these vibrations move through fluid in the inner ear, and they are amplified and translated into electrical impulses that the brain receives and processes as sound. We have little control over this mechanical process. Hearing is distinct even among other senses like vision, in which we can choose to close our eyes, or taste or touch, in which we can move our bodies to elect what we will or will not sense. The mechanical nature of hearing is significant beyond the level of physical processes. Because people have little control over which sound waves enter our ears and what our ears process as sound through hearing, we have adapted attentive strategies to focus on or ignore certain parts of what we hear. In other words, because we cannot close our ears, if we do not want to pay attention to something, we direct our attention elsewhere: we keep hearing but stop listening. Listening, the process by which we attend to auditory stimuli, involves choice. This distinction is central in this chapter and, I argue, in the way we understand hearing and listening to specific voices in a variety of contexts.

Scholarly responses to minoritarian voices frequently engage a discourse of not being heard. In this passive construction, suggesting that someone is not being heard erases the people who should be doing the hearing. It focuses on the idea of the voice: it should be louder, it needs to be amplified, it requires something to make it hearable. Ignoring the hearer (or nonhearer) is a kind of walking away from blame and walking away from responsibility. As explained by Malea Powell, sometimes learning to listen means fully sensing that which was already present; we should not assume that a voice has just begun speaking simply because we have finally learned to listen for it.[21] If, for example, Indigenous female rappers are not being heard, the passive construction and this use of hearing suggests that they should be doing something different if they want to be heard. An unasked question that needs to be addressed is this: Even if they are heard, will they be listened to?

In this analysis, then, I move toward listening. Who is listening? Who is not listening? What does listening require of the speaker and of the listener? Given this relationship, who is invited to listen, and who is asked not to listen? Listening intentionally requires attention and action. If hearing is about sound vibrations reaching the inner ear, then listening is about paying attention to these vibrations, noticing them, and doing something with them. Through sonic sovereignty, artists articulate their own audiences, often in contrast to default listening publics of an assumed mainstream market. The insider, or at least somewhat exclusive, listenership is clear from the very outset of the album *For Women By Women.*

On "Introduction," Eekwol speaks over sparse instrumentals: "Welcome to For Women By Women. This project is for women and those who identify as women. If you are a man or identify as such, this is not for you." T-Rhyme offers a negative "uh-uh," and Eekwol continues, "Please click the button embodying the black square and walk away. We will wait." A pause follows. If the listener does not press stop, the track continues, with Eekwol interjecting tips on how to find the stop button. All listeners hear this waiting; silence speaks. This break is an uncharacteristic sonic move in popular music, as the flow of the song is interrupted. By choosing to remain silent for a long moment, the artists create an unsettling rupture. If the track is allowed to play on, the listener hears a slightly puzzled, "Why are you not pressing it? Why are you not doing as I say?" If it continues, the song offers sighs from both rappers and then the promise that they will not apologize if anyone still listening does not like what they hear. Eekwol warns, "You're not gonna like it," and a delay effect creates the sound of her voice reverberating, stretching out in time and emphasizing these words. The MCs make a strategic choice to exclude those who may not understand or support the project.

Throughout the album and related live performances, being both by and for womxn is clear in lyrical topicality, as well as approach. Eekwol and T-Rhyme broach topics not heard on every rap album: how to face attempts to demean strong womxn, the need for Indigenous language revitalization, how to choose to manifest rage, the gendered wage gap in the music business, gender-based violence, and victim shaming. And as they trade verses live and on the recording, they have nothing but support for each other. Pairing humor with rage, T-Rhyme and Eekwol respond to experiences of bias within the recording industry with this performative intervention that is the kernel for other related actions. Like Tribe Called Queenz, *FWBW* addresses spaces, attitudes, language, access, and safety.

An intersectional analysis of *FWBW* illuminates the types of power that impact expressions by Indigenous female and nonbinary hip hop artists. Analyzed alongside other hip hop projects, the following segments demonstrate the types of power that constrain creative activity as well as the ways in which socio-musical activities lay bare and alter these dynamics. In Patricia Hill Collins and Sirma Bilge's analysis of what intersectionality can do as an analytic tool, they disaggregate the kinds of power that circumscribe behavior along four domains: structural, disciplinary, interpersonal, and cultural.[22] I leverage the intersectional framework identified by Kimberlé Crenshaw as detailed by Collins and Bilge by using its focal points of critical inquiry and critical praxis to facilitate a better understanding of how musical activity participates in multiple and shifting emplacements of its maker-listeners. This is particularly relevant for womxn's cyphers and musical projects designed for womxn listeners. As both analytic and practice, intersectionality as used here responds to critiques about its limitations. Conscious of the potential for intersectionality's absorption into depoliticized processes due to what Jennifer Nash calls its "elasticity," its use here hews toward its deployment as both critical and generative praxis: "intersectionality is an antisubordination project, one committed to foregrounding exclusion and its effects."[23] When undertaken with rematriation, intersectionality is a defiant project that refuses hierarchies and creates or re-creates alternative structures.

The use of this analytic proceeds from the vantage point that womxn experience the effects of gender bias in the music industry based on divergent ways in which people are racialized.[24] These ascriptions vary across time and contexts for the same individuals. The following four sections probe interlocking ways in which the self-ascription and other-ascription of gender identity, heritage, race, sexual orientation, and family status are mutually influential, though never equivalent. In each section, I identify how power operates in one of these interconnected dimensions. Taken together, they help to explain the context in which *FWBW* and related projects emerge, and they show ways in which musicians are intervening and reforming established dynamics.

## Structural Power: Structural Exclusion versus Strategic Exclusivity

Musicians, industry professionals, and fans are affected by structural power, or power at the institutional and organizational level. Participants' experiences are shaped by the rules and operations of established entities. The manner in which the music industry is structured creates discrete impacts on a range of musicians, listeners, and other music professionals. As described in chapter 1, settler colonial state policies have restructured social organization in a way that both creates and reflects race and gender policing. These have targeted Indigenous womxn through specific policies such as the Indian Act; Audra Simpson identifies how the "the snaking, dividing, and yet organizing logic of raced and gendered heteropatriarchy" concretized as it "sought to divest Indian women from land by divesting them of their legal rights as Indians."[25] This policing is also manifest in interactions from the quotidian to the policy level that target gender and sexual expression as a tool of control. By disciplining bodies and regulating the population, in the Foucauldian sense of bio-power, the colonial state produces what Scott Morgensen describes as "white national heteronormativity that regulates Indigenous sexuality and gender by supplanting them with the sexual modernity of settler subjects."[26]

Implicit and explicit gender and racial bias profoundly affects media-entertainment industries. Due to intersecting forms of bias, fewer female and nonbinary people access training in production and recording, and those who do face unequal treatment. Starker even for womxn of color, this exclusion resonates through music broadcasting and streaming, described in chapters 2 and 3. Consequently, attitudes impact opportunities that are made available and unavailable to women and nonbinary creatives and other professionals. This bias is heard in the output of the popular music industry. A survey of gender representation in popular music charting in the top one hundred showed a dearth of women on both the creative and business sides of the music industry. The imbalance is strikingly large: just 16.8 percent of artists were women in 2017. From 2012 to 2017, 12.3 percent of songwriters were women, and only 2 percent of producers were women. Among producers, just 0.3 percent were women from a racially underrepresented group.[27] Womxn who do write, engineer, and produce encounter having their expertise minimized, undercut, and not heard. Bias in the music industry against female identified and/or perceived artists limits opportunities for individual womxn. It also shrinks the kinds of stories the music industry is able to tell. Summarizing the effects of this discrimination, Smith, Choueiti, and Pieper find, "The lack of women in roles responsible for creative direction across visual and audio entertainment is troubling. This appears to reflect deeply-held biases related to women and leadership. . . . Addressing these beliefs is paramount to opening doors for women in all creative roles, and offering females a chance to shape the cultural narratives and landscape in which entertainment is made."[28]

Industry gatekeeping is experienced as structural exclusion. The lack of authority in the hands of womxn, particularly womxn of color, influences how decisions are made and which voices are heard—and silenced—at all levels. Womxn's leadership does not guarantee antisexist behavior. As rap scholar Tricia Rose points out, "since sexism socializes all men and women, we have to work against it; being anti-sexist doesn't come naturally in a system that rewards us for participating."[29] Structures of power are likely to reproduce the forces that keep those who are currently in charge at the top. To obtain success, female artists are told, they need to enact mainstream stereotypes that are expected of them. Rose reports, "young women are also coerced into participating [in a sexist system] by the dictates of record-industry marketing." Music industry insider Glen Ford shares a telling example of the external imposition of racialized sexual tropes: "A young female artist broke down at my kitchen table one afternoon, after we had finished a promotional interview. 'They're trying to make me into a whore,' she said, sobbing, 'They say I'm not "street" enough.' Her skills on the mic were fine. 'They' were the A&R [artists and repertoire] people from her corporate record label."[30] Diversifying management—in race, gender, and ideas—would open the door to varied ways of being a successful artist.

While streaming audio and social media sites create some opportunities for independent musicians to impact current hits playlists, as described in chapter 2, the bottom-up transformational potential of online music distribution is structurally limited. For example, annual *Billboard* data for US year-end pop hits shows a sharp decline in the (already lower) number of female performers who reach the top of the charts, starting in 2013—the year that streaming audio was first considered in these figures.[31] In popular music, in particular, the role of gatekeepers is still strong: high-ranking individuals and groups often decide what music gets played on-air, nonneutral broadcast standards influence who can be heard, and hierarchical access to decision-makers impacts artists' ability to get on a record label, an awards shortlist, or onstage at a club or a festival, all of which are traditionally key for artists to get to audience members' ears.

Efforts to address these imbalances are being led by womxn from within music industries. For example, leaders and volunteers with She Is The Music (SITM) provide mentorship, workshops, and professional connections for female-identified and nonbinary musicians and industry professionals. SITM has also launched a global database to connect womxn in the music industry around the world.[32] Other organizations such as Women in Music, Femme House, SoundGirls, and We Are Moving The Needle support girls, women, and nonbinary people seeking to enter or advance within popular music professions. Projects including *FWBW*, Tribe Called Queenz, and First Ladies Crew provide resources and stage space for female-identified and gender-nonconforming musicians, both through mutual amplification of group members and through members' mentorship of younger musicians.

Music awards offer opportunities for special recognition, prestige, and additional audience reach.[33] Yet music by womxn performers, composers, engineers, and producers is troublingly underrepresented at the level of nomination. That is, before high-profile decisions about awards are made, gatekeeping often prevents female creatives from being in the running. In the US-based Grammy Awards, fewer than 10 percent of nominees were women between 2013 and 2018.[34] For awards with an official nomination process, female creatives report submitting music to boards and not arriving at the nomination stage, generally without explanation. Even within a substream of the music industry dedicated to Indigenous artists, the structural exclusion of womxn continues. Disparity among official gatekeepers is acute in hip hop. Industry insiders note the lack of female hip hop artists nominated for the Aboriginal Peoples' Choice Music Awards (APCMA), renamed the Indigenous Music Awards (IMA) in 2015. Industry professionals secure the pool of nominees. Under the APCMA iteration, public voting influenced the winner. According to the IMAs, "Voting will be conducted by Industry music professionals ONLY. There is no public voting."[35] All of the Indigenous Music Awards' Rap/Hip Hop nominees in 2018 were solo male artists or all-male groups (Chase Manhattan, Lil Mike & FunnyBone, Snotty Nose Rez Kids, StenJoddi, and Supaman). This was also the case in 2017, when the nominees were B. of Dakota South Records, City Natives, Chase Manhattan, Joey Stylez, J-Rez, and Rellik. The awards were on hiatus in 2016, and the 2015 Rap/Hip Hop nominees (Chief Rock, City Natives, Cody Coyote, Drezus, and Hellnback) and 2014 nominees (K.A.S.P., Mike Bone, Shawn Bertrand, Supaman, and Winnipeg Boyz) followed the same pattern: not a single female artist was nominated for the Best Rap/Hip Hop Album between 2014 and 2018. JB the First Lady was finally nominated for this category in 2019. The other four nominees— Artson, Buggin Malone, Hellnback, and Jah'kota—were all male, and the award went to Buggin Malone.[36] These music awards oversights, felt as snubs and erasures, constitute a larger pattern of minimizing voices within industry structures.

As praxis, an intersectional critique of inequity as it affects Indigenous womxn both lays bare overlapping forms of bias and reveals the ways in which artists can articulate sovereignty through musical sound. All of the aspects of power described here—including structural power— impact womxn differently based on how they are read racially, ethnically, and with regard to status and heritage. A critique of power inequity as it impacts Indigenous womxn is necessarily an intersectional one. Mishuana Goeman (Tonawanda Band of Seneca) and Jennifer Nez Denetdale (Diné) recognize the effects of racism, sexism, and discrimination even as they identify the controversial nature of "Native feminism" as a term. Though colonial histories cannot be separated from feminism as a historical social project, "a monolithic approach to a Native feminism is not possible," they explain; "the false dichotomy of feminist and non-feminist is oversimplified and undermines Native women's approaches to decolonization."[37]

While some strains of feminism do not support, and even work against, Indigenous sovereignty and self-determination, others engage in antisexist and antiracist work in a manner that supports decolonial action. As such, Goeman and Denetdale "affirm the usefulness of a Native feminism's analysis and, indeed, declare that Native feminist analysis is crucial if we are determined to decolonize as Native peoples."[38] As Joyce Green (English, Ktunaxa, and Cree-Scots Métis) defines it, "Feminism is an ideology based on a political analysis that takes women's experiences seriously, and it is played out politically by women's groups that generally have characteristic processes of organization and of action."[39] Indigenous or Aboriginal feminism, then, "brings together the two critiques, feminism and anti-colonialism, to show how Aboriginal peoples, and in particular Aboriginal women, are affected by colonialism and by patriarchy."[40] Acknowledging that some Indigenous women face pushback for using terms such as "feminism" or organizing for women, Green identifies that definitions of "tradition" are contested, may reinforce gender hierarchies that disempower women, and are difficult to disaggregate from colonial ideas of gender norms. In the *FWBW* project and Indigenous-led womxn's cyphers, some artists and listeners find power in remembering and reactivating matriarchy. T-Rhyme and Eekwol recall the ways in which women's leadership is part of Nehiyaw heritage and, in so doing, provide an interpretation of "traditional" as that which privileges women's power. An act of asserting sovereignty, claiming one's own terminology is part of the work of bringing into being this matriarchal power structure.

## Disciplinary Power: Indigenous Womxn and Decolonization

Artists, media professionals, and fans experience the effects of disciplinary power in the music industry. Even if rules and procedures, on their face, allegedly apply to all, their effects on people change based on aspects of social positions. Rules may be enforced or ignored, depending on the parties involved. In the music industry, as in other sectors of the labor market, the effects of disciplinary power are acutely felt in

salary and related working conditions. In addition to monetary compensation, disciplinary power is felt in who performs which kinds of
labor, how people's work is counted, and the degrees of safety people
experience in work environments. There are many ways to be counted;
in the face of inequitable monetary compensation, artists share credibility and retell stories. Some forms of storytelling are continuations
of history and connect it to what comes next. Recognition of teachers
and creative influence is common in hip hop, where knowledge is a
core element.

Listen. How is history told and continued? An upbeat guitar melody starts the song "Would You." A driving snare enters next, then a
kick drum deepens the bass. Snare and kick drum tussle with each
other, eventually settling into a syncopated beat that creates a sense of
forward-moving energy. Over this mix, T-Rhyme starts rapping with a
speech-effusive flow. A quarter of the way through her first sixteen-bar
verse, she starts naming names: "Comprehend my metaphors, hip hop
forever more / Give me TLC, I'm diggin' on you like a record store."
She slows her flow and punches out the words, "De La Soul, always c'est
la vie." Throughout the verse, she weaves in other Black US-based hip
hop legends, notably Mary J. Blige and the collective Native Tongues,
whose collaborators included Monie Love and Queen Latifah. Braiding
in these influences, T-Rhyme ends in the present, "you gotta understand the modern woman's hustle."

Historically the creative labor of womxn in hip hop, particularly Black
womxn and Latinas and to a degree also Indigenous womxn, has been
underacknowledged.[41] As hip hop has gone the way of many other cultural expressions and been codified as a music genre, the process of can-
onization has increased the focus on a small subset of male artists and
male-fronted groups, minimizing both female music professionals and
the creative work of people, notably womxn, who never made a living
from music. A key example of this is the way early hip hop practices are
remembered today. Those artists who are typically deemed part of the
hip hop canon—who make lists of names in textbooks and coffee-table
books—are typically young men.[42] Hip hop heads remember how the
now-canonized greats started as teenagers playing their moms' records.
The musical curation of these Black and Latina womxn produced many
of the sounds and the breaks that are foundational in hip hop practice.

Their names were often written on the records their children played, yet they are not remembered in writing about this period. This exists within a larger gloss that does not always recognize the range of Afro-diasporic, Indigenous, Puerto Rican, and other Latinx influences in early hip hop.[43] Another simplification occurs in the retelling of the moment rap music started to become a commodity that could be sold on records and aired on the radio. Music producer and founder of Sugar Hill Records Sylvia Robinson was instrumental in creating this change. She produced the Sugarhill Gang's "Rapper's Delight," which has become the signifier of the market shift. This record is undoubtedly significant. Robinson's others are as well. Cheryl Keyes highlighted many groups and songs that were important in the 1970s through the 1990s that are now often sidelined in subsequent histories. Sugar Hill arranged a national tour, an important step in commercializing rap as a genre. The rap trio Sequence, composed of Angie B., Cheryl the Pearl, and Blondie, released the commercially successful "Funk You Up" on Sugar Hill Records.[44] This misremembering is evinced in breakdance histories and retellings of graffiti greats, cutting across hip hop's elements.[45]

Telling these histories is part of hip hop culture. As a practice, hip hop since its inception has centered on learning from others: learning from elders in the scene, learning respect for others and for a culture. T-Rhyme reflects on the importance of recognizing hip hop's origins in Black America, a refrain that Eekwol has often taken up as well. T-Rhyme understands her expression in hip hop as a branch of a tree. She explains, "We just happen to branch off and have created our own stories and voices. We're all on the same tree. You know. That's the only way that I can really think about it. The roots are there. We've all grown throughout this scene and this medium, but we're just a different branch of it." It is crucial to acknowledge the foundational creativity of Black artists.[46] She continues, "We will always acknowledge because we know that historically we have never really been acknowledged fairly or properly within our own culture or our own history. It doesn't make any sense to not do the same for the culture that we borrow from." T-Rhyme connects her own recognition of musical influences to the intentional erasure of Indigenous legacies and presence. In our conversation, we talked through the many foundational and creative roles of Black womxn, spanning early hip hop through the genre's golden age and into the present. Musically citing young creatives in early hip hop brings forward the contributions of a wide range of Black, Latinx, and Indigenous womxn and men and puts listeners into conversation across time with the people from whom artists learn. Through each one teach one, the conscious hip hop legacy, artists model from earlier innovators through their lyrics, conversations, and ongoing efforts to mentor young people.

*FWBW* acknowledges the importance of Black womxn's labor, even as the rappers' own labor is undervalued. These moments of sharing credibility and bringing forward past musical innovators in *FWBW* reflect a larger trend in substreams of hip hop by Indigenous artists: musicians articulate localized expressions of Indigeneity while continually honoring Black American hip hop artists. Acting through knowledge, the fifth element of hip hop, artists re-member their own creative influences, including womxn of color whose stories need to be told and retold.

Wage disparity affects womxn, and especially womxn of color. Its impacts on Indigenous womxn are egregious. The kinds of labor expected of womxn vary based on cultural norms; womxn navigating multiple cultural spaces may be asked to do specialized work across both or all of them. Eekwol and T-Rhyme do many kinds of labor as rappers and members of their communities, incorporating personal and public-facing kinds of work: making and sharing music, raising children, storytelling, mentoring, and teaching through rap. Finding time to write the music for *FWBW* was sometimes a challenge alongside all the other work the artists do in their lives. T-Rhyme reflects that on occasion she would need to recalibrate to be able to do the work, so they would start a writing session with a smudge. Then,

T-RHYME: Our kids would be playing around. And we'd sit there and take that moment to write down ideas for a song [*Eekwol affirming*]. And then when we'd go home//
EEKWOL: Then back to something completely different//
T-RHYME: Back to real life.[47]

T-Rhyme recalls that there were even times when she had not gotten a chance to write beforehand, but Eekwol adjusted and offered to record first while T-Rhyme wrote verses in studio.

When the artists discuss this album, both of them talk about motherhood specifically. They describe themselves as being busy moms, talk about their kids playing together, and identify how important it is to have support in order to write and also be present for their children. They both reference caregiving and recognize intergenerational care in Indigenous communities. This valued and valuable labor typically does not take center stage in settler music industry activity.[48] Overlapping life responsibilities create a specific set of needs for music recording: to make music, rappers must access a studio where they can record at night after their kids are in bed, and where they deeply trust the personnel.

Like other workers, musicians require compensation to keep doing their craft; gendered and raced inequalities in pay affect those in the music industry. The effects of wage inequity as a form of disciplinary power are felt by rappers, DJs, producers, and others. Taking this issue public, Eekwol rapped about not getting equitable pay at shows. After narrating getting ready to perform, she raps, "Hold up! / How come I'm the only rapper here wearing makeup? / And I'm probably the only rapper here walking out with a pay cut. / And I'm probably the only rapper here hearin' a 'hey girl, what's up.'"[49] Eekwol lyrically recounts her experience performing, in which she is expected to put in additional time to prepare her look for an event, faces pay inequity, and is singled out with unwanted sexual and/or romantic attention while she is rapping. Access for women and nonbinary people to stage time, airtime, inclusion in playlists, and nominations for awards has financial repercussions. In an immediate sense, workers do not earn royalties if their music is not played. The professional exposure, or lack thereof, further accrues to influence how much of a living an artist can make. The financial stability that comes from opportunities to interface with audiences then impacts how much time an artist can afford to spend making more music. Layering upon itself, this impacts the ability to obtain future performance contracts, which impacts future exposure, and so on.

Getting booked less often, and paid less when they are, drives some artists to seek other sources of revenue. Eekwol and T-Rhyme proactively chose to seek grant funding.[50] Not only can alternative revenue streams provide an opportunity for musicians who get paid less at the door or for recording or streaming sales, but they also can allow artists to make music that is challenging and thus might not sell well. This freedom allows for creative moves—such as excluding one audience segment in order to carefully craft a message to another segment that less frequently is at the center of music and marketing decisions.[51] Focusing on one's message and creative freedom, regardless of audience response, is a privilege that is only possible when artists have the material means available to make music. With this support, artists can write and perform music that expresses uncomfortable ideas that challenge the consumption patterns of a promotion economy.

A minor-key melody in treble electronics repeats over an ominous bass line. The driving sound increases in volume, mounting in intensity. Listeners might respond to these cues, taught through television and movie soundtracks as well as popular music, without conscious thought. These are cues used often for tension and even danger. The rapper begins, "on a spiritual journey, I'm takin' trips every day." This is not a quiet journey, nor is it one that takes place outside the built environment; there are no ocean or wind sounds or soothing slow melodies. She continues, "maniacal panic attacks, take 'em away." The music contributes to, rather than relieves, this mania, the repetition circling on itself. The rapper elaborates, "the masculine mentality divides society; the problem with bein' brilliant is the constant anxiety." The music in "Pressure" on *FWBW* offers just a few moments of respite in this stressful pattern: the sound of rattles cuts through when the rapper urges the listener, "dance until the sunrise." Listeners get a moment of reprieve, to possibly breathe with the rattle. Then it stops, and the pressure returns. At the end of her verse, the rapper finishes, "we will never back down, beats kickin' in," and the melody changes, still ominous but less oppressive.

Whether the rhythmic patterns are heard as a whole or each analyzed toward their cumulative effect, they are disorienting, especially on the repeated chorus. A duple beat is consistent in the instrumentals, yet the MC's words don't quite fit. She raps, "The pressure is on. We handling, we handling it / World is so wrong. We balancing, we balancing it / Journey's so long. We traveling, we traveling it / Word is our bond. You panicking, you panicking yet." Each gerund (handling, balancing, traveling, panicking) is repeated, the beat misaligned with the natural stress of the word, so that each time a three-syllable word is repeated, it feels like it doesn't quite land. We are tumbling with the speaker, unsettled, and by the end of the chorus, may yet be panicking. In the third verse, the rappers trade narration, each keeping up rapid-fire delivery as they talk about a woman preparing against, and responding to, a physical attack by a man: mace, sweat, kicking down a door, nightmare, roar. The verse ends with T-Rhyme rapping, "I'm silent no longer." Then the chorus returns, and the final statement is Eekwol's repeated words, "the pressure is on." This is a song about stress and pressure; it works through a musical language that can create these same feelings. The song uses repetition, which could sound like a vicious cycle, or share a feeling of anxiety, or explore how the rapper feels pressure, and then works through spiritual practice to process difficult emotions. With each repetition, what resonates?

Eekwol and T-Rhyme recorded *FWBW* at a friend's home studio in Saskatoon. Not only was the engineer familiar with their voices from previous projects, but recording was able to fit into the musicians' lives due to the proximity of the studio and their ability to record there after hours. As a family friend, the engineer was a trusted person, and his studio was a safe place. T-Rhyme and Eekwol echo each other on why this was important to the project:

> T-RHYME: [Our friend has] a studio in his home. So we would go//
> EEKWOL: Yeah, so we could go there at night. [*T-Rhyme affirming*] Our husbands would put our kids to bed. [*T-Rhyme affirming*] We'd just hang out.
> T-RHYME: And that's another thing too, that shout-out to our partners for being so supportive and believing in what we do//
> EEKWOL: Not making us feel bad//
> T-RHYME: Like, truly//
> EEKWOL: Like, it's a burden.
> T-RHYME: They really see what we do as important and valuable.

This passage demonstrates intersecting ideas on the musicians' labor. First, they do other work besides making this album—paid labor and raising their families—so they need a time outside of those hours to do the recording and a space where they can (safely) do so. Second, implicit in their appreciation for the work-sharing of child rearing that their partners do is the understanding that not all men would willingly perform such labor for their own children; "making us feel bad" or not doing the work are alternatives that some choose. These women musicians have male partners with whom they are coparenting and raising children, and yet the attitude they encountered toward affective labor is one faced by many: the gendering of care labor is neither inevitable nor always assigned in a binary manner.[52] However, in many situations, it is assumed first to fall to womxn. These realities reveal that, while a studio might on paper be available to anyone who pays for the time, womxn frequently perform other kinds of labor, leaving less free time for creative projects. Social norms keep some spaces homosocial. Bedroom studios and private practice spaces for hip hop artists have often operated as spaces in which men teach other men, as Mark Katz has found.[53] This particular home studio is owned by a friend of Eekwol's brother; family connections make it a viable option.

The power dynamics operative in music spaces do not end with physical recording studios, informal learning spaces, or performance venues. Online venues for musical interaction are far from immune to the kinds of social dynamics that operate offline. While some early adopters had utopic visions of online spaces offering equity that does not exist offline, animosity that people express in offline spaces also appears in online venues. Players of online music note that musicians sometimes intentionally play over each other in online performance spaces, simply because some take joy from creating disruption.[54] Many popular musicians must operate in a music scene that spans online and offline spaces. The twenty-first-century music market typically requires that musicians, or their agents, promote shows and sell music in the hybrid sphere and interact with fans across a physical/digital divide. The neoliberal music industry economy is structured so that musicians themselves take on much of this online labor. Intentionally irritating or harassing others online for fun is so common that it has had its own verb since the 1990s: "griefing." Some people take it a step further, using digital tools to inflict harm on others or enacting physical violence that was threatened in internet-mediated spaces. Threats, violence, and erasure are more than individual acts; digital tools reinforce biases at the structural level. These inequities disproportionately affect womxn of color.[55]

Women and nonbinary people face far more threats and harassment online than men do. When a University of Maryland study created sample online accounts and monitored them for responses, "accounts with feminine usernames incurred an average of 100 sexually explicit or threatening messages a day. Masculine names received 3.7."[56] These threats negatively impact womxn's ability to operate in online communication spaces.[57] Aggression can render participation in venues helpful for promotion, like social media and personal websites, less available, thus inhibiting womxn's use of these spaces for professional connections and promotions. It can also hamper the use of media circulation sites, such as YouTube, or online communities dedicated to interactive music learning; sites for learning new skills and promoting music or music videos are especially important for independent artists, so compromised access to these is particularly detrimental. T-Rhyme has seen people use the comments sections on music she shares online to post negative responses to and about her, as well as to attempt to inflame negative competition between female musicians. She details that men would say something such as "'So-and-so was the best.' 'So and so is way better than you guys and blah blah blah,' you know, pitting us against each other." Eekwol immediately affirmed, "Oh, of course." T-Rhyme stated, with her voice showing a determination born of experience, "I would just be like, delete," and Eekwol immediately affirmed this. Again, they attempt to excise those who will not truly listen from their audience, removing their commentary from the space of online dialogue and, hopefully, from their own, and their listeners', attention. In some instances, it is possible for musicians to draw on community support and stability to reshape online spaces. Yet the additional toll caused by womxn's unequal access to space is costly, and instances of sexual assault and misogynist violence spurred through online harassment are serious and real.[58]

## Interpersonal Power: Raced and Gendered Behavior Expectations

From the recording studio to the performance space, musicians and fans experience power at the interpersonal level. Face-to-face, online, on the airwaves, and stage-to-audience, music performance demonstrates how people are divergently advantaged and disadvantaged in social relationships. Artists and professionals reference these dynamics overtly, as when they identify variations in treatment and opportunities for female, male, and nonbinary colleagues and the way these differ based on other characteristics, notably race, class, sexual orientation, and status.[59]

Interpersonal relationships draw on and perpetuate ideas about support and competition. Eekwol, T-Rhyme, and other womxn MCs have experienced interactions in which they have been told that there is not room for multiple womxn in hip hop; due to assumptions about who can participate, many people in the music industry have only been able to imagine a token female rapper, rather than an industry in which people of all genders can participate at multiple levels. This limitation interacts with, and is fueled by, interpersonal dynamics: many female MCs have been encouraged by men to compete against other womxn, an attitude rooted in a heteropatriarchal mind-set. As T-Rhyme told Eekwol, "You've never encouraged me to go after and be competitive with another woman, but I've had many men come up to me and told me to go after and be competitive with other women." Eekwol explains that this is due to an industry attitude she has faced again and again, that "there can't be another woman who raps." T-Rhyme's take on this bias is that "it's that whole smashing that patriarchy within even our own relationships, because my partner, he would never tell me to go out there and be better than [Eekwol]. He's always saying, 'You are *as good as.*'" Recognizing the interpersonal power dynamics that could proscribe choices, sonic sovereignty is enacted as people refuse these limitations, instead personally refocusing on a mind-set that offers a more beneficial approach.

Interpersonal dynamics gain relevance beyond daily interactions in music scenes: hip hop artists are expected to enact a musical persona onstage and when conducting activities related to their music, such as in interviews and social media posts. In hip hop, some genre-based codes of behavior elicit machismo from performers onstage. This may be expected of people of all genders, though there is a smaller subset of established acceptable roles for womxn.[60] These norms are raced and classed; they manifest themselves in hip hop in particular ways. As Gwendolyn Pough asserts, "The only difference between rappers and the 'suits' in the boardroom is race and socioeconomic status. While rap does give us some startling, and indeed, ugly representations of female objectification, rap is not responsible for other travesties, such as the feminization of poverty, welfare reform, and the glass ceiling."[61] Expected interpersonal dynamics include limited roles for men; until the early 2010s, a highly individualist rags-to-riches machismo based in tropes of monoracial Black masculinity circumscribed onstage and public interactions of many male rappers and DJs.[62] A battle-oriented machismo is expected of rappers who span gender identities. This attitude encapsulates performative self-aggrandizement. T-Rhyme and Eekwol explain:

> T-RHYME: I would always be rapping about how dope I was. How I'm better than you. How I was//
>
> EEKWOL: How you were supposed to rap//
>
> T-RHYME: Yeah, yeah, yeah. How we're supposed to always *battle, battle, battle.*

The objectification of womxn specifically and the objectification of Indigenous peoples of all sexes are processes that are both integrated into settler colonial logics. Interpersonal dynamics take on an added level of codified ritual behavior in performance spaces, albeit in insidious ways that can be overlooked or minimized. Audiences are also implicated in these dynamics. Machismo expected of audience members—male hip hop heads, and sometimes nonmale ones as well, perform aggressive behavior, such as shouting, jostling, and demonstratively taking up space at shows. In these spaces, forms of raced and gendered behaviors are circumscribed. As hip hop musicians and fans respond to the social conditions in which they speak and listen, they encounter a heteropatriarchy that is inextricably linked to settler colonialism; in the performance space, musicians and fans negotiate racialized gender.[63] To make sense of these dynamics, I look to Imani Kai Johnson's account of marginalized femininities that are discouraged in public spaces. Johnson argues for the importance of "badass femininity" and other alternative femininities that womxn express in hip hop spaces while articulating the multiple forms of constraint that limit varied expressions of gender. In these spaces, a "conventional notion of masculinity," read in a hip hop battle space as involving aggression, threats, and sexual domination, is expected of male-identifying participants.[64] In Eekwol's words, "There's a lot of misogyny in hip-hop. Any time you watch any videos, you're going to see the obvious stereotypes about women. You either have to be super sexualized or thugged out. I've never subscribed to that."[65] These dominant gender norms have historically limited the range of performances that are permitted in hip hop spaces. Circumscribed gendered ways of relating to each other, which crystallize in live shows, extend to relation-ships beyond the moment of the performance. Gesture, tone, physical approach, and degree of attentiveness vary for fans on the basis of how their gender and race are perceived. Online and in live event spaces, some fans take musicians and fellow fans less seriously when they present traditional femininities or perform nonnormative masculinities.[66]

Tangible examples of interpersonal power dynamics are found at shows, studios, and industry events. These can be so out of balance that musicians' and fans' physical safety is threatened. A pattern emerges in which womxn are at times expected to tolerate harassment or to perform sexually to advance within the industry. In performance spaces, womxn—both performers and audience members—may not be safe. As T-Rhyme explains, "We need to remind men, especially, that they need to continue to respect our work and respect our spaces and respect our voices and our roles in this scene and to not be predatory or discrediting in any way, to who we are as females in this scene." Sexual violence that impacts power dynamics in music industry spaces mirrors that of larger society, in which female and gender-nonconforming people are targeted. This violence disproportionately affects Indigenous womxn.[67] Tina Beads and Rauna Kuokkanen explain the ongoing necessity of anti-racist and antipoverty work, detailing that these connect to work against sexism and that all three are paramount in ensuring the safety of Indigenous womxn and, in their words, in "achieving equality."[68]

T-Rhyme articulates how critical it is to reestablish interpersonal dynamics that ensure the safety of womxn: "That's one thing that I care about the most. I don't ever want to hear another story about girls going to shows and feeling unsafe, or scared or worried or [*pause*] abused. I want them to continue to uplift and revive this matriarchy." This pause, heard as silence, is more-than. Sonic sovereignty operates through sound and silence; here this pause is weighty with meaning. In this silence that speaks, T-Rhyme takes a pause that invites in multiple meanings and experiences. Like a generative refusal, a pause like this could be a turning point: the speaker making the choice to name the uncomfortable reality of violence against women and girls. A pause like this can also provide a breath, preparation for the realization to come. A pause like this can make space for summation and for listeners to reflect on their knowledge—direct or indirect—of the situations

T-Rhyme names; moments and histories of threats and of gender-based violence echo with each other and with the conversation.[69] The timing of the call in which the need for matriarchy is asserted—while discussing gender-based violence—carries meaning. Violence experienced in the present demonstrates the urgency of the need for change. As Eekwol and T-Rhyme rap, "the pressure is on." Bias, harassment, and violence against womxn imbue popular music spaces with alarming regularity; LGBTQ2+ people, particularly Native female and nonbinary LGBTQ2+ people, experience discrimination, threats, and violence disproportionally due to overlapping and ongoing impacts of heteropatriarchy and coloniality.[70] How are musicians, and audiences, responding to threats to bodily sovereignty?

In the face of violence, claiming sovereignty entails calling into being matriarchy, which includes a commitment to reinstantiate—in the space of the performance and then aspirationally into the future—a social dynamic that is remembered forward from the past. This system is not a mere reversal, maintaining dyads of power in which womxn are placed in a position of control. Rather, this process, which some scholars and musicians refer to as "rematriation"—and which I examine further in the next section—requires a renegotiation of social dynamics and a reinterpretation of social responsibility. Such an understanding of gendered relationships centers on responsibility toward self, other, and community, not a simple ascription of who may and may not wield power to control others. Marginalized femininities are valued, and while womxn reassume responsibilities and types of authority, these need not mirror patriarchal power-distribution logics and the settler colonial process of objectification. Understandings of gendered responsibility extend to women, men, and two-spirit and nonbinary individuals. Constructions of masculinity, too, draw on historical ideas of gender that are band and region specific while also operating in conversation with stereotypes promulgated in settler society.[71] Responsibility extends further to nonhuman animals, spirits, and other actors. The emphasis on responsibility expands how power can be understood. Yet some discussions of Indigenous sovereignty overemphasize responsibility and fail to account for the rights to autonomy that it entails. Sonic sovereignty encompasses the both-and: connection through responsibility and that Indigenous peoples and groups are already entitled to self-determination.

The matriarchy that the musicians call forward—through the rematriation that they themselves participate in—is a form of social organization that will replace the colonial heteropatriarchal one in which desire to exert physical power over others is a core tenet underpinning the ideology. The work of projects including *FWBW*, Tribe Called Queenz, First Ladies Crew, and their members' solo output takes place under inequitable political conditions. It acknowledges them—directly and indirectly—not to be resigned to them but to name them in order to upend them.

Speaking sovereignty into being, a sound practice is offered: storytelling. Rappers' roles as storytellers come into play in this process, as they can transmit narratives that need to be shared, including those of physical abuse and threats thereof. Given the reality of the disproportionate effects of violence, Indigenous womxn in music play a crucial role: they tell stories that need to be heard, featuring stories that extend beyond their own personal experience that touch people they know. There are costs to telling these stories, especially to unsympathetic ears. Creating an exclusive listenership provides some measure of safety. Amid the rampant problem of violence against Native women, the process of self- and group representation that challenges negative stereotypes is an ongoing negotiation.

In the Downtown Eastside of Vancouver, where many Indigenous women have been targeted, Dara Culhane problematizes portrayals of Indigenous women and gender-based violence. While media have covered stories of missing and murdered Indigenous women in this area, this coverage has both exoticized and underrepresented the voices of Native womxn who are directly impacted. Together, media tendencies of negative overexposure and undervaluing womxn's self-representation are "constitutive of a regime of disappearance."[72] Through sustained strategic action, Indigenous womxn and their families have worked to address this multilayered problem.[73] As in Vancouver, on the unceded land from which JB the First Lady raps, artists confront racialized gender-based violence around Canada and across borders. Musical interventions and public events have the potential to create attention around this issue and even to ameliorate the situation. However, performing and recording music that highlights gender-based violence risks commodifying the pain of the womxn against whom such violence is levied.

Careful audience creation is one strategy to use music in a way that acknowledges and attempts to avoids this potential pitfall.[74]

Media professionals acting in their roles as public figures could provide an opportunity to intervene, telling stories in a manner that derives from their own vantage point and speaks to their particular goals. Yet, as described in chapter 2, the limitations of people's professional roles may constrain their expressive choices. Streetz DJ Miss Melissa was motivated to participate in community events that use music as an antiviolence strategy. As a professional radio DJ, Miss Melissa has worked as a popular morning-show host who talks about everything from Justin Bieber to presidential motorcades to what members of the Wu-Tang Clan are doing now. A charismatic and humorous storyteller, she has also talked about socially conscious trends in hip hop from Winnipeg's North End neighborhood and how her role as a figure in the local music scene can influence listeners. After participating as an attendee of No Stone Unturned, she became a host as well. This community event, led by Indigenous women in Winnipeg, was designed to bring music and art alongside speaking and witnessing in a public gathering place, giving families of missing women an opportunity to tell their stories and connect with others and giving the community an opportunity to provide resources and support. While appearing in a hosting capacity is similar to Miss Melissa's work role at Streetz, she participated as an individual. Her industry role has been to manage the music library and DJ on-air; in her personal role, she took part in strategic audience creation. In the No Stone Unturned venue, musicians whose music airs on Streetz have performed with this particular audience in mind. With a connection to the cause, this self-selecting group of performers and hosts thus creates a supportive atmosphere for an intentionally crafted listenership.

Eekwol and T-Rhyme have embraced this role as storytellers for their albums' listeners, as well for audiences at touring shows. In songs for this project and others, they assert their voices in a literal fashion: storytelling, expressed through their voices, produces sound waves that travel to the ears of audience members. Eekwol is one among many rappers who point to the utility of hip hop for telling stories that need to be heard; sometimes the people who experienced them do not wish to share such personal stories directly or do not have access to the same kind of platform that successful rappers have. Eekwol explained that her song "Too Sick," about a woman in an abusive relationship, was based on experiences of women she knew. Yet the first-person narrative and sincere delivery made some listeners mistakenly assume that she was talking about a personal experience. As storytellers, musicians take on a responsibility to these people and these stories. As T-Rhyme explains, "We can share stories, and we can take on those stories as if they're our own. And that's okay. Because sometimes that person will not have the strength to share it on their own. . . . As artists, we're almost given this role and position that we carry everybody else's—we carry the world literally on our shoulders, and we just release everything bit by bit."

## Cultural Power and Rematriation: Language, Religion, and Frames for Expression

To complement this discussion of experiencing power at the interpersonal level, I turn to an analysis of cultural power. In particular, musicians, music professionals, and fans experience cultural power through the worldviews to which we are exposed, linguistic frames through which experience is known, the manner in which media sources depict expressive culture, and the narratives that are reproduced. The narratives that locate Indigeneity vis-à-vis modernity, which were exposed in chapter 1, intersect with those about gender, sexuality, and race that can normalize false statements and make one opinion seem as if it were fact. Continuing the long trajectory of expressing cultural power through song, the hip hop in this chapter presents its own stories and its own power.

*FWBW* is one such example that invoked other formations of cultural power. Collaboratives First Ladies Crew and Tribe Called Queenz have also done this work; they provide additional models for how spaces can be curated. First Ladies Crew emerged as a collective out of East Vancouver, British Columbia, on Coast Salish Territory.[75] Cofounder JB the First Lady, of the Nuxalk and Cayuga Six Nations, explains how the matriarchy of her heritage can be transmitted via hip hop: "Our ancestors, the matriarchs, were the speakers, the keepers of ceremony, and our oral history. As a young person, an activist talking about women's rights or about murdered and missing Indigenous women, hip-hop has been the best venue to connect with not only my peers and young people, but also the greater public that may have barriers to listening to the stories of First Nations' Indigenous people." She notes that the way the group worked together "wasn't a hierarchy": "We were walking together, holding hands together."[76] This structure of social relations diverges from that which musicians typically experience in the mainstream industry. JB has performed with fellow artists Mama Es, Miss Christie Lee, and the duos Rapsure Risin and Dani and Lizzy; the musicians also feature and support each other on their own projects.[77] Dani and Lizzy, too, reflect on the process of making music alongside other womxn. After working largely with boys, they explain that they first anticipated lyrical battle with other female MCs. Then, they found instead, "No, this is dope. We can actually hang out with girls who are into the same things."[78] Germinating in this space, JB's album *Righteous Empowered Daughter* addresses violence against Indigenous women and girls, notably the crisis of missing and murdered women. Several of the tracks on this album feature collaborating activists and musicians who create art that moves into decolonial action. On "All My Relations," for example, she and Kimmortal speak to concerns facing women and two-spirit people, thinking forward into "magic and decolonization."

Where else can a listener feel "magic and decolonization"? As the heartbeat of "Revitalize" on *FWBW*, the bass drum and snare drum repeat to create a regular four-beat pattern. The rhythmic sound of a record scratching punctuates the beat at steady intervals. A solo flute melody soars over these patterns, the line first rising in pitch and then falling, then rising again, reaching upward. This too, repeats, making space for the voices that enter. T-Rhyme raps her words in the chorus in a steady rhythmic flow. Each time she arrives at the word "revitalize," it is doubled by a second voice. Sonically, she is not alone. The chorus ends as she urges listeners to join her: "raise your fists high while we rise." Then, breaking with the rhythmic regularity of the song, a spoken voice enters with a question, "How do we become resilient?" This narrator offers her own answer: "It's feeling the blood of the women ancestors in my veins. Finding our voice. And being strong enough and brave enough to get up and talk about our experience." She calls for, and participates in, rematriation. Her last word, too, is echoed: "revitalization."

Offered as an alternative to repatriation by Penelope Myrtle Kelsey, rematriation entails the regeneration of the role of being responsible for land and community.[79] For Eve Tuck and Rubén Gaztambide-Fernández, rematriation is a form of "ethical relationality, an 'ecological' understanding of human relationality that does not deny difference, seeks to understand mutual implication, puts Indigenous epistemologies at the forefront, and requires a more public form of memory."[80] Musical practice is a fitting vehicle for the kind of resilience through vocalization that Eekwol and T-Rhyme espouse through their music and touring and that JB the First Lady and others articulate through cyphers and collaborations. Relationships that artists develop with fellow performers, audiences, and learners through mentorship and professional activities span time and geography. This decolonial practice is sparked in sounds. In the face of genocidal violence and dispossession, Heather Davis asserts,

> Art practices alone cannot adequately address everything that needs to change, . . . [yet] they can provide modes of critique, of resistance, of brilliant propositions, and ingenious models of relationality. Through decolonial (self-)love and rematriation, art can create avenues for Indigenous women and trans people to be the holders of their multiple and diverse identities. And settler allies can use their privileged access as platforms for Indigenous voices to be amplified, to begin to affect and infect the colonial structures of the nation-state, to slowly, but ever so surely, shift those structures towards modes of Indigenous-led governance and imaginaries.[81]

For Kelsey, Davis, and others, rematriation fundamentally entails repairing relationships to land and a rejection of colonialist powers.

Listen as JB the First Lady and collaborator Dioganhdih call to, for, and through rematriation. A minor melody played by electronic flute outlines two chords, first A minor, then B diminished. The melody repeats, solidifying one chord then the other: A minor, B diminished. The solo flute fills the aural space for four bars, then a beat drops in. The bass-register electronics slide around, a buzzy timbre sounds largely percussive even as the line outlines an A octave. The flute flips into a higher register immediately, widening the melodic range to play the same melody, outlining A minor and B diminished an octave higher. The two musical lines, one low bass and the other high treble, leave the middle register open for the voice that enters. The rapper steps into the space made for her with a lyrical realization: "Now I see reality / unmask the truth, they're killin' the youth." Over her sixteen-bar verse, the rapper, too, plays with the tension. She runs over the ends of bars to put an important word on the stressed first beat: "Makin' Native cartoons to get away with abuse / They blame us in the news." The chosen words pop out from the flow: "abuse," "news." As she keeps rapping in "Front Lines," JB untangles complexity but rhythmically gives the listener the key words: "They blame us in the news, but they excuse the accused." She elaborates how jurors fail to deliver guilty verdicts and the legal system and RCMP fail Indigenous peoples as media stereotypes make it easier to blame the very people who are wronged.

The flute outlines the chords but does not play them together; the harmonic rhythm is slow. First the A minor chord emerges, then the B diminished, over and over again. Tension builds slowly but steadily; musical devices tighten as they do in Eekwol and T-Rhyme's song "Pressure." Here, too, the loops activate this feeling. The tension repeats and does not resolve. The flute melody drops octaves. It silences some of the pattern, skipping notes when the rapper pauses; the human voice and electronic instrument voice emphasize each other as they work together: "Genocide, in slo-mo / I see you Justin, uh, Trudeau / White paper, uh, two-point-oh." Her contemporary words echo the 1969 White Paper "Statement of the Government of Canada on Indian Policy, 1969." Since version 1.0 was delivered by Justin Trudeau's father and his colleagues as part of an assimilation project, what does the listener hear as version 2.0? JB sparks many ideas and makes space for listeners to bring more: the court system of the settler state, reconciliation policy, the RCMP investigation into missing and murdered women.

A second rapper enters for the second verse, their tone more nasal. They bring the "heat from the East" and introduce themselves on the verse: "I'm a Haudenosaunee queer that was raised as a deer / Ain't had a drink in seven years / Now I'm livin' in the clear / Put that pain in the rear / Front lines without fear." Dioganhdih establishes who they are when they add their voice as a featured artist on this track on JB the First Lady's album.[82] They are ready to lead, and already leading, on the front lines. In an interview, they explain, "I was born on Haudenosaunee Territory, on what is now known as Upstate New York. Today's colonized terms call it a reservation on the Onondaga Nation, which, along with the Mohawk Nation, is a part of the Iroquois Confederacy. But I'm not actually Onondaga, I'm Mohawk through my father and my mother is Cherokee and Armenian." They continue, acknowledging that settler colonialism can make tracing one's own family ties a challenge: "Knowing where you come from is a privilege, especially for Natives, who through forced removal and assimilation were stripped of their homelands and cultures. Being a queer Indigenous person, I've been searching for a community that accepts and can hold my intersections."[83]

As a whole, JB the First Lady's 2018 album *Righteous Empowered Daughter* showcases multiple womxn and queer and two-spirit rappers living in Canada and the United States. On "Front Lines," Dioganhdih's verse connects thematically back to the chorus and the song's overall musical atmosphere. The chorus repeats, "When the tension is high / relatives with the signs / women warrior, front lines / This is, this is our time." The musical tension holds and builds, but instrumentally, melodic lines step back and make space for each rapper's voice to cut through and take prominence in the aural space. As Dioganhdih continues their verse, they deliver a message of sovereignty that is repeated across their other music and performances: "Yeah, we gon' rise. It's a prophecy, our time, my life, my line. My choice, my voice. Huh. Clanada and the United Snakes, Turtle Island come back, this is the break." As they described at a performance, "it's a matter of upholding our own sovereignty."[84] This rapped line is exactly that—a call to recognize sovereignty that already exists. And it is delivered with a little humor. The wordplay on "Clanada" and the "United Snakes" is clever; the reference to the racist Ku Klux Klan and the sly snakes that could recall USAmerican political rallies from colonists under the Gadsden flag through the Tea Party movement show a racist and colonial orientation at the very core—the names—of the present-day nation-states. This kind of humor with a sting is part of what the rapper often delivers. As they put it, "The only way I can move through the world is with comedic breaks. Humor is relatable and available, a necessary element in healing. It's a reprieve from all the processing, grieving, shedding of trauma, and bullshit that we carry. Plus, it stings a li'l less when realities are muddled with satire."[85] Dioganhdih takes the listener into the break. Their call, "Turtle Island, come back," leads to a fuzzy glissando; the pitch in the background rises as the chorus returns. A voice repeats, both calling for and stating that women warriors are on the front lines. The instrumentals cut out and let the voice resonate. The final sound is a strong assertion: "This is, this is our time."

The cultural power at work that disadvantages womxn, and particularly Indigenous womxn and other womxn of color, is clearly operative in hip hop. Yet it extends far beyond performance spaces, as do efforts to call attention to, and even dismantle, its power. Cultural power is expressed and felt through storytelling: in narrative, poetry, song, and in daily word choices.[86] Musicians point to repeated terms and familiar feedback leveled exclusively against them and other womxn artists. One of these is the prevalence among some reporters and industry workers of the label "femcee." The enduring use of the term crystallizes the structural exclusion faced by womxn in the popular music industry. The use of this word, applied to female MCs, highlights the gender of female artists, while reserving the generic term "MC" for males. Discursively, this both calls further attention to womxn's gender, which artists report is already highlighted by men to an often uncomfortable degree, and also suggests that the purportedly unmarked category is in fact gendered male, as is the profession of the MC. Focusing on womxn as female MCs suggests a lack of seriousness afforded to female artists and also reflects a pervasive notion that female artists are a novelty and thus that there is limited space for them among artist rosters or at shows. A perception of limited opportunities for female artists can also dovetail with attempts to encourage female artists to compete against each other for limited space, rather than increasing the space available for their music. Feminists worked hard to remove phrases such as "female doctor" from socially acceptable discourse; these exert a similar form of misogynist discursive power as "femcee," yet some people in the music industry continue to use the latter term to describe professional musicians.

As epochal forces that impact gender roles, Christianity and the English language have both altered the dynamics of cultural power. T-Rhyme has seen the power of English in her own lifetime. She recalls that her grandmother did not discern between feminine and masculine pronouns either in her native Cree or in the English she learned later in life. Based on the norms she learned in school, T-Rhyme made this gendered language distinction and even corrected her own grandmother for getting this "wrong." Upon reflection now, both T-Rhyme and Eekwol identify that Cree and English have different approaches to gender. While there is nothing incorrect about the Cree linguistic approach, the cultural power of the English language and its use in school and other official institutions are so great that many people, the rappers vividly recall, were raised believing in Cree as an inferior form of communication. In contrast, Eekwol has since been taught, "Women went hunting too. If a woman was a good hunter, a good shot, she went too. No problem. . . . Because tipi camps were hard to survive. You needed the best people to do the jobs to survive. A lot of men stayed home and took care of kids because they were better at nurturing. One of my young two-spirit friends talks about how two-spirit were the ones that took care of kids because they were so nurturing." Inherited norms relating to sexuality and sexual orientation, too, are often both strongly influential and strategically invisibilized. Musicians reference how ideas of homophobia and fear of two-spirit and related identities came with heteropatriarchal ideas brought by colonization. The idea that pre-contact societies had different, and more tolerant, notions of sexuality and sexual orientation emerges in contemporary discourse, in repeated colloquial language such as "Tipis don't have closets."

Discussing cultural power in the context of these projects requires an acknowledgment of the bicultural experiences of the artists and of some audience members.[87] The overwhelming power of majoritarian Anglophone settler culture cannot be denied; its impact circumscribes the very language—linguistic and musical—that the artists often operate in. For *FWBW*, Nehiyaw culture, with its own set of prevailing values and attitudes, also actively shapes interactions. T-Rhyme, Eekwol, and I discussed how matriarchy is a prevailing facet of Nehiyaw culture, as well as of some other Indigenous and non-Indigenous cultures. Its impact is felt in interactions T-Rhyme and Eekwol have in the present. For example, both musicians are inspired by their grandmothers. The matriarchal influence also extends to both women's partners: Eekwol's husband grew up speaking Cree and learning from his grandmother, and T-Rhyme's non-Indigenous partner was raised by a strong woman, they explained.

Eekwol speaks about the gender roles that are part of her Nehiyaw heritage, as does T-Rhyme, who also has Denesuline roots. They both refer to commonalities among other Native North American pre-contact cultures, a refrain I have heard from womxn and men across the United States and Canada. Native North American cultures are incredibly diverse; cultural differences are even more varied when considered across time.[88] In urban areas, where these cyphers operate, many musicians and audience members find intertribal Indigeneity to be relevant, often in addition to one or more Nation-specific identities.[89] Indigenous womxn's perspectives are impacted by far more intersecting axes than gender and class; Devon Mihesuah has found in her historical research that these elements include "race (or races), tribal social systems, factionalism, culture change, physiological appearance, and personal motivations."[90] As Eekwol and T-Rhyme reference, gender identity and sexual orientation are also elements that impact experience and viewpoint. Mihesuah's category "personal motivations" serves as a reminder that individual goals and viewpoints intersect with all of these categories; there are as many nuances to belief systems as there are individuals. As Mihesuah reflects when presenting the individual life story of one Comanche elder, "Just as tribes differ from each other in history and cultural adherence, individual tribespeople vary within the same tribe."[91] Her careful historical analysis, which accounts for these axes, has yet identified many commonalities among Native North American groups that differ from major trends in settler society: "The spiritual traditions of many tribes include a female divine spirit," whereas Euro-Christian conversion required allegiance to a single male-gendered deity; in many cases, women "did indeed have religious, political, and economic power."[92] This research highlights, for the twenty-first century, knowledge about a variety of nonpatriarchal governance systems and attitudes across Indigenous North American tribes prior to sustained, transformational contact with settlers.

Interventions that would move women, men, and nonbinary people toward parity in the music industry would begin to correct entrenched difference in treatment, but it is not sufficient: addressing the raced implications of colonial relations, too, is imperative. Colonial heteropatriarchy is a way of organizing the world. This system accrues privileges and power asymmetrically based on gender ascription; it is rooted in the idea that these unmeritoriously assigned power hierarchies are necessary and appropriate for social functioning. Verna St.

Denis (Cree and Métis) argues that Western patriarchy is a problem for Indigenous women and men, as well as everyone else living with the system. Achieving parity within this system is not a sufficient goal, as "equality is not enough and does little to address colonial relations."[93] She advocates for not abandoning men and the ways they have been mistreated by Western patriarchy but also not being complacent with patriarchal ideas and forces.[94] Rearticulating sovereignty—particularly as it relates to cultural sovereignty and womxn's bodily sovereignty—acts as a refusal against Euro-American colonial gender structures, instead choosing contemporary iterations of pre-contact ideas of gender and sex, including those that do not fit in the English language or USAmerican and Canadian social organization at present. Enacting refusal is one strategy for musicians to challenge colonial ideologies and practices; it forms a key component of sovereignty through musical expression.[95]

This struggle is one in which many people and groups are implicated and from which many will benefit. Coauthors Qwo-Li Driskill, Chris Finley, Brian Joseph Gilley, and Scott Lauria Morgensen highlight the importance of artists, particularly LGBTQ2+ and female and nonbinary artists, in imagining the future and doing the work to get us there: "Artists are the visionaries leading us to a bright future, to mourning the past in productive ways, and to sensuously stunning us in the present." They articulate, "we—as Indigenous people, as GLBTQ2 people, as feminists, and as allies in numerous struggles—must engage in long-term, multifaceted, decolonial activism and scholarship that centralize analyses of, and resistance to, heteropatriarchal colonial systems in all of their manifestations."[96] Projects, collaborations, and cyphers created by and for womxn contend with structural, disciplinary, interpersonal, and cultural power. Indigenous womxn and their allies face barriers to access for some mainstream spaces. Artists' responses encompass various strategies for creating their own listenerships. As was described in chapter 3, sometimes "alternative" listenerships influence the mainstream listenerships from which they were excluded. The work done in these spaces, however, need not center the desires of a mainstream audience. The second half of this chapter explores what these exclusive listenerships make possible and suggests future directions for artist-audience engagement.

## Backspin: Why Is This Still Happening?
## Or, Have We Heard This All Before?

In "Real as It Gets," *FWBW* first exposes gendered expectations and then defies them. Eekwol raps that she's real in sweatpants stained with hot sauce, cataloging the beauty expectations and appearance-based feedback launched at womxn and especially those who perform onstage. Building to the song's hook, she turns around the negative use of the word "pussy," operationalizing it as an expression of strength: "Pussy? Weak? Tch, you must be crazy. / I don't know anything stronger that can push out a baby. / So, of course, no question, this is for the ladies. / Take myself out the corner, don't need no Patrick Swayze." Perhaps her listeners cringed while watching this 1987 version of a damsel-in-distress narrative in *Dirty Dancing*, or maybe her audience is only laughing for the first time now because of the juxtaposition. In any case, her words wryly touch the absurdity of the male hero swooping into this mainstream teen love story for people who don't need to be saved, don't want to be saved, or won't be saved by anyone but themselves.

Gendered expectations for behavior can be so ubiquitous that they may not be readily apparent until disrupted in some manner. That is, many observers will assume a naturalness to face-to-face dynamics, not becoming aware of their highly gendered nature unless something happens to alter them. A phenomenological approach to gender expectations, theorized by Judith Butler in the late 1980s, has since informed decades of research in gender studies, queer theory, and even in musical practices. Butler argues, "if gender is instituted through acts which are internally discontinuous, then the *appearance of substance* is precisely that, a constructed identity, a performative accomplishment which the mundane social audience, including the actors themselves, come to believe and perform in the mode of belief."[97] This idea of identity construction is so ubiquitous that it is worked and reworked in twenty-first-century popular culture.[98] Theorized in practice by performers for decades, if listener-viewers understand gender to be a "stylized repetition of acts" that the actors have come to believe are natural, then revealing that belief offers the first step toward reperforming gender in another manner. Stage performers, notably musicians, are well positioned to help crack the illusion of naturalness and offer reperformances of gender that overflow into quotidian activities. And they have been doing so for years. Yet musicians and fans active in the twenty-first century continue to experience prescripted interpersonal dynamics, which can still conceal their own artificially imposed nature. Social sanctions are high; the illusion is often convincing. Eekwol and T-Rhyme have been performing for decades; a hip hop show in which, exceptionally, the audience was primarily female served as a pivot in the way they think about audience dynamics, as will be explored later in this chapter.

In popular music leading up to and through the 1990s, musicians and fans who read Butler and contemporary gender theorists created music, wrote zines, and enacted performance dynamics that were explicitly in conversation with this scholarship. On Le Tigre's self-titled 1999 album, they explore the influence of feminist culture producers in the song "Hot Topic," including Leslie Feinberg, whose writing explores sexual orientation as it intersects with class; academic Mab Segrest, who is known for her feminist antiracist writing; and postcolonial critical theorist Gayatri Spivak. Their lyrics call attention to social regulations, which, based on the context of the song, could reasonably be interpreted as those rules related to gendered expectations and racial biases: "So many rules and so much opinion / So much bullshit, but we won't give in." Decades before #MeToo pushed questions about if and how audiences could appreciate films and television made by men who harass and rape womxn, their "What's Ya Take on Cassavettes" debates how audience members reconcile the misogyny, possible genius, and alcoholic ramblings they encounter in the filmmaker's output. All of the members of punk band Huggy Bear, women and men, have identified in interviews specific theorists who inspire their music and performance practice, such as bell hooks, Julia Kristeva, and Hélène Cixous. Girls Rock Camps across the United States in the 2000s perform covers of Bikini Kill's 1993 "Rebel Girl"; girls develop their artistic takes on the emphatic, fast chords and lyrics such as, "When she talks, I hear the revolution"; "That girl thinks she's the queen of the neighborhood / I got news for you, she is!"

As in rock and punk, hip hop, R&B, and neosoul music based specifically in critical feminist theory and artistic practice led up to the turn of the previous century. Feminist and womanist messaging has long been present in hip hop; the messaging of *FWBW* and related cyphers is both precedented and still necessary. Erykah Badu's "Bag Lady," released in

2000 on her album *Mama's Gun*, is a musical reworking of *For Colored Girls Who Have Considered Suicide When the Rainbow Is Enuf*, the 1975 play by Ntozake Shange that presents twenty poems through individual women's personal stories about being Black and female in the United States. "Ladies First," by Queen Latifah and featuring Monie Love, has become a kind of anthem. Released in 1989 on the album *All Hail the Queen*, Queen Latifah opens, "A woman can bear you, break you, take you / Now it's time to rhyme, can you relate to / A sister dope enough to make you holler and scream." Specifically countering a stereotype that women can't rap, she replies, "Stereotypes, they got to go," and then the two women groove through two more verses of fast-flowing rhymes.[99] Holler, scream, rap along. This is a litany of strength and a remembering of leaders. This style of honoring and remembering forward extended into the 1990s; it continues into the changing hip hop atmosphere of the twenty-first century.

## Humor and Rage

Continuing in this legacy of storytelling through song, Eekwol and T-Rhyme offer the refreshing pairing of humor and rage. By creating an exclusive listenership, they are able to play up humor that will resonate with this chosen audience and share anger in a way that might be misunderstood by other hearers. The musicians' strategy is effective in part because it is fun, and funny. Eekwol makes a wry nod to the discomfort of wearing high heels and then half jokes that they're applying lipstick while plotting revolution. T-Rhyme's fast wordplay is witty, balancing internal and end rhymes, in a way that makes me smile and tip my hat to her at the same time. They both make creative twists with pop culture references that make me laugh out loud. And they are unapologetically real. The MCs rap about anger, rage, panic, and pressure. Bolstered by tension in the instrumentals, the rage and pressure at times become visceral. When I listen, I hear moments of anger that are pieces of narrative, and I also feel something in the telling, and the listening, that offers a way not to bottle the rage but to turn it toward motivation for action.

A comedic approach to rage-inducing situations is part of how Indigenous humor is often described, for example, by Dioganhdih earlier in this chapter, and the way humor operates in *FWBW* also extends past any single definition.[100] This attitude finds a productive fit in hip hop: The practice emerged in a space of block parties and get-togethers, the influences of toasting and comedic jabs bringing together the razor's edge of jesting and jousting. Simultaneously, signifyin' had artists— especially rappers—speaking truths in a kind of nuanced metaphor, saying that which needed to be said but could not be directly spoken. The practice also came up in a space where violent physical conflict was subsumed in proxy battles of breaking and rapping. Later artists define hip hop by its very use of anger. Given a sense of humor that is more than purely funny, attributes of hip hop and Indigenous humor speak to each other. Rage is embedded in the humor, and vice versa; both must be expressed so as not to consume the speaker, as well as in order to create a crucible for further action.

This finely tuned humor and specifically pitched rage is operative in performance contexts besides Indigenous hip hop; José Muñoz found in his groundbreaking *Disidentifications* that "comedy does not exist independently of rage" in queer of color performance art. The rage that is voiced in performance "is sustained and it is pitched as a call to activism, a bid to take space in the social that has been colonized by the logics of white normativity and heteronormativity."[101] Manifestations of rage in hip hop that are related to gender- and race-based discrimination resonate in some ways with this description. In the words of Audre Lorde, "Every woman has a well-stocked arsenal of anger potentially useful against those oppressions, personal and institutional, which brought that anger into being."[102] The cyphers and projects discussed here all hinge on angry vocalizations and physical gestures that provide mental reprieve for the artists and audiences and that impel both groups to manifest, and then transform, that rage into ongoing action that further centers their own experience at the expense of the settler heteropatriarchy. In these spaces, what Muñoz found is nuanced. Where he has found "activism," what emerges in these spaces is instead a different form of engagement.

In many North American Indigenous contexts, the idea of "activism" does not resonate quite as it does in Muñoz's definition. Dioganhdih explained at a performance, "It's often hard to differentiate between activism and music and life."[103] They say that many Indigenous people are not given a choice as to whether to be politically active. On the

228 | THIS MUSIC IS NOT FOR YOU

reservation where they have lived, for example, they are "inherently political," because the US-Canada border and multiple state and provincial
borders were placed across the land.[104] Without asking to be put in the
middle, they and their family, then, contend with land borders, border
patrol personnel, and companies that use the water that flows across
these borders. This idea of finding oneself dealing with externally imposed commercial and governmental structures echoes what pop musician, throat singer, and Inuk performance artist Tanya Tagaq explained
to me: "The idea of activism I kind of have to scoff at it. Because when
you live it . . . it's not being an activist, it's just being a human being in
the day to day."[105] Their responses parallel those of many Indigenous
musicians who find that responsibility is not reserved for a small group
of activists but for everyone. Additionally, those who are impacted by
the systems that cause the rage cannot choose to avoid confronting the
situation. It is crucial, too, to note that expressions of rage-work differ when performed by queer bodies; the artists in Muñoz's study move
through the world in a particular way and experience the world and its
power dynamics in a manner that cannot be divorced from their queer-
ness. A variation in lived experience impacts rappers and other hip hop
musicians, as their bodies that expel and transform this rage have been
shaped, and continue to be impacted, by external realities.

*FWBW* is one of many projects and spaces where humor shines
alongside antiracist and feminist action. Humor is central to storytelling in Anishinaabeg and Nehiyaw traditions, so its prevalence in rapped
lyrics is in many ways unsurprising. For humor to exist with and even
through accounts of discrimination and violence, and charges for action, is consistent with these storytelling practices. In Janice Acosta
and Natasha Beeds's pun-laden collaborative account of Nehiyaw/Cree
humor, they explain, "Cree-ative humor encourages us to laugh at everything. Nothing is exempt; the more sacred the idea, the better it is
to poke fun at."[106]

In a similar humor-centered approach, conceptions of humor within
and beyond Nehiyaw contexts are operational in performance environments.[107] This hip hop space, like many of its predecessors, invites jocu-
larity. Yet here, humor and survival are intertwined: in the words of Vine
Deloria, "When a people can laugh at themselves and laugh at others
and hold all aspects of life together without letting anybody drive them

to extremes, then it seems to me that that people can survive."[108] Storytelling, a tool for enacting sonic sovereignty, can incorporate humor in radical ways. According to Louise Profeit-Leblanc's analysis of the performative and orality in storytelling, both factors carry over into the space of music performance. This storyteller, from the Nacho N'yak Dun First Nation in northern Yukon, prepares readers for her telling by reminding them that "stories like this one are meant to be told, spoken, shared with a listener, with many nuances, sound effects, and cadences of language and much pointing of the mouth, the chin, and the nose." Sound, gesture, and embodied telling are part of the story, as are pauses and silence. The audience must prepare for another world, "a world where many of the simple things in life are so horrendous that the only way to stay sane is simply to laugh about it all."[109] Humor is functional. Anishinaabe writer Lawrence W. Gross finds that it allows communities to deal with stress in ways that can be generative: "Along with many other Native American peoples, the Anishinaabe have seen the end of our world, which has created tremendous social stresses. The comic vision of the Anishinaabe is helping us overcome that trauma and helps explain how we are managing to survive."[110] Sovereign approaches to humor can come together with self-directed approaches to rage. On *FWBW*, for example, Eekwol raps, "I've gotta learn, teach, fight, and pray / so this rage comes out in productive ways." Hierarchical organization of power, felt across its structural, interpersonal, cultural, and disciplinary aspects, creates feelings of domination in which bodies sit. They also move, scream, sing, listen, pray, maneuver, and dance. As a space and an action created by participating bodies, in a cypher, people feel and act in a temporary collectivity.

## The Hip Hop Cypher and Sovereign Space

In hip hop, the cypher is a way to gather. Often in a circle, rappers trade verses and listen to each other. Cyphers for womxn encounter many of the same questions that other separate spaces face. Eekwol, T-Rhyme, and I discussed how the very act of creating a separate space for womxn in some ways acknowledges the kind of gender binary system that is supported by the patriarchal constructs they are working against. Yet creating an alternative space acts as a productive response to the kinds of bias and gendered violence that people experience. And, when created carefully, it can be more equitable than the strict binary hierarchy against which it is counterposed. Why argue for inclusion in a flawed system? Cyphers, festivals, and performance nights that showcase female and nonbinary artists can both offer the access womxn are denied in mainstream venues and model alternative ways of interacting. Spaces that support Indigenous womxn as part of these efforts enact alternate possibilities. Mainstream music structures might or might not learn from these; they are not centered in these efforts. Musicians instead choose whom to invite in order to do necessary work that would be challenging with an unsympathetic audience.

Instead of competing for artificially scarce resources, it is possible to find mutual success. Accepting the narrative that only a few can be heard is a form of acquiescence to a heteropatriarchal mind-set that suggests that only token womxn or people of color may excel; thinking through sonic sovereignty suggests other ways of interacting. Opting out of forms of competition that pigeonhole womxn does not necessarily preclude rappers from participating in the sometimes-jovial yet serious competition based on skills, ubiquitous in hip hop through battling. This is the case for members of *FWBW*, as well as for other cyphers focused on female and nonbinary musicians. Participants in *FWBW*, Tribe Called Queenz, and First Ladies Crew do not eschew rap battling. Some insist on the importance of battling with men, in statements they make verbally and through showing up prepared for a (usually) good-natured battle. T-Rhyme makes this distinction with a bit of a knowing laugh. She explains that her partner sometimes tells her she's "better than certain men in the scene." He will say, "'You're better than that guy. I was there.' But he never tries to pit me against my sisters. And that to me is so imperative in that whole allyship, too, right? So it's just changing all these narratives in these ways of thinking within our own communities and in our own relationships. It is so important."

*FWBW* was conceived as a collaboration. It came into the world because of Eekwol and T-Rhyme's work, and the musicians collaborate with, and credit, others. This collectivity presents an alternative to entrenched power structures. When the title song was released on December 21, 2018, T-Rhyme offered thanks (in English and Cree) and

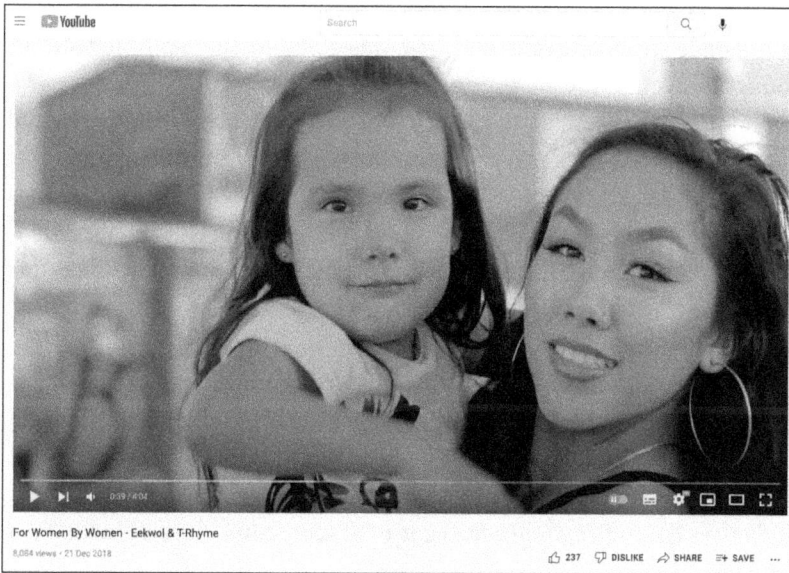

Figure 4.5. "FWBW" music video cover still. (YouTube, www.youtube.com/watch?v
=6kqUdA9IA-0)

acknowledgment to many collaborators. The artists credit the videogra-
pher Enkrypt for her work.[111]

As the musicians take time to thank many contributors to the project, they recognize the specialized labor and knowledge of a network of
people who dedicated time to making it a reality. This embodies a spirit
of collaboration and also contrasts with experiences musicians have in
other spaces. Not only do some musicians find it difficult to access the
support they need, but–intentionally or not—others sometimes act in
ways that undercut their productivity. When discussing the project after
a show, Eekwol, T-Rhyme, and I were not even able to have an uninter-
rupted conversation about their work. We were speaking in a gallery
space. This was a showcase of hip hop visual art, which coincided with
a hip hop festival. While we were talking, a man came up to the table
where we were seated. He lingered in order to overhear some of our conversation and then proceeded to speak about his own work experience.
Though no one encouraged him to go on, he did at some length. When
we reflected at the end of our conversation, both rappers mentioned that
this interjection was one of the reasons that the project was so necessary.

We were having a conversation about Eekwol and T-Rhyme's artistry, and a male stranger decided that he was going to take up time with his thoughts, even in the absence of our professed interest.

In hip hop collectives, the subject of collaboration is ever present, and Indigenous womxn's leadership is invaluable in creating and maintaining group success. The groups also leverage solidarity with non-Indigenous and mixed-heritage audience members and music professionals. Multiple Indigenous group members acknowledge their own hip hop learning from Black American musicians in conversation and in their music. The *FWBW* album, for example, offers a witty layering of nods to Black female rappers, as referenced in the first section of this chapter. Tribe Called Queenz includes non-Indigenous hip hop artists.[112] Tribe Called Queenz, First Ladies Crew, and the *FWBW* project work with musicians and other music professionals who do not identify as Indigenous. Across groups, audiences fail to fit into neat categories of race, ethnocultural identity, or heritage.

Returning to the "us" whom this project is for, it becomes clear that musicians and audience members are invited to think through all the aspects of who they are and who they can become. The process of becoming involves reflecting on how the very constitution of the self is circumscribed by the way the cultural power of norms and expectations delineate behavior. It may seem somewhat obvious to say that messages of worth, possibility, and expectation are leveraged differently on individuals on the basis of gender, race, and class. Yet it is crucial to continually acknowledge and respond to the many ways in which this power is felt in the day-to-day and to seek ways in which to rearticulate the self as sovereign.

In the following excerpt of conversation, Eekwol and T-Rhyme dialogue about what "us" means. In so doing, they develop understandings of the personal importance of projects such as *FWBW* for the artists, audiences, and young listeners. The "us" is created strategically, as there is work to do.

> T-RHYME: It's imperative that we understand who we are. Our bodies are our bodies, and we carry all this power and knowledge and teachings, and we just gotta keep this conversation going. And you know,

teaching your kids and everything too, because they are the ones that
have to, have to . . . [*pause*]

EEKWOL: Carry it on.

T-RHYME: Yeah, exactly. Because unfortunately a lot was lost.

EEKWOL: Mmhmm [*affirmative*].

T-RHYME: Our culture and our language was lost. . . . You know, I'm
just starting to learn things now in my culture, in my language, and I
feel like I'm being reborn in a way because it's like the rebirth of my
Indigeneity, I guess. You know?

EEKWOL: Mmhmm [*affirmative*].

LP: Yeah.

T-RHYME: Because I walked this Earth only knowing one thing for so
long. Now I'm finally understanding my own fire.

"For us" comprises the artists: they have done their own healing work
through rap and performance; they continue to do work that helps them.
T-Rhyme elaborates: "It's been really eye opening, even for me, because I
am very much guilty of—back in the day, I would slut shame. I would put
down other women, I would fight other women, I would discredit. I did
all these toxic things because I wasn't happy with myself. I wasn't proud of
who I was, and I didn't know or see my worth. And now that I've grown
and I've experienced and I've done so many things that have shifted my
thoughts and perspectives." She continues, "You can't have movements
without growth. You can't have any of that."

From "for us" to "by us," the artists call into conversation articulations of personal bodily self-determination with the collectively produced sovereignty of dialogic performance spaces. The work done by
the "us" of this project is at once personal and connected to community.
This resonates with a growing body of Indigenous feminist literature.
Shirley Green identifies that her sense of self has been impacted by not
learning her heritage language, Ktunaxa, and that this loss enforced
class-based codes and stems from bias against Indigenous people and
against womxn: "My mother denied her heritage and ours because of the
pressures of a racist, sexist society, where to be Indian was to be viewed
as being a low-class person, with few opportunities for education, employment, growth or progress within the dominant white society."[113]

Reclaiming cultural knowledge and practices, as T-Rhyme and Green describe, is a personal challenge that has effects beyond the individual. Green elaborates, "It is only by reclaiming our heritage that we can gain an understanding of who we are and enable us to achieve our full potential, as Aboriginal women."[114]

## Funding Indigenous Music: Support for Strategic Exclusivity and Audience Making

When T-Rhyme and Eekwol wrote their funding application to the Canada Council for the Arts, which Eekwol described as "poetic" and "full of passion," the artists were responding to their frustration about gendered disparities they see around them in the music industry. The album was to be a way to directly address the inequities Indigenous womxn face attempting to get heard; securing funding would also be a substantive way for them to alter the playing field, at least for this project.

Some granting agencies have established dedicated funds for Indigenous arts activities. The Canada Council for the Arts, a prominent example, has publicized that it "is committed to reaffirming and revitalizing its relationship with First Nations, Inuit and Métis peoples in Canada. The Canada Council believes that an approach that respects First Nations, Inuit and Métis artistic expression, cultural protocols, Indigenous rights and Indigenous worldviews will stimulate First Nations, Inuit and Métis artists, artistic practices, and communities."[115] The Canada Council has identified that artists with and without formalized institutional training can qualify; its grant website has featured work by First Nations, Inuit, and Métis artists prominently among its funded projects.[116] The council specifies that the granting project respects self-determination and, as such, "will be guided by Indigenous values and worldviews, administered by staff of First Nations, Inuit and Métis heritage, and assessed by First Nations, Inuit and Métis individuals."[117]

Eekwol and T-Rhyme used funding from the Canada Council to produce the album *For Women By Women*. Under the Canada Council's Creating, Knowing and Sharing program, which is specifically for art and culture activities of First Nations, Inuit, and Métis artists, Eekwol was awarded CAD$18,100 in the 2017 grant cycle. She reports that she found the grant helpful in freeing the duo from commercial expectations, letting them instead focus on what they needed to say.[118] Creating a strategically exclusive listenership comes with real monetary costs; working musicians, especially those who are structurally excluded from mainstream industry access, need support to shoulder these costs.

Presenting at festivals across Canada and beyond borders, *For Women By Women* was supported by government and private funders at multiple levels that facilitate these events. T-Rhyme and Eekwol were featured performers at the sākihiwē festival in the summer of 2019. Formerly Aboriginal Music Week, this festival was in its tenth year in 2019. Hosted by Aboriginal Music Manitoba in Winnipeg, it features First Nation, Métis, Inuit, Native American, and Indigenous artists in multiple venues across the city. The sākihiwē festival is supported by federal, provincial, and city funding sources, incorporating heritage and arts funding streams. These include the government of Canada (Department of Canadian Heritage), the Canada Council for the Arts, the Province of Manitoba, the Manitoba Arts Council, and the Winnipeg Arts Council. Funding streams such as these have the potential to expand access to making and distributing music. Studio-quality hardware, software, and either personnel, training, or a combination thereof can be expensive and out of reach for many artists. This is compounded for artists who are already performing many kinds of labor and/or for whom safety is another barrier to studio access. Early revenue (for recording) and non-unit-based revenue (e.g., not per ticket or per album) frees artists to express themselves without fear of covering production costs and helps increase equity for female and nonbinary Indigenous artists.

## For Whom, by Whom

To those who have wondered, is speaking only to womxn retrogressive? Or why would artists exclude possible audience members? A moment from a live performance shows the clarity and generative energy that come from strategic refusal. The Sorority was originally composed of Toronto-based musicians pHoenix Pagliacci, Keysha Freshh, Haviah Mighty, and Lex Leosis. The MCs got together in 2016 for a cypher, and it was such a success that they continued to perform together. Each artist continues her own projects as well. Reformed as a trio (pHoenix

Pagliacci moved on to other undertakings), they have performed with other groups who are gaining an increasing following in Canada and beyond, such as the duo Snotty Nose Rez Kids from the Haisla Nation. When The Sorority toured in Saskatoon, they invited Eekwol and T-Rhyme to open for their show. As they discuss the show, both rappers affirm and build on the idea that this show broke from expected gender norms of artist—and audience—behavior:

> EEKWOL: That show was the first time in my life there were these
>   amazing MCs onstage//
> T-RHYME: All four of them//
> EEKWOL: Like we were on first, of course [*laughs*]. And I look, and the
>   audience was mostly women [*T-Rhyme emphatically affirming*]. It
>   sent chills through me. Women and those who identify as. So it was
>   this amazing powerful performance 'cause they're so good. But it
>   was a safe space, and everybody was just vibing out and good//
> T-RHYME: And it was cool//
> EEKWOL: It wasn't a bunch of men in the center being all like, "Rah,
>   rah, rah." It was weird.

At this show, Eekwol and T-Rhyme experienced an audience rapport that challenged norms they had experienced before, and they found power in the performance coming from the artists, which was reflected in the good vibes of the audience. In our conversation, it became clear that this moment brought their previous performing experiences into sharp relief: men at the center had always been the norm. These MCs are often expected to perform in spaces that are *first for men* and largely controlled *by men*, though this default is rarely expressed in such terms. Safety here is crucial. In unsafe spaces, the power to define oneself, and even to maintain one's own bodily integrity, is not respected. This all-womxn show is a manifestation of the power in refusal. Clarity emerges when the musicians say "No"—they understand something that they had perhaps felt before but never quite articulated, as they experience altered gender performance in this closer-to-homosocial space. As in Simpson's working of potentials of refusal, something new is known here. While working toward possible futures, a generative space comes into being, even if only temporarily. The "rah, rah, rah" machismo that fans often perform is absent; the space to listen and dance is safer, as in other popular music shows in which audience dynamics are intentionally managed to become safer spaces for womxn fans.

Let us return now to listening. Audience creation is about active listening. It involves listeners showing up at artists' shows. They dance along; they sing or rap the lyrics with the musicians. Listening is active engagement and embodied engagement; it is an engagement that happens outside the brain that other people are able to perceive. An interpersonal connection is operational here: this is a listening that happens with other people. Someone is rapping or singing or playing; listeners sense vibrations to the ear and the brain, then do something with those vibrations. Listening does not stop at being at both ends of those sound waves; there is a relationship that is created through them that invites subsequent action.

Sonic sovereignty is invoked through this building of relationships on both ends of sound waves. Unlike a mechanical process of hearing, listening builds the archive of the body: the listener can transform as she listens; she becomes a witness and changes through the witnessing. What she carries forward, then, is her experience and the experiences of others whose narratives fold together through musical storytelling. And through music listening, so often a chosen repeated process, she changes with each iteration, over time, as her archive of bodily knowledge expands with each experience.

Witnessing a story requires action with it; as T-Rhyme expressed, "If you stand with us, then *you stand with us.*" Yet even in the moment, a relational bond is created through participatory listening. This listening involves choice, power, and agency. Yes, the listener is drawn into relationship and responsibility through having chosen to listen. An autonomous choice has created an interdependent relationship. An embodied webbing of networked experiences comes into being in the performance space. The musician, as speaker, rapper, player of music, is curating the music, shaping the sound waves. Given the relationship that will be created through the physical connection of sound vibration, why would she not also curate the audience? Artists in these cyphers and projects are directly acting on their ability to set up conditions in which listening is directed in some way. Their active choices direct the engaged listener, for example, by requiring a commitment or by needing to know that people can talk about things like pay inequality and gender-based violence and that no one is going to question the legitimacy of these experiences. Sonic sovereignty becomes operational in this listening relationship: the musicians sculpt the listenership, just like they sculpt the sound created for it. And to be part of the relationship, the hearer must choose to become a listener.

In this chapter, I have engaged in an intersectional analysis of overlapping dimensions of power—as Collins and Bilge describe—in order to reveal how behavior is circumscribed. The reflections with and through *FWBW* and the related projects First Ladies Crew and Tribe Called Queenz offer a way of analyzing sexist and racist biases in the music industry; these reflect gendered, raced, and classed expectations that persist in twenty-first-century settler colonial states. Faced with structural barriers that minimize their access to a mainstream music industry, these artists respond with strategic exclusivity, crafting their own listenerships in order to laugh together, rage together, and take over physical and sonic space on their own terms.

Consciously having these conversations leads to productive intersectional ends. While artists and audiences have sometimes sidestepped direct conversations about race, increasingly, non-Black artists (Indigenous and non-Indigenous) and listeners are acknowledging the importance of engaging in antiracist work, working against anti-Blackness, and figuring out how to participate in such efforts. This process involves recognizing anti-Blackness when it occurs in many communities, including communities of color and hip hop circles, and working to combat it. This overlaps with ongoing efforts to name and work against misogyny, homophobia, ableism, and class bias.

The way hip hop musicians tell stories is important in its own right. It is also crucial because the stories they tell influence contemporary behavior. These stories support efforts such as working with young people. For Eekwol and T-Rhyme, this is the relationship building of rematriation, which takes form through mentoring womxn. It also encompasses taking time to understand and support the needs of two-spirit people. As Eekwol recalls, she is frequently approached by two-spirit young people for guidance writing lyrics. As a result, she explained, "we've established this thing. It's called the Indigenous Poets Society. And it started in Saskatoon and continues to grow and branch out. And there's a huge group of two-spirit young people that are active participants in that. Some of the meetings are held at the pride spaces. So that's another solidarity that happens through lyric writing [*T-Rhyme affirms*]—just being able to talk about your experience and talk about culture." Generating resources for allied causes, the *FWBW* album-release show was a benefit concert that raised funds for the Unist'ot'en Camp; the Indigenous Poets Society hosted.[119]

The way the music industry works for the musicians in this chapter, or does not work, reflects larger ways in which society works, and does not work, for certain people: Indigenous women, nonbinary people, two-spirit people, girls, women, women of color, white women, and so on. The cyphers and projects highlighted here create a separate space. In some ways, this might feel retrogressive. After all, many women's music spaces no longer exist, notable women-owned labels have folded, and some industry professionals and artists alike are questioning whether Indigenous music categories and award shows are still necessary. Music industry operations, impacted globally by neoliberalism, create financial conditions in which artists must often make allowances for the mainstream ear.[120] However, as Eekwol and T-Rhyme found performing with The Sorority, making music in spaces designed for womxn is neither old-fashioned nor reactionary. In *FWBW*, artists and listeners find power in saying this music is not for you; this music is for *us*, for the people who need to hear it. They access power by refusing to please or conform.

The music industry as a whole, and the way that it operates, relies on an assumed masculine audience. For example, a hip hop audience has been imagined to keep tuning in to mainstream radio and streaming audio and buying music and tickets to shows, even if those media deploy homophobic or misogynist language or messaging. *FWBW* and cyphers for womxn reveal that there has long been an unnamed but assumed masculine performer and listener. Now, artists like Eekwol and T-Rhyme are marking their listeners—as nonbinary or two-spirit or female—and saying, "We are making music for *you*." This is an end to the fiction of the generic listener: the specific kind of power dynamic at play was so convincing at normalizing a narrative of the unmarked listener that many people were not conscious of the fact that the listener was, in fact, marked. *FWBW* and related cyphers, then, are not really new, but they are newly transparent. One of the crucial interventions of this project is that it reveals how *not* new it is, how in many ways significant portions of the industry have been for men by men, though they rarely name themselves as such. The declamatory transparency of *FWBW* and related projects links to a long line of new and ancient ways of listening. These lead into other kinds of innovation, which take into account older ways of storytelling. If decolonization is to continue through artistic interaction, then silence and sound will be tools by which musicians undertake this work. Next, chapter 5 elaborates on both current and storied forms of musical interventions and invites the reader into relational listening.

# 5

# Decolonial Listening?

Press play. Again. A single guitar chord. A voice singing a solo phrase. A second, then a third chord, then a repeated progression. Chord tones held, unbreaking, emphasizing the same three-chord movement. Low bass rumbles. The voice returns, rapping this time, playing with internal and end rhymes. Eyes closed, hear the word stress shift. "In the battles with my*self*, I'm continually *fa*cing. Feel the stress of the world on my shoulders and *fate*." Where are you now? What do you hear this time? Words pop: Out yet. Outset. Change. Outfit. Camo. Ammo. Warrior. Rambo. A rhythm, a punch, a pattern, a poem. A torrent of syllables: "dont-reh-pree-sent-our-lea-der-ship-eye-reh-pree-zent-im-pow-er-mint-wer-kin-on-thuh-ground-cuz-eye-have-ih-shoes-with-thuh-guh-ver-mint-who-ih-shoe-out-uh-po-luh-gees-while-sti-kin-to-thuh-pah-lih-cee-while-deh-fih-nit-lee-prah-bu-blee-kee-pin-us-in-pah-ver-tee." Disambiguate, re-form: "I don't belong to the queen / so as long as I dream / That means a sleep with a song that forever will be / Sung from the heart, so whenever I speak / The truth comes out and it's settin' me free."[1] Repeat: "I don't belong . . ."

This is the voice of Leonard Sumner, aka Lorenzo, and the instrumentals are from the song "They Say." Heard in chapter 2 at an Idle No More event, what happens when you listen again now? Choose again, hear again, listen again. Skip back, pick up the needle, fast forward. In this chapter, I invite the reader to experiment with and practice the possibilities of decolonial listening. Far from committing all possible aspects of decolonial listening to the page, I instead challenge the reader to find those listening possibilities that are the most relevant and resonant to them, to you, to wherever and whoever you are.

Like my collaborators, I am speaking into and through a flawed lived reality. Attempts at audibility grapple with the structures that are set up to *not* listen to certain voices and stories. Commercial systems invite particular forms of engagement. Even the logics of being understood as subjects are predicated on raced and gendered notions of what it is to be human: experiencing the power of these self-concealing structures, people cobble together self-making behaviors from modernity's detritus. And so our prose is imprecise. Sometimes, carefully chosen words conceal, inadvertently corroborate, participate in structures they wish to disavow. These actions emerge between the utterance and the hearer, in the relationships formed through the activity of speaking-listening. This is why we listen and relisten: to invite alternate ways of processing the sound, feeling it in transformed and transformational manners, understanding our own misperceptions, taking time to resonate anew. There are ways to listen that can alter the mainstream. There is little ease in this unsettling process.

We can be deafened by the (sounds of the) words we think we know. No longer listening but feeling the known grooves of familiar patterns of consonants and vowels, we may search our own minds and not hear the sounds that sparked the personal reverie. Because of limitations imposed by familiarity, I want to push at the boundaries of genre. The expression of more-than-text can, and does, happen in musical expressions that stem heavily from lyrics and wordplay. Deeply attending to this is a worthy project for a perceptive listener. Yet, for those who spend much of our lives speaking, reading, and interacting with lexical text, it can be easier to listen closely when words as we usually understand them are absent. These are sounds to which even word-focused listeners can attune ready ears: punk-inflected scream-singing where timbre and tone share emotion and story; the cool, deep power of a whisper, its volume compelling the auditor to strain their ears to listen, to enter into an altered listening posture to grasp at meaning; the hypnotic power of a repeated instrumental line, the brain invited into a loop, the ears refined to listen for microchanges as the melodic and dynamic range shrinks. With these sounds come individual experience, the indexical associations that auditors carry: disappointment, rage, or power in a stark whisper; fury, determination, erotic charge in a guttural yell; comfort, meditative bliss, panicked self-reflection, or spiritual practice that come with the trance of repeated sound. Memory, future hope, lived and relived experience: these may come fully consciously or less so. And yet they begin with the fleshy pinnae of the ears and then reverberate through the body and its brain.

Reverberation: Decolonial Sounds, Audience
Interpretations, and Sonic Possibilities

The singer pushes air from her lungs, which vibrates her vocal folds. The small membranes across her larynx quiver, small changes in the mucous folds creating outsized variations in pitch, timbre, and volume. She holds a microphone near her lips. The mechanical tool responds to her phonations. Like the singer, the microphone has a diaphragm. The singer uses this muscle to produce and control her sound. The microphone's diaphragm is at her mercy; it vibrates as her sound hits it and then produces electrical pulses. One of the singer's hands is glued to this machine. With the other, she beckons. Muscles, tendons, and bones in her fingers, hand, and arm work together to produce recognizable gestures. She moves her whole body back and forth in the space, bare feet turning on stage floor. With her onstage is a violinist. He snakes his hand up and down the instrument's finger board, pressing firmly and lightly to create pitches and to set off the harmonic series that rises above them. Animal hair and sticky rosin make the strings vibrate and make his ears, and the audience's ears, vibrate too. The skin on a drum head is hit by a percussionist, the vibrating membrane adding to the sound waves in the room. As I listen, my body moves in complementary motion with the sounds produced by the bodies onstage. When they stop playing, a silence blooms, followed by a burst of applause. All around me, knees unbend, and leg muscles launch audience members to their feet, a standing ovation the physical manifestation of our appreciative listening.

In this performance, Inuk musician Tanya Tagaq and bandmembers Jean Martin and Jesse Zubot improvise around a planned musical structure. Black-and-white images flicker behind them. The film, *Nanook of the North*, was originally silent, yet these performers bring sound back into the space. The voice that Tagaq produces defies easy categorization. It is her own artistic version of the ongoing tradition of Inuit throat singing. It is punk-inflected. It carries some of the extremes of the human and machine voices of rock musicians, who scream and whisper, who make feedback sounds with their microphones that squeal and grind. It carries some of the sounds associated with other kinds of throat singing, the more-than-human voices of water, wind, seals, and geese.

The film that Tagaq and her team voice is infamous now as an example of a southern filmmaker getting it wrong, not hearing Inuit voices, and projecting his own vision for an underinformed non-Inuit public.[2] It is also known by some Inuit viewers of Tagaq's generation and older as a recording of elders now gone, the strength of ancestors documented for future generations to see and honor.[3] And it is known as a way that Allakariallak (the man who played Nanook) and other Inuit actors were not the victims they might have seemed, as they wink back through the director's misunderstandings, creating the possibility for their own narrative.[4] I listen here for the way Tagaq's voice brings the human voice of a contemporary Inuk subject through this 2012 piece and its subsequent reperformances.[5] And I also listen for the expanse of the landscape she carries from the film—ice, air, water, land, and more—as well as the more-than-human animals and spirits she invokes. Sonic sovereignty entails actors making choices about how they invite listening and about audiences choosing to engage with the range of sonic possibilities. Throughout this book, I have provided moments when readers can listen to Indigenous musicians insisting on their fundamental humanity in all of its complexity, and I have also detailed the ways in which that humanity is strategically and consistently denied for colonialist purposes. Listening implies an ethical relationship. Here, I invite you to listen through a decolonial soundscape and ask, What happens when listeners pay attention to artists' demands to be heard on their own terms?

## A Live Rendition of *Nanook of the North*

I felt Tagaq take over an auditorium during her tour stop in Los Angeles in 2016. In her introduction to the staged reperformance of the film *Nanook of the North*, Tagaq prepared the audience in her treble speaking voice for the film we were about to see. She let us know with a bit of a wink that in the pseudodocumentary, we were going to see some things that were not quite true. The film started, and the trio began to play. Throughout the evening, Martin used his drum set and also triggered the recorded backing track. Sometimes the band followed the film literally: there was a moment in which we as an audience saw dogs on-screen, and Martin brought in the sound of barking dogs, creating the effect of diegetic sound. Zubot too sometimes text-painted the sound: a tremolo to announce anticipation, such as when Nanook and his companions were getting close to prey on a hunt.

It felt like a marathon. But only afterward. The concert lasted for about an hour and a half; the group voiced the entire film without pause. Then, the audience launched quickly into a standing ovation and applauded and applauded and applauded. The trio left the stage, and Tagaq looked moved by our response. She covered her mouth with her hand, thanking us, seeming almost surprised that we had enjoyed it so much. The ensemble came back onstage and presented an encore, no filmic images to divide our attentive focus, percussion and then violin and then voice.

Throughout the performance, Tagaq's voice is human and more-than-human. Her bodily gestures extend her vocal vibrations. Electronic amplification expands her technical body, a microphone becoming an extension of a limb. She holds long notes on resonant vowels, gradually swelling and decreasing the volume as the vowels color slightly but otherwise continue unchanged. She pulses breathy sounds, barely aspirating a start to each one. The mechanics of breathing, of controlling pitch and volume and line, take center stage. She continues a sound for longer than feels possible. At times, Tagaq seems to be in a duet with herself. She produces sounds as she inhales and as she exhales. Higher-pitched notes and sounds of breath speak to each other. Breath might be hers or that of the wind sweeping the frozen landscape behind her.

At one moment, the film projects the scene of a seal hunt behind the musicians. When the seal is cut open, Tagaq continues singing into the mic she holds in one hand. She opens the other and hovers it along the front of her body, slit in the center like the seal. As in her album *Animism*, a violent connection crystallizes between a woman's body and another animal body, blood and sexuality mingling. During the scene of the hunt, she strides past Martin on the drums, going out far house left, moving as Inuk hunter Nanook stalks his prey. She crouches down, making low guttural sounds with her open throat. These sounds are not lexical text in any human language. Is this throaty pulsating voice the seal? The emotions of the hunter? The energy created between beings sensing each other? As Nanook harpoons the seal and tries to bring the animal to the top of the sea ice, she pulls with her body, with the cord, and with her voice. I hear her pulling us up above the surface of the ice.

Through her sound, I hear her as hunter, as narrator, as seal, as space between. I feel us, the audience, as the harpoon in the seal, being dragged to the surface by her song.

Another moment, another set of listeners, and still the same voice guides the story. A clock ticks. Time passes audibly, yet a disorienting fray of moments crowd too quickly into the passing seconds. A city bus drives through falling snow. Lights flash on a neon sign, in the headlights of cars at night, on a taxi's running meter. Brick. Chain-link fence. An escalator. A departing subway car. Hundred-dollar bills fall, then burn with bright reds, oranges, and yellows. Whirling through city streets at a dizzying pace, time only slows down to a less frantic clip when a woman takes center screen; she patiently applies oil-black mascara and blood-red lipstick. The ticking clock is joined by other percussive sounds to make a full drum beat; the sharp click of drumsticks and more resonant bass tones fill out the sonic range. And a voice enters. The voice shares a hum, low and buzzy, coming and going at intervals. With a pitched tone, higher in range, the singer provides a repeated single note that cuts through the building low instrumental lines. She does not need words as she keeps singing, her voice directing the song's building energy. Her breath is audible, another rhythmic line that drives the music. A police car appears, lights flashing, and anonymous bodies in full tactical gear raise guns and aim. They do not fire.

Instead, a partially obscured figure raises her hands, and the viewer is transported through a light tunnel into a forest. The singing carries the viewer, and the music continues with its hums, pitched song, and breath sounds. Daylight blazes away the darkness, and three wolves maneuver through snow. Red from the woman's lipstick reemerges in this forest: the flash of a pair of eyes, moving cells, blood in the water. A fox hunts. Polar bears wrestle in the water. Birds pick apart a carcass in the snow. Blood drips from human fingertips. The viewer becomes other-than-human, running along the snowy forest floor at the height of a fox. Low to the ground, the music video's audience pads across a fallen tree. Like a gust of wind, the audience flies through clouds as the singer continues to inhale and exhale, propelling listeners with her breath. There is no more ticking clock, not even the drum set. A strong buzzy vocal phrase marks a turn in the song. Just the complex voice and instrumentals play now, as a figure raises her hands and walks into the snow. Only then does the singer stop. Tagaq's voice, which guides her music video "Uja" from her 2014 album *Animism*, brings her audience through locations, experiences, bodies, and beings.[6]

## Listening beyond the Logics of Settler Colonialism: To Be More-than-Human

Decolonial listening expands listening to, for, and with the human. Determining who qualifies as human under reigning societal power structures is not now—and never has been—a neutral process. As *Sonic Sovereignty* has detailed, efforts to mark Indigenous communities as located in an elsewhen and Black North Americans as fundamentally located elsewhere were part of the founding of Canadian and USAmerican nation-states; these related otherings are perpetuated into the present.[7] With the continuation of colonial (and neocolonial) power relations, these and other marked groups are constituted, in the words of Homi Bhabha, as "otherwise than modernity."[8] In some spheres, an assumed primacy of humans over other beings is being questioned, decentered, and in some cases, a memory of a time before human-centrism is being rekindled. Simultaneously, the fight for Black and Indigenous women, men, and others to be universally understood and recognized as always fully human is an ongoing struggle; lives literally depend on the success of this project. Tensions over the relative value of people's lives are refracted through the words of Audre Lorde: "Women of color in america have grown up within a symphony of anger, at being silenced, at being unchosen, at knowing that when we survive it is in spite of a world that takes for granted our lack of humanness, and which hates our very existence outside of its service."[9] When Tagaq opens the sonic range of her response, listeners can hear something different than a rehumanizing of strategically dehumanized Inuit subjects. Sonic sovereignty here is not someone giving voice to a silenced person, to Nanook or Allakariallak or Nyla; it is expressed through the music's ability to alter the manner in which humans and other-than-humans are recognized: heard, seen, understood, and valued.

Listening to and seeing this place and these beings again, refracted through Tagaq's music, how is it possible for settler, newcomer, and non-Inuit Indigenous listeners to work through our own listening positions?

What would it mean for settler listeners to let go of human primacy? How could Inuit listeners, if they wish, listen through adaptive Inuit Qaujimajatuqangit, perhaps focusing not just on human agents but on the values that James Tester and Peter Irniq define as "Avatimik Kamattiarniq 'the treatment of nature with respect, recognizing that what is done to something has implications for something else and that actions can have good and bad consequences,'" as well as "Iliijaaqaqtallniq 'prohibiting treating animals with disrespect'" and "Papattiniq 'the idea that nature is not a commodity'"?[10]

One hearing of Tagaq and her collaborators' performance of *Nanook* is that the musicians respond to a film in which Inuit subjects are silenced and objectified and re-present it with the voices of Nanook and Nyla at the center. This is one way the project can be, and has been, celebrated, and it can offer a model for other aesthetic interventions. In the face of ignorance and inequity, there is power not only in how musicians perform their voices but in how audiences listen as people who have been objectified articulate themselves as autonomous subjects.[11] What if the refraction through the subjectivity of a modern Inuk multigenre musician creates something more than the updating of one human voice for another? Expansive listenings can be consonant with ideas of Indigenous futurity that resonate throughout this book; past and future connect through storytelling. So as vocal folds vibrate, air pulses, and ears quiver, a resonance emerges in which beings cry out against anthropocentrism even as they insist that basic affordances of decency be extended to all, particularly those who have been otherized again and again. These cries complement rather than overpower each other.

The way the subjects and objects were positioned in the original silent film reserves lexical speech for the narrator. The viewer sees director Flaherty's perspective. The audience reads his words on slides that introduce the film and then that intercut various scenes to demonstrate how he frames each one. Contemporary rereadings such as Michelle Raheja's demonstrate how the Inuit actors do not blindly play along; they maintain human agency through alternative readings of visual sovereignty. And also, some Inuit families' appreciation for this footage is rooted in respect for the strength and skill of Nanook, Nyla, and the other people on-screen. The viewers, too, are not necessarily blindly playing along with the director. Yet, by associating speech only with the southern explorer-narrator, the northern characters fail to become human subjects in the modernist sense—they are presented without language. Nanook and Nyla are shown with family and doing activities, but they are also shown with other animals and interacting with the landscape in a way that shows a distanced fascination: they travel with dogs that accompany them; Nanook and the other men hunt a seal; they build shelter from packed snow. The filmic representation allows the narrator to maintain a distance from the actors on-screen and to present the land and animals as distant, and fascinating, others. The men hunt with then-outmoded tools, and Nanook infamously shows bafflement at then-modern technology, biting a record when he sees it at the trading post. If the viewer only stays in Flaherty's gaze, they might not see Nanook and Nyla as fully modern or even as fully human, per Flaherty's depiction.

Because one way of accessing the rights and privileges of the nation-state is to seize voice and to speak in the language understood by the colonizer, it is possible to make the actors intelligible to a colonial audience, to make the Inuit subjects human in their minds, by having them speak in English in a way that is designed for the colonial ear. But other interpretive frames for listening are possible. What if the voicing does not rely on the modernist, Eurocentric notion of the kind of object allowed to become a subject, the kind of self that is allowed to live and to access self- and group determination? What if the voice that emerges refuses to frame itself in order to be intelligible to the southern colonial audience?

Often in the performance, the voice that Tagaq produces—with her body, processed through technological tools, bolstered by her collaborators—extends past the limitations of quotidian human vocal production. Some of this comes from her use of techniques from throat singing. As Inuk throat singer Marie Belleau described it to me, "It's as if you have a watch mechanism that's all rusty, that's a regular person's throat. In order to throat sing, you have to slowly move it, slowly oil it, start getting the rust off to start producing all the sounds."[12] Some of this range also comes from the techniques of rock and punk music, which push timbres of the voice into fuzzy, gritty, and growly places where the tone of the singer can carry much more meaning than any lyric to which the techniques are applied. And some comes from the tools of contemporary music production used by the performers—looping, re-playing of previously sampled sounds, amplification.

Together, the artists create such an expanse of timbres, tones, pitches, and volumes that ears can be entranced by this vast palette and stop hunting for lyrics in English or any human language. An invitation to listen past lexical text extends the possibilities to deeply attend to sonic production made by an expanded sense of human vocalization, as well as by nonhuman animals. Heard in this way, Nyla and Nanook can become subjects without having to mediate through a human-centered idea of subjecthood. The vast array of sounds that revoice the film allow them to express thought and volition through musical expression that is not reliant on human language. If the point of definition of subjecthood maintains the modernist Eurocentric model, this is problematic. However, in the immersive performance experience, it could be otherwise. As Robin Wall Kimmerer (Potawatomi) explains, "In the Western tradition there is a recognized hierarchy of beings, with, of course, the human being on top—the pinnacle of evolution, the darling of Creation—and the plants at the bottom. But in Native ways of knowing, human people are often referred to as 'the younger brothers of Creation.' We say that humans have the least experience with how to live and thus the most to learn—we must look to our teachers among the other species for guidance."[13] Kimmerer teaches students the grammar of animacy as a way to instill respect for other-than-human beings; it also moves listeners outside the limits of the English language, in which rock and fox and moss become things. This inanimate grammar has too often been applied to people as well, dehumanizing subjects as racialized and gendered people became objects. Quoting Thomas Berry, Kimmerer reflects on the ethical need to de-objectify: "We must say of the universe that it is a communion of subjects, not a collection of objects."[14] Through rosin on strings, flickering light, high harmonics, the barking of dogs, breath processed through electronics, and a singing voice that pulls and pulls long notes, the listener could let go of a hierarchical point of departure. Instead, the connection between humans and other-than-human animals and spirits need not denigrate the status of humans. That is, connections among people and other beings do not imply that any specific peoples are less than, or nonhuman, or nonsubjects. Rather, it suggests that to be a subject is a possibility that was already taken up by Nyla and Nanook. Taken further, it is possible that subjecthood is not contingent on species. The audience's ears could hear wolves, seals, spirits, wind in this way: all might be subjects. English, or other lexical text, is not a prerequisite for subjecthood, nor must association with wolves, seals, spirits, or wind suggest a denigration of status for other beings. The functions of song surpass those of the English language; this is a strength and a space of possibility.

So, too, can a listener expansively perceive the narrator's transformation in "Uja." In the built environment of the city, human animals are centered. The music video starts by focusing on people, their things, their roads, their structures, their weapons. A mechanical clock ticks, framing the soundscape. Other-than-human animals, while undeniably present in built environments, are neither seen nor heard here. Then the central figure invites the audience to transform. The viewer sees her face, her mouth, her deft application of mascara, how she is treated in the human-centered environment as a gendered and raced being within a stratified society. Then, the viewer moves away from the built environment, running as a fox and flying as a bird and seeing through their eyes. This environment, too, has its logics and its rules, blood in the water a reminder of the reality of struggle that permeates the lives of other-than-humans as well.[15] Yet, when the audience moves with the narrator away from the human-centered environment, new questions about what is possible emerge. The fox must live within the structures and relationships of its environment, but it is not bound by the rules of human policing in the colonialist nation-state. Breath and melody take the fore, as the clock disappears, and then the percussive loops drop out entirely. As the audience sees the human face fade and hears mechanized sound dissipate, listeners can ask, What is possible through the active choosing to be read on one's own terms, choosing to cast the other-than-human as just as valorized and valuable as the human, and (temporarily) inhabiting a nonhuman, who has the ability not to bow to human laws?

## Repeat

Membranes vibrate, ossicles amplify, and nerves fire. Again. And again. A DJ's hands spin and stop a platter. Fingers grasp and twist a dial. The volume adjusts, quieter and louder; the balance shifts: bass, mid, treble.

Filters cut off certain sounds but, in so doing, allow others to come to prominence. Some sounds crisp and clarify, some widen and buzz, some disappear, cut off at the pass. Thumbs and indexes move sliders. Pitch adjusts. All of these movements of hands, wrists, and arms make the sound waves that hit the ears. Changes, more and less subtle, move dancing bodies on a packed floor. Recorded or broadcast, they move dancers in an apartment or twitch toes and bop knees on buses and subway cars.

The sounds are those of electronic instruments, crafted, triggered, and ordered by human ears and hands. The synthesized drums drive a fast, clear four-beat pattern. Kick and snare set a groove. A midregister pitched drum spits out a much faster duple pattern. The timbre buzzy and resonant, it crashes out four bars on a single pitch and then repeats the same rhythmic pattern a fourth lower for four more bars. A recorded track might not loop and linger as long as one played live, but the structure for the entrancing is here. Looping, immersive, and on the right speaker system, the frequencies vibrate spaces and bodies. On "Sila," a human voice speaks into a pause in the looping, Tanya Tagaq's voice breathing in amid A Tribe Called Red's instrumentals.[16] On the track as a whole, the singer's voice becomes part of the rhythmic play, through both her own direct expression and the treatment of the vocal line in the mix. No words are needed to bring the listener-dancer through repetition and change, a flow that varies in tempo, ebbs and flows in volume, and does not fear what emerges in a loop. Are you daydreaming? Are you imagining? Does your affective response bypass conscious thought? Is the kinaesthetic prominent in your listening body? I think about how I have felt in live performances by A Tribe Called Red, dancing loops with sonic loops. I see video projections that glitch and restart, a GIF re-performed with a new soundtrack that gives it a new valence. I hear this reference and smile. I wonder what this sample is. The room is packed. The club is strangely empty. I shiver as I converse with others, sweaty post-dancing on a cold sidewalk after a show. To whom and to what do you listen? To what aspects do you choose to attend? Where are you, when are you, who are you with? How do you move? How do you feel?

On the same album, a low wah-wah bass melody evokes a spaceship floating, or it evokes some kind of descent downward, or it evokes nothing and just rumbles. Voices sing in a human unison—clear but wide enough to feel real and yet not quite perfect—the presence of multiple singers amplified by the sound of multiple people beating a drum, also in unison. The singer-drummers, Northern Voice, continue; the bass cuts out, and a pop dance drumbeat frames a moving four on the floor. The rapper starts with what he says he can't imagine: a mother's pain. Does she face the death of her child? Whose life has become the canvas that can never be completed? The rapper tells what he can imagine, too. Leonard Sumner continues with his own feelings: "My energy is depleted, but I wanna stand and fight. So we can meet the spirits that have traveled back into the light." Spirits move across time and place; they are here. Sumner feels the weight of time and history in a live present. He raps, "I feel the fears and depression, fears and aggression, woven into society from years of oppression." What's in your mind when you hear him say, "The violence is normalized, the silence is horrifying. Truth is denied, and the fact is more are dying"? He feels his own feelings but hears the feelings of others. As the song launches from verse to chorus, the music of Northern Voice goes from background to foreground. Sumner raps, "You don't have to tell me how you feel, 'cause I can hear it in their cries," and the singing soars.

Sumner reflected on his experience doing shows with A Tribe Called Red, reformed as The Halluci Nation. Years after he first edged his way onto festival stages, through tours, and into awards shows, he describes, "people are tuning into a lot more Indigenous musicians now more than ever." His audiences, which he identifies as having Indigenous and non-Indigenous listeners, are "pretty receptive to the things [he] had to say" and "familiar with the struggle." And critically, he finds that music and stories like his often get "mainstream attention."[17] This attention is hard-won. It is incomplete. It requires sustained listening from a wide listenership. And it implies listeners' ongoing responsibility and action.

Keep listening. The second rapper starts a new verse: "It's hard to listen, but listen." Pause. Are you listening? Shad continues, "'Cause it's much harder living it than listening to the hardships." He listens; he asks others to listen: "Still the heart's conditioned to condition the air. When they air their conditions, keep cool. But the more tears, sometimes the clearer the vision." He raps about his country, disappointments and possibility, protests, and the many places he can find truth. Like Sumner, Shad leads to the chorus by speaking and then by listening. He raps, "Tell them what they must know. Turn it up loud when we bust flows. Not in

254 | DECOLONIAL LISTENING?

hushed tones, speaking up, let the trust grow." And he prepares to watch and to listen: "Now you don't gotta tell me how you feel, 'cause I can see it in your eyes. You don't gotta tell me that the pain is real, 'cause I can hear it in your cry." Northern Voice plays out the bridge. Sumner raps about the plan that was and is settler colonial policy, linking decades and centuries in a fast rapped flow. Separation. Slaughter. Missing daughters. The '60s scoop. Residential schools. Occupation. Starvation. How do you feel when you listen? When you hear him rap, "It's a nation with racism here since the start of it. Hard to let go 'cause it's carved in the heart of it. Relation to the land and our rise were a part of it. Roots where I stand, I could never depart from it"? He makes space, invites the listener to pay attention to what they can hear in the cries, and the singer-drummers have the last word.

## Coda

We do not have to stop at hearing; we can listen. And the "we," here, is paramount. This work will not be done alone by a single listener, nor should any singer be expected to shift global systems on their own. Listening matters because it draws beings together, it brings bodies into relationship with each other, it articulates our connections. We listen because we cannot individualize ourselves out of society's problems. The neoliberal promise of the individual has left us alone and lonely. So listen. The logics used to transform beings and places into objects for domination constitute the ongoing forces of colonialism; their overthrow is at the center of decolonial projects. Relistening to beings *as* beings, as subjects (whether human or other-than-human and valued regardless), is at the core of sonic sovereignty. The speaker-listener-listener relationships, physical, embodied ones of subject to subject, enact sonic sovereignty.

This next act of listening is for you. There is space for experimentation, for respectful curiosity. Open your ears. I invite you to come into the act of listening. Choose an artist who is local to where you are now or whose people are from the Indigenous territory on which you are sitting. Maybe you choose a hip hop artist or a pop musician or a group whose work pushes at the limits of genre. Maybe there are lyrics or there are none, or they are in a language you are learning or that you cannot understand. What stories are being told, with and without text? If you do not yet know to whom you might listen, spend time learning more. Open your ears, turn on the speakers, buy a ticket to a live show, let your body reverberate. To whom do you choose to listen? How do you listen? What happens during the listening? What will happen after?

# ACKNOWLEDGMENTS

This project was possible because of many collaborators over years. I acknowledge all the musicians, listeners, and producers I worked with for sharing time and stories with me and for finding insights together, both those listed here and those unnamed. Many thanks to the entire staff at CIUR-FM, particularly Dave McLeod, Alex Sannie, Paul Rabliauskas, and Miss Melissa. I have enjoyed sharing time and thoughts with all of you. Further, I appreciate current and former staff of CBC Manitoba for offering their perspectives, particularly Sandy Thacker and Kim Wheeler. I am grateful to everyone at UMFM, especially Jared McKetiak and Michael Elves. Thanks to Lori Faber, Kitty Alfonso Gurneau, Jordan Gurneau, Mike Marin, Cindy Soto, and Negwes White for dialogue about hip hop from Chicago to California. Frank Waln shared a keen awareness not only about his own work but also about a larger musical context in Chicago. I appreciate the time I spent with the hardworking people who make Indigenous Music Week and the sākihiwē festival a reality, and I particularly learned much from Alan Greyeyes. Andrew Balfour kept me on my toes in our discussions about composition and contemporary Indigenous music of many genres and also gave me the honor of singing in some of his work. I have been enriched by spending time with a larger community of hip hop artists and media professionals in Winnipeg, including Dane Goulet, Billy Pierson, Tyler Rogers, Patrick Skene, Leonard Sumner, Elliott Walsh, and the community at Graffiti Art Programming and Studio 393. Material proceeds from work like this are neither guaranteed nor the point, but I am honored to donate to nonprofits that support emerging Indigenous artists. Thanks to Suzette Amaya, Marie Belleau, Drezus, Inez, Chase Manhattan, Samian, Beka Solo, and Tanya Tagaq for helping me to hear ever more layers of connections. To Eekwol and T-Rhyme, I am so grateful for the work you do and honored that you came to California to share it.

I was fortunate to spend time with many talented people at the University of Manitoba during the course of this research. Thanks, Sherry Farrell Racette, for your creativity and insight. Robert-Falcon Ouellette and I shared many discussions about ethnomusicology in Canada, Métis music, and community radio. I am honored to have been able to host interviews on the radio program *At the Edge of Canada: Indigenous Research*. I thank Niigaan Sinclair for welcoming me into the Native Studies Colloquium and appreciate fellow researchers with whom I dialogued.

To Robert Loiselle, Katherine Styrchak, François Fouquerel, and your families, thank you for showing me the wonderful and critical work that can be done in community. I am deeply grateful. To Katherine for teaching me how to fall and get up again in the snow, to Robert for first introducing me to Wab Kinew and inviting me to guest teach a class on hip hop poetry, and to François for starting this journey with me many years ago. Katherine, Robert, and François, you have been with me from conversations in the woods to winter concerts in snow and into writing across years. To you, I say merci and miigwech.

I appreciate invitations to present material as this project has come together. Thanks to generous audiences at Columbia University, the University of Toronto, Brandon University, and the University of Manitoba, especially scholars Aaron Fox, Nasim Niknafs, Jon-Thomas Godin, Colette Simonot, and James Maiello. I thank colleagues and friends at SEM, IASPM, and the Show & Prove Hip Hop Studies Conference, with special shout-outs to Elyse Carter Vosen, Beverley Diamond, Imani Kai Johnson, Heather MacLachlan, and Chris Scales.

I am grateful to have done much writing in community. I so appreciate feedback and support from Donatella Galella and the Performing Difference team at the University of California, Riverside, and colleagues with the California Center for the Native Nations, as well as Crystal Baik, Jordan Beltran Gonzales, Tammy Ho, Emily Hue, Anthea Kraut, David Martinez, Stephen Sohn, and Deborah Wong. Dialogue shaped this book over the years. Thanks to Faye Ginsburg, Mishuana Goeman, Michelle Raheja, and Richard Sutherland for workshopping chapters with me.

It takes material resources to make scholarship move forward. I recognize the support of the National Endowment for the Humanities

Faculty Fellowship, a Fulbright Fellowship, a Hellman Fellowship, the Center for Ideas and Society, and the University of California, Riverside Academic Senate. Thank you to these funders for seeing possibility in this research. Thanks to the team at NYU Press, particularly editors Karen Tongson and Henry Jenkins, as well as this book's anonymous peer reviewers for their thoughtful suggestions. Marc Kuegle, much appreciation for your spot-on cover art, and also to Sly Skeeta for contributing to such a powerful image.

To my entire family, I appreciate you more than words can ever say. Friends who have sustained me: some of you see your names in the previous paragraphs, and some of you get to hear my voice when you call me in the middle of the night. To Diana Saltanovitz, who helped me love music from before I can remember, and to Katie Saltanovitz, Michael Przybylski, Susan Edwards, Dean Bradley, Joanne Knutson, Jeff Knutson, Raluca Albu, Carlin Thomas, Morgan Stirling, and so many others—you know who you are. I could not have done this without my partner, Erin Nathalie Edwards. Every day I am grateful for our fabulous kids. If I can be as supportive to others as those named and unnamed here have been to me, I will be a fortunate scholar, musician, and person.

# NOTES

## INTRODUCTION

1. The word "Indigenous" is used differently in a variety of contexts and times, as are terms such as "Native American" and "First Nations." "Indigenous," the term most often used in recent academic work, and "Native," which is also used by hip hop listeners and performers who have participated in this project, serve when this book is not referring to a specific person's self-identification. Some artists use "Aboriginal" as a term to refer to First Nations, Métis, and Inuit groups living in present-day Canada.

2. Adam Krims, *Rap Music and the Poetics of Identity* (Cambridge: Cambridge University Press, 2000).

3. Alan Lechusza, "Without Reservations: Native Hip Hop and Identity in the Music of W.O.R." (PhD diss., University of California, San Diego, 2009); Neal Ullestad, "American Indian Rap and Reggae" (paper presented at the annual conference of the NAAAS, NAHLS, NANAS, and IAAS, Baton Rouge, LA, 2007).

4. Audra Simpson and Andrea Smith, eds., *Theorizing Native Studies* (Durham, NC: Duke University Press, 2014).

5. Eve Tuck and K. Wayne Yang, "Decolonization Is Not a Metaphor," *Decolonization: Indigeneity, Education, & Society* 1, no. 1 (2012): 1–40.

6. Leanne Betasamosake Simpson, *Dancing on Our Turtle's Back* (Winnipeg, MB: ARP Books, 2011), 16.

7. Pamela Palmater, "Canada 150 Is a Celebration of Indigenous Genocide," *Now Toronto*, 29 March 2017, https://nowtoronto.com.

8. Sofia Johansson, "Music in Times of Streaming: Transformation and Debate," in *Making Media*, ed. Mark Deuze and Mirjam Prenger (Amsterdam: Amsterdam University Press, 2019), 309.

9. Alan B. Krueger, *Rokonomics* (New York: Currency, 2019).

10. Nielsen Company, "The Nielsen Total Audience Report," 31 July 2018, www.nielsen.com; "How Canada Listens: Fall 2018," *Numeris*, 21 February 2019, http://en.numeris.ca.

11. Radio broadcaster Streetz FM is commonly referred to as Streetz.

12. Since this time, the group changed its name to The Halluci Nation; terminology in this book follows the group's name at the referenced time unless otherwise noted.

13. These events are cataloged in sources such as The Kino-nda-niimi Collective, *The Winter We Danced: Voices from the Past, the Future, and the Idle No More Movement* (Winnipeg: ARP Books, 2014).

14. Pauline Oliveros, *Deep Listening: A Composer's Sound Practice* (Bloomington, IN: iUniverse, 2005), xv.
15. A Tribe Called Red, *We Are the Halluci Nation* (Radicalized Records, 2016).
16. Faye D. Ginsburg, "Screen Memories: Resignifying the Traditional in Indigenous Media," in *Media Worlds: Anthropology on New Terrain*, ed. Faye D. Ginsburg, Lila Abu-Lughod, and Brian Larkin (Berkeley: University of California Press, 2002), 37–57.
17. Lorna Roth, *Something New in the Air* (Montréal: McGill-Queen's University Press, 2005); Richard Sutherland, "Sound Recording and Radio: Intersections and Overlaps," in *Cultural Industries.ca: Making Sense of Canadian Media in the Digital Age*, ed. Ira Wagman and Peter Urquhart (Toronto: James Lorimer, 2012), 33–52; CRTC, "Canadian Content Requirement for Music on Canadian Radio," modified 22 June 2022, www.crtc.gc.ca.
18. Jarl Ahlkvist "Programming Philosophies and the Rationalization of Music Radio," *Media Culture & Society* 23 (2001): 339–58; Gillian Turnbull, "Radio Mondo: Transcending the Boundaries of Community Radio in Alberta," in *Post-Colonial Distances: The Study of Popular Music in Canada and Australia*, ed. Beverley Diamond, Denis Crowdy, and Daniel M. Downes (Newcastle, UK: Cambridge Scholars, 2008), 131–44.
19. Eric Weisbard, *Top 40 Democracy* (Chicago: University of Chicago Press, 2014).
20. Cyphers are ways to gather in which musicians show off skills and generate new ideas. A cypher can also be defined as the circle of freestyle rappers or breakers who take turns to spit verses or trade moves.

CHAPTER 1. HIP HOP AND CONTEMPORARY URBAN INDIGENEITY

1. Field notes from 22 February 2013.
2. Samian rapped in French; English translation by the author.
3. Speech-effusive flow is rap delivery with a large volume of syllables. It can include irregular rhythms; lyric and metrical accents may not overlap. See Krims, *Rap Music and the Poetics of Identity*. An organizing element of music, the beat is a strong pulse that occurs at a regular interval. It can also be felt as a pulse to which listeners move their bodies and to which DJs attune themselves so they can match or play with patterns. See Mark J. Butler, *Playing with Something That Runs: Technology, Improvisation, and Composition* (New York: Oxford University Press, 2014).
4. "Mixed heritage" refers to people who identify with multiple backgrounds. Like multiracial identification, this is not as straightforward as a single term might suggest. This book uses the terms "mixed" and "mixed heritage" to reflect terminology used by many people who identify with ancestry from multiple places and groups. It follows more specific or alternative terminology when chosen by individuals. The repetition of the term "mixed" is a reminder that categories including "Indigenous," "Black," "Latinx," and "settler" are often overlapping, with regard to personal background.

5. While Indigenous peoples are often racialized, Indigenous groups express concerns that are explicitly related to sovereignty. Music research about genres that began in the United States often focuses on black/white divides; analysis of other categories came later to music scholarship. Indigeneity is often ignored in studies of popular music and music technology.

6. Liz Przybylski, "Bilingual Hip Hop from Community to Classroom and Back: A Study in Decolonial Applied Ethnomusicology," *Ethnomusicology* 62, no. 3 (2018): 375–402.

7. Krims, *Rap Music and the Poetics of Identity*; Tricia Rose, *Black Noise: Rap Music and Contemporary Culture in Black America* (Hanover, NH: Wesleyan University Press, 1994); Mark Katz, *Capturing Sound: How Technology Has Changed Music* (Berkeley: University of California Press, 2004); Joseph G. Schloss, *Making Beats: The Art of Sample-Based Hip-Hop* (Middletown, CT: Wesleyan University Press, 2004).

8. Liz Przybylski, "Hip Hop Dialogues: Sampling Women's Hand Drum Songs and the Canadian Popular Mainstream," in *Popular Music and the Politics of Hope: Queer and Feminist Interventions*, ed. Susan Fast and Craig Jennex (New York: Routledge, 2019), 187–205.

9. Joshua Tucker, "Permitted Indians and Popular Music in Contemporary Peru: The Poetics and Politics of Indigenous Performativity," *Ethnomusicology* 55 (3): 387–413.

10. See also Monique Giroux, "'From Identity to Alliance': Challenging Métis 'Inauthenticity' through Alliance Studies," *Yearbook for Traditional Music* 50 (2018): 91–118.

11. Liz Przybylski, "Rapping to and for a Multivocal Canada: Je m'y oppose au nom de toute la nation," in *We Still Here: Hip Hop North of the 49th Parallel*, ed. Charity Marsh and Mark Campbell (Montréal: McGill-Queens Press, 2020), 65–96.

12. Rinaldo Walcott, *Black like Who? Writing Black*, 2nd ed. (Toronto: Insomniac, 2003).

13. This geographic specificity becomes audible in hip hop anthems from the 2010s, "AbOriginal" and "Red Winter." In these music videos, Lakota rapper Frank Waln and Cree/Saulteaux rapper Drezus, respectively, incorporate Lakota rabbit dance songs and round dance into hip hop. These videos, which circulated online during Idle No More, deploy functions of place that ground the rappers in community and experience even as they demonstrate the fluid transborder movement integral to contemporary Indigenous cultural production. Consult Liz Przybylski, "Customs and Duty: Indigenous Hip Hop and the US-Canada Border," *Journal of Borderlands Studies* 33, no. 3 (2018): 487–506. See also Murray Forman, "'Represent': Race, Space, and Place in Rap Music," *Popular Music* 19, no. 1 (2000): 65–90.

14. Richard Majors and Janet Mancini Billson, *Cool Pose: The Dilemmas of Manhood in America* (New York: Lexington Books, 1992).

15. The internationalization of US-based conceptions of race affects the reception of hip hop in Canada; this parallels Derek Pardue's study on Blackness and hip hop

in Brazil, Ian Condry's work in Japan, and Nitasha Sharma's analysis of Desi hip hop. Derek Pardue, "Hip Hop as Pedagogy: A Look into 'Heaven' and 'Soul' in São Paulo, Brazil," *Anthropological Quarterly* 80, no. 3 (2007): 673–709; Ian Condry, *Hip-Hop Japan: Rap and the Paths of Cultural Globalization* (Durham, NC: Duke University Press, 2006); Nitasha Sharma, *Refiguring American Music: Hip Hop Desis: South Asian Americans, Blackness, and a Global Race Consciousness* (Durham, NC: Duke University Press, 2010).

16. Shawn Wilson, *Research Is Ceremony: Indigenous Research Methods* (Black Point, NS: Fernwood, 2008), 6.

17. Linda Tuhiwai Smith, *Decolonizing Methodologies: Research and Indigenous Peoples*, 2nd ed. (London: Zed Books, 2012), 201.

18. Deborah Kapchan, "Learning to Listen: The Sound of Sufism in France," *World of Music* 51, no. 2 (2009): 81.

19. Kara Keeling, "Looking for M—: Queer Temporality, Black Political Possibility, and Poetry from the Future," *GLQ* 15, no. 4 (2009): 566–67.

20. Laura Harjo, *Spiral to the Stars: Mvskoke Tools of Futurity* (Tucson: University of Arizona Press, 2019), 216.

21. Tiffany Lethabo King, *The Black Shoals: Offshore Formations of Black and Native Studies* (Durham, NC: Duke University Press, 2019), ix–xi.

22. Qwo-Li Driskill, Chris Finley, Brian Joseph Gilley, and Scott Lauria Morgensen, eds., *Queer Indigenous Studies: Critical Interventions in Theory, Politics, and Literature* (Tucson: University of Arizona Press, 2011).

23. Acadien musician Zachary Richard explained, "L'histoire des Métis et de Louis Riel m'a toujours inspiré. Elle me rejoint et me parle. Il était d'ailleurs facile pour ce francophone et Acadien que je suis de m'identifier aux luttes, à la résilience et à la fierté du peuple métis." (The history of the Métis and of Louis Riel has always inspired me. It reaches me and speaks to me. That made it easy for me as a Francophone and as an Acadien to identify with the struggles, the resilience, and the pride of the Métis people.) Daniel Bahuaud, "La cloche de Batoche, en chanson," *La Liberté*, 1 August 2013, www.la-liberte.ca. Richard worked with the translator Jules Chartrand to create lyrics in Michif.

24. For example, Navajo religious songs alter the world as they are articulated. See Kimberly Marshall, *Upward, Not Sunwise* (Lincoln: University of Nebraska Press, 2016).

25. Nonlinear temporality is also connected to what Tavia Nyong'o calls "black polytemporality," which queerly resists linear time, and J. Halberstam's notion of queer time, in which freedom from heteronormative life-stage markers makes alternate temporalities available. See Jack Halberstam, *In a Queer Time and Place* (New York: New York University Press, 2005); Tavia Nyong'o, *Afro-Fabulations: The Queer Drama of Black Life* (New York: New York University Press, 2019).

26. See, for example, Paul Khalil Saucier, *Native Tongues: An African Hip-Hop Reader* (Trenton, NJ: Africa World, 2011).

27. Examples include Ray Barnhardt and Angayuqaq Oscar Kawagley, "Indigenous Knowledge Systems and Alaska Native Ways of Knowing," *Anthropology and Education Quarterly* 36, no. 1 (2005): 8–23; Maximilian Christian Forte, *Indigenous Resurgence in the Contemporary Caribbean: Amerindian Survival and Revival* (New York: Peter Lang, 2006); Rodolfo Kusch, *Indigenous and Popular Thinking in América* (Durham, NC: Duke University Press, 2010).

28. Christopher Scales, "First Nations Popular Music in Canada: Musical Meaning and the Politics of Identity," *Canadian University Music Review* 19, no. 2 (1999): 94–101.

29. Mishuana Goeman, "Indigeneity," in *Gender: Sources, Perspectives, and Methodologies*, ed. Renée C. Hoogland (New York: Macmillan, 2016), 152. In response to the variety of ways that individuals identify, both parenthetical and in-text references to Indigenous affiliation are used for musicians and scholars in this book.

30. Usage changes over time and location. For a comparison of terminology leading up to the mid-1990s, see Alan B. Anderson, "Review Essay: The 'Fourth World' of Indigenous Peoples: A Review of the Concept and the Literature," *Native Studies Review* 9, no. 1 (1993–94): 126–32. Deprivation and injustice continue in many definitions of "Indigenous" or "Indigenous people," a feature that raises conversation and, in some cases, concern. If the histories accrued in this terminology are always definitionally related to privation, do these not center inappropriately on colonizers rather than the peoples themselves? And if the definition is oppositional and based in a specific power asymmetry, what happens after decolonization?

31. Gregory Younging, *Elements of Indigenous Style: A Guide for Writing by and about Indigenous Peoples* (Edmonton: Brush Education, 2018); Journalists for Human Rights. Indigenous Reporters Program, *Style Guide for Reporting on Indigenous People*, December 2017, www.jhr.ca.

32. For additional examples of digital Indigeneity spanning global contexts, including Andean, Taiwanese, and Sami online or recorded music scenes, see Thomas R. Hilder, Henry Stobart, and Shzr Ee Tan, eds., *Music, Indigeneity, Digital Media* (Rochester, NY: University of Rochester Press, 2016).

33. Rights to cultural expression are articulated in this document, alongside rights to safety, health, self-determination, spiritual practices, educational systems, political systems, and land, among others. It expresses equality of Indigenous peoples in terms of protections, as in Article 1: "Indigenous peoples have the right to the full enjoyment, as a collective or as individuals, of all human rights and fundamental freedoms as recognized in the Charter of the United Nations, the Universal Declaration of Human Rights and international human rights law" (4) and then specifically enumerates rights of Indigenous peoples in response to particular threats. Article 8 begins, "Indigenous peoples and individuals have the right not to be subjected to forced assimilation or destruction of their culture." The first point of article 8, section 2, reads, "States shall provide effective mechanisms

for prevention of, and redress for: (*a*) Any action which has the aim or effect of depriving them of their integrity as distinct peoples, or of their cultural values or ethnic identities" (5). United Nations, "Declaration of the Rights of Indigenous Peoples," adopted 13 September 2017.

34. Klisala Harrison, "Indigenous Music Sustainability during Climate Change," *Current Opinion in Environmental Sustainability* 43 (2020): 28.

35. One common critique is that, in an effort to define similarities across locations, unique experiences can be flattened. See also José Barreiro, "Taíno Survivals: Cacique Panchito, Caridad de los Indios, Cuba," in *Indigenous Resurgence in the Contemporary Caribbean*, ed. Maximilian C. Forte (New York: Peter Lang, 2006), 21–39.

36. Joanne Barker, ed., *Critically Sovereign: Indigenous Gender, Sexuality, and Feminist Studies* (Durham, NC: Duke University Press, 2017).

37. Cris Derksen, Melody McKiver, Ian Cusson, Beverley McKiver, Jeremy Dutcher, Sonny-Ray Day Rider, Michelle Lafferty, Corey Payette, Jessica McMann, and Andrew Balfour, "Indigenous Musical Sovereignty," *IPAA News*, 22 February 2019.

38. Scholarly discussions of what is deemed "music" tend to have less purchase in popular music industry spaces. Additionally, claiming the title "Indigenous music" can itself be contested. There is no universally agreed-on definition of the kind of connection that is required in order for a musician or group to confirm community acceptance or cultural continuity, though there are many examples of musics that are widely accepted within this title and others that have stirred notable controversy. For more on a pop musician exploring the experience of being adopted out of an Indigenous family, see Liz Przybylski, "Media Review of *Unreserved*," *Yearbook for Traditional Music* 51 (2019): 333–35.

39. See Eric Lott, *Love and Theft: Blackface Minstrelsy and the American Working Class* (New York: Oxford University Press, 1993); Maureen Mahon, *Right to Rock: The Black Rock Coalition and the Cultural Politics of Race* (Durham, NC: Duke University Press, 2004).

40. Tricia Rose, *The Hip Hop Wars* (New York: Basic Books, 2008), 5.

41. Cheryl Keyes, *Rap Music and Street Consciousness* (Urbana: University of Illinois Press, 2002).

42. Cornel West, "On Afro-American Popular Music: From Bebop to Rap," *Black Sacred Music* 6, no. 1 (March 1992): 282–94.

43. Portia Maultsby and Mellonee Burnim, eds., *Issues in African American Music: Power, Gender, Race, Representation* (New York: Routledge, 2016); Rose, *Black Noise*.

44. Fernando Orejuela, introduction to *Black Lives Matter and Music: Protest, Intervention, Reflection*, ed. Fernando Orejuela and Stephanie Shonekan (Bloomington: Indiana University Press, 2018), 38.

45. See also Diamond, Crowdy, and Downes, *Post-Colonial Distances*.

46. Kent A. Ono, *Contemporary Media Culture and the Remnants of a Colonial Past* (New York: Peter Lang, 2009), 7.

47. Patrick Wolfe, "Settler Colonialism and the Elimination of the Native," *Journal of Genocide Research* 8, no. 4 (2006): 387–409.

48. Haunani-Kay Trask, "The Color of Violence," *Social Justice* 31, no. 4 (2004): 8. On the economic effects of neocolonialism, see, for example, Homi K. Bhabha, *The Location of Culture* (London: Routledge, 1994).

49. King, *Black Shoals*, 40.

50. Simone Browne, *Dark Matters: On the Surveillance of Blackness* (Durham, NC: Duke University Press, 2015); Michael Pisani, *Imagining Native America in Music* (New Haven, CT: Yale University Press, 2005); Jennifer Stoever, *The Sonic Color Line: Race and the Cultural Politics of Listening* (New York: New York University Press, 2016).

51. Katherine McKittrick, *Demonic Grounds: Black Women and the Cartographies of Struggle* (Minneapolis: University of Minnesota Press, 2006).

52. Rinaldo Walcott, *Black like Who? Writing Black*, 2nd ed. (Toronto: Insomniac, 2003), 144.

53. Stacy L. Smith, Marc Choueiti, and Katherine Pieper, *Inequality in 800 Popular Films: Examining Portrayals of Gender, Race/Ethnicity, LGBT, and Disability from 2007–2015* (Los Angeles: Media, Diversity, & Social Change Initiative, 2016).

54. Tatiana Cirisano, Srishti Das, and Hannah Kahlert, *Be the Change: Women in Music 2022* (MIDiA Research, TuneCore, and Believe, 2022), www.tunecore.com; Stacy L. Smith, Katherine Pieper, Hannah Clark, Ariana Case, and Marc Choueiti, "Inclusion in the Recording Studio? Gender and Race/Ethnicity of Artists, Songwriters & Producers across 800 Popular Songs from 2012–2019," USC Annenberg Inclusion Initiative, January 2020; Alanna Stuart and Kim de Laat, *Closing the Gap: Impact and Representation of Indigenous, Black and People of Colour (IBPOC) Live Music Workers in Canada* (Canadian Live Music Association, 2022), www.canadianlivemusic.ca.

55. The term "womxn" comes from scholarship and practice that decenter cisgender identities and resist a strict binary idea of gender. It is used here as an expansive term, including girls, as well as cis and trans* women. See note 2 in chapter 4 for further details.

56. Dawn Norfleet, "Hip-Hop and Rap," in *African American Music*, ed. Mellonee V. Burnim and Portia K. Maultsby (New York: Routledge, 2006), 379 (emphasis in original).

57. Norfleet, 379.

58. Liz Pelly, "Discover Weakly: Sexism on Spotify," *Baffler*, 4 June 2018, https://thebaffler.com.

59. Smith, Choueiti, and Pieper, *Inequality in 800 Popular Films*, 18–19.

60. Silvia Rivera Cusicanqui, "Ch'ixinakax utxiwa: A Reflection on the Practices and Discourses of Decolonization," *South Atlantic Quarterly* 111, no. 1 (2012): 95–109.

61. Michelle Raheja, *Reservation Reelism: Redfacing, Visual Sovereignty, and Representations of Native Americans in Film* (Lincoln: University of Nebraska Press, 2010), 197; Joanne Barker, *Sovereignty Matters: Locations of Contestation and Possibility*

*in Indigenous Struggles for Self-Determination* (Lincoln: University of Nebraska Press, 2005).

62. Even with this wide address, the song uses Lakota text to convey a culturally specific relationship to water. For an explanation of ecological stewardship and Lakota ways of knowing, consult Joshua Thunder Little and Liz Przybylski, "Hearing Resistance through Wolakota: Lakota Hip Hop and Environmental Activism," *MUSICultures* 49 (2022), 45–69.

63. Michelle Raheja, "Visual Sovereignty," in *Native Studies Keywords*, ed. Stephanie Nohelani Teves, Andrea Smith, and Michelle H. Raheja, 25–34 (Tucson: University of Arizona Press, 2015), 28.

64. Jolene Rickard, "Diversifying Sovereignty and the Reception of Indigenous Art," *Art Journal* 76, no. 2 (2017): 82.

65. Beverly R. Singer, *Wiping the War Paint off the Lens: Native American Film and Video* (Minneapolis: University of Minnesota Press, 2001), 2.

66. Robert A. Warrior, *Tribal Secrets: Recovering American Indian Intellectual Traditions* (Minneapolis: University of Minnesota Press, 1995); Taiaiake Alfred, "Sovereignty," in *Sovereignty Matters: Locations of Contestation and Possibility in Indigenous Struggles for Self-Determination*, ed. Joanne Barker (Lincoln: University of Nebraska Press, 2005).

67. Vine Deloria Jr. links sovereignty to kinship responsibilities and commitment to mutual aid. See Deloria, "Intellectual Self-Determination and Sovereignty: Looking at the Windmills in Our Minds," *Wicazo Sa Review* 13, no. 1 (1998): 25–31.

68. L. Simpson, *Dancing on Our Turtle's Back*, 19.

69. Qwul'sih'yah'maht (Robina Anne Thomas), "Honoring the Oral traditions of the Ta't Mustimuxw (Ancestors) through Storytelling," in *Research as Resistance: Critical, Indigenous and Anti-oppressive Approaches*, ed. Leslie Brown and Susan Strega (Toronto: Canadian Scholars' Press, 2005), 127–51.

70. Leanne Betasamosake Simpson, "Indigenous Resurgence and Co-resistance," *Critical Ethnic Studies* 2 no. 2 (2016): 19.

71. Wilson, *Research Is Ceremony*, 27.

72. "Musical messaging" refers to all of the content conveyed by multiple elements of this music. In recordings, these include melody, harmony, rhythm, lyrics, timbre, instrumentation, samples and other citations, and other elements. In music videos, these expand to include visual elements. In live shows, these also include performance elements.

73. Leonard Sumner, interview with author, 6 July 2021.

74. Tucker, "Permitted Indians," 388.

75. Barker, introduction to *Critically Sovereign*, 3.

76. Max Carocci, "Living in an Urban Rez," in *Place and Native American Indian History and Culture*, ed. Joy Porter (New York: Peter Lang, 2007).

77. Bear Witness, quoted in Liz Przybylski, "Indigenous Survivance and Urban Musical Practice," *Revue de recherche en civilisation américaine* 5 (2015): 9, http://rrca .revues.org.

78. Carol Edelman Warrior, "Indigenous Collectives: A Meditation on Fixity and Flexibility," *American Indian Quarterly* 41, no. 4 (2017): 388.

79. Cusicanqui, "Ch'ixinakax utxiwa," 96.

80. This book uses the words "reserve" and "reservation"; the former is prevalent in Canadian contexts and the latter in USAmerican contexts. Jessica Martin, "Majority of American Indians Move off Reservations, but Their Cultural, Financial Services Remain Behind," *Washington University in St. Louis Newsroom*, 12 April 2007.

81. Canadian government reporting includes the categories Métis, Inuit, Registered Indian, and Non-Status Indian. The definition and use of these categories is a contested and evolving process. Andrew J. Siggner, "Urban Aboriginal Populations: An Update Using the 2001 Census Results," paper presented at Not Strangers in These Parts: Urban Aboriginal Peoples, University of Western Ontario, 2002.

82. Tradition can be productively framed, following Adrienne L. Kaeppler, as "an ongoing process." See Kaeppler, "The Beholder's Share: Viewing Music and Dance in a Globalized World," *Ethnomusicology* 54, no. 2 (2010): 189. I refer to "traditional" music as that which demonstrates rootedness in historical cultural practices. This can be fully compatible with contemporary practices. Further, I propose that tradition may be enacted with and through urban landscapes and digital technologies.

83. Grant Leigh Saunders, "B.L.A.C.K.," 2006, https://vimeo.com/59720608.

84. Theories of cities as places of loss have been critiqued in scholarship of the first decade of the twenty-first century. See Wayne Warry, *Ending Denial: Understanding Aboriginal Issues* (Toronto: University of Toronto Press, 2009); Deborah Davis Jackson, *Our Elders Lived It: American Indian Identity in the City* (DeKalb: Northern Illinois University Press, 2002). Cultural change, too, is not necessarily negative. See Catherine James, "Cultural Change in Mistissini: Implications for Self Determination and Cultural Survival," in *Aboriginal Autonomy and Development in Northern Quebec and Labrador*, ed. Colin H. Scott (Vancouver: UBC Press, 2001). Even the juxtaposition of urban with rural is often reductive. See Marianne Ignace, "Why Is My People Sleeping—First Nations Hip Hop between the Rez and the City," in *Aboriginal Peoples in Canadian Cities: Transformations and Continuity*, ed. Heather A. Howard and Craig Proulx (Waterloo, ON: Wilfrid Laurier University Press, 2011).

85. Rickard, "Diversifying Sovereignty," 83.

86. Tuck and Yang, "Decolonization Is Not a Metaphor," 5.

87. Andrew Armitage, *Comparing the Policy of Aboriginal Assimilation: Australia, Canada, and New Zealand* (Vancouver: UBC Press, 1995), 185–88. See also David B. MacDonald and Graham Hudson, "The Genocide Question and Indian Residential Schools in Canada," *Canadian Journal of Political Science / Revue canadienne de science politique* 45, no. 2 (2012): 427–49.

88. Carmen Robertson and Sherry Farrell Racette, *Clearing a Path: New Ways of Seeing Traditional Indigenous Art* (Regina, SK: University of Regina, Canadian Plains

Research Center, 2009); K. Tsianina Lomawaima, Brenda J. Child, and Margaret L. Archuleta, *Away from Home: American Indian Boarding School Experiences, 1879–2000* (Phoenix: Heard Museum, 2002); Eric Taylor Woods, "A Cultural Approach to a Canadian Tragedy," *International Journal of Politics, Culture, and Society* 26, no. 2 (2013): 173–87.

89. Wolfe, "Settler Colonialism," 399.

90. Indigenous music scholars including Wanta Jampijinpa Patrick connect musicians in the global hip hop diaspora to New York's hip hop history. The celebration of hip hop as a way to fight adversity is often hailed even when it arrived through commercial channels, as in Australia and Aotearoa–New Zealand. Australian Aboriginal hip hop artist Jimblah traces his interest to his teenage years, when he learned of hip hop as a way oppressed peoples expressed their voices. He explains, "these are things people don't normally talk about in such a forthright manner— racism and oppression." Andrew Taylor, "Hip Hop a Poor Cop in a White Man's World," *Sydney Morning Herald*, 13 July 2013. Thelma Thomas, aka MC Trey, has worked as a rapper and hip hop educator in Indigenous communities in Australia. For her, hip hop culture is "a powerful culture which can unite many. It can also be a powerful platform to voice issues." Maxine Johns to Ms Hennessey Speaks, *Ms Hennessey Speaks* (blog), 17 June 2013, https://mshennesseyspeaksblog.com. See also Kirsten Zemke White, "'This Is My Life': Biography, Identity, and Narra- tive in New Zealand Rap Song," *Perfect Beat* 8, no. 3 (2007): 31–52.

91. Jeffrey O. G. Ogbar, "Slouching toward Bork: The Culture Wars and Self-Criticism in Hip-Hop Music," *Journal of Black Studies* 30, no. 2 (1999): 164–83; Jayna Brown, "Hip Hop, Pleasure, and Its Fulfillment," *Palimpsest* 2, no. 2 (2013): 147–50.

92. In the first decades of the twenty-first century, an expansion of media outlets emerged in which Indigenous narrators took more narrative control. The launch- ing of CBC's Indigenous channels and expansion of public programming by In- digenous artists for diverse audiences are part of this trend. For more on the need to correct anti-Indigenous biases in popular journalism, consult Mark Cronlund Anderson and Carmen L. Robertson, *Seeing Red: A History of Natives in Canadian Newspapers* (Winnipeg: University of Manitoba Press, 2011).

93. Beverley Diamond, "Deadly or Not: Indigenous Music Awards in Canada and Australia," in Diamond, Crowdy, and Downes, *Post-Colonial Distances*, 187.

94. Frank Waln, interview with author, 7 June 2013.

95. For more on political resonances of the culture wars, see Richard Jensen, "The Culture Wars, 1965–1995: A Historian's Map," *Journal of Social History* 29 (1995): 17–37. Contentious discussions about rap music have had echoes in Canada.

96. Mark Anthony Neal, "Postindustrial Soul: Black Popular Music at the Cross- roads," in *That's the Joint! The Hip-Hop Studies Reader*, ed. Murray Forman and Mark Anthony Neal (New York: Routledge, 2004), 371; Rose, *Hip Hop Wars*.

97. Davarian L. Baldwin, "Black Empires, White Desires: The Spatial Politics of Iden- tity in the Age of Hip Hop," in Forman and Neal, *That's the Joint!*, 166.

98. Majors and Billson, *Cool Pose*, 4.

99. Beretta E. Smith-Shomade, "'Rock-a-Bye, Baby!': Black Women Disrupting Gangs and Constructing Hip-Hop Gangsta Films," *Cinema Journal* 42, no. 2 (2003): 25–40.

100. Ann Laura Stoler, "Making Empire Respectable: The Politics of Race and Sexual Morality in Twentieth-Century Colonial Cultures," *American Ethnologist* 16, no. 4 (1989): 634–60; Driskill et al., *Queer Indigenous Studies*.

101. Rashad Shabazz, "Masculinity and the Mic: Confronting the Uneven Geography of Hip-Hop," *Gender, Place & Culture* 21, no. 3 (2014): 376.

102. David M. Jones, "Postmodernism, Pop Music, and Blues Practice in Nelson George's Post-Soul Culture," *African American Review* 41, no. 4 (2007): 669.

103. The degree to which Indigeneity coincides with classifications of race and ethnicity is contested. Throughout this book, I use the term "race" as my collaborators do, which is often to address the manner in which Indigenous people are constructed as different (typically as opposed to white, Black, Latinx, or Asian Canadians and Americans) based on perceived phenotypical characteristics or family lineage. "Status" refers to the recognition, or lack of recognition, that an Indigenous person, family, or group is granted by the state. Kimberly TallBear, "DNA, Blood, and Racializing the Tribe," *Wicazo Sa Review* 18, no. 1 (2003): 81–107; Augie Fleras, "Race Relations as Collective Definition: Renegotiating Aboriginal-Government Relations in Canada," *Symbolic Interaction* 13, no. 1 (1990): 19–35.

104. Imani Perry, *Prophets of the Hood: Politics and Poetics in Hip Hop* (Durham, NC: Duke University Press, 2004); Maultsby and Burnim, *Issues in African American Music*. See also Keyes, *Rap Music and Street Consciousness*; Rose, *Black Noise*. Hip hop's connections to North American concepts of Blackness impact the ways it is construed globally. Hip hop is racialized as Black in Australia. See Peter Dunbar-Hall and Chris Gibson, *Deadly Sounds, Deadly Places: Contemporary Aboriginal Music in Australia* (Randwick: University of New South Wales Press, 2004).

105. Jones, "Postmodernism, Pop Music, and Blues Practice," 679.

106. Dunbar-Hall and Gibson, *Deadly Sounds, Deadly Places*, 126.

107. Wolfe, "Settler Colonialism," 387–88. See also Dustin Tahmahkera, "'We're Gonna Capture Johnny Depp': Making Kin with Cinematic Comanches," *American Indian Culture and Research Journal* 41, no. 2 (2017): 23–42.

108. Beth Piatote, *Domestic Subjects* (New Haven, CT: Yale University Press, 2013).

109. Audrey Smedley, "'Race' and the Construction of Human Identity," *American Anthropologist* 100, no. 3 (1998): 696.

110. Russell Thornton, "Tribal Membership Requirements and the Demography of 'Old' and 'New' Native Americans," *Population Research and Policy Review* 16, nos. 1–2 (1997): 33–42.

111. The term "Aboriginal" was used at the time of this data collection.

112. Siggner, "Urban Aboriginal Populations," 16.

113. Giroux, "From Identity to Alliance," 114.

114. Julie Burelle, *Encounters on Contested Lands: Indigenous Performances of Sovereignty and Nationhood in Québec* (Evanston, IL: Northwestern University Press, 2019), 16.

115. Burelle, 6.

116. Adam Gaudry and Chris Andersen, "Daniels v. Canada: Racialized Legacies, Settler Self-Indigenization and the Denial of Indigenous Peoplehood," *TOPIA: Canadian Journal of Cultural Studies* 36 (2016): 24, 29. See also Tuck and Yang, "Decolonization Is Not a Metaphor."

117. Jo-Anne Fiske, "Political Status of Native Indian Women: Contradictory Implications of Canadian State Policy," *American Indian Culture and Research Journal* 19, no. 2 (1995): 1–30. On the legal history of the Indian Act, John Borrows summarizes, "The *Act* flows from the idea that Indigenous people are inferior and must be schooled in Canadian forms to hasten assimilation." Borrows, "Unextinguished: Rights and the Indian Act (Canada)," *University of New Brunswick Law Journal* 67 (2016): 5.

118. Joanne Barker, "Gender, Sovereignty, Rights: Native Women's Activism against Social Inequality and Violence in Canada," *American Quarterly* 60, no. 2 (2008): 259–66.

119. Fleras, "Race Relations as Collective Definition."

120. Bonita Lawrence, "Gender, Race, and the Regulation of Native Identity in Canada and the United States: An Overview," *Hypatia* 18, no. 2 (2003): 3–31.

121. Into the twenty-first century, Canada continued to use a regimented system involving precise legal definitions of different categories of "Status Indian" based on parentage.

122. Janice Acoose, *Iskwewak—Kah' Ki Yaw Ni Wahkomakanak: Neither Indian Princesses nor Easy Squaws* (Toronto: Women's Press, 1995), 46–48.

123. "An Act further to amend 'The Indian Act, 1880,'" S.C. 1884, c. 27. (47 Vict.), assented to 19 April 1884, chap. 27, sec. 3.

124. Joseph Weiss, "Giving Back the 'Queen Charlotte Islands': The Politics of Names and Naming between Canada and the Haida Nation," *Native American and Indigenous Studies* 7, no. 1 (2020): 76–77.

125. John Milloy, "Indian Act Colonialism: A Century of Dishonour, 1869–1969," research paper for the National Centre for First Nations Governance, 2008. Kwakwaka'wakw people maintained ceremonial practices in "underground potlatches" during the government ban and explain the ongoing healing and cultural functions of music, dance, and ceremony. Douglas Deur, Kim Recalma-Clutesi, and William White, "Benediction: The Teachings of Chief Kwaxsistalla Adam Dick and the Atla'gimma ("Spirits of the Forest") Dance," in *Plants, People, and Places*, ed. Nancy J. Turner (Montréal: McGill-Queen's University Press, 2020), xvii–xxiv. Hilistis Pauline Waterfall describes how, after returning from residential school, she participates in Heiltsuk cultural renewal through potlatch, which includes matrilineal and patrilineal family lineage recognition. She describes, "I learned about ceremonies that included youth coming of age, mourning

ceremonies, washing or purification ceremonies, traditional wedding ceremonies, and so on." Waterfall, "Healing through Culture," in *Memory*, ed. Philippe Tortell, Mark Turin, and Margot Young (Vancouver: Peter Wall Institute for Advanced Studies, 2018), 15.

126. Rosanna Deerchild, *Unreserved*, CBC Radio, 4 January 2019, www.cbc.ca.

127. Suzy Malik, "Anything Goes: Kinnie Starr's Bright and Fiery Rhymes," *Crooked Q*, 3 June 2013.

128. Kinnie Starr, *Anything* (MapleMusic Recordings, 2006).

129. Starr.

130. Deerchild, *Unreserved*.

131. Winnipeg's Most is the iteration of trio Jon C, Charlie Fettah, and Brooklyn, which later reformed as Winnipeg Boyz with just Jon C and Charlie Fettah.

132. This list is not complete, but it can spark listening for many artists who either came into the scene or increased in popularity through Indigenous music industry structures during the time period in focus here. Other sections of this chapter address influential artists prior to this time.

133. Listen for this style on Joey Stylez, *The Black Star* (Stressed Street, 2009).

134. Joey Stylez, "Living Proof," YouTube, 4 June 2008, www.youtube.com/watch?v =AnEZnYIlwzU.

135. On the song, a resonant drum beat indexes a big drum, such as one that is used in powwow. Chase and Jeezy convey the timbre of a resonant drum from a sound in the producer's electronic instrument library. Chase described the artists working toward the sound they had in mind while using the tools at hand. Chase Manhattan, interview with author, 16 August 2013.

136. Sometimes called a "rental assistance community," this housing development is designed for residents who cannot afford market-rate housing and, somewhat ironically, collects reduced rents from Native American residents so they can live on urban Native land.

137. A 49 is a gathering held in the evening after a powwow that offers performance opportunities as well as communal listening and dancing to popular forms of music, including hip hop. It is often characterized in contrast to the spiritual and ceremonial music of the powwow. Music lyrics are often comedic and can riff freely on a variety of topics, including sex, without breaching protocol. See Daniel J. Gelo, "Powwow Patter: Indian Emcee Discourse on Power and Identity," *Journal of American Folklore* 112, no. 443 (1999): 40–57.

138. WithOut Rezervation, *Are You Ready for W.O.R.?* (Canyon Records, 1994).

139. The term "lyrical topicality" refers to clusters of themes that emerge in lexical text.

140. Litefoot, *Seein' Red* (Red Vinyl Records, 1994); Julian B., *Once Upon a Genocide* (Sound of America Records, 1994).

141. See DM#1761182, "Application by Native Communications Inc. to amend a condition of license of CIUR-FM (Streetz-FM) Winnipeg, MB Permitting the level of Canadian Music Selections to be lowered from 40% to 35%: Supplementary Brief."

Canadian Radio-television and Telecommunications Commission, "Closed Part 1 Applications," https://applications.crtc.gc.ca.

142. DM#1761182.

143. Winnipeg has seen controversies indicative of the complex and changing relationships between various Indigenous groups and the settler state, as in public debate about the opening of the Canadian Museum for Human Rights, multiple Idle No More rallies, large public gatherings in support of missing and murdered Indigenous women and girls, and marches to honor the lives of young people who have been killed, such as Tina Fontaine.

144. These connections resonate in projects such as the sākihiwē festival's mentorship programs and in artists such as Leonard Sumner and The Halluci Nation finding success on Australian tours and Indigenous music events in the Commonwealth.

145. City of Winnipeg, "Census Information: 2016 Census," www.winnipeg.ca.

146. Arthur Manuel and Ronald M. Derrickson, *Unsettling Canada* (Toronto: Between the Lines, 2015).

147. Festival du Voyageur, "Notre Organisme," https://heho.ca. The festival's publicity materials describe music, cuisine, and performances as cultural activities.

148. Burelle, *Encounters on Contested Lands*, 28.

149. For analysis of pathologizing discourses, see Dara Culhane, "Their Spirits Live within Us: Aboriginal Women in Downtown Eastside Vancouver Emerging into Visibility," *American Indian Quarterly* 27, no. 2 (2003): 595–606.

150. Gerald Vizenor, *Manifest Manners: Narratives on Postindian Survivance* (Lincoln: University of Nebraska Press, 1999), 12.

151. Harjo, *Spiral to the Stars*, 199.

152. A Tribe Called Red, press kit bio.

153. Barker, introduction to *Critically Sovereign*, 18.

154. Frank Waln, quoted in Christina Rose, "Frank Waln, Hip Hop Artist, Ready for Anything," *Native Sun News*, 22 April 2013.

155. Eekwol, interview with author, 2 March 2017, Winnipeg, MB.

## CHAPTER 2. THE REMAKING OF A HIP HOP MAINSTREAM THROUGH ONLINE AND BROADCAST MEDIA

1. Aboriginal Music Week is a festival composed of concerts, workshops, and networking events. In 2018, it was renamed sākihiwē, meaning "love another" in Cree.

2. Elizabeth Cook-Lynn, "The Radical Conscience in Native American Studies," *Wicazo Sa Review* 7, no. 2 (1991): 9–13.

3. Deloria, "Intellectual Self-Determination and Sovereignty," 25–31.

4. The Broadcasting Act outlines federal policies in Aotearoa–New Zealand. Section 37d, regarding promotion of New Zealand content in programming, reads, "The Commission shall, in the exercise of its functions under sections 36(1)(a) and 36(2)(a) and (b),—(d) ensure that, in its funding of sound radio broadcasting, reasonable provision is made to assist in the production and broadcasting of

drama programmers and in the broadcasting of New Zealand music." The commission explicitly includes Maori music in its purview; the first function of the commission is "to reflect and develop New Zealand identity and culture by—(i) promoting programmes about New Zealand and New Zealand interests; and (ii) promoting Maori language and Maori culture." Broadcasting Act of 1989, reprint as at 21 March 2017, administered by the Ministry for Culture and Heritage, Te Puni Kōkiri, and the Ministry of Justice, www.legislation.govt.nz. In Australia, the Broadcasting Services Act of 1992, compiled 23 June 2017, details on-air and on-line broadcasting regulations and names governmental interest in "ensur[ing] the maintenance and, where possible, the development of diversity, including public, community and indigenous broadcasting, in the Australian broadcasting system in the transition to digital broadcasting." Australian Government, Broadcasting Services Act 1992, section 3, www.legislation.gov.au. The Australian Communications and Media Authority also includes provisions for media of Australian origin; see Australian Communications and Media Authority, "Standards and Codes," www.acma.gov.au.

5. The CRTC home page introduction reads, "We are an administrative tribunal that operates at arm's length from the federal government. We are dedicated to ensuring that Canadians have access to a world-class communication system that promotes innovation and enriches their lives." CRTC, home page, https://crtc.gc.ca.

6. CIUR-FM operates in the Native-licensed category as set out by the CRTC.

7. Often, these roles fall on the same people—managers flex engineering skills; music directors announce on air; marketing, branding, and event coordinating fall into the cubicle of one worker.

8. Sara Ahmed, *What's the Use? On the Uses of Use* (Durham, NC: Duke University Press, 2019).

9. While in a city with an intertribal population, Ramirez finds, "there is no guarantee of Native solidarity in an urban area," cities often provide meeting spaces for Native residents to "share common experiences of displacement, racist treatment, and colonization." Renya K. Ramirez, *Native Hubs: Culture, Community, and Belonging in Silicon Valley and Beyond* (Durham, NC: Duke University Press, 2007), 171.

10. Malea Powell, "Listening to Ghosts," in *Alt Dis: Alternative Discourses and the Academy*, ed. Christopher L. Schroeder, Helen Fox, and Patricia Bizzell (Portsmouth, NH: Boynton/Cook Heinemann, 2002), 17–18.

11. David Newhouse and Evelyn Peters, ed., *Not Strangers in These Parts* (Ottawa: Policy Research Initiative, 2003).

12. Powell, "Listening to Ghosts," 18.

13. See note 12 in the Introduction about the name change to The Halluci Nation. This is a group of DJs whose membership has changed over time. They sample and collaborate with competition powwow musicians and other Native North American music as they create their beats. They also critique images of Indigenous people in the media by recontextualizing segments of video alongside their remixes.

14. C. Matthew Snipp, "Sociological Perspectives on American Indians," *Annual Review of Sociology* 18 (1992): 351–71; Joane Nagel, "The Political Mobilization of Native Americans," *Social Science Journal* 19 (1982): 37–46; Nicholas C. Peroff and Danial R. Wildcat, "Who Is an American Indian?," *Social Science Journal* 39, no. 3 (2002): 349–61.

15. Janusz Mucha, "From Prairie to the City: Transformation of Chicago's American Indian Community," *Urban Anthropology* 12, nos. 3–4 (1983): 337–71; Vine Deloria Jr., "Native Americans: The American Indian Today," *Annals of the American Academy of Political and Social Science* 454 (1981): 139–49.

16. Judit Szathmári, "Urban Adjustment," *Hungarian Journal of English and American Studies* 8, no. 2 (2002): 133–52.

17. Tucker, "Permitted Indians," 388.

18. Scales, "First Nations Popular Music in Canada."

19. Carocci, "Living in an Urban Rez."

20. Morgan Baillargeon, "Urban Native Life," Canadian Museum of Civilization, www.civilization.ca.

21. Ramirez, *Native Hubs*, 180.

22. Baillargeon, "Urban Native Life."

23. Graffiti Art Programming offers workshops and drop-in sessions in which youth work on music, dance, and visual arts.

24. Canada's international role in Indigenous media production is further solidified through ventures such as the National Film Board's Indigenous Cinema projects, the ISUMA collective of Inuit video companies, and a plethora of impactful Indigenous community radio stations. See also Roth, *Something New in the Air*.

25. Ginsburg, "Screen Memories," 41.

26. Ginsburg, 41.

27. Leonard Sumner, interview with author, 16 May 2014.

28. Leonard Sumner, interview with author, 6 July 2021.

29. Streetz, "About Us," accessed 3 April 2014, www.streetzfm.ca. The station used the term "Aboriginal" to refer to First Nations, Inuit, and Métis groups.

30. Meta titles were consistent in 2013 and 2014. See www.streetzfm.ca.

31. Shad, "Brother (Watching)," on *The Old Prince* (Black Box Recordings, 2007).

32. Shad.

33. Shabazz, "Masculinity and the Mic."

34. McKittrick, *Demonic Grounds*, 92.

35. David Jones finds that hip hop is "widely presumed, in fact, to be the musical style with the most current relevance to everyday African American life" ("Postmodernism, Pop Music, and Blues Practice," 668). Layli Phillips, Kerri Reddick-Morgan, and Dionne Stephens write that hip hop's "perspective is still centered in the experiences of the underdogs and it still expresses the cultural flair of African American and Latino people." Phillips, Reddick-Morgan, and Stephens, "Oppositional Consciousness within an Oppositional Realm: The Case of Feminism and

Womanism in Rap and Hip Hop, 1976–2004," *Journal of African American History* 90, no. 3 (2005): 254.

36. Robert Alexander Innes and Kim Anderson, "Introduction: Who's Walking with Our Brothers?," in *Indigenous Men and Masculinities: Legacies, Identities, Regeneration*, ed. Innes and Anderson (Winnipeg: University of Manitoba Press, 2015), 4.

37. Halifu Osumare, "Global Hip-Hop and the African Diaspora," in *Black Cultural Traffic: Crossroads in Global Performance and Popular Culture*, ed. Harry J. Elam Jr. and Kennell Jackson (Ann Arbor: University of Michigan Press, 2005), 266.

38. Imani Kai Johnson, "From Blues Women to B-Girls: Performing Badass Femininity," *Women & Performance: A Journal of Feminist Theory* 24, no. 1 (2014): 15.

39. Daniel Traber, "The Identity Joke: Race, Rap, Performance in Cb4," *American Studies* 52, no. 1 (2012): 126.

40. Forman, "Represent," 89.

41. T. Rose, *Hip Hop Wars*, 119. Nelson George, *Hip Hop America* (New York: Viking, 1998), 67.

42. George, *Hip Hop America*, 67.

43. Traber, "Identity Joke," 124.

44. Reiland Rabaka, *Hip Hop's Inheritance: From the Harlem Renaissance to the Hip Hop Feminist Movement* (Lanham, MD: Rowman and Littlefield, 2011), 205.

45. Roopali Mukherjee, "Bling Fling: Commodity Consumption and the Politics of the 'Post-Racial,'" in *Critical Rhetorics of Race*, ed. Michael G. Lacy and Kent A. Ono (New York New York University Press, 2011), 186.

46. Annette J. Saddik, "Rap's Unruly Body: The Postmodern Performance of Black Male Identity on the American Stage," *TDR* 47, no. 4 (2003): 111.

47. Antigovernment and oppositional messaging are among these tropes, yet the specifics of the antiauthoritarian content are important: messages that shore up urban credibility and masculine power are genre typical. See Jennifer C. Lena, *Banding Together: How Communities Create Genres in Popular Music* (Princeton, NJ: Princeton University Press, 2012).

48. Mireille Miller-Young, "Hip-Hop Honeys and Da Hustlaz: Black Sexualities in the New Hip-Hop Pornography," *Meridians: Feminism, Race, Transnationalism* 8, no. 1 (2008): 261–92.

49. bell hooks, "Eating the Other: Desire and Resistance," in *Media and Cultural Studies: Keyworks*, ed. Meenakshi Gigi Durham and Douglas M. Kellner (Malden, MA: Blackwell, 1992), 366.

50. See also Harry Justin Elam and Kennell A. Jackson, eds., *Black Cultural Traffic: Crossroads in Global Performance and Popular Culture* (Ann Arbor: University of Michigan Press, 2005); E. Patrick Johnson, *Appropriating Blackness: Performance and the Politics of Authenticity* (Durham, NC: Duke University Press, 2003); Perry, *Prophets of the Hood*.

51. Aisha Durham, Brittney C. Cooper, and Susana M. Morris, "The Stage Hip-Hop Feminism Built," *Signs* 38, no. 3 (2013): 730.

52. Quoted in Durham, Cooper, and Morris, 730.

53. L. H. Stallings, "Hip Hop and the Black Rachet Imagination," *Palimpsest* 2, no. 2 (2013): 137.

54. This "cool" relates back to Shad's perceptions of how he is seen. See also Majors and Billson, *Cool Pose.*

55. Billboard, "Chart History: Kardinal Offishall," www.billboard.com.

56. Walcott, *Black like Who?*, 12.

57. This history of slavery and economic reliance on the transatlantic slave trade in Canada is underacknowledged. Canadian historian Natasha Henry wrote in 2010, "To this day, it is still not common historical knowledge in Canada that Africans were enslaved in both French and British colonies from as early as 1628. Furthermore, very few Canadians are aware that at one time their nation's economy was firmly linked to African slavery through the building and sale of slave ships, the sale and purchase of slaves to and from the Caribbean, and the exchange of timber, cod, and other food items from the Maritimes for West-Indian slave-produced goods such as rum, tobacco, cotton, coffee, molasses, and sugar." Henry, *Emancipation Day: Celebrating Freedom in Canada* (Toronto: Natural Heritage Books, 2010), 41. See also Peggy Bristow, Dionne Brand, Linda Carty, Afua P. Cooper, Sylvia Hamilton, and Adrienne Shadd, eds., *"We're Rooted Here and They Can't Pull Us Up": Essays in African Canadian Women's History* (Toronto: University of Toronto Press, 1994).

58. McKittrick, *Demonic Grounds*, 99.

59. Brett Rushforth, "'A Little Flesh We Offer You': The Origins of Indian Slavery in New France," *William and Mary Quarterly* 60, no. 4 (2003): 777–808; Aline Helg, *Slave No More: Self-Liberation before Abolitionism in the Americas*, trans. Lara Vergnaud (Chapel Hill: University of North Carolina Press, 2019); Gregory Wigmore, "Before the Railroad: From Slavery to Freedom in the Canadian-American Borderland," *Journal of American History* 98, no. 2 (2011): 437–54.

60. Peggy Bristow, "'Whatever You Raise in the Ground You Can Sell It in Chatham': Black Women in Buxton and Chatham, 1850–65," in Bristow et al., *"We're Rooted Here and They Can't Pull Us Up,"* 71.

61. For more on Shadd Cary and publications by Black Canadian women, see Bristow et al., *"We're Rooted Here and They Can't Pull Us Up."*

62. See Bristow, "Whatever You Raise in the Ground," 110.

63. Webster, feat. Karim Ouellet, "QC History X," *Le vieux d'la montagne* (Universal / Coyote Records, 2007).

64. David McLeod, interview with author, 6 February 2014, updated in conversation 3 April 2014.

65. McLeod, interview with author, 6 February 2014.

66. For an application of the mainstream ear, see chapter 4; see also Stoever, *Sonic Color Line.*

67. David McLeod, interview with author, 11 April 2014.

68. Leonard Sumner, interview with author, 16 May 2014.
69. Guy Morrow, "The Music Industry in Australia and Canada," in Diamond, Crowdy, and Downes, *Post-Colonial Distances*, 191–214.
70. Przybylski, "Indigenous Survivance and Urban Musical Practice."
71. Tuck and Yang, "Decolonization Is Not a Metaphor," 10.
72. Matthew Wildcat, "Fearing Social and Cultural Death: Genocide and Elimination in Settler Colonial Canada: An Indigenous Perspective," *Journal of Genocide Research* 17, no. 4 (2015): 391–409.
73. Audra Simpson, *Mohawk Interruptus: Political Life across the Borders of Settler States* (Durham, NC: Duke University Press, 2014), 7.
74. CBC News, "Winnipeg's Most Buys Headstones for Slain Women," 15 November 2012, www.cbc.ca.
75. These are detailed in chapter 3's analysis.
76. Jean LaRose to Robert A. Morin, "Re: Broadcasting Notice of Public Hearing CRTC 2008-3 Native Communications Inc. Winnipeg, Manitoba Application No. 2007-116," 7 May 2008, https://aptn.ca.
77. Indigenous urban artists in daily rotation in the early 2010s included Winnipeg's Most, Wab Kinew, Lorenzo, The Link, Plex, Beatrice Love, Young Kidd, Joey Stylez, Inez, Sherry St. Germain, Drezus, Feenix, JB the First Lady, Shadow, Kamea, Zane Gold, and Vibez. Canadian urban artist heard daily during the same period included SJ Stacks, The Happy Unfortunate, Lyrical Militant, Belly, Six Sigma, Kay, Len Bowen, Try Nyce, Rupness Monsta, Brakada, Rational, Chad James, Sketch Williams, Dele-O, Boombox Saints, Goody, Saint Kris, Rawg, Madchild, Masia One, Grand Analog, The Lytics, Thunderhiest, K'Naan, Swollen Members, Kardinal Offishall, Classified, Abstract Artform, Magnum KI, Peter Jackson, Flo, Pip Skid, Drake, Berris Smith, Choclair, Shad, D-Sisive, The Weeknd, Keshia Chante, R.O.Z., and K-os. See DM#1761182, "Application by Native Communications."
78. McLeod, interview with author, 11 April 2014.
79. Miss Melissa, interview with author, 30 April 2014. For dialogue segments in this book, participant initials indicate the speaker, except where musicians elected to use their one-word stage names.
80. Alex Sannie, interview with author, 12 February 2014.
81. Miss Melissa, email message to author, 12 May 2014.
82. Miss Melissa, email message to author, 14 May 2014.
83. Clint Bracknell and Casey Kickett (2017) identify that popular programming on Noongar radio is listened to by Noongar and white Australian audiences. It is primarily designed to serve Noongar listeners but also reaches others as secondary audiences. The authors find that music radio programming changed perceptions that white Australians held of Indigenous peoples in Western Australia. Clint Bracknell and Casey Kickett, "*Inside Out*: An Indigenous Community Radio Response to Incarceration in Western Australia," *ab-Original* 1 no. 1 (2017): 81–98.

84. Beka Solo, interview with author, 23 June 2022. Beka Solo began performing with a duo, Rich n Beka; the group's music and details are available at www .richnbekamusic.com.

85. Helene Vosters, *Unbecoming Nationalism: From Commemoration to Redress in Canada* (Winnipeg: University of Manitoba Press, 2017), 188.

86. For example, Kanaka Maoli rapper Krystilez has both acted as a DJ on a Clear Channel–owned radio station and garnered respect on the underground hip hop circuit. Stephanie Teves, "Bloodline Is All I Need: Defiant Indigeneity and Hawaiian Hip-Hop," *American Indian Culture and Research Journal* 35, no. 4 (2011): 73–101.

87. See Jillian Hernandez, "Carnal Teachings: Raunch Aesthetics as Queer Feminist Pedagogies in Yo! Majesty's Hip Hop Practice," *Women & Performance* 24, no. 1 (2014): 88–106.

88. KTV, "Wab Kinew—Good Boy w/ Lorenzo & Troy Westwood," YouTube, 1 March 2011, www.youtube.com/watch?v=c9K3n_fNp64.

89. Sumner, interview with author, 16 May 2014.

90. Walcott, *Black like Who?*, 114.

91. Walcott, *Black like Who?*, 115.

92. Sumner, interview with author, 16 May 2014.

93. Sumner, interview with author, 6 July 2021. Sumner elaborates, "I see the similarities between [Black people being targeted and] Indigenous people being targeted. . . . It all goes back to the power structures and how all the laws are based around protecting land-owning white men. And so everything else is going to become an issue when that's what your foundation is based on."

94. Jill Doerfler, Niigaanwewidam James Sinclair, and Heidi Kiiwetinepinesiik Stark, eds., *Centering Anishinaabeg Studies: Understanding the World through Stories* (Winnipeg: University of Manitoba Press, 2013), 235.

95. Doerfler, Sinclair, and Stark, 235.

96. Stirrup's analysis, while focused on visual art, is applicable to the multimodal manners in which Anishinaabeg story is shared. David Stirrup, "Aadizookewininiwag and the Visual Arts: Story as Process and Principle in Twenty-First Century Anishinaabeg Painting," in Doerfler, Sinclair, and Stark, *Centering Anishinaabeg Studies*, 298.

97. Sumner, interview with author, 16 May 2014.

98. Sumner, interview with author, 16 May 2014.

99. Sumner, interview with author, 6 July 2021.

100. Sumner, interview with author, 10 September 2013.

101. Sumner, interview with author, 10 September 2013.

102. Sean Lee Fahrlander, "Names by Which the Spirits Know Us," in *Genocide of the Mind: New Native American Writing*, ed. MariJo Moore (New York: Nation Books, 2003), 178.

103. Sumner, *Rez Poetry*. The album title uses the term "rez," short for "reservation" or "reserve." The term "rez" is used south of the US-Canada border in the same manner. Leonard Sumner, *Rez Poetry* (Broken Reel Records, 2013).

104. Sumner, interview with author, 10 September 2013.

105. Sumner, interview with author, 16 May 2014.

106. In hip hop, cultural continuity can be understood in a variety of ways. Chase Manhattan cites contemporary powwow; Samian and Drezus cite throat singing and hand drum music, respectively. In "They Say," a hand drum and sung outro appends the piece. Like these musicians and others, Sumner makes references to land and its continuing importance to Indigenous communities in his lyrics. He and the musicians with whom he works reference treaty lands and policies, in addition to Sumner's ongoing attention to cultural sovereignty. Sumner, interview with author, 10 September 2013.

107. Sumner, interview with author, 6 July 2021.

108. Government regulations also impact staff members' music choices. The relationship between broadcast radio rules and music programming is explored from a regulatory perspective in chapter 3.

109. Streetz has been designed to follow the "urban" format, a standard category in radio genres. This encompasses hip hop, R&B, and dance music.

110. This gendering of technologized musical activity has been heard since the beginning of the twentieth century, when the player piano was introduced as a technologized version of the popular parlor instrument. Manufacturers aimed to increase sales by associating it with manliness and machinery. During the postwar period, the phonograph was linked to hi-fi technology; advertising strategies promoted the male music technology connoisseur. See Trevor J. Pinch and Karin Bijsterveld, "'Should One Applaud?': Breaches and Boundaries in the Reception of New Technology in Music," *Technology and Culture* 44, no. 3 (2003): 536–59; Craig H. Roell, *The Piano in America, 1890–1940* (Chapel Hill: University of North Carolina Press, 1991); Keir Keightley, "'Turn It Down!' She Shrieked: Gender, Domestic Space, and High Fidelity, 1948–59," *Popular Music* 15, no. 2 (1996): 149–77.

111. Robin M. James, "Deconstruction, Fetishism, and the Racial Contract: On the Politics of 'Faking It' in Music," *CR: The New Centennial Review* 7, no. 1 (2007): 45–80.

112. James, "Deconstruction, Fetishism, and the Racial Contract," 76.

113. Tara Rodgers, "On the Process and Aesthetics of Sampling in Electronic Music Production," *Organised Sound* 8, no. 3 (2003): 313–20.

114. Julia Emberley, *Defamiliarizing the Aboriginal: Cultural Practices and Decolonization in Canada* (Toronto: University of Toronto Press, 2007), 21.

115. See, for example, Ramirez's interviews with young women who have heard the slur "squaw" used against them, detailed in *Native Hubs*. These interviews also detail women's experiences with other sexist assumptions and practices. Additionally, Janice Acoose writes of the power and damage of the "squaw" and "drudge" stereotypes waged against Indigenous women: "I implore readers to look to their own ideological foundation as a way of understanding personal perceptions and cultural attitudes towards Indigenous women" (*Iskwewak—Kah' Ki Yaw Ni Wahkomakanak*, 40).

116. Jesse Stewart, "DJ Spooky and the Politics of Afro-Postmodernism," *Black Music Research Journal* 30, no. 2 (2010): 340.
117. Mark Katz, *Groove Music: The Art and Culture of the Hip-Hop DJ* (New York: Oxford University Press, 2012); Katz, "Men, Women, and Turntables: Gender and the DJ Battle," *Musical Quarterly* 89, no. 4 (2006): 580–99.
118. Suzanne G. Cusick, "Gender, Musicology and Feminism," in *Rethinking Music*, ed. Nicholas Cook and Mark Everist (Oxford: Oxford University Press, 2001), 471–98.
119. This distinction is even more stark when dance is associated with the feminine. See Nabeel Zuberi, "Is This the Future? Black Music and Technology Discourse," *Science Fiction Studies* 34, no. 2 (2007): 283–300.
120. Sam McKegney, ed., *Masculindians* (Winnipeg: University of Manitoba Press, 2014); Emberley, *Defamiliarizing the Aboriginal*; Innes and Anderson, *Indigenous Men and Masculinities*.
121. Ayana Byrd, "Claiming Jezebel: Black Female Subjectivity and Sexual Expression in Hip-Hop," in *Reconstructing Gender: A Multicultural Anthology*, ed. Estelle Disch (New York: McGraw-Hill, 2009); Joan Morgan, *When the Chickenheads Come Home to Roost* (New York: Simon and Schuster, 2000).
122. Liz Przybylski, *Hybrid Ethnography: Online, Offline, and In Between* (Los Angeles: Sage, 2020).
123. I further this discussion in chapter 4.
124. Hyunsuk Im, Haeyeop Song, and Jaemin Jung, "The Effect of Streaming Services on the Concentration of Digital Music Consumption," *Information Technology & People* 33, no. 1 (2020): 160–79.
125. Przybylski, "Customs and Duty," 10.
126. Users have little control over how the platform operates. Like commercial radio or streaming services, the social media user is not the end consumer; social media companies profit by selling users to advertisers as targeted audiences. Shelly Knotts, "Changing Music's Constitution: Network Music and Radical Democratization," *Leonardo Music Journal* 25 (2015): 49.
127. Tall Paul, 14 October 2016, Facebook.
128. Users engage in identity work by curating their pages and shaping networked communities. Jennifer S. Evans-Cowley, "Planning in the Age of Facebook: The Role of Social Networking in Planning Processes," *GeoJournal* 75, no. 5 (2010): 407–20. Indigenous social media posters have used platforms to rally followers for causes such as preventing pipeline expansion and protecting sacred sites and for international movements such as #IdleNoMore. See also Cutcha Risling Baldy, "The New Native Intellectualism: #ElizabethCook-Lynn, Social Media Movements, and the Millennial Native American Studies Scholar," *Wicazo Sa Review* 31, no. 1 (2016): 90–110.
129. Anderson and Robertson, *Seeing Red*; Gina Masullo Chen, *Online Incivility and Public Debate: Nasty Talk* (New York: Palgrave Macmillan, 2017).
130. This is also a play on the group name N.W.A.

131. For other Indigenous digital media projects, see Brian Hochman, *Savage Preservation* (Minneapolis: University of Minnesota Press, 2014).

132. Jean Burgess and Joshua Green, *YouTube: Online Video and Participatory Culture* (Cambridge, UK: Polity, 2009).

133. Thomas Allmer, "(Dis)Like Facebook? Dialectical and Critical Perspectives on Social Media," *Javnost—The Public* 21, no. 2 (2014): 39–55.

134. S. Vosoughi, D. Roy, and S. Aral, "The Spread of True and False News Online," *Science* 359 (2018): 1146–51; Tarleton Gillespie, *Custodians of the Internet: Platforms, Content Moderation, and the Hidden Decisions That Shape Social Media* (New Haven, CT: Yale University Press, 2018).

135. Tom Johnson, "Chance the Rapper, Spotify, and Musical Categorization in the 2010s," *American Music* 38, no. 2 (2020): 176–96; Lyndsey Havens, "Chance the Rapper's 'Coloring Book' Is First Streaming-Only Album to Win a Grammy," *Billboard*, 28 February 2017, www.billboard.com; Joe Caramanica, "Chance the Rapper Releases 'Coloring Book,' with Spirit," *New York Times*, 18 May 2016, www.nytimes.com.

136. Kris Ex, "Chance the Rapper: Coloring Book," *Pitchfork*, 17 May 2016, https://pitchfork.com; Jack Hamilton, "Chance the Rapper's *Coloring Book* Is the First True Gospel-Rap Masterpiece," *Slate*, 16 May 2016, https://slate.com.

137. Marisa Elena Duarte, *Network Sovereignty: Building the Internet across Indian Country* (Seattle: University of Washington, 2017).

## CHAPTER 3. RADIO SILENCE

1. CRTC, "Broadcasting Decision CRTC 2008-195," Ottawa, 21 August 2008, www.crtc.gc.ca.

2. Kim Wheeler, "Winnipeg's Streetz FM Caters to Urban Aboriginal Youth Market," *CBC Music*, 27 April 2012, http://music.cbc.ca. This chapter uses the call letters CIUR when referring to the station's official licensing paperwork or features that were the same across the Streetz and Rhythm branding changes. Otherwise, the more specific Streetz and Rhythm titles are used as relevant.

3. In Canada, the term "newcomer" refers to recent immigrants.

4. "Time spent per listener at 16.6 hours per week. Nearly half of radio tuning is done at home, over a third in the car and 20% at work." Numeris, *How Canada Listens*, Fall 2017 Radio Diary Survey, http://assets.numeris.ca.

5. Nielsen, "Audio Today: Radio 2016—Appealing Far and Wide," February 2016, www.nielsen.com.

6. Manuel Pacheco Coelho and José Zorro Mendes, "Digital Music and the 'Death of the Long Tail,'" *Journal of Business Research* 101 (2019): 459.

7. Heikki Hellman and Arto Vilkko, "Is There Diversity on Popular Music Radio? Developing a Methodology for a Quantitative Analysis of Radio Playlists," *Journal of Radio & Audio Media*, 8 December 2019.

8. The Streetz and Rhythm Facebook pages are public.

9. This post was set to be visible to everyone.

10. Facebook responses to Rabliauskas's post, 2 April 2014.

11. Michael Redhead Champagne, "Lessons from the Streetz," *North End MC* (blog), 30 December 2011, https://northendmc.wordpress.com.

12. Comments on Streetz Facebook page, 2 April 2014.

13. Turnbull, "Radio Mondo," 132.

14. Bill Curry, "CBC Funding under Microscope in Conservative Surveys," *Globe and Mail*, 23 September 2011; Suevon Lee, "Big Bird Debate: How Much Does Federal Funding Matter to Public Broadcasting?," *ProPublica*, 11 October 2012; Laura Kane, "More CBC Cuts Include Making Radio 2 Online-Only: Watchdog Group," *City News*, 22 May 2014; Marion Ménard, *CBC/Radio Canada: Overview and Key Issues*, ed. Legal and Social Affairs Division (Ottawa: Library of Parliament, 2013).

15. CBC Manitoba's *Scene* centers on concerts, art, and events in Manitoba and previews music events in Winnipeg. Radio Canada covers local Francophone content. See CBC Manitoba, "Scene," www.cbc.ca.

16. Canadian Heritage, "Northern Native Broadcast Access Program (NNBAP) & Northern Distribution Program (NDP) Evaluation: Final Report," 25 June 2003, 5, http://publications.gc.ca.

17. NCI's estimated total budget was $1,391,108, and NNBAP funded $641,108. Canadian Heritage, 88.

18. LaRose, "Re: Broadcasting Notice of Public Hearing," 3.

19. Per DM#1761182, "about 8% of its annual operating budget of NCI-FM Radio Network from Canadian Heritage, as per programming commitments none of Canadian Heritage's funding is utilized towards Streetz-FM." DM#1761182, "Application by Native Communications," 3. NCI continued to receive Canadian Heritage funding when it operated Rhythm, notably through a $450,956 contribution through the NNBAP, granted May 20, 2015. As in previous awards, this was earmarked for media in northern Manitoba, which does not include Winnipeg. See Government of Canada, "Government Grants and Contributions," GC-2015-Q1-02006, https://open.canada.ca.

20. CRTC, "Diversity of Voices—Winnipeg," www.crtc.gc.ca.

21. "Campus" category stations are the Winnipeg Campus / Community Radio Society Inc. and UMFM Campus Radio Inc.; "Community-Based" covers Nostalgia Broadcasting Cooperative Inc. and Radio communautaire du Manitoba inc.; there were no "Religious" licensed stations as of 2018.

22. David McLeod, interview with author, 6 February 2014, updated in conversation 3 April 2014.

23. The station highlights that its "radio network currently reaches 98% of Manitoba: from Churchill to Winnipeg—'you are in NCI country!'" NCI, "About Us," www.ncifm.com.

24. Sutherland, "Sound Recording and Radio"; CRTC, "Canadian Content Requirement for Music on Canadian Radio."

25. McLeod, interview with author, 3 April 2014.

26. Streetz, "About Us," www.streetzfm.ca. Meta titles were consistent in 2013 and through the branding change into 2014.

27. Over Streetz's time on air, it courted listeners from overlapping groups of Black, Indigenous, Filipinx, white, and other listeners. Compared to other Winnipeg stations, it had more focus on reaching nonwhite listenerships.

28. Browne, *Dark Matters*.

29. Alex Sannie, interview with author, 12 February 2014.

30. CRTC, "Broadcasting Decision CRTC 2008-195."

31. McLeod, interview with author, 3 April 2014. It should be noted that NCI operates under a different structure than commercial stations. The music director at CIUR, for instance, does not take direction from a national office that selects music for the station to play, therefore giving the station more flexibility in which artists it broadcasts. On the relationship between local and national criteria in programming, consult Eric W. Rothenbuhler, "Programming Decision Making in Popular Music Radio," *Communication Research* 12, no. 2 (1985): 209–32. For more on commercial radio and music programming decisions, see Jarl A. Ahlkvist, "Programming Philosophies and the Rationalization of Music Radio," *Media, Culture & Society* 23 (2001): 339–58.

32. Inez Jasper is sometimes referred to exclusively as Inez.

33. Non-Indigenous Canadian rappers including Shad and Drake are also mainstays.

34. McLeod, interview with author, 3 April 2014.

35. Cusicanqui, "Ch'ixinakax utxiwa," 105–6.

36. Jolene Rickard, "Sovereignty: A Line in the Sand," *Aperture*, no. 139 (1995): 51.

37. Barker, *Critically Sovereign*; Doerfler et al., *Centering Anishinaabeg Studies*; Duarte, *Network Sovereignty*; Harjo, *Spiral to the Stars*; Raheja, "Visual Sovereignty."

38. Maile Arvin, Eve Tuck, and Angie Morrill, "Decolonizing Feminism: Challenging Connections between Settler Colonialism and Heteropatriarchy," *Feminist Formations* 25, no. 1 (2013): 8–34.

39. Simpson describes an embodied sovereignty that extends into the past and into the future. See chapter 1; L. Simpson, *Dancing on Our Turtle's Back*.

40. Frank Waln's use of Lakota Rabbit Dance songs is an example of this specificity, in contrast to artists such as Drezus who rely on intertribal musical references. Przybylski, "Customs and Duty."

41. Waaseyaa'sin Christine Sy, "Relationship with Land in Anishinaabeg Womxn's Historical Research," in *Reshaping Women's History: Voices of Nontraditional Women Historians*, ed. Julie A. Gallagher and Barbara Winslow (Urbana: University of Illinois Press, 2018), 227.

42. Sy, "Relationship with Land"; David McNally, *Ojibwe Singers* (St. Paul: Minnesota Historical Society Press, 2009).

43. Many North American Indigenous nations have teachings about a white buffalo. Anishinaabe teachings tell of how the White Buffalo Calf Woman shared the seven sacred teachings; for many people, a white buffalo is an enduring sign of connection to Creator. See David Bouchard and Joseph Martin Tehanakerehkwen,

*The Seven Sacred Teachings of White Buffalo Calf Woman, Niizhwaaswi Aanike'iniwendiwin: Waabishiki Mashkode Bizhikiins Ikwe* (North Vancouver, BC: More than Words, 2009).

44. See chapter 1 for a description of a 49, the celebratory and less formal gathering held after a powwow.

45. At the time, the awards show was called the Aboriginal Peoples' Choice Music Awards (APCMA).

46. The group's Soundclick page was active in 2004–5.

47. Sannie, interview with author, 12 February 2014.

48. Sumner, interview with author, 6 July 2021.

49. Staff often use "mainstream" to cue a non-Indigenous listenership. There is some slippage here as the term often cues a white audience and may also imply settler Canadians of other racial backgrounds. This usage of "mainstream" to mean non-Indigenous is consistent in scholarship about Indigenous music. See Scales, "First Nations Popular Music in Canada."

50. NCI, Application 2007-1163-1, received 20 August 2007. See CRTC, "Broadcasting Decision CRTC 2008-195."

51. See DM#2199354-2014-0928-5-APP-CIUR-FM Winnipeg, Manitoba Renewal Licensing Application, 11 September 2014, https://applications.crtc.gc.ca. In the application, hip hop appeared under music enjoyed by MJ, one of the hosts of *The Rise Up Show*, and by Anthony Carvalho, the host of *Mid-day* who took over part of the slot made vacant by Alex Sannie's departure. DJ Dow Jones, host of the Friday-evening pregame show (9–10 p.m.), is a former performer and cofounding member of Mood Ruff, a hip hop group that started in Winnipeg in 1994.

52. McLeod, interview with author, 3 April 2014.

53. Alex Sannie talks about the particular bias he hears as a Black Canadian. He has encountered anti-Black negative assumptions that some listeners have about hip hop as an entire genre. Not of Indigenous heritage himself, he recounts some anti-Native attitudes he has heard in Winnipeg. Sannie described that he is aware of these societal biases as he thinks through how he talks about music by Black and Indigenous artists that plays on-air and online.

54. McLeod, interview with author, 3 April 2014.

55. NCI pays attention to radio reach and marketing data. The numbers from listening surveys influence decision-making, as do the focus groups the station has held. For more on listener data, see BBM Canada, "Top Line Radio Statistics," http://assets.numeris.ca.

56. Miss Melissa, interview with author, 30 April 2014. The term "quality" here could refer to the production value of songs and also gestures to the class subtexts referenced previously.

57. In contrast to liberal multiculturalism, while "Indigenous peoples do form important alliances with people of color, Indigenous communities' concerns are often not about achieving formal equality or civil rights within a nation-state, but instead achieving substantial independence from a Western

nation-state—independence decided on their own terms" (Arvin, Tuck, and Morrill, "Decolonizing Feminism," 10).
58. Lawrence, "Gender, Race, and the Regulation of Native Identity," 5.
59. Weisbard, *Top 40 Democracy*, 18.
60. DM#2199354-2014-0928-5-APP-CIUR-FM Winnipeg.
61. DM#2199354-2014-0928-5-APP-CIUR-FM Winnipeg.
62. DM#2199354-2014-0928-5-APP-CIUR-FM Winnipeg.
63. The teenage market is not traditionally attractive to radio advertisers, though it was part of Streetz's audience.
64. Weisbard, *Top 40 Democracy*, 4.
65. Media companies (including Spotify, Pandora, and Deezer) arranged their business models to track and profit from this information. See Eric Drott, "Music as a Technology of Surveillance," *Journal of the Society for American Music* 12, no. 3 (August 2018): 233–67.
66. While regulations are generally more specific than acts, both are legislation passed by Parliament that transmit rules or requirements. See CanLII, "Radio Regulations, SOR/86-982 (1986) (Can.)," http://canlii.ca; Freya Zaltz, email message to author, 8 July 2014.
67. The CRTC has been given authority by Parliament. The CBSC was proposed as an effort by commercial broadcasters to handle complaints. This was approved by the CRTC. Should a party that files a complaint against the CBSC be unsatisfied with the result, that party retains the right to bring the complaint to the CRTC.
68. Freya Zaltz, email message to author, 26 June 2014.
69. Morrow, "Music Industry in Australia and Canada."
70. CRTC, "The MAPL System—Defining a Canadian Song," www.crtc.gc.ca.
71. CRTC, "Our Mandate for Canadian Content," www.crtc.gc.ca.
72. Scott Henderson, "Canadian Content Regulations and the Formation of a National Scene," *Popular Music* 27, no. 2 (2008): 307–15.
73. Sannie, interview with author, 12 February 2014.
74. Sannie.
75. Greg Hobbs, "Maestro Fresh-Wes Hip Hop Classic Gets Thumbs-Up from Canadian Songwriters' Hall of Fame," *CBC News*, 19 November 2019.
76. See also Przybylski, "Rapping to and for a Multivocal Canada."
77. Some US-based musicians described challenges crossing into Canada for shows, and vice versa.
78. Thomas King, *The Inconvenient Indian: A Curious Account of Native People in North America* (Minneapolis: University of Minnesota Press, 2013), xv–xvi.
79. Miss Melissa, interview with author, 30 April 2014.
80. Music genre affects the Canadian content requirement. The 35 percent standard applied to "popular music"; "jazz" and "classical" genres have a lower standard percentage, as does "ethnic" music during "ethnic" broadcasting periods. See CRTC, "Canadian Content Requirements for Music on Canadian Radio." See also Sutherland, "Sound Recording and Radio."

81. In September 2012, NCI filed a request with the CRTC to reduce the Canadian selections on CIUR-FM from 40 percent to 35 percent. This request was denied. CRTC, "Broadcasting Decision CRTC 2013-69," Ottawa, 20 February 2013, www .crtc.gc.ca.

82. See DM#1761181-2012-1125-0-APP-Amendment to license CIUR Winnipeg MB, 7 September 2012, https://crtc.gc.ca.

83. The CRTC noted timing as a reason for the denial: "given that CIUR-FM's third year of operation started on 1 September 2011 and the application was posted in September 2012, the Commission considers that NCI did not allow sufficient time to assess the impact of a 40% level of Canadian music before applying for a reduction." CRTC, Broadcasting Decision CRTC 2013-69, Ottawa, 20 February 2013, https://crtc.gc.ca.

84. See DM#1761182, "Application by Native Communications," 1.

85. DM#1761182, 3.

86. Cusicanqui, "Ch'ixinakax utxiwa."

87. Walcott, *Black like Who?*, 116.

88. Walcott, 118.

89. Bruno Cornellier, "The Thing about Obomsawin's Indianness: Indigenous Reality and the Burden of Education at the National Film Board of Canada," *Revue canadienne d'études cinématographiques / Canadian Journal of Film Studies* 21, no. 2 (2012): 6.

90. Casey Mecija, "Good-Bye Ohbijou: Notes on Music, Queer Affect, and the Impossibilities of Satisfying Multicultural Ideals in Canada," in *Diasporic Intimacies: Queer Filipinos and Canadian Imaginaries*, ed. Robert Diaz, Marissa Largo, and Fritz Pino (Evanston, IL: Northwestern University Press, 2018), 119.

91. Marissa Largo, "Reimagining Filipina Visibility through 'Black Mirror': The Queer Decolonial Diasporic Aesthetic of Marigold Santos," in Diaz, Largo, and Pino. *Diasporic Intimacies*, 99.

92. T. Rose, *Hip Hop Wars*; Alan Light, "About a Salary or Reality? Rap's Recurrent Conflict," in Neal and Forman, *That's the Joint!*; Betty Houchin Winfield and Sandra Davidson, eds., *Bleep! Censoring Rock and Rap Music* (Westport, CT: Greenwood, 1999), 137–45.

93. David McLeod, interview with author, 11 April 2014.

94. Canadian Radio-television and Telecommunications Commission, "Broadcasting Decision CRTC 2013–69," https://crtc.gc.ca.

95. David McLeod, interview with author, 6 February 2014, updated in conversation 3 April 2014.

96. Martin Patriquin, "Straight Outta Winnipeg," *Maclean's*, 13 December 2010.

97. Devon, "Mr. Metro" (independent release, 1990).

98. Sannie, interview with author, 12 February 2014.

99. The Broadcasting Act requires programming of a "high standard." This has generally been understood by the CRTC to block obscenity and profanity, though neither word is strictly defined. Further, exceptions are made, for example, during

certain times of day or when listeners are forewarned. Regulations handled by the FCC in the United States are also open to some interpretation but contain specific guidelines. See FCC, *Commission's Rules Concerning Commercial Radio Operators* (Washington, DC: FCC, 2014); FCC, *Obscene, Indecent and Profane Broadcasts* (Washington, DC: FCC, 2014). In both countries, individual broadcasters may set formal or informal practices regarding what may be aired, on the basis of their own standards or perceptions of what the regulatory policy means.

100. The CRTC only handles complaints against radio broadcasters that are public (CBC), campus, community licensed, or Native licensed.

101. Rhythm 104.7, "About Us," http://rhythm1047.com.

102. While legislation is amended by the government, this is done upon the CRTC's recommendation. This is analogous with the functioning of the FCC in the United States. Both operate as arms-length regulators. Freya Zaltz, email message to author, 25 December 2014.

103. Sannie, interview with author, 12 February 2014.

104. Sannie.

105. On audience construction for radio, see also Eric W. Rothenbuhler, "Commercial Radio as Communication," *Journal of Communication* 46, no. 1 (1996): 125–43.

106. Turnbull, "Radio Mondo," 132.

107. Antoine Hennion, "The Production of Success: An Anti-Musicology of the Pop Song," in *Pop Music and Easy Listening*, ed. Stan Hawkins (Farnham, UK: Ashgate, 2011).

108. Fabian Holt, *Genre in Popular Music* (Chicago: University of Chicago Press, 2007), 17.

109. Turnbull, "Radio Mondo," 132.

110. McLeod, interview with author, 11 April 2014.

111. Weisbard, *Top 40 Democracy.*

112. Language, whether rapped or spoken, is racially coded. See H. Samy Alim, "Translocal Style Communities: Hip Hop Youth as Cultural Theorists of Style, Language, and Globalization," *Pragmatics* 19, no. 1 (2009): 103–27. Other aspects of sonic expression, such as timbre, pitch register, and genre, too, have raced associations. This idea was applied to hip hop in chapter 1; its history on radio is traced in Stoever, *Sonic Color Line.*

113. McLeod, interview with author, 11 April 2014.

114. David McLeod, Facebook post, 5 May 2014.

115. Bonita Lawrence and Enakshi Dua, "Decolonizing Antiracism," *Social Justice* 32, no. 4 (2005): 137.

116. Many prominent Indigenous popular music projects have been shortlisted, such as Streetz favorite A Tribe Called Red in 2013.

117. Camerata Nova changed its name to Dead of Winter in 2021.

118. Dutcher joined the label in August 2017. See RPM.fm, "Jeremy Dutcher Joins RPM Records, Announces Forthcoming Single 'Honour Song,'" 18 August 2017, http://rpm.fm.

119. These include the Indigenous Music Awards, the sākihiwē festival, Aboriginal Music Program Mentors, and, as already mentioned, APTN and NCI.

## CHAPTER 4. THIS MUSIC IS NOT FOR YOU

1. T-Rhyme, *Diary of a Mad Red Woman* (independent release, 2016); Eekwol, *Good Kill* (independent release, 2015).

2. The musicians whose work informs chapter 4 use expansive notions of the idea of women. I use the term "womxn" to recognize this definition. Following my collaborators, "womxn" explicitly includes trans* women. The term "womxn" is age expansive, including girls. It operates as a stand-in for a vast group that is often included in the music scenes in chapter 4, including nonbinary, two-spirit, agender, and female identifying people. As identified in chapter 1, the term "womxn" is from practice and scholarship that intentionally decenter cisgender identities. I use the term to include nonbinary and two-spirit people, as expressed by Eekwol, T-Rhyme, and others. The terminology is particularly apt in this chapter because it releases the nominative from its reliance on "men." "Womxn" is more than half of a binary. See also The Cruel Ironies Collective, "Cruel Ironies: The Afterlife of Black Womxn's Intervention," in *To Exist Is to Resist: Black Feminism in Europe*, ed. Emejulu Akwugo and Sobande Francesca (London: Pluto, 2019), 181–94; Lara Medina and Martha R. Gonzales, eds., *Voices from the Ancestors: Xicanx and Latinx Spiritual Expressions and Healing Practices* (Tucson: University of Arizona Press, 2019).

3. T-Rhyme and Eekwol, interview with author, 8 December 2018, updated in dialogue with interviewees, 3 April 2019, Culver Center of the Arts, Show & Prove. Subsequent quotations from musicians in this chapter are from this same dialogue unless otherwise noted.

4. I invited T-Rhyme and Eekwol to be part of a hip hop festival and conference. They performed in California in December 2018. After the show, two of my students stayed to talk with them. One student has been actively developing her musical career. The other young woman, while not planning a specific musical career, came to a realization in my hip hop class that her interest in graffiti was much more important to her than she knew, and she started making visual art again. Both students talked to T-Rhyme and Eekwol about what it was like to see them perform and found inspiration in doing so. The rappers reflected to me on the importance of this interaction to them. They also talked about being introverts, and one of my students talked with them about feeling shy and yet finding space for herself in hip hop. This interaction expresses one of T-Rhyme's stated goals: "We want to be good medicine for other people."

5. Music connected to Idle No More, NoDAPL, and other movements has explicitly called for governments and corporate entities to respect the land rights held by Indigenous peoples. It has also garnered attention from audiences through online music videos. See chapter 1 for more details, as well as the exploration of pop

songs in Idle No More in chapter 2 and Przybylski, "Indigenous Survivance and Urban Musical Practice."

6. These projects, based in current-day Canada, resonate with other cyphers for and by female and nonbinary artists. Connections are particularly strong with those in Australia, Aotearoa–New Zealand, and to a certain extent, the United States. As a way to come together, a cypher is an object and a practice, a circle in which people gather to take turns freestyling, and the act of gathering and improvisation.

7. Audience curation depends on both the technical ability to project or restrict sound and the creation of a feeling of welcome for the invited listeners. The previous chapters dealt directly with the ability to get sound on-air or online, so that listeners access it. This chapter further interrogates the question of what it means to make certain listeners welcome or unwelcome, with regard to both musical address and creating the conditions for desired listening attitudes and the following of chosen protocols in the spaces of the cypher and performance.

8. A. Simpson, *Mohawk Interruptus*.

9. A. Simpson, 185.

10. José Esteban Muñoz, *The Sense of Brown* (Durham, NC: Duke University Press, 2020), 6.

11. Interrelated and nonidentical conceptions of gender and sexuality beyond two-spirit and Nation-specific identities include Third Gender and IndigiQueer. See also Mark Rifkin, *When Did Indians Become Straight? Kinship, the History of Sexuality, and Native Sovereignty* (Oxford: Oxford University Press, 2011); Jenny L. Davis, "More than Just 'Gay Indians': Intersecting Articulations of Two-Spirit Gender, Sexuality, and Indigenousness," in *Queer Excursions: Retheorizing Binaries in Language, Gender, and Sexuality*, ed. Lal Zimman, Jenny L. Davis, and Joshua Raclaw (Oxford: Oxford University Press, 2014), 62–80.

12. Female-fronted punk bands rocked North America, Europe, and beyond in the 1980s and '90s, and rock music education spaces have continued this trend even after feminist-separatist political power was reduced in its mainstream versions starting in the mid-'90s. The Michigan Womyn's Festival, whose regulations around who could participate were debated among feminists in its later years, came to an end in 2015.

13. Artist response to lyrics at Genius.com, Solange Knowles, "F.U.B.U.," https://genius.com.

14. T-Rhyme, post to Facebook, 18 January 2019.

15. Liz Przybylski, "Singing Resilience: Indigenous Women's Leadership Counteracting Gender-Based Violence," in *Violence and Indigenous Communities*, ed. Susan Sleeper-Smith, Jeff Ostler, and Josh Reid (Evanston, IL: Northwestern University Press, 2021), 203–21.

16. A. Simpson, *Mohawk Interruptus*, 156.

17. Stoever, *Sonic Color Line*, 11.

18. Stoever, 22–23.

19. The manner in which this dynamic has played out at Indigenous music labels is outlined in Scales, "First Nations Popular Music in Canada." This topic is discussed in detail in chapters 1 and 2.
20. McKittrick, *Demonic Grounds*, 18.
21. Powell, "Listening to Ghosts."
22. Patricia Hill Collins and Sirma Bilge, *Intersectionality* (Malden, MA: Polity, 2016). See also Kimberlé Crenshaw, "Mapping the Margins: Intersectionality, Identity Politics, and Violence against Women of Color," *Stanford Law Review* 43, no. 6 (1990): 1241–99.
23. Jennifer C. Nash, *Black Feminism Reimagined: After Intersectionality* (Durham, NC: Duke University Press, 2019), 24, 25. Intersectionality as analytic has come from Black feminist theory; the hip hop practices in this chapter are rooted in, and recognize, the creative labor of Black womxn hip hop artists. The citational practices in the music analyzed here, and the musicians who make them, continue to recognize this.
24. The effects of categorization vary based on the ways in which people define themselves, and see themselves defined by others, in terms of Nation or band-specific identity, a more globalized Indigenous identity, and/or a mixed-race or mixed-heritage affiliation.
25. Simpson, *Mohawk Interruptus*, 149.
26. Scott Lauria Morgensen, "Settler Homonationalism: Theorizing Settler Colonialism within Queer Modernities," *GLQ* 16, nos. 1–2 (2010): 106. See also Michel Foucault, *The History of Sexuality: An Introduction, Volume 1*, trans. Robert Hurley (New York: Vintage Books, 1990).
27. Smith, Choueiti, and Pieper, *Inequality in 800 Popular Films*, 3–4.
28. Smith, Choueiti, and Pieper, 25.
29. T. Rose, *Black Noise*, 387.
30. T. Rose, 387.
31. Emily Blake, "On the Charts, It's Ladies First," *Rolling Stone* 1353/1354 (1 July 2021): 30.
32. She Is The Music, https://sheisthemusic.org.
33. Diamond, Crowdy, and Downes, *Post-Colonial Distances*. Media activity and awards focus attention on Indigenous musicians in positive ways, yet these also monetize Indigenous performance, which raises questions about representation and selling Indigenous musical knowledge. This is particularly the case when stories unique to specific groups are taken up by multicultural narratives.
34. Smith, Choueiti, and Pieper, *Inequality in 800 Popular Films*, 5.
35. Indigenous Music Awards, "Rules and Regulations," 2018, www .indigenousmusicawards.com (emphasis in original).
36. Indigenous Music Awards, "Nominees," 2019, www.indigenousmusicawards.com.
37. Mishuana Goeman and Jennifer Nez Denetdale, "Native Feminisms: Legacies, Interventions, and Sovereignties," *Wicazo Sa Review* 24, no. 2 (2009): 10.
38. Goeman and Nez Denetdale, 10.

39. Joyce Green, "Taking Account of Aboriginal Feminism," in *Making Space for Indigenous Feminism*, 2nd ed., ed. Joyce Green (Winnipeg, MB: Fernwood, 2017), 20.

40. Green, "Taking Account of Aboriginal Feminism," 23.

41. Hernandez, "Carnal Teachings."

42. "Rapper's Delight" is on the National Recording Registry of the Library of Congress in the United States. As of 2019, the only other recordings in the Rap/Hip Hop category to be included are "The Message" by Grandmaster Flash and the Furious Five, *Fear of a Black Planet* by Public Enemy, "Dear Mama," by Tupac Shakur, *3 Feet High and Rising*, by De La Soul, *The Miseducation of Lauryn Hill* by Lauryn Hill, *Straight Outta Compton* by N.W.A., *Raising Hell* by Run-DMC, and *The Blueprint* by Jay-Z. Library of Congress, "Complete National Recording Registry Listing," www.loc.gov.

43. Raquel Z. Rivera, *New York Ricans from the Hip Hop Zone* (New York: Palgrave Macmillan, 2003); Lechusza, "Without Reservations"; Raegan Kelly, "Hip-Hop Chicano: A Separate but Parallel Story," in *It's Not about a Salary: Rap, Race, and Resistance in Los Angeles*, ed. Brian Cross (New York: Verso, 1993), 65–76.

44. Keyes, *Rap Music and Street Consciousness*, 71.

45. For more on sovereignty as enacted through dance, see Mique'l Dangeli, "Dancing Chiax, Dancing Sovereignty: Performing Protocol in Unceded Territories," *Dance Research Journal* 48, no. 1 (2016): 75–90; and Jacqueline Shea Murphy, *The People Have Never Stopped Dancing* (Minneapolis: University of Minnesota Press, 2007).

46. This chapter focuses on how artists reference Black musicians and music in their own work. Many Indigenous artists who appear throughout this book offer similar recognition in interviews, lyrics, and other musical forms of homage.

47. In interview passages, // indicates that the speakers build directly on each other's ideas without pause.

48. This tension emerges in various ways. Witness, for example, the debate around Lauryn Hill's decision to prioritize raising a child when at a high point in her career and the largely unquestioned assumption that she would either focus on a hip hop career or care for her baby. Listen for her awareness of, and response to, public pressure within her track "To Zion." Hill is one of many rappers who experienced a role shift upon becoming a mother: the roles available to female performers in mainstream rap have often placed a sexualized, young-looking persona at odds with a maternal persona.

49. Eekwol and T-Rhyme, "As Real as It Gets," *For Women By Women* (independent release, 2019).

50. In Canada, funding for Indigenous-musician-led projects appears in some federal, provincial, and foundation-based programs. These monies do not sufficiently support the wealth of creative projects that have been undertaken during 2008–18 or that continue to be undertaken. And yet there is even less financial and other material support available for Indigenous womxn musicians who are US-based, particularly at the federal and state levels.

51. When I talked with Eekwol and T-Rhyme initially, the artists were not sure how the album would do with regard to popularity. However, grant funding allowed for a certain freedom of approach and the ability not to hyperfocus on sales and recuperating costs. Yet, since the release, the album has attracted praise from reviewers and audiences, and touring with the new project has opened up performance invitations. Said another way, an album that was birthed in response to frustration with the music industry has done relatively well in it. Even so, grants come with their own requirements with regard to outcomes and reporting, including attendant priorities and limitations or regulations based on the granting agency's goals. Musicians can walk a fine line between their goals and funders' goals, and some choose not to accept funding from particular industries or parties on the basis of their own ethical standards.

52. Sara Ahmed, *The Promise of Happiness* (Durham, NC: Duke University Press, 2010); Encarnación Gutiérrez-Rodríguez, *Migration, Domestic Work and Affect: A Decolonial Approach on Value and the Feminization of Labor* (New York: Routledge, 2010).

53. Katz, "Men, Women, and Turntables." Physical safety can become a concern for nonbinary people, men, and boys as well. Violence can also come from people known to the musician. Harassment and violence have been directed toward boys and men in male homosocial spaces, as attested in credible allegations against formerly trusted male hip hop figures.

54. William Cheng, "Role-Playing toward a Virtual Musical Democracy in *The Lord of the Rings Online*," *Ethnomusicology* 56, no. 1 (2012): 31–62.

55. Andrew L. Yarrow, "Online, Offline," in *Man Out: Men on the Sidelines of American Life* (Washington, DC: Brookings Institution Press, 2018), 109–24; Safiya Noble, *Algorithms of Oppression* (New York: New York University Press, 2018).

56. Jamie Bartlett, Richard Norrie, Sofia Patel, Rebekka Rumpel, and Simon Wibberley, *Misogyny on Twitter* (London: Demos, 2014), https://demos.co.uk.

57. Amanda Hess, "Why Women Aren't Welcome on the Internet," *Pacific Standard*, 6 January 2014, https://psmag.com.

58. William Cheng, "Coming through Loud and Queer: Ethnomusicological Ethics of Voice and Violence in Real and Virtual Battlegrounds," in *Queering the Field: Sounding Out Ethnomusicology*, ed. Gregory Barz and William Cheng (New York: Oxford University Press, 2019), 307–32.

59. These moments are myriad and arc across this book as a whole. They come in instants and build over time. An MC recounted anti-Black comments and racially charged club attire. A radio DJ identified times that urban Indigenous professionals face anti-Indigenous bias. Another MC remembered aggressive posturing of male fans at hip hop shows. A media producer opined on the way women are belittled in media spaces and strategized how to navigate the attitudes that build from small interactions to large consequences. These also come in subtler forms, in attitudes that women, men, and nonbinary people internalize and may not realize they are enacting, believing, and perpetuating. Patterns of interpersonal

behavior reveal mind-sets impacted by racial bias and heteropatriarchal thinking that influence the relationships people have with each other.

60. Many roles are based on the limited opportunities for Black women in hip hop: embodying a hip hop machismo, as in the persona of an artist such as openly lesbian rapper Young M.A.; maternal, as attributed to later-career Queen Latifah; or overtly sexualized, as ascribed to the public presence of Foxy Brown. Queen Latifah plays with some of these expectations in her 2009 album *Persona* (while encouraging young women in some rapped verses). Janelle Monae calls attention to gendered expectations of rappers in "Django Jane." See also Miller-Young, "Hip-Hop Honeys and Da Hustlaz"; Tricia Rose, "There Are Bitches and Hoes" in *Gender, Race, and Class in Media*, ed. Gail Hines and Jean Humez (Thousand Oaks, CA: Sage, 2015), 386–90; Perry, *Prophets of the Hood*.

61. Gwendolyn D. Pough, "'Do the Ladies Run This . . . ?': Some Thoughts on Hip-Hop Feminism," in *Catching a Wave: Reclaiming Feminism for the 21st Century*, ed. Rory Dicker and Alison Piepmeier (Boston: Northeastern University Press, 2003), 232–43.

62. Some non-Black artists have parroted this stereotype, as well as a few other available roles, such as the comedian, in the vein of Flavor Flav, or the professor, as in the serious political leader à la Chuck D and Tupac. Eminem famously used the role of comedian, poking fun at himself using negative stereotypes associated with poor white USAmericans, to establish himself according to a legible set of interpersonal dynamics as a white rapper. See Traber, "Identity Joke"; Karin L. Stanford, "Keepin' It Real in Hip Hop Politics: A Political Perspective of Tupac Shakur," *Journal of Black Studies* 42, no. 1 (2011): 3–22; Loren Kajikawa, "My Name Is: Signifying Whiteness, Rearticulating Race," in *Sounding Race in Rap Songs* (Berkeley: University of California Press, 2014), 118–42.

63. As detailed in chapter 2, Rinaldo Walcott, Katherine McKittrick, and other scholars have traced how Black communities have been discursively relocated outside Canada, despite histories of Black Canadians that stretch back pre-confederation. This insidious invisibility and inaudibility encounters Afro-diasporic sonic practices in hip hop, through which North American ideas of Blackness become hyperaudible.

64. I. Johnson, "From Blues Women to B-Girls."

65. Devin Pacholick, "Eekwol Fights for Aboriginal Women's Rights through Hip-Hop," *Noisey*, 13 January 2016.

66. McKegney, *Masculindians*.

67. Vivian O'Donnell and Susan Wallace, "Women in Canada: A Gender-Based Statistical Report: First Nations, Inuit and Métis Women," Statistics Canada, 2011, www150.statcan.gc.ca; Amnesty International Canada, "Violence against Indigenous Women and Girls in Canada: A Summary of Amnesty International's Concerns and Call to Action," Amnesty International, February 2014, www.amnesty.ca.

68. Tina Beads and Rauna Kuokkanen, "Aboriginal Feminist Action on Violence against Women," in Green, *Making Space for Indigenous Feminism*, 229.

69. For some artists, making music can be intertwined with efforts to respond to sexual violence on a wide scale. Tsilhqot'in rapper/producer Beka Solo explains, "There's a message that I need to get out to the public." It is essential to address sexual abuse publicly; "it's a problem everywhere." She focuses on possibilities to communicate about it and heal from it, saying, "For me being in music and learning to be a strong voice, I feel like my job as an artist is to teach people I interact with that they have the ability to heal; they have the ability to have a limitless vision. Because before colonization, our people were really powerful people. . . . That's why I'm so drawn to music. Because music is the easiest way to communicate with people." Interview with author, 23 June 2022.

70. Qwo-Li Driskill, Chris Finley, Brian Joseph Gilley, and Scott Lauria Morgensen, "The Revolution Is for Everyone: Imagining an Emancipatory Future through Queer Indigenous Critical Theories," in Driskill et al., *Queer Indigenous Studies*, 211.

71. Innes and Anderson, *Indigenous Men and Masculinities*.

72. Culhane, "Their Spirits Live within Us."

73. Sarah Deer, *The Beginning and End of Rape: Confronting Sexual Violence in Native America* (Minneapolis: University of Minnesota Press, 2015).

74. While this is an ongoing conversation, musicians and organizers recommend allowing families and individuals to portray their own narratives. Additionally, organizers including Barbara Smith, who began No Stone Unturned after her sister disappeared, emphasize that it is crucial to move audiences from empathy to action. This involves pressuring police to intensify search efforts for Indigenous women, raising funds, distributing a toolkit to families of missing women, and connecting to other public events, such as the annual Women's Memorial March.

75. JB the First Lady speaks to similarities across Indigenous groups. Many musicians respond to Nation-specific cultural practices and norms. Cayuga Six Nations members come from the Haudenosaunee confederacy in the East. Coast Salish artists come from a different place culturally and geographically than Nehiyaw artists; experiences of colonization and treaty diverge. Nuxalk peoples never entered into treaty. They share significant commonalities with other Coast Salish societies.

76. Andrea Warner, "Inside Canada's Indigenous Hip-Hop Scene with the First Ladies Crew," *Pitchfork*, 17 August 2015, https://pitchfork.com.

77. Mel Mundell remembers hearing Platypus Toof in Vancouver at a show shared with First Ladies Crew. Beforehand, "the male sound engineer decided to give her an impromptu 101 on her own equipment rather than listen to her sound set-up needs." Mel Mundell, "JB the First Lady and the First Lady Crew: First Nations Female Hip Hop," Bitch Media, 5 April 2011, www.bitchmedia.org.

78. Warner, "Inside Canada's Indigenous Hip-Hop Scene."

79. Penelope Myrtle Kelsey, *Reading the Wampum: Essays on Hodinöhsö:Ni' Visual Code and Epistemological Recovery* (Syracuse, NY: Syracuse University Press, 2014).

80. Eve Tuck and Rubén Gaztambide-Fernández, "Curriculum, Replacement, and Settler Futurity," *Journal of Curriculum Theorizing* 29, no. 1 (2013): 84.

81. Heather Davis, "Decolonization Proposition 2: On Colonial Patriarchy and Matriarchal Decolonization," in *Desire Change: Contemporary Feminist Art in Canada*, ed. Heather Davis (Montréal: McGill-Queen's University Press, 2017), 134.

82. This musician is credited as Dio Ganhdih on JB the First Lady's 2018 album *Righteous Empowered Daughter*. More recent publicity materials and releases, such as the 2019 single "Native New Yorker," use Dioganhdih.

83. Anjum Mubarak Asharia, "Take a Walk with Dio Ganhdih," *Mask Magazine*, April 2016, www.maskmagazine.com.

84. Dioganhdih, comments at live performance, Bennington College, Bennington, VT, 12 October 2020, livestreamed on Twitch.tv.

85. Asharia, "Take a Walk with Dio Ganhdih."

86. This is felt in the very use of colonial languages as dominant modes of communication.

87. In music literature, musico-cultural knowledge is discussed through bimusicality. Many participants have fluency and comfort in more than two cultural languages. However, the word "multicultural" has a political connotation that makes it an inadequate descriptor of this phenomenon.

88. Gendered attitudes with which settlers arrived, too, vary based on the time, social location, and point of origin.

89. Coalition building among Indigenous groups where multiple communities have come to share urban spaces is common, as is the increased relevance of intertribal and multitribal identity markers. See Renya K. Ramirez, *Native Hubs: Culture, Community, and Belonging in Silicon Valley and Beyond* (Durham, NC: Duke University Press, 2007).

90. Devon Abbott Mihesuah, "Commonalty of Difference: American Indian Women and History," *American Indian Quarterly* 20, no. 1 (1996): 15.

91. Mihesuah, introduction to *First to Fight*, by Henry Mihesuah (Lincoln: University of Nebraska Press, 2002), xiii.

92. Mihesuah, "Commonalty of Difference," 20.

93. Verna St. Denis, "Feminism Is for Everybody," in Green, *Making Space for Indigenous Feminism*, 43.

94. St. Denis, 46.

95. Ahmed, *What's the Use?*

96. Driskill et al., "Revolution Is for Everyone," 220, 212.

97. Judith Butler, "Performative Acts and Gender Constitution: An Essay in Phenomenology and Feminist Theory," *Theatre Journal* 40, no. 4 (1988): 520. Butler's influential book *Gender Trouble: Feminism and the Subversion of Identity* was first published in 1990 by Routledge.

98. Many listeners are more familiar with performers' articulations than Butler's, yet her message resonates: "gender is in no way a stable identity or locus of agency from which various acts proceed; rather, it is an identity tenuously constituted in

time—an identity instituted through a stylized repetition of acts" (Butler, "Performative Acts and Gender Constitution," 519). This contestation in some ways contributes to the very questioning of separate spaces for women.

99. With echoes supporting her lyrics, Queen Latifah raps, "Some think that we can't flow (can't flow); Stereotypes, they got to go (got to go); I'm a mess around and flip the scene into reverse; (With what?) With a little touch of Ladies First." This flip and reverse language is heard in other late-1990s and early-2000s hip hop, yet this performance is part of more than a gender reversal via a flipping of the script. The strength of women is articulated here on its own terms.

100. Thomas King describes how scholarship characterized Native humor as about survival and community, yet he resists defining it exclusively. See King, "Performing Native Humor," in *Me Funny: A Far-Reaching Exploration of the Humor, Wittiness and Repartee Dominant among the First Nations People of North America, as Witnessed, Experienced and Created Directly by Themselves, and with the Inclusion of Outside but Reputable Sources Necessarily Familiar with the Indigenous Sense of Humour as Seen from an Objective Perspective*, ed. Drew Hayden Taylor (Vancouver: Douglas and McIntyre, 2005), 169–83. See also Angel M. Hinzo and Lynn Schofield Clark, "Digital Survivance and Trickster Humor: Exploring Visual and Digital Indigenous Epistemologies in the #NoDAPL Movement," *Information, Communication & Society* 22, no. 6 (2019): 791–807.

101. José Esteban Muñoz, *Disidentifications* (Minneapolis: University of Minnesota Press, 1999), xi–xii. Muñoz defines white normativity, like heteronormativity, as specifically not "linked to predetermined biological coordinates" (xii); this clarification offers a warning that normative attitudes and practices can come from many corners.

102. Audre Lorde, *Sister Outsider* (Berkeley, CA: Crossing, 1984), 127.

103. Dioganhdih, comments at live performance.

104. Dioganhdih.

105. Przybylski, "Singing Resilience," 212.

106. Janice Acosta and Natasha Beeds, "Cree-atively Speaking," in Taylor, *Me Funny*, 85–97.

107. Writing in English can occlude some meaning. Calling Cree the "funniest of all languages," Tomson Highway explains that if he were writing in Cree, "and you were reading it that way, then what you would be doing is laughing, laughing constantly, laughing so hard your sides would hurt. Somewhere deep inside of you, there would be a zany sensation perpetually on the verge of exploding into a wild cry of intoxicating, silly, giddy pleasure." Highway, "Why Cree Is the Funniest of All Languages," in Taylor, *Me Funny*, 160–61.

108. Vine Deloria Jr., *Custer Died for Your Sins: An Indian Manifesto* (New York: Macmillan, 1969), 167.

109. Louise Profeit-Leblanc, "Ruby Lips," in Taylor, *Me Funny*, 146.

110. Lawrence W. Gross, "The Comic Vision of Anishinaabe Culture and Religion," *American Indian Quarterly* 26, no. 3 (2003): 437.
111. T-Rhyme, public post to Facebook, 21 December 2018. The post linked to the music video on YouTube.
112. Cyphers for womxn function as spaces for Indigenous/non-Indigenous solidarity beyond nation-state borders. One such example is the collective Fempre$$ in Australia.
113. Shirley Green, "Looking Back, Looking Forward," in *Making Space for Indigenous Feminism*, ed. Joyce Green (Winnipeg, MB: Fernwood, 2007), 172.
114. S. Green, 172.
115. Canada Council for the Arts / Conseil des arts du Canada, *Applicant Profiles*, PDF guide published February 2019, 61, https://canadacouncil.ca.
116. See Canada Council for the Arts /Conseil des arts du Canada, "Grants," https://canadacouncil.ca.
117. Canada Council for the Arts / Conseil des arts du Canada, "Creating, Knowing and Sharing: The Arts and Cultures of First Nations, Inuit and Métis Peoples," https://canadacouncil.ca. Because nation-states and funding bodies continue to define categories including First Nations, Métis, and Inuit for their own use, politics of recognition are at play. See Karrmen Crey, "Screen Text and Institutional Context: Indigenous Film Production and Academic Research Institutions," *Native American and Indigenous Studies* 4, no. 1 (2017): 61–88.
118. This came up in conversation and has also been reported in news sources such as the CBC. Madeline Kotzer, "Recognizing the Power We Have," *CBC News*, 27 October 2018. This chapter uses rappers' stage names, per their requests. The Canada Council publishes grantees legal names.
119. The Unist'ot'en Camp was designed to promote Indigenous healing and oppose pipeline expansion.
120. The grant structures that Eekwol and T-Rhyme accessed create some opportunities beyond per-unit sales; these same structures allow decision-making based on funder priorities rather than just ad-sales potential for media distribution, as was analyzed in chapters 2 and 3. For more on neoliberal capitalism's effects on the music industry and the ways racialized gender construction intersects with neoliberalism in hip hop and wider cultural industries, see also Robin James, *The Sonic Episteme: Acoustic Resonance, Neoliberalism, and Biopolitics* (Durham, NC: Duke University Press, 2019); Jalondra Davis, "Ladyhood in Distress: Neoliberalism and Black Politics in Nicole Sconiers's *Escape from Beckyville: Tales of Race, Hair, and Rage*," in *Challenging Misrepresentations of Black Womanhood: Media, Literature and Theory*, ed. Marquita M. Gammage and Antwanisha Alameen-Shavers (New York: Anthem, 2019), 95–114; and Jacob Rekedal, "Martyrdom and Mapuche Metal: Defying Cultural and Territorial Reductions in Twenty-First-Century Wallmapu," *Ethnomusicology* 63, no. 1 (2019): 78–104.

CHAPTER 5. DECOLONIAL LISTENING?

1. Leonard Sumner, "They Say," *Rez Poetry*, retranscribed by author.
2. Robert Flaherty, dir., *Nanook of the North* (1922), feat. Allakariallak and Nyla (Criterion DVD, 2013). The director staged many scenes in which he asked Inuit actors to use older technology, despite presenting the film as a kind of documentary. It is criticized for exacerbating a depiction of Indigenous peoples as premodern. The silent film contains written commentary about, but not by, the on-screen actors.
3. Tagaq is a residential-school survivor. She learned throat singing from recordings. She has explained that many viewers who suffered the ruptures of residential school watched *Nanook* and found a sense of pride in the strength of these elders shown on-screen.
4. In a reading of visual sovereignty, Michelle Raheja suggests that Inuit actors and members of the technical team were fully aware of what Flaherty was doing and can be seen as doing their own crafting from behind and in front of the camera. Raheja, "Reading Nanook's Smile: Visual Sovereignty, Indigenous Revisions of Ethnography, and 'Atanarjuat (The Fast Runner),'" *American Quarterly* 59, no. 4 (2007): 1159–85.
5. See also Przybylski, "Singing Resilience."
6. Tanya Tagaq, *Animism* (Six Shooter Records, 2014).
7. Glen Coulthard, *Red Skin White Masks* (Minneapolis: University of Minnesota Press, 2014); Heather A. Howard and Craig Proulx, eds., *Aboriginal Peoples in Canadian Cities: Transformations and Continuity* (Waterloo, ON: Wilfrid Laurier University Press, 2011); Tiffany Lethabo King, Jenell Navarro, and Andrea Smith, eds., *Otherwise Worlds: Against Settler Colonialism and Anti-Blackness* (Durham, NC: Duke University Press, 2020).
8. Bhabha, *Location of Culture*, 9.
9. Lorde, *Sister Outsider*, 129.
10. James Tester and Peter Irniq, "Inuit Qaujimajatuqangit: Social History, Politics and the Practice of Resistance," *Arctic* 6, supp. 1: "Arctic Change and Coastal Communities" (2008): 51. My reading makes no claim to specific Inuit cultural knowledge. Rather, it is a reminder that the focus on human primacy over other beings is a culturally situated focus and not a given. Readers may find it helpful to consider the description offered by Natasha Thorpe, Naikak Hakongak, Sandra Eyegetok, and the Qitirmiut Elders: "Inuit Qaujimajatuqangit (IQ) is 'what has always been known' or, in other words, Inuit knowledge, insight, and wisdom that is gained through experience, shared through stories, and passed from one generation to the next. More than just knowledge, as it is typically termed, IQ includes a finely tuned awareness of the forever changing relationship between Inuit and nuna, hila, wildlife, and the spiritual world." Thorpe, Hakongak, Eyegetok, and Qitirmiut Elders, *The Tuktu and Nogak Project: A Caribou Chronicle* (Ikaluktuuttiak, NT: Qitirmiut Elders and the *Tuktu* and *Nogak* Project, 2001), 24. This

knowledge system is dynamic and responsive to listeners who are raised into it: "IQ passed from one generation to the next is filtered through the listener and understood within the listener's experience or ability. IQ changes with each new listener in a way that is iterative and adaptive so that IQ of the past is contributed to that of the present" (26–27).

11. For further exploration of multiple positionalities and possibilities in listening, consult Dylan Robinson, *Hungry Listening: Resonant Theory for Indigenous Sound Studies* (Minneapolis: University of Minnesota Press, 2020).

12. Przybylski, "Rapping to and for a Multivocal Canada," 78–79.

13. Robin Wall Kimmerer, *Braiding Sweetgrass: Indigenous Wisdom, Scientific Knowledge and the Teachings of Plants* (Minneapolis: University of Minnesota Press, 2013), 12.

14. Kimmerer, "Learning the Grammar of Animacy," *Anthropology of Consciousness* 28, no. 2 (2017): 132.

15. Warrior asserts that other-than-human relatives, including those who are typically ignored, can be "some of our most eloquent teachers" ("Indigenous Collectives," 388).

16. A Tribe Called Red, "Sila," *We Are the Halluci Nation* (Radicalized Records, 2016).

17. Leonard Sumner, interview with author, 6 July 2021.

# INDEX

Page numbers in italic indicate figures.

## ABOUT THE AUTHOR

LIZ PRZYBYLSKI, PhD, is a pop music scholar working in hip hop in Canada and the US. An Associate Professor of Ethnomusicology at the University of California, Riverside, Liz is the author of *Hybrid Ethnography* (2020), and an awardee of the National Endowment for the Humanities Faculty Fellowship.

www.ingramcontent.com/pod-product-compliance
Lightning Source LLC
Chambersburg PA
CBHW032101040426
42336CB00040B/628